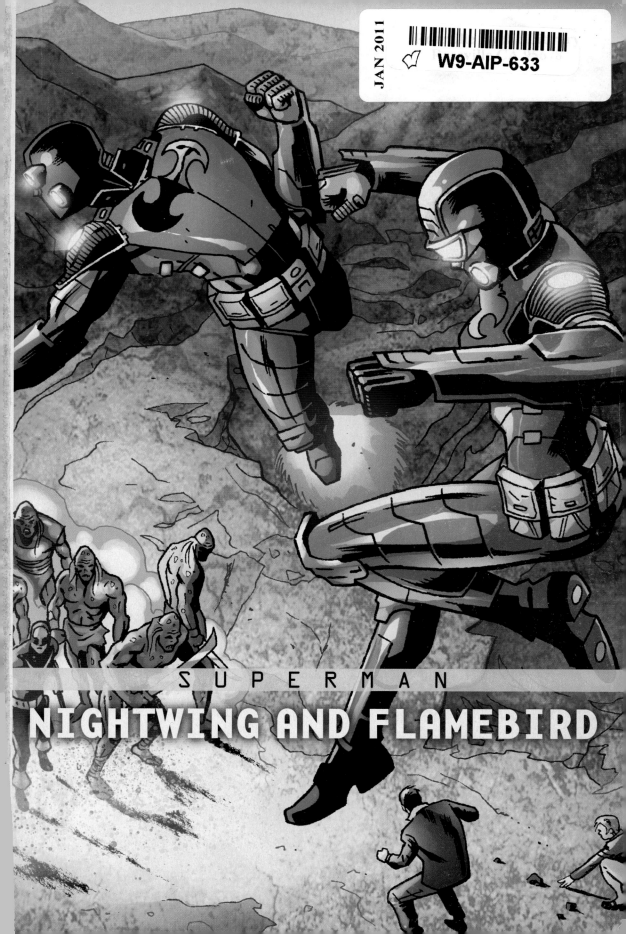

SUPERMAN

NIGHTWING AND FLAMEBIRD

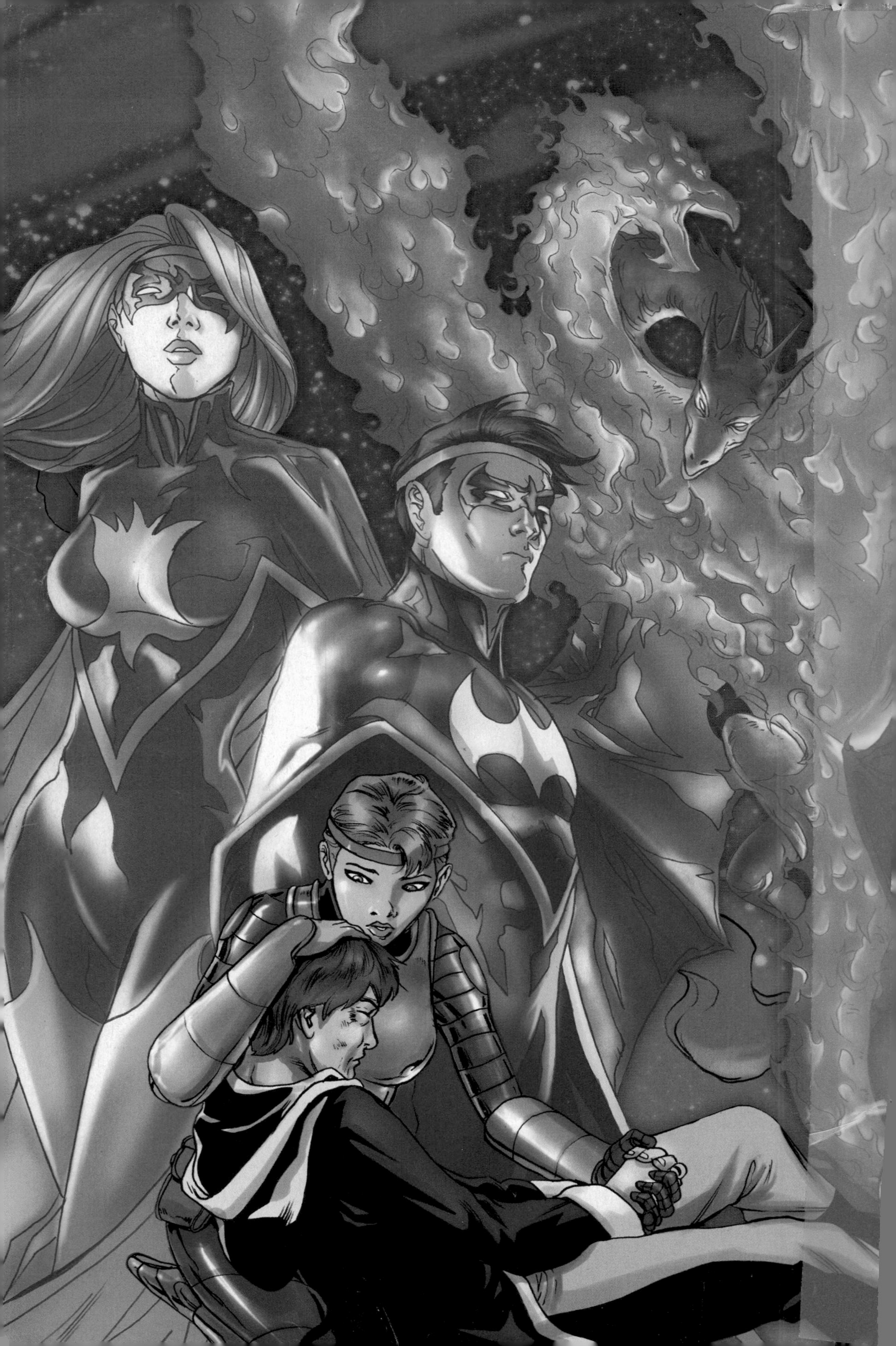

SUPERMAN

NIGHTWING AND FLAMEBIRD

GREG RUCKA
WRITER

EDDY BARROWS
SIDNEY TELES
DIEGO OLMOS
PERE PÉREZ
PENCILLERS

RUY JOSÉ
JÚLIO FERREIRA
SANDRO RIBEIRO
DIEGO OLMOS
BIT
PERE PÉREZ
INKERS

ROD REIS
MAZI
COLORISTS

ROB LEIGH
LETTERER

SUPERMAN CREATED BY
JERRY SIEGEL AND
JOE SHUSTER

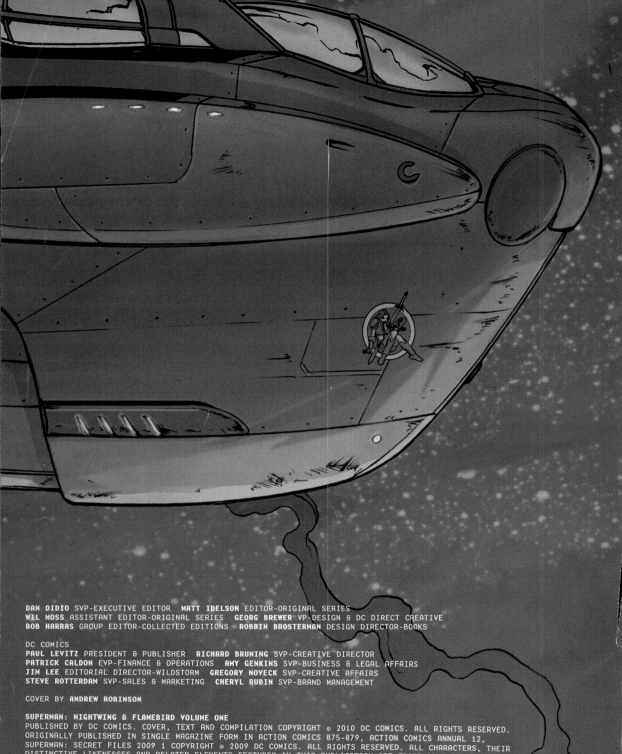

DAN DIDIO SVP-EXECUTIVE EDITOR **MATT IDELSON** EDITOR-ORIGINAL SERIES
WIL MOSS ASSISTANT EDITOR-ORIGINAL SERIES **GEORG BREWER** VP-DESIGN & DC DIRECT CREATIVE
BOB HARRAS GROUP EDITOR-COLLECTED EDITIONS **ROBBIN BROSTERMAN** DESIGN DIRECTOR-BOOKS

DC COMICS
PAUL LEVITZ PRESIDENT & PUBLISHER **RICHARD BRUNING** SVP-CREATIVE DIRECTOR
PATRICK CALDON EVP-FINANCE & OPERATIONS **AMY GENKINS** SVP-BUSINESS & LEGAL AFFAIRS
JIM LEE EDITORIAL DIRECTOR-WILDSTORM **GREGORY NOVECK** SVP-CREATIVE AFFAIRS
STEVE ROTTERDAM SVP-SALES & MARKETING **CHERYL RUBIN** SVP-BRAND MANAGEMENT

COVER BY **ANDREW ROBINSON**

SUPERMAN: NIGHTWING & FLAMEBIRD VOLUME ONE
PUBLISHED BY DC COMICS. COVER, TEXT AND COMPILATION COPYRIGHT © 2010 DC COMICS. ALL RIGHTS RESERVED.
ORIGINALLY PUBLISHED IN SINGLE MAGAZINE FORM IN ACTION COMICS 875-879, ACTION COMICS ANNUAL 12,
SUPERMAN: SECRET FILES 2009 1 COPYRIGHT © 2009 DC COMICS. ALL RIGHTS RESERVED. ALL CHARACTERS, THEIR
DISTINCTIVE LIKENESSES AND RELATED ELEMENTS FEATURED IN THIS PUBLICATION ARE TRADEMARKS OF DC COMICS.
MILESTONE CHARACTERS ARE COPYRIGHT © MILESTONE MEDIA PARTNERS, INC. ALL RIGHTS RESERVED. THE STORIES,
CHARACTERS AND INCIDENTS FEATURED IN THIS PUBLICATION ARE ENTIRELY FICTIONAL. DC COMICS DOES NOT READ
OR ACCEPT UNSOLICITED SUBMISSIONS OF IDEAS, STORIES OR ARTWORK.

DC COMICS, 1700 BROADWAY, NEW YORK, NY 10019. A WARNER BROS. ENTERTAINMENT COMPANY
PRINTED BY RR DONNELLEY, SALEM, VA, USA 12/8/2010 FIRST PRINTING.
SC ISBN:978-1-4012-2639-8

WHAT CAME BEFORE

It began with an epic battle between Earth's greatest hero, SUPERMAN, and the evil alien BRAINIAC. During that clash, Superman discovered the lost CITY OF KANDOR trapped in the depths of the alien's ship, 100,000 Kryptonian inhabitants inside. Superman was reunited with his people, but at a huge personal cost: he was unable to save the life of his adoptive father, JONATHAN KENT.

Kandor was freed and relocated to Earth, but the uneasy alliance between humans and Kryptonians quickly degenerated into violence and tragedy. A secret government organization, PROJECT 7734, helped orchestrate the aggression between the two races. 7734's leader is GENERAL SAM LANE, a man thought long dead, and he gave the order to assassinate ZOR-EL, SUPERGIRL's father and the leader of the Kryptonians. Meanwhile, a team of Kryptonians brutally murdered several of Metropolis's SCIENCE POLICE on American soil.

In an effort to resolve the growing conflict, Zor-El's widow, ALURA, took charge of the Kryptonians and combined Brainiac's technology with Kandor's to create a new planet — NEW KRYPTON. The planet established an orbit opposite Earth's own. It appeared that the conflict had ended… but looks can be deceiving.

When Alura released GENERAL ZOD from the Phantom Zone and gave him command of New Krypton's army, Superman was forced to make the hardest decision of his life: he would move to New Krypton to keep Zod in check.

Amid the escalating tensions and Superman's absence, new and old heroes alike have risen to protect the Earth.

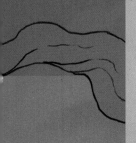

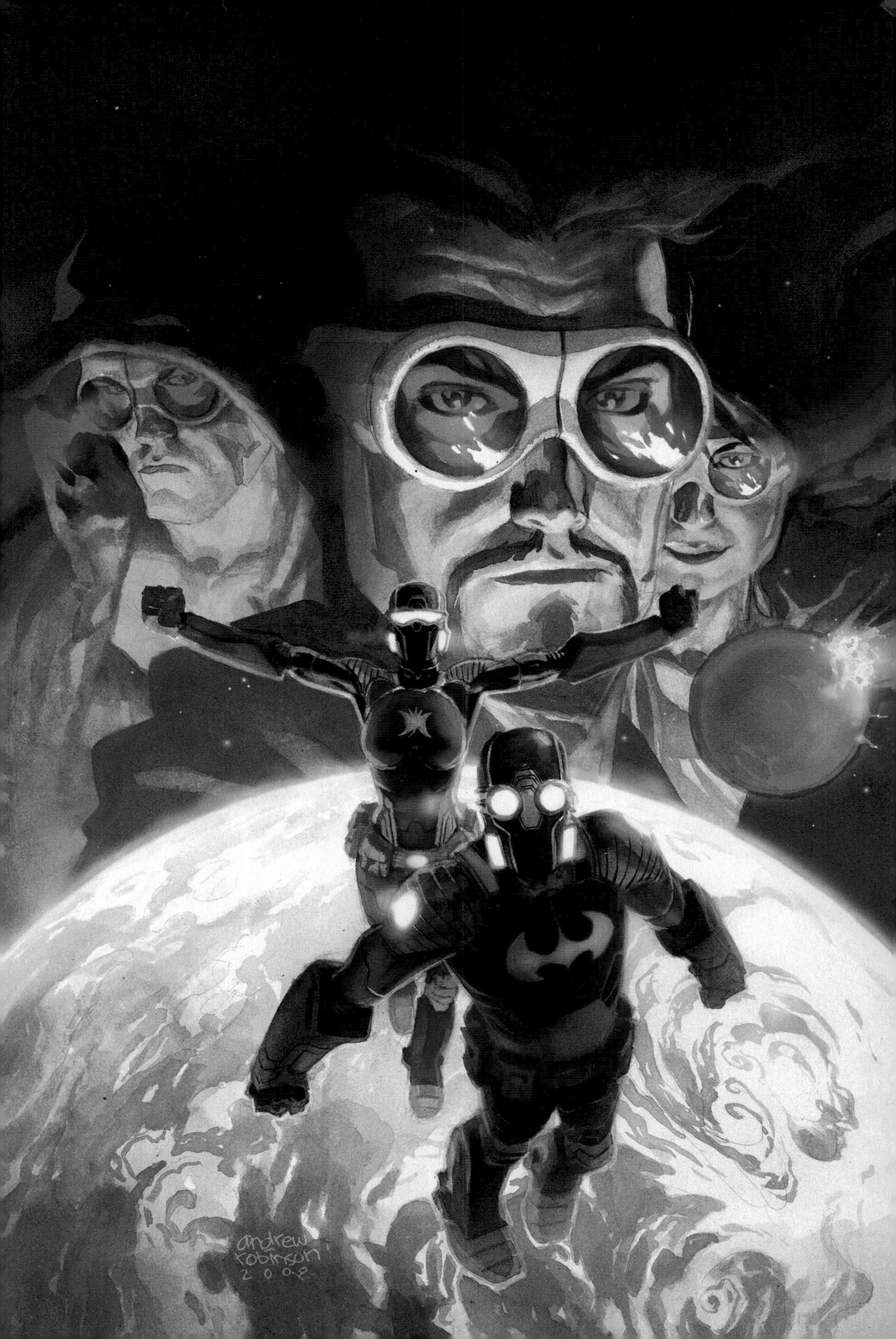
andrew robinson 2008

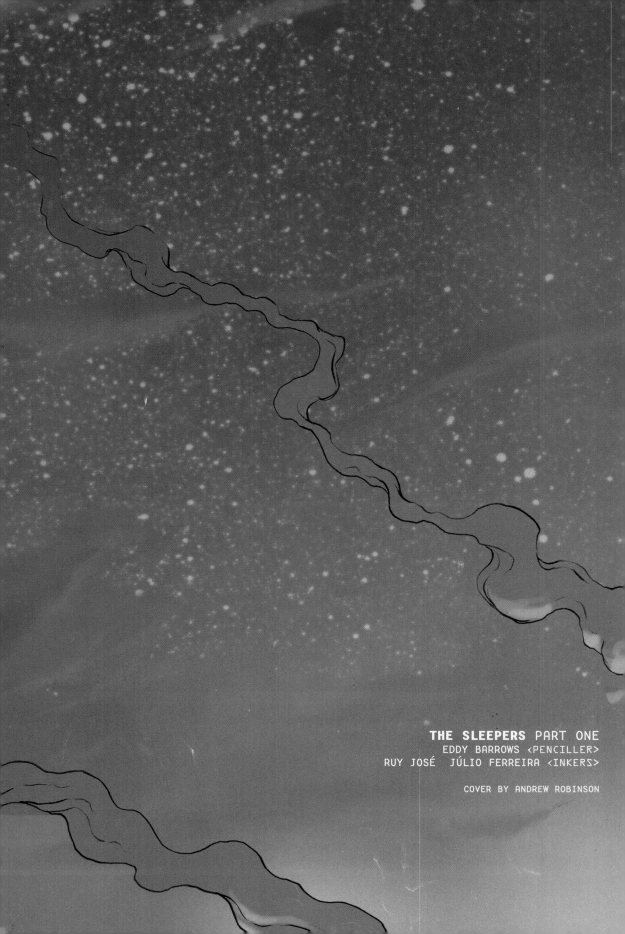

THE SLEEPERS PART ONE
EDDY BARROWS <PENCILLER>
RUY JOSÉ   JÚLIO FERREIRA <INKERS>

COVER BY ANDREW ROBINSON

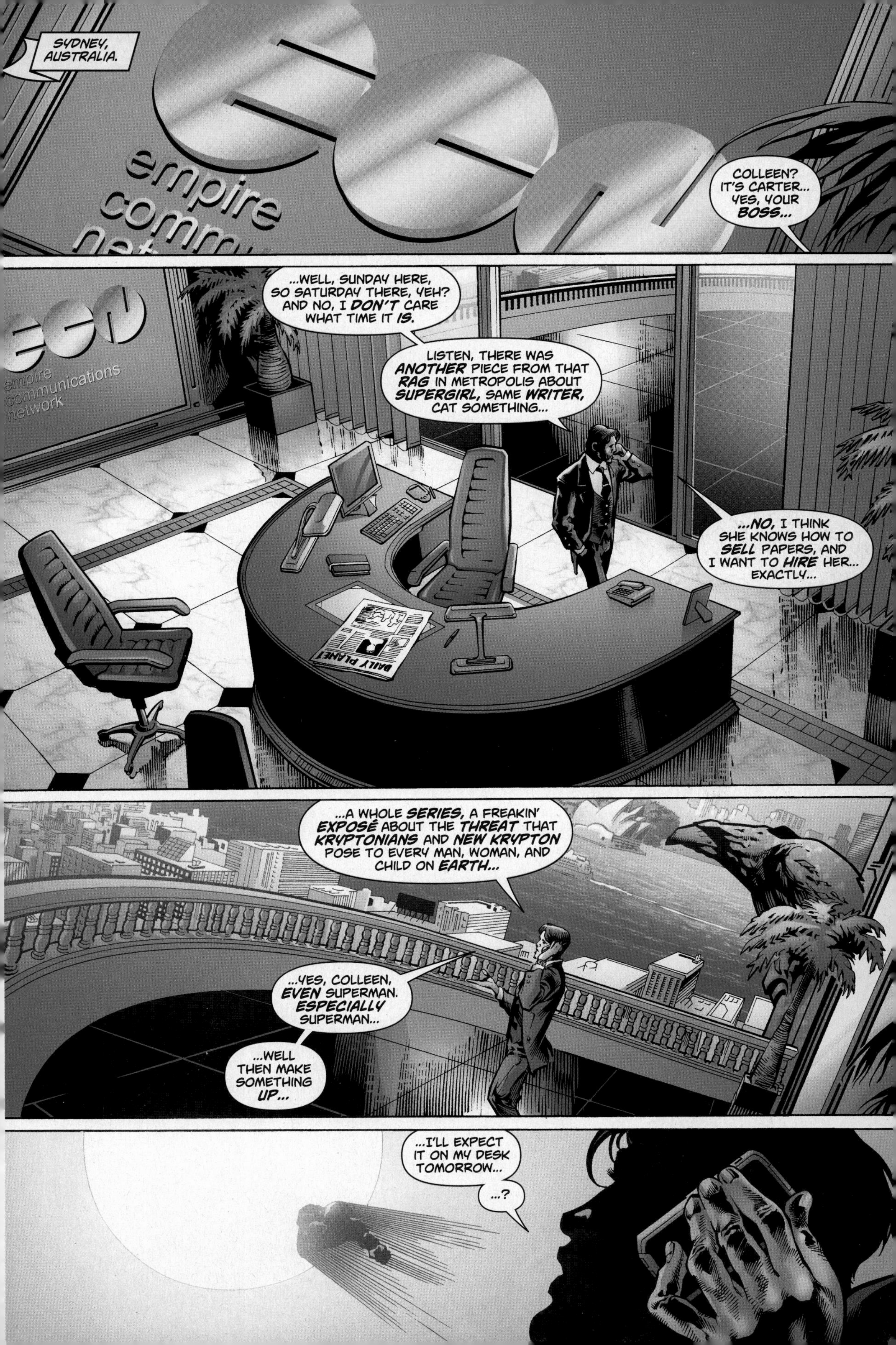
SYDNEY, AUSTRALIA.
empire commu net
COLLEEN? IT'S CARTER... YES, YOUR BOSS...
ECN empire communications network
...WELL, SUNDAY HERE, SO SATURDAY THERE, YEH? AND NO, I DON'T CARE WHAT TIME IT IS.
LISTEN, THERE WAS ANOTHER PIECE FROM THAT RAG IN METROPOLIS ABOUT SUPERGIRL, SAME WRITER, CAT SOMETHING...
...NO, I THINK SHE KNOWS HOW TO SELL PAPERS, AND I WANT TO HIRE HER... EXACTLY...
DAILY PLANET
...A WHOLE SERIES, A FREAKIN' EXPOSÉ ABOUT THE THREAT THAT KRYPTONIANS AND NEW KRYPTON POSE TO EVERY MAN, WOMAN, AND CHILD ON EARTH...
...YES, COLLEEN, EVEN SUPERMAN. ESPECIALLY SUPERMAN...
...WELL THEN MAKE SOMETHING UP...
...I'LL EXPECT IT ON MY DESK TOMORROW...
...?

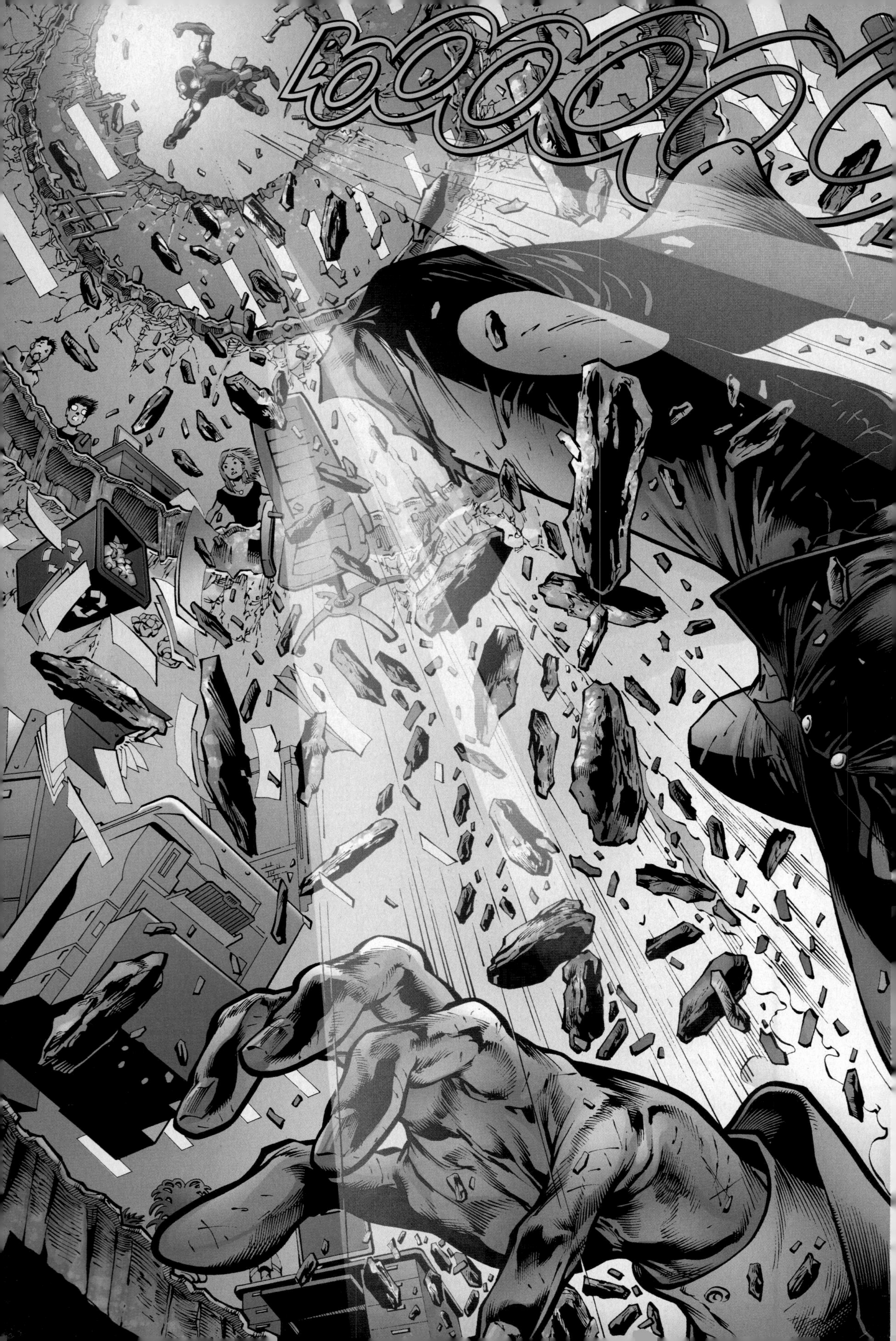
BOOOOOO

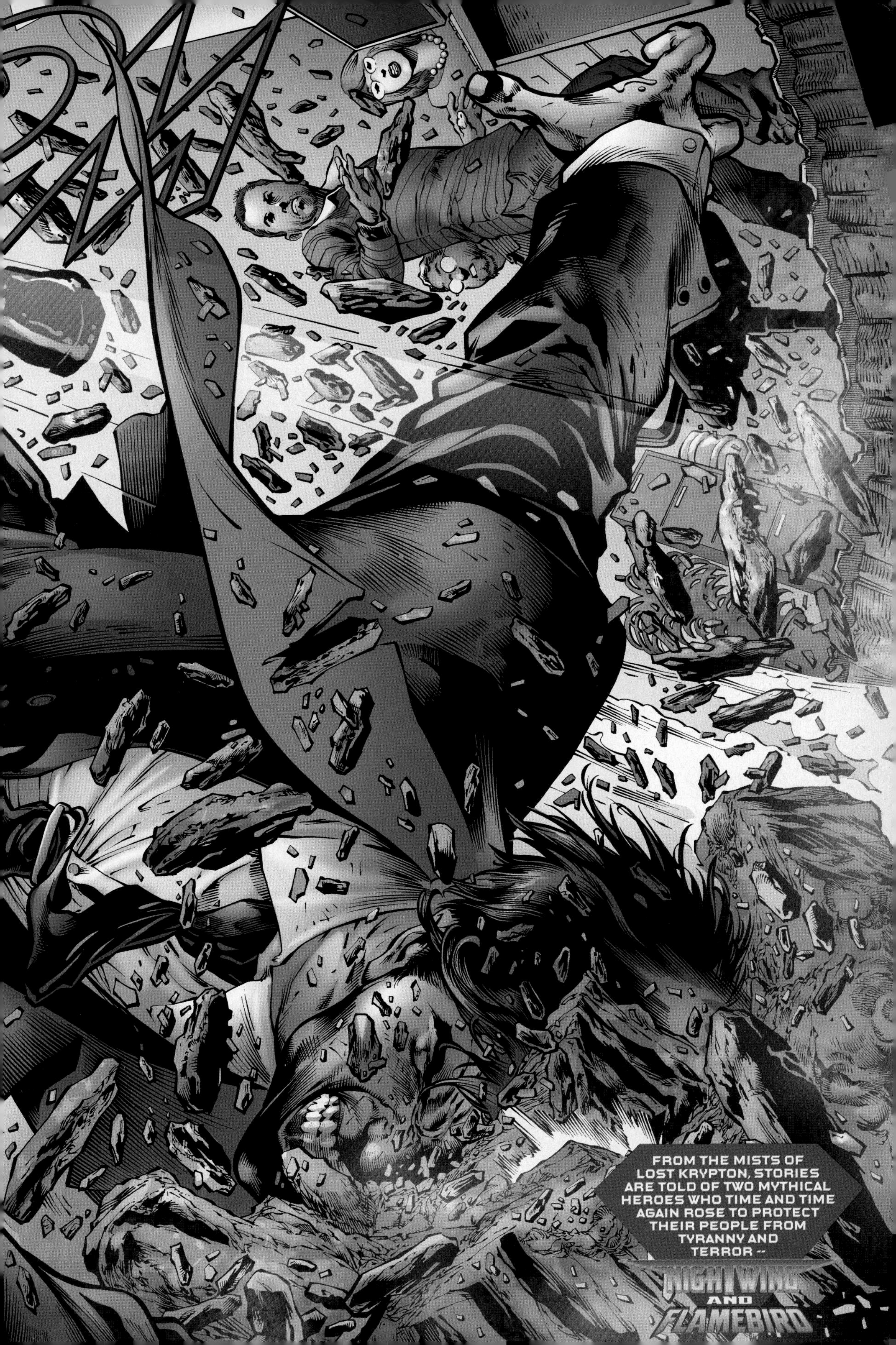
FROM THE MISTS OF LOST KRYPTON, STORIES ARE TOLD OF TWO MYTHICAL HEROES WHO TIME AND TIME AGAIN ROSE TO PROTECT THEIR PEOPLE FROM TYRANNY AND TERROR --
NIGHTWING AND FLAMEBIRD

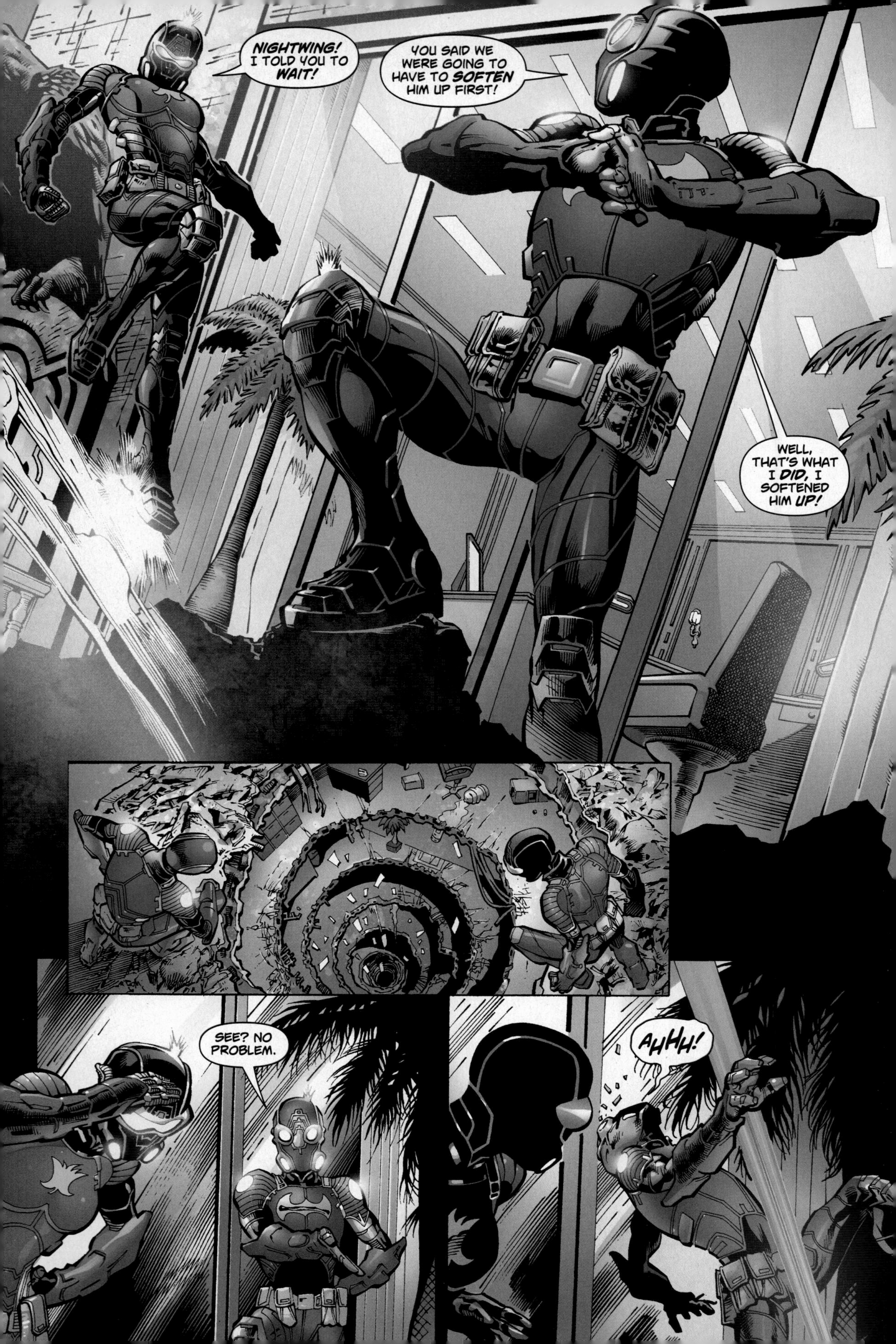
NIGHTWING! I TOLD YOU TO WAIT!
YOU SAID WE WERE GOING TO HAVE TO SOFTEN HIM UP FIRST!
WELL, THAT'S WHAT I DID, I SOFTENED HIM UP!
SEE? NO PROBLEM.
AHHH!

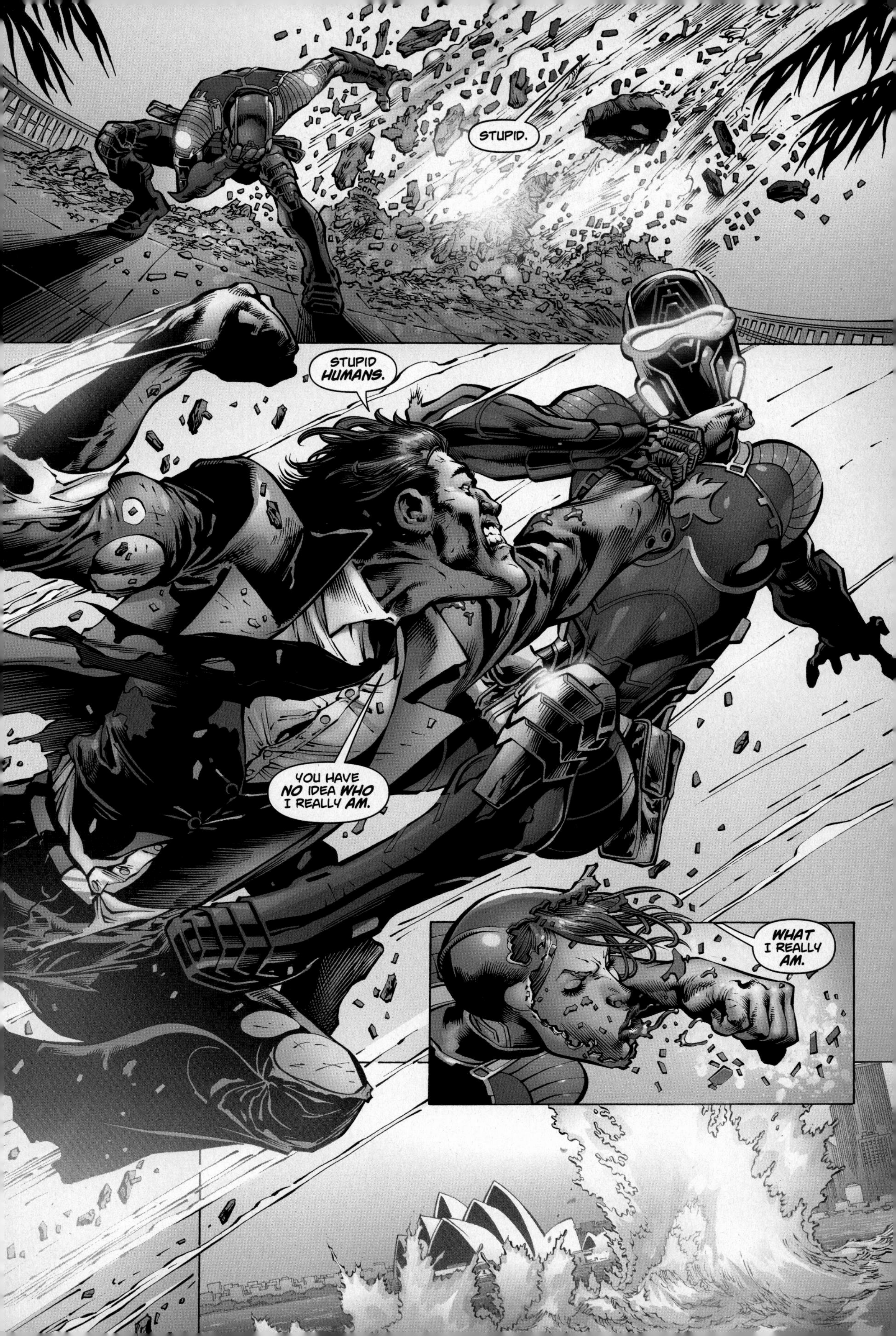
STUPID.
STUPID HUMANS.
YOU HAVE NO IDEA WHO I REALLY AM.
WHAT I REALLY AM.

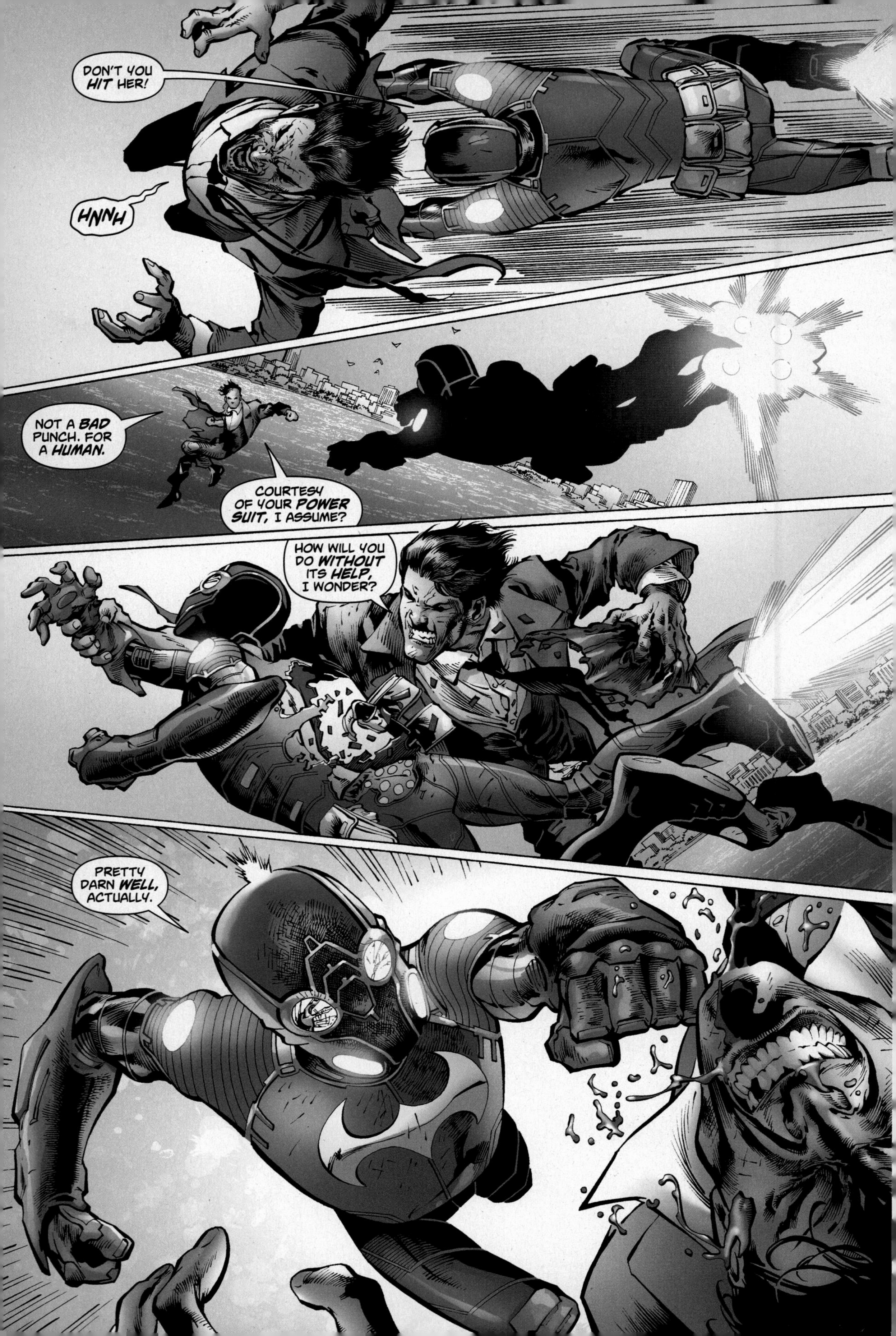
DON'T YOU HIT HER!
HNNH
NOT A BAD PUNCH. FOR A HUMAN.
COURTESY OF YOUR POWER SUIT, I ASSUME?
HOW WILL YOU DO WITHOUT ITS HELP, I WONDER?
PRETTY DARN WELL, ACTUALLY.

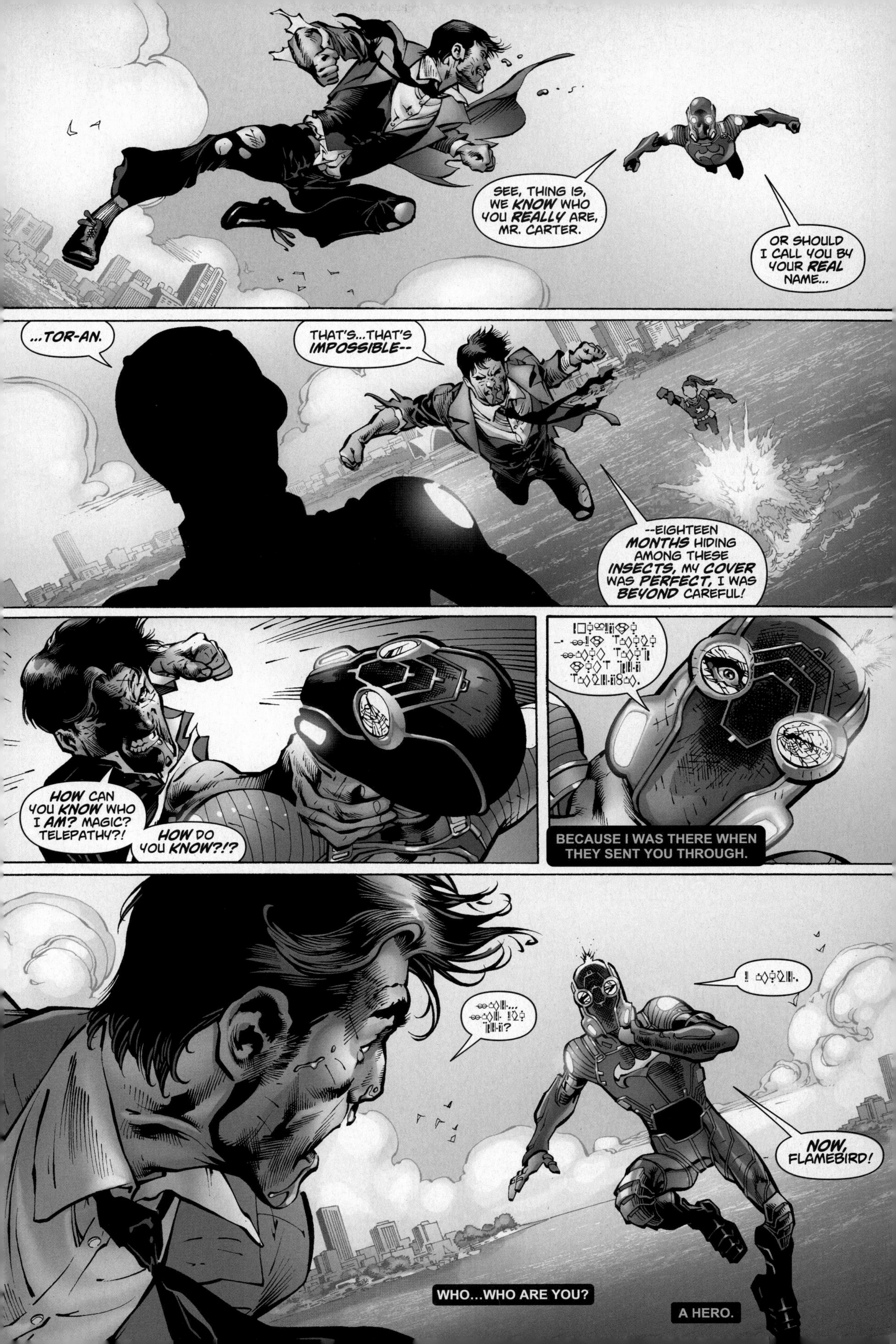
SEE, THING IS, WE KNOW WHO YOU REALLY ARE, MR. CARTER.
OR SHOULD I CALL YOU BY YOUR REAL NAME...
...TOR-AN.
THAT'S...THAT'S IMPOSSIBLE--
--EIGHTEEN MONTHS HIDING AMONG THESE INSECTS, MY COVER WAS PERFECT, I WAS BEYOND CAREFUL!
HOW CAN YOU KNOW WHO I AM? MAGIC? TELEPATHY?!
HOW DO YOU KNOW?!?
BECAUSE I WAS THERE WHEN THEY SENT YOU THROUGH.
NOW, FLAMEBIRD!
WHO…WHO ARE YOU?
A HERO.

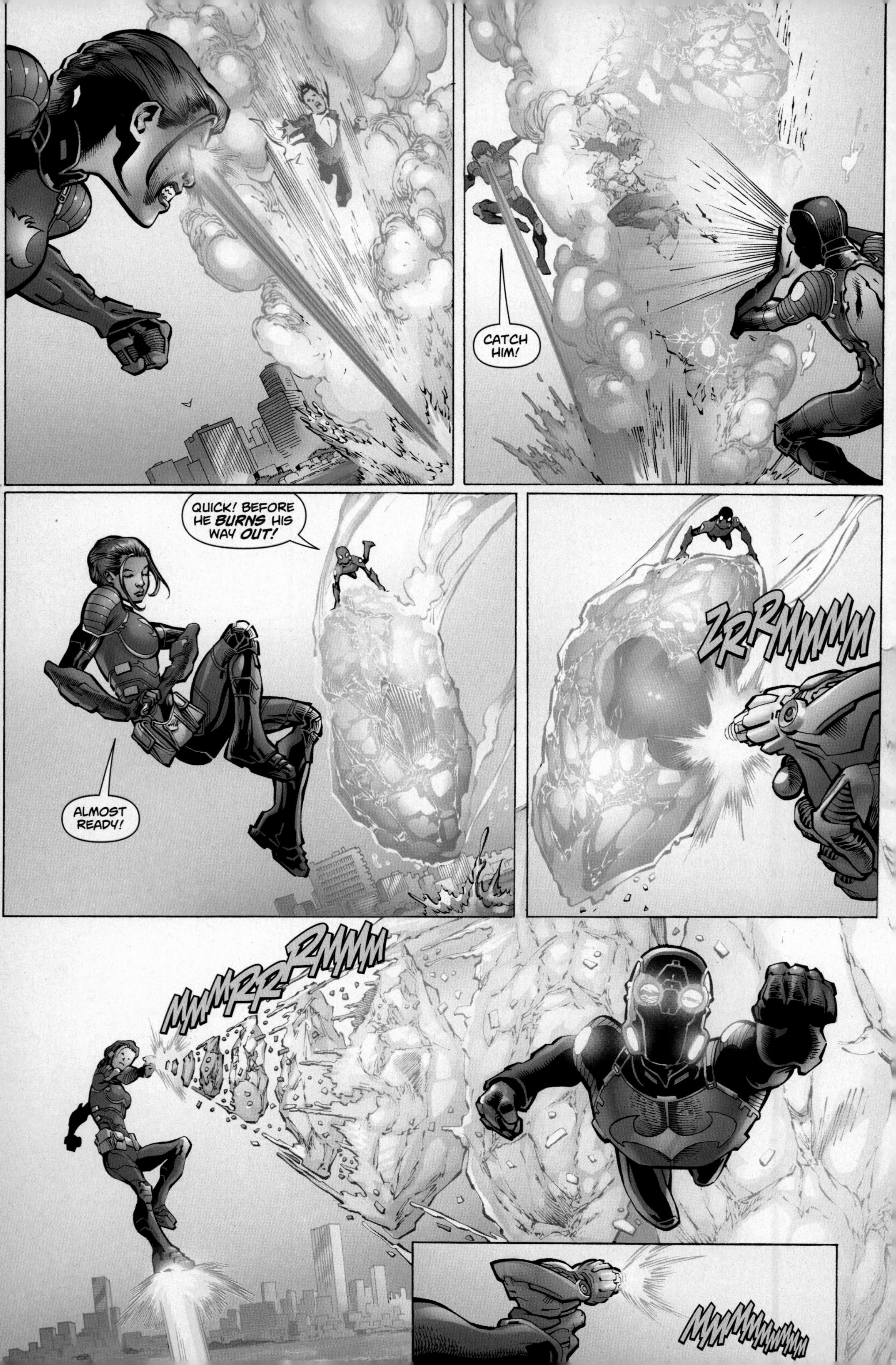
CATCH HIM!
QUICK! BEFORE HE BURNS HIS WAY OUT!
ALMOST READY!
ZRRMMMMM
MMMRRRMMMM
MMMMMMMMM

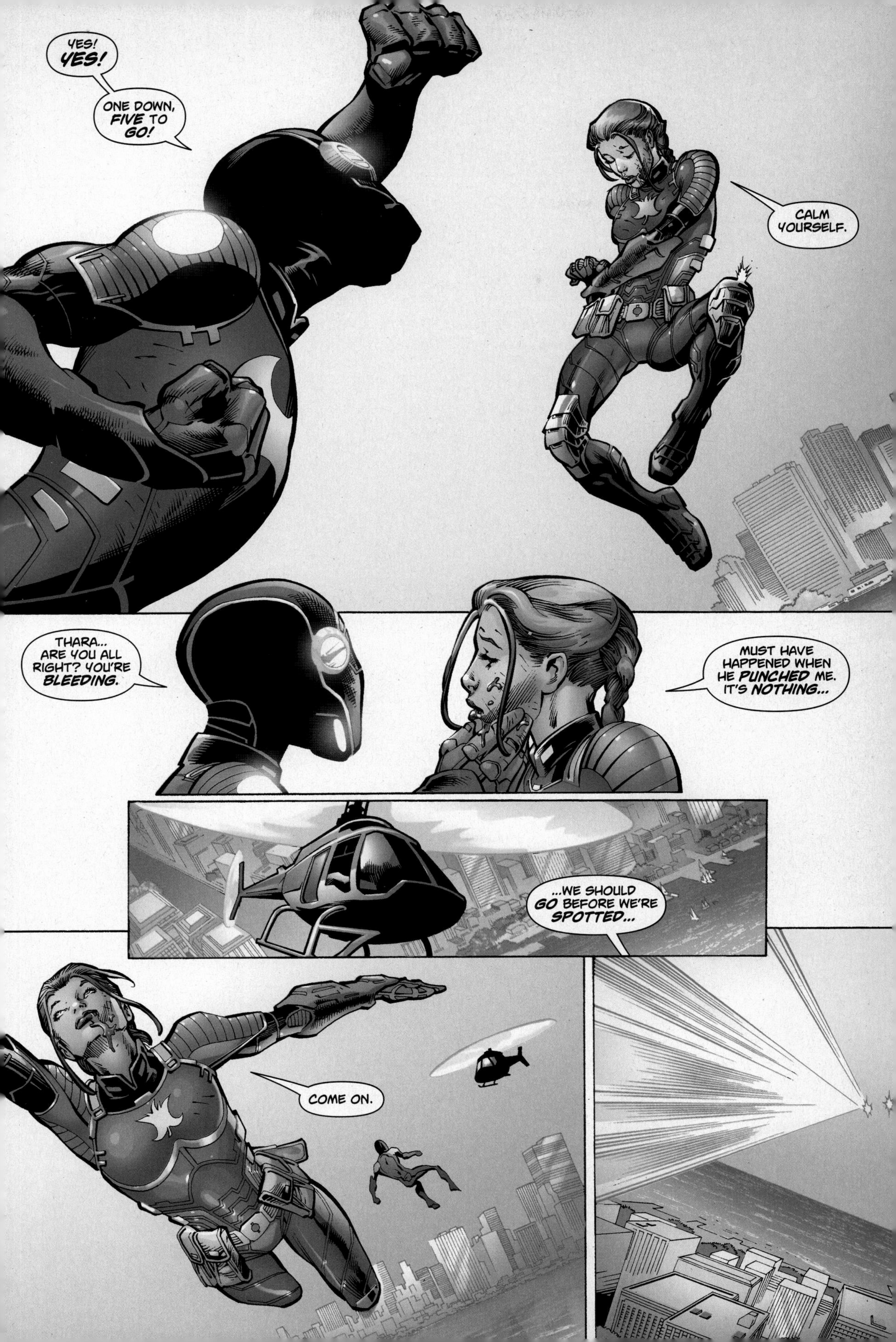

YES! YES!
ONE DOWN, FIVE TO GO!
CALM YOURSELF.
THARA... ARE YOU ALL RIGHT? YOU'RE BLEEDING.
MUST HAVE HAPPENED WHEN HE PUNCHED ME. IT'S NOTHING...
...WE SHOULD GO BEFORE WE'RE SPOTTED...
COME ON.

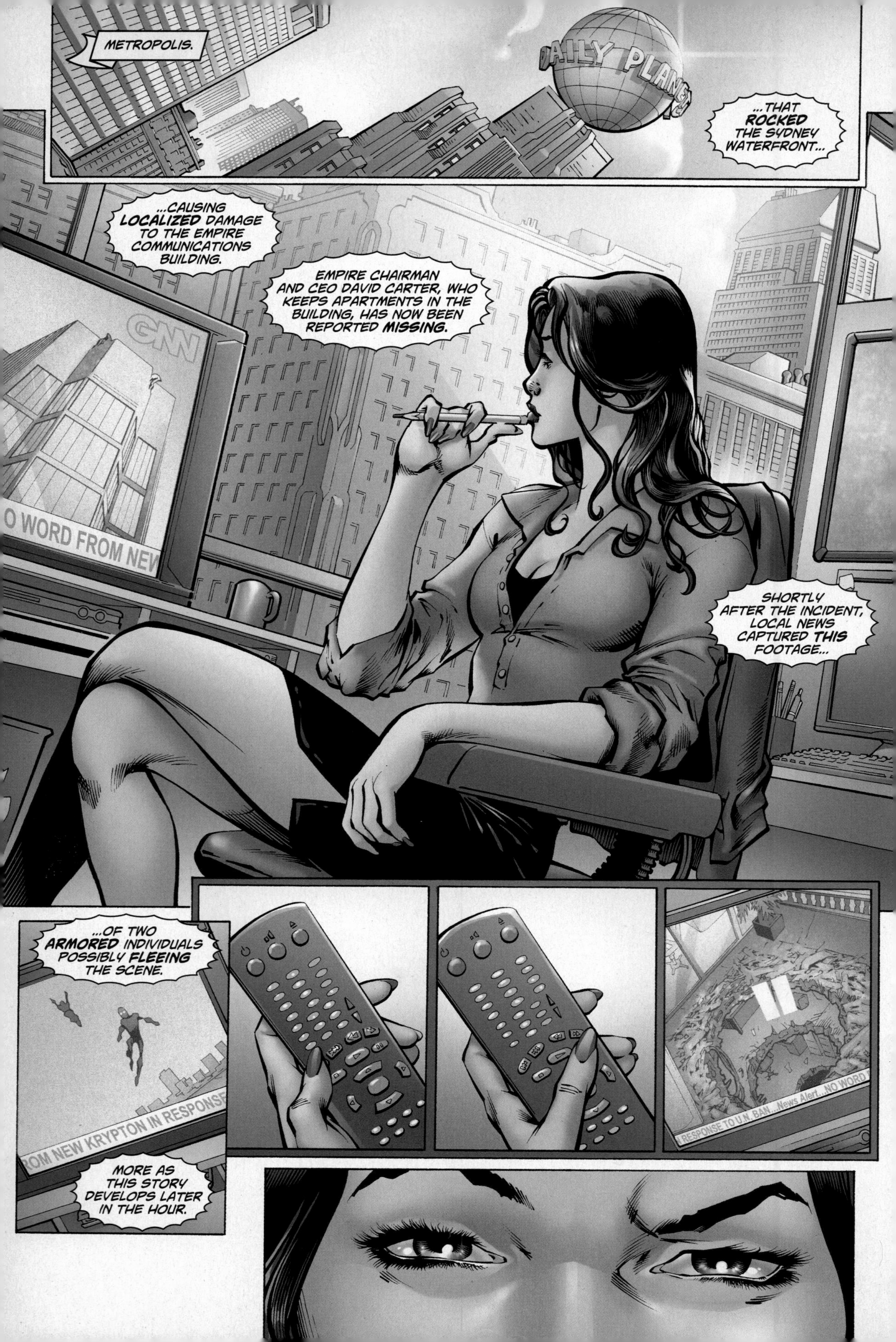

METROPOLIS.
DAILY PLANET
...THAT ROCKED THE SYDNEY WATERFRONT...
...CAUSING LOCALIZED DAMAGE TO THE EMPIRE COMMUNICATIONS BUILDING.
EMPIRE CHAIRMAN AND CEO DAVID CARTER, WHO KEEPS APARTMENTS IN THE BUILDING, HAS NOW BEEN REPORTED MISSING.
GNN
O WORD FROM NEW
SHORTLY AFTER THE INCIDENT, LOCAL NEWS CAPTURED THIS FOOTAGE...
...OF TWO ARMORED INDIVIDUALS POSSIBLY FLEEING THE SCENE.
ROM NEW KRYPTON IN RESPONSE
MORE AS THIS STORY DEVELOPS LATER IN THE HOUR.
I RESPONSE TO U.N. BAN...News Alert...NO WORD

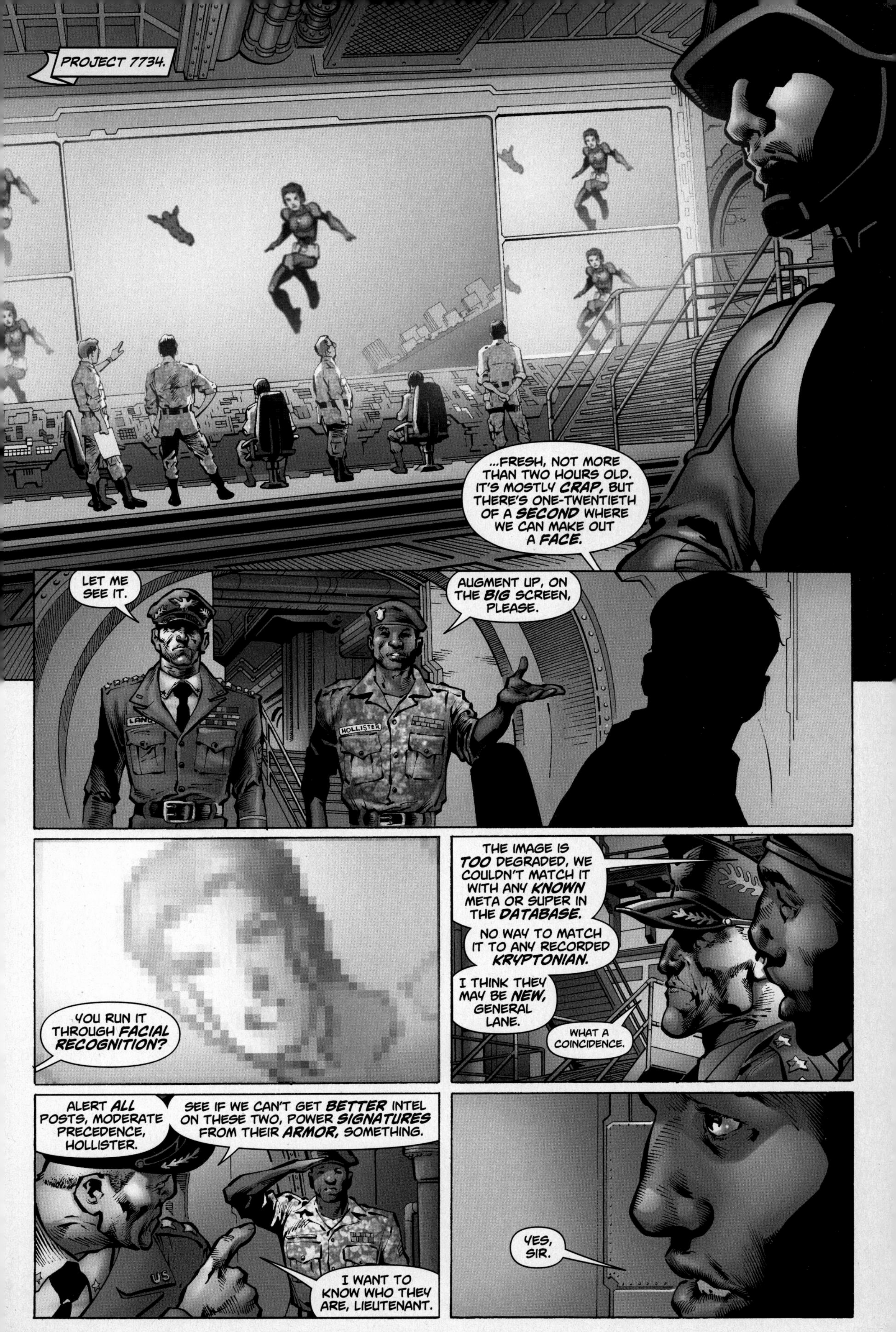
PROJECT 7734.
...FRESH, NOT MORE THAN TWO HOURS OLD. IT'S MOSTLY CRAP, BUT THERE'S ONE-TWENTIETH OF A SECOND WHERE WE CAN MAKE OUT A FACE.
LET ME SEE IT.
AUGMENT UP, ON THE BIG SCREEN, PLEASE.
LANE
HOLLISTER
YOU RUN IT THROUGH FACIAL RECOGNITION?
THE IMAGE IS TOO DEGRADED, WE COULDN'T MATCH IT WITH ANY KNOWN META OR SUPER IN THE DATABASE.
NO WAY TO MATCH IT TO ANY RECORDED KRYPTONIAN.
I THINK THEY MAY BE NEW, GENERAL LANE.
WHAT A COINCIDENCE.
ALERT ALL POSTS, MODERATE PRECEDENCE, HOLLISTER.
SEE IF WE CAN'T GET BETTER INTEL ON THESE TWO, POWER SIGNATURES FROM THEIR ARMOR, SOMETHING.
US
I WANT TO KNOW WHO THEY ARE, LIEUTENANT.
YES, SIR.

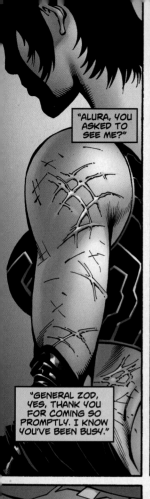

"ALURA, YOU ASKED TO SEE ME?"

"GENERAL ZOD, YES, THANK YOU FOR COMING SO PROMPTLY. I KNOW YOU'VE BEEN BUSY."

"I CAN ALWAYS MAKE TIME FOR YOU. WE ARE OF LIKE MIND, AFTER ALL: EACH OF US COMMITTED TO THE DEFENSE OF OUR PEOPLE."

"THAT'S WHY I WANTED TO SPEAK WITH YOU. I'M AFRAID I MAY HAVE... COMPROMISED OUR DEFENSES."

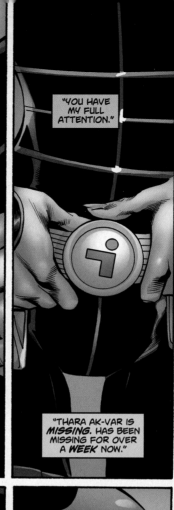

"YOU HAVE MY FULL ATTENTION."

"THARA AK-VAR IS MISSING. HAS BEEN MISSING FOR OVER A WEEK NOW."

"I DON'T UNDERSTAND."

"THARA WAS THE CHIEF OF OUR SECURITY, GENERAL. SHE PERMITTED MY HUSBAND TO BE MURDERED BY THOSE HUMAN ANIMALS."

"I SEE. AND YOU FEAR SHE'S DEFECTED?"

"THARA IS... DELUSIONAL, GENERAL. EVEN BEFORE KANDOR WAS RESTORED SHE SPOKE TO MY HUSBAND AND ME ABOUT DREAMS SHE WAS HAVING..."

"...OF A VOICE THAT CALLED OUT TO HER FROM THE PHANTOM ZONE. A BOY ASKING FOR HER HELP..."

"...WARNING HER ABOUT YOU AND LIEUTENANT COMMANDER URSA."

"..."

"...GENERAL?"

"AK-VAR, YOU SAID?"

"THARA AK-VAR, YES. HER PARENTS BOTH SERVED UNDER YOU, DIDN'T THEY?"

"I BELIEVE THEY DID. THANK YOU FOR BRINGING THIS TO MY ATTENTION, ALURA..."

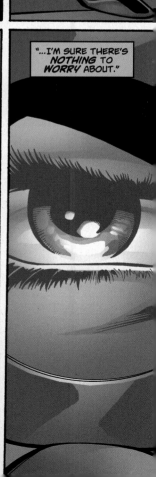

"...I'M SURE THERE'S NOTHING TO WORRY ABOUT."

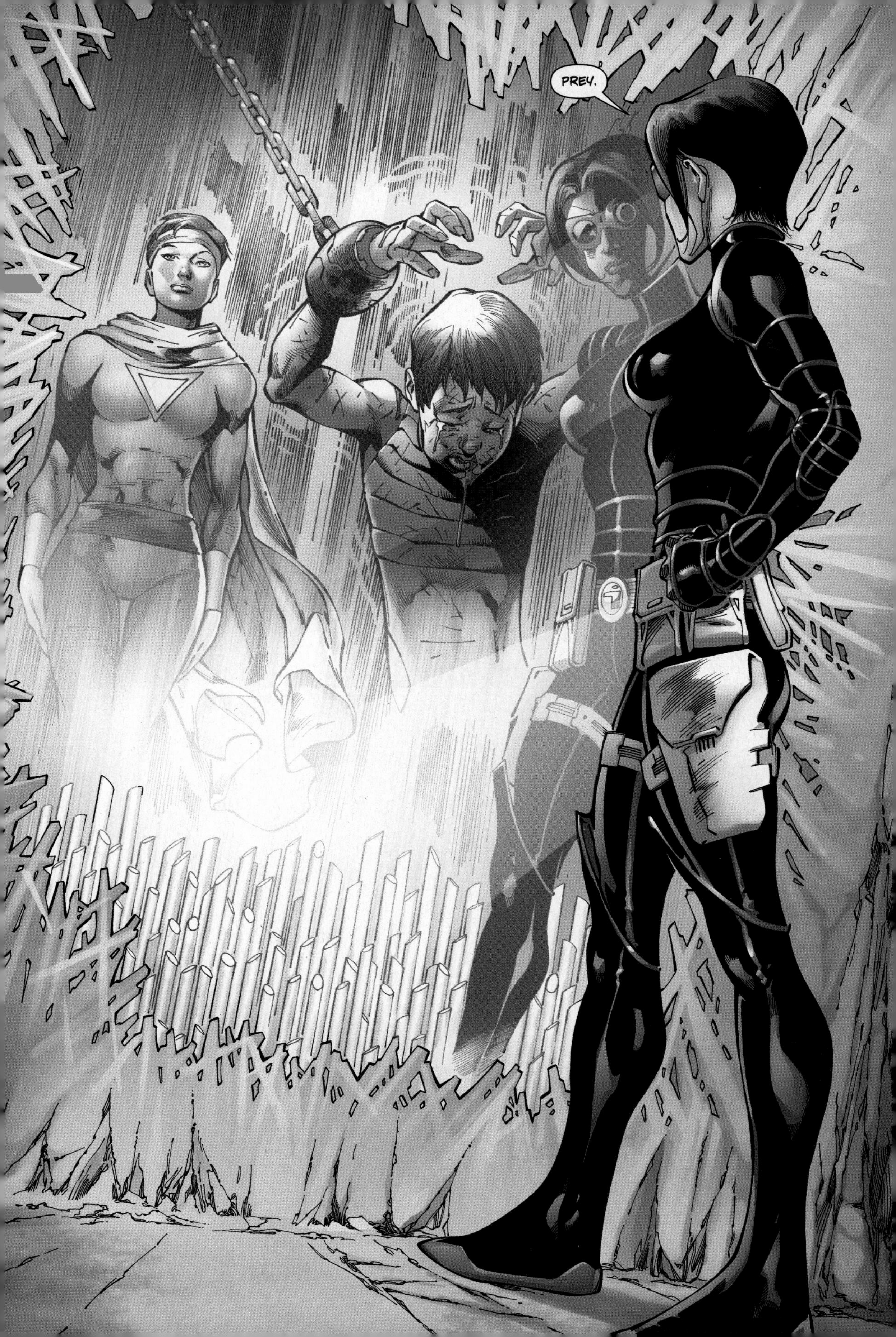
PREY.

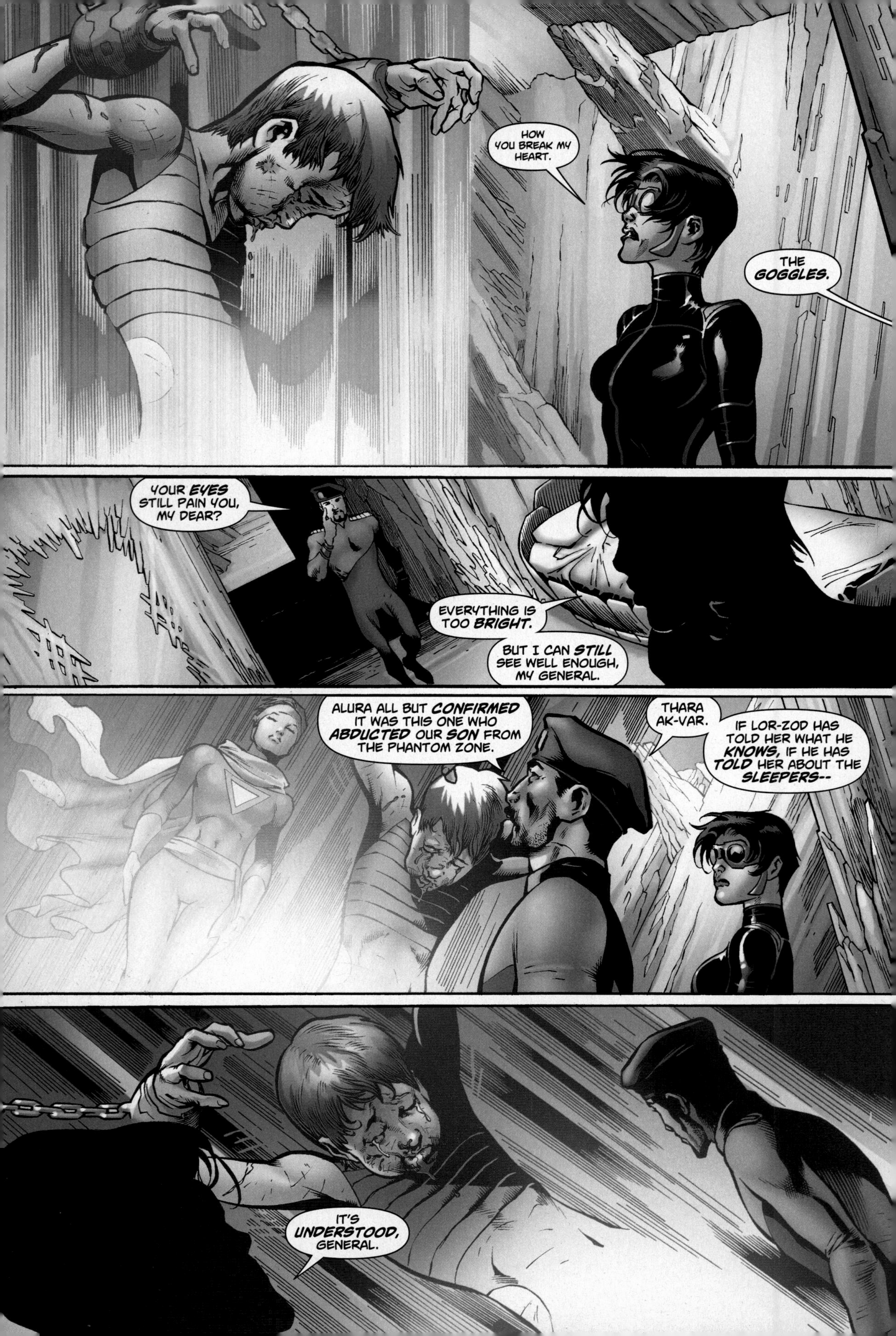
HOW YOU BREAK MY HEART.
THE GOGGLES.
YOUR EYES STILL PAIN YOU, MY DEAR?
EVERYTHING IS TOO BRIGHT.
BUT I CAN STILL SEE WELL ENOUGH, MY GENERAL.
ALURA ALL BUT CONFIRMED IT WAS THIS ONE WHO ABDUCTED OUR SON FROM THE PHANTOM ZONE.
THARA AK-VAR.
IF LOR-ZOD HAS TOLD HER WHAT HE KNOWS, IF HE HAS TOLD HER ABOUT THE SLEEPERS--
IT'S UNDERSTOOD, GENERAL.

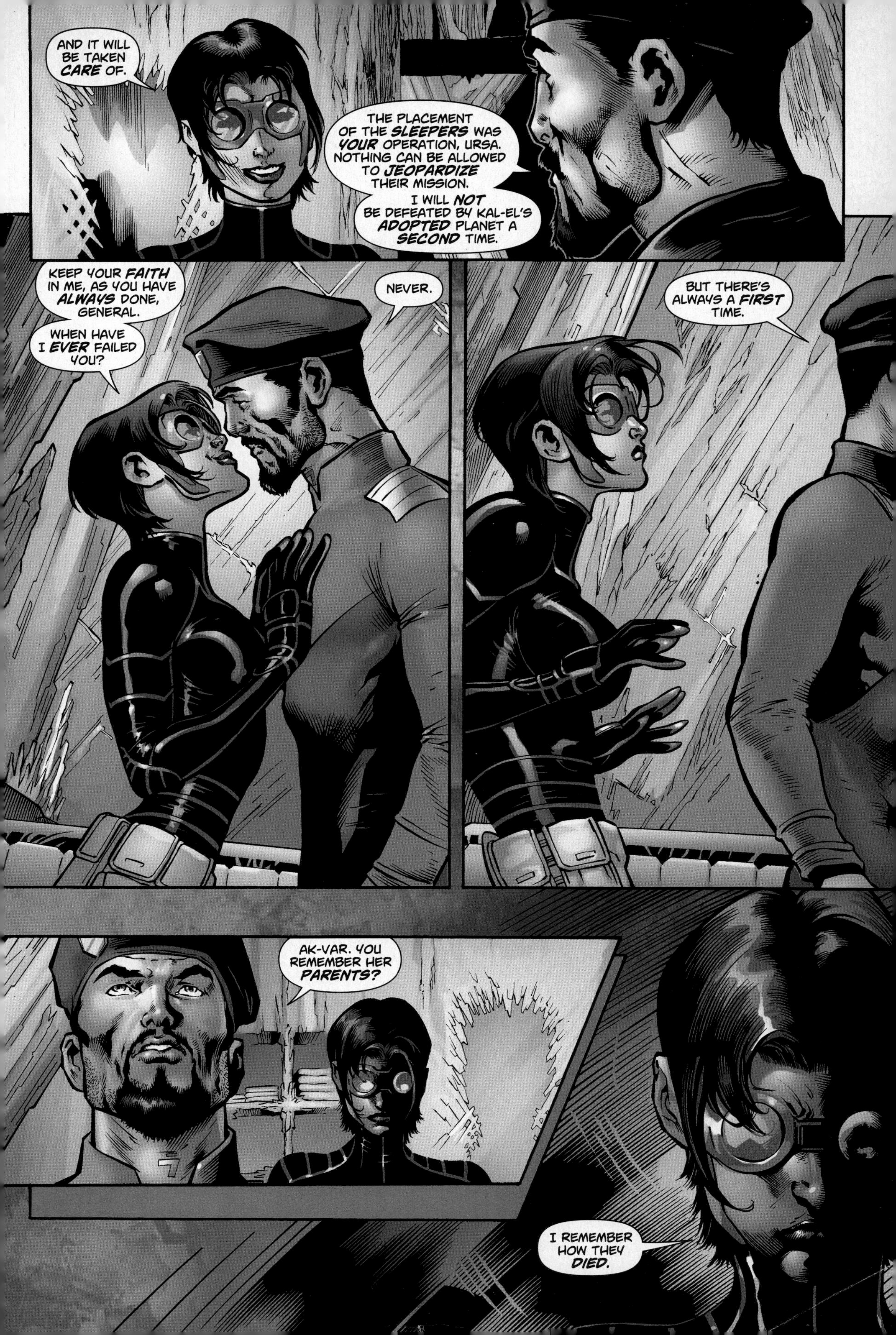
AND IT WILL BE TAKEN CARE OF.
THE PLACEMENT OF THE SLEEPERS WAS YOUR OPERATION, URSA. NOTHING CAN BE ALLOWED TO JEOPARDIZE THEIR MISSION.
I WILL NOT BE DEFEATED BY KAL-EL'S ADOPTED PLANET A SECOND TIME.
KEEP YOUR FAITH IN ME, AS YOU HAVE ALWAYS DONE, GENERAL.
WHEN HAVE I EVER FAILED YOU?
NEVER.
BUT THERE'S ALWAYS A FIRST TIME.
AK-VAR. YOU REMEMBER HER PARENTS?
I REMEMBER HOW THEY DIED.

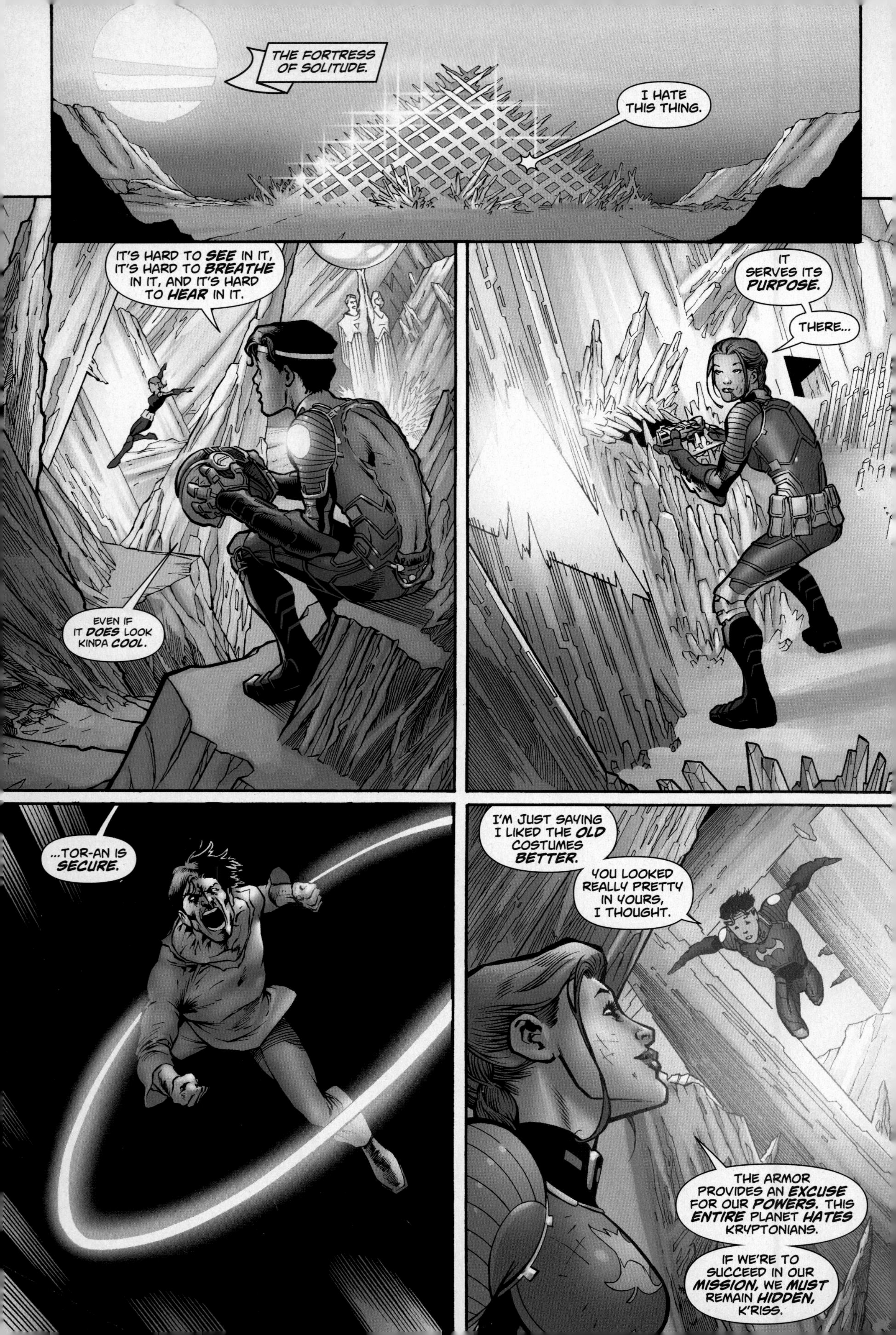
THE FORTRESS OF SOLITUDE.
I HATE THIS THING.
IT'S HARD TO SEE IN IT, IT'S HARD TO BREATHE IN IT, AND IT'S HARD TO HEAR IN IT.
EVEN IF IT DOES LOOK KINDA COOL.
IT SERVES ITS PURPOSE.
THERE...
...TOR-AN IS SECURE.
I'M JUST SAYING I LIKED THE OLD COSTUMES BETTER.
YOU LOOKED REALLY PRETTY IN YOURS, I THOUGHT.
THE ARMOR PROVIDES AN EXCUSE FOR OUR POWERS. THIS ENTIRE PLANET HATES KRYPTONIANS.
IF WE'RE TO SUCCEED IN OUR MISSION, WE MUST REMAIN HIDDEN, K'RISS.

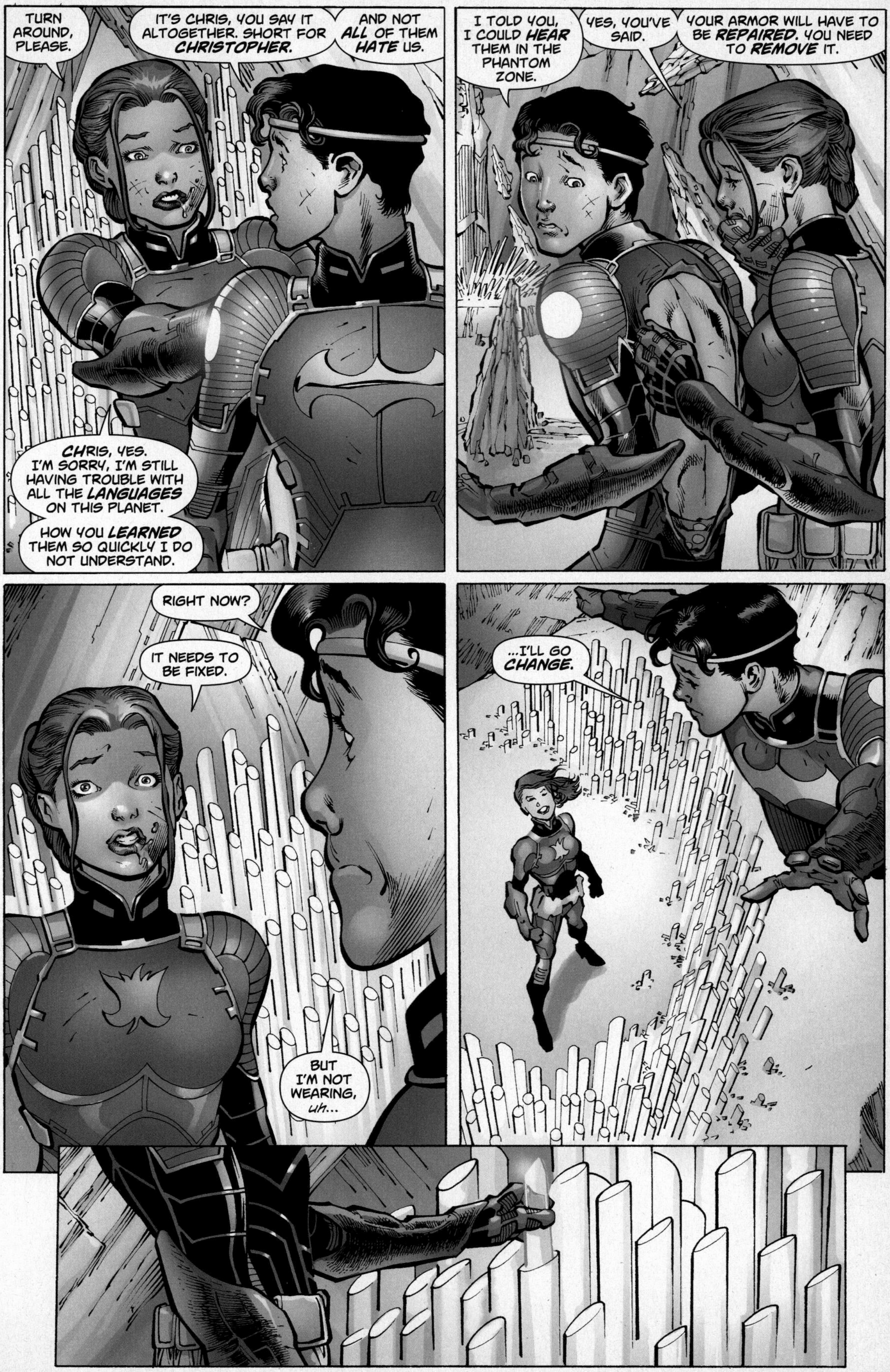
TURN AROUND, PLEASE.
IT'S CHRIS, YOU SAY IT ALTOGETHER. SHORT FOR CHRISTOPHER.
AND NOT ALL OF THEM HATE US.
CHRIS, YES. I'M SORRY, I'M STILL HAVING TROUBLE WITH ALL THE LANGUAGES ON THIS PLANET.
HOW YOU LEARNED THEM SO QUICKLY I DO NOT UNDERSTAND.
I TOLD YOU, I COULD HEAR THEM IN THE PHANTOM ZONE.
YES, YOU'VE SAID.
YOUR ARMOR WILL HAVE TO BE REPAIRED. YOU NEED TO REMOVE IT.
RIGHT NOW?
IT NEEDS TO BE FIXED.
BUT I'M NOT WEARING, uh...
...I'LL GO CHANGE.

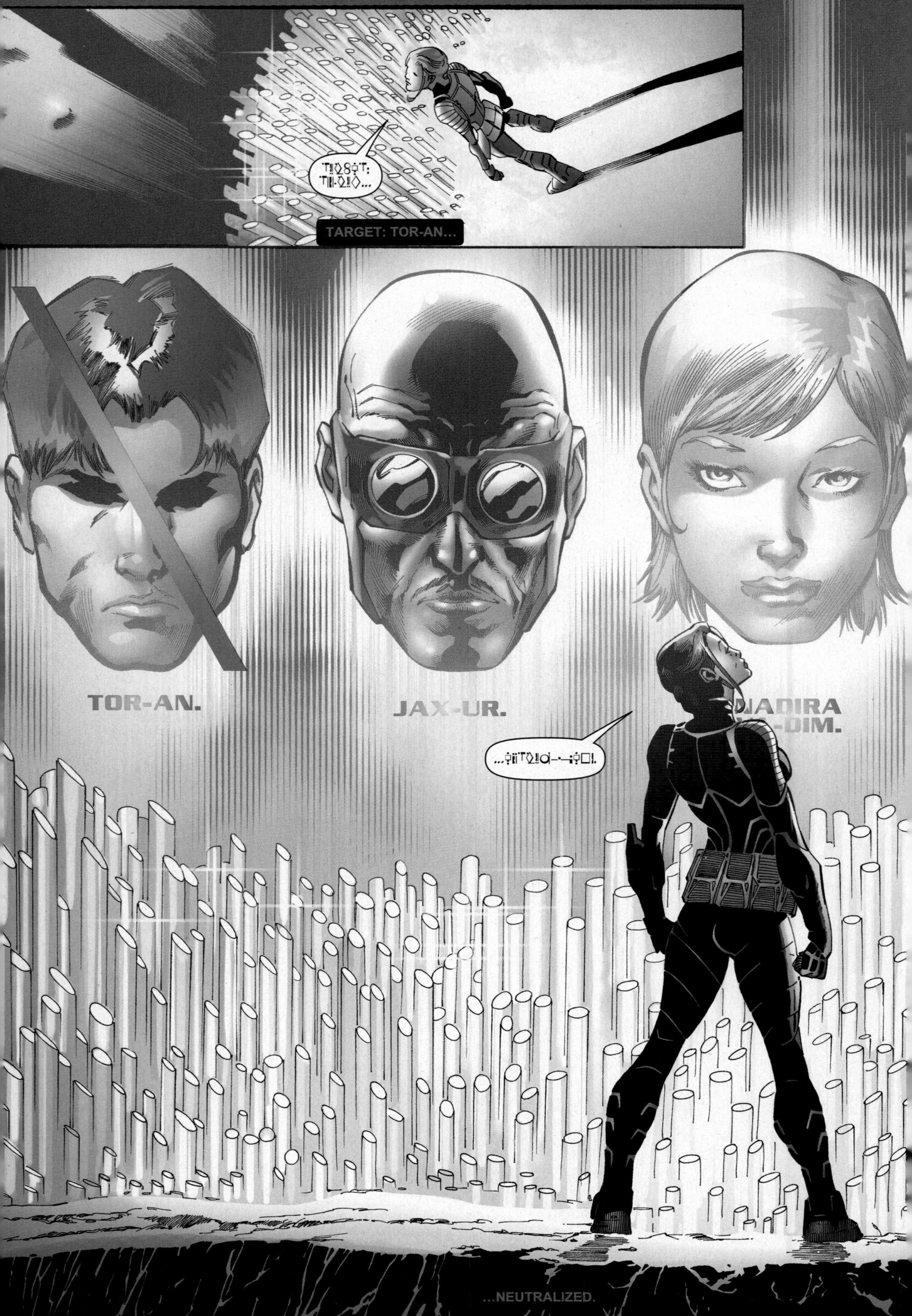

TARGET: TOR-AN...
TOR-AN.
JAX-UR.
NADIRA
-DIM.
...NEUTRALIZED.

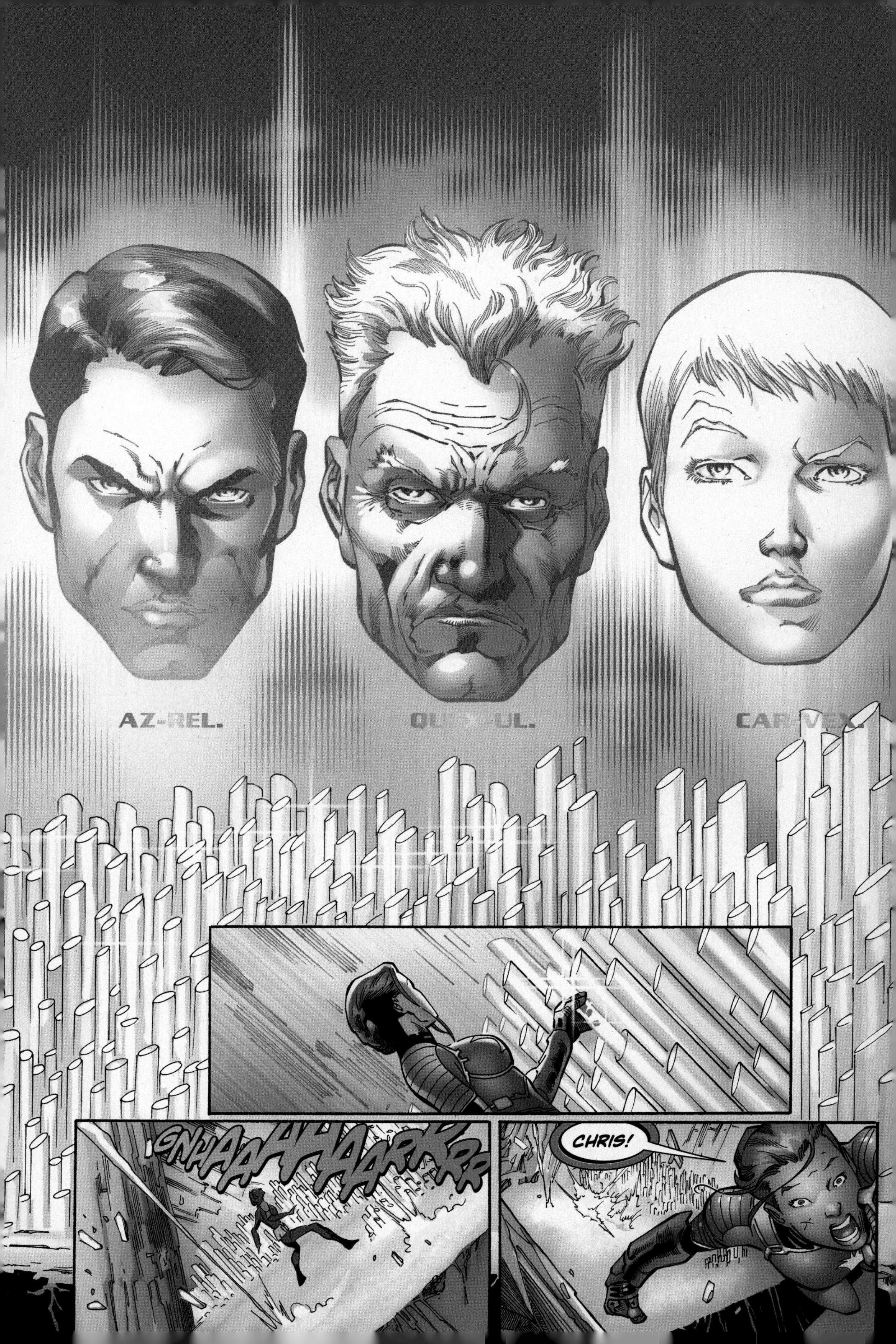
AZ-REL.
QUEX-UL.
CAR-VEX.
GNHAAAHHAARKRR
CHRIS!

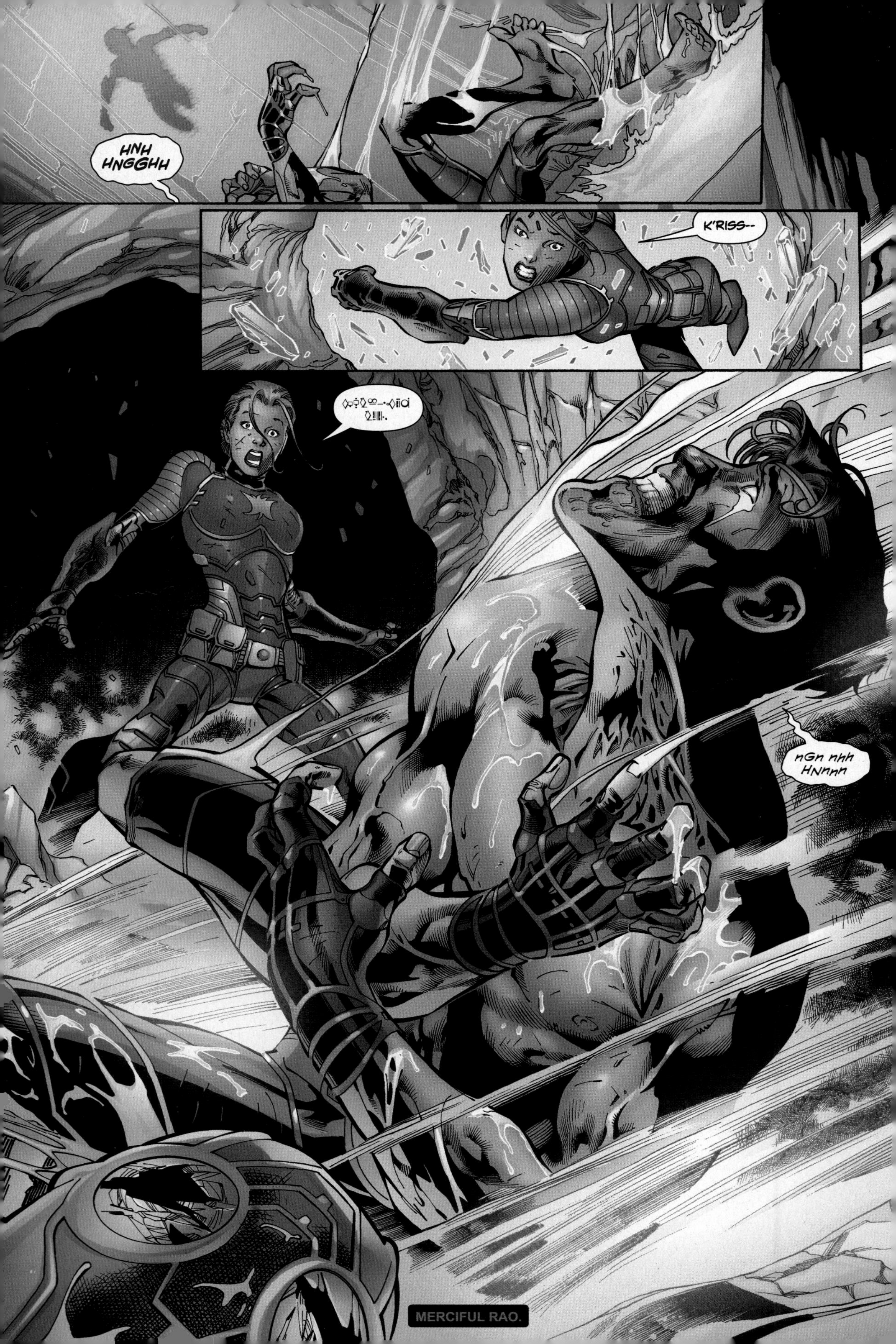
HNH HNGGHH
K'RISS--
nGn nhh HNnnn
MERCIFUL RAO.

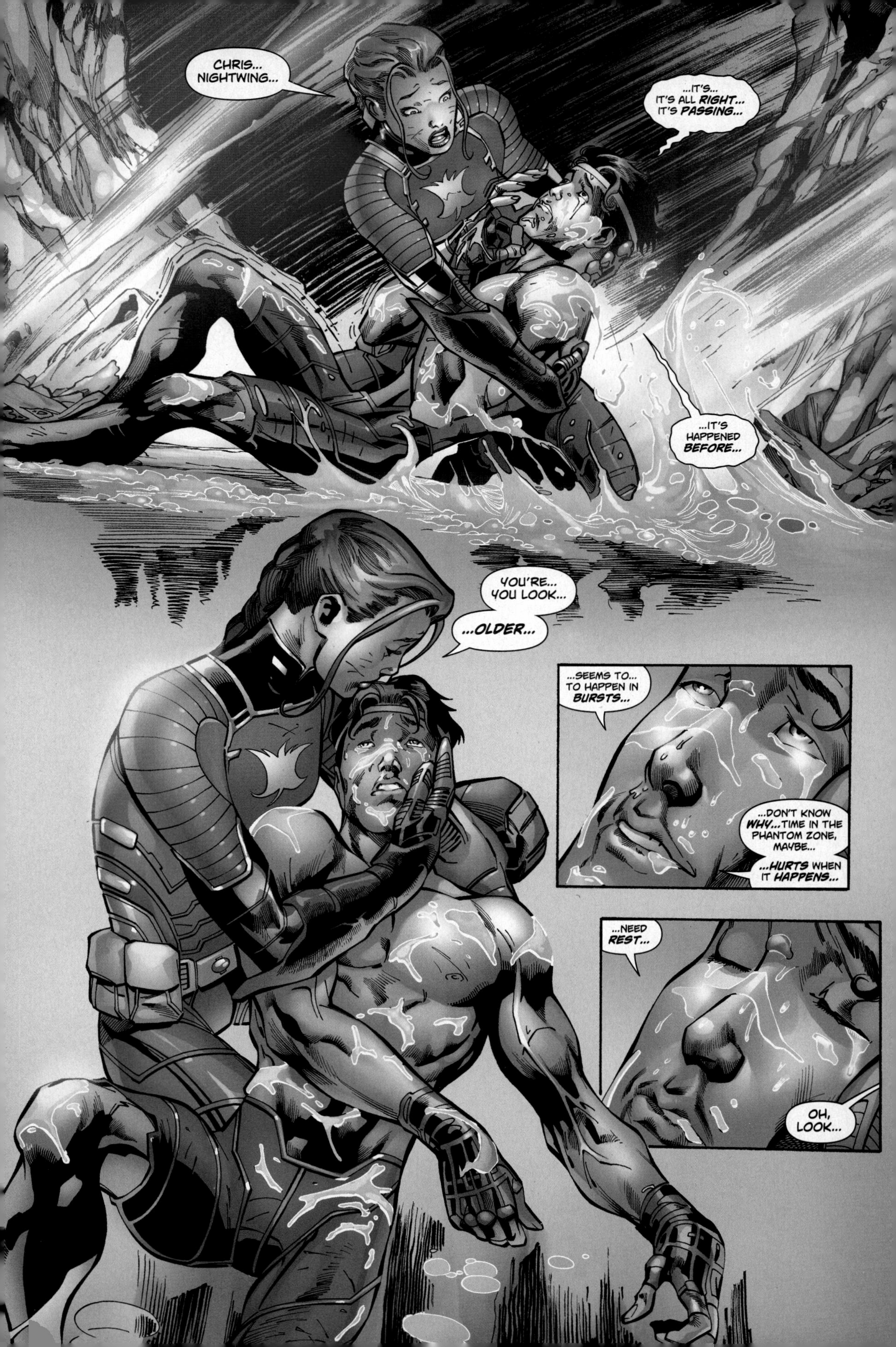
CHRIS... NIGHTWING...
...IT'S... IT'S ALL RIGHT... IT'S PASSING...
...IT'S HAPPENED BEFORE...
YOU'RE... YOU LOOK...
...OLDER...
...SEEMS TO... TO HAPPEN IN BURSTS...
...DON'T KNOW WHY... TIME IN THE PHANTOM ZONE, MAYBE...
...HURTS WHEN IT HAPPENS...
...NEED REST...
OH, LOOK...

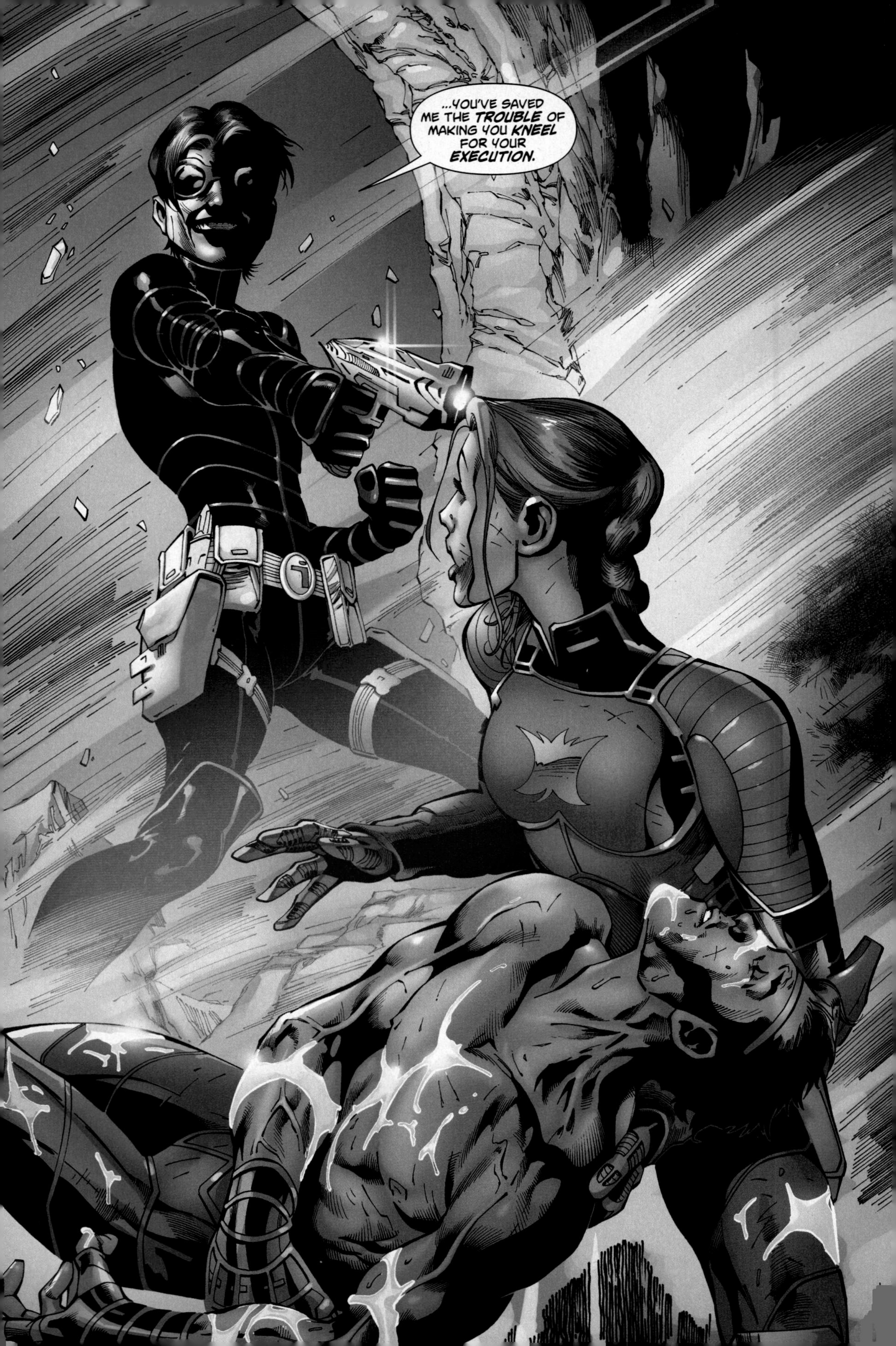
...YOU'VE SAVED ME THE TROUBLE OF MAKING YOU KNEEL FOR YOUR EXECUTION.

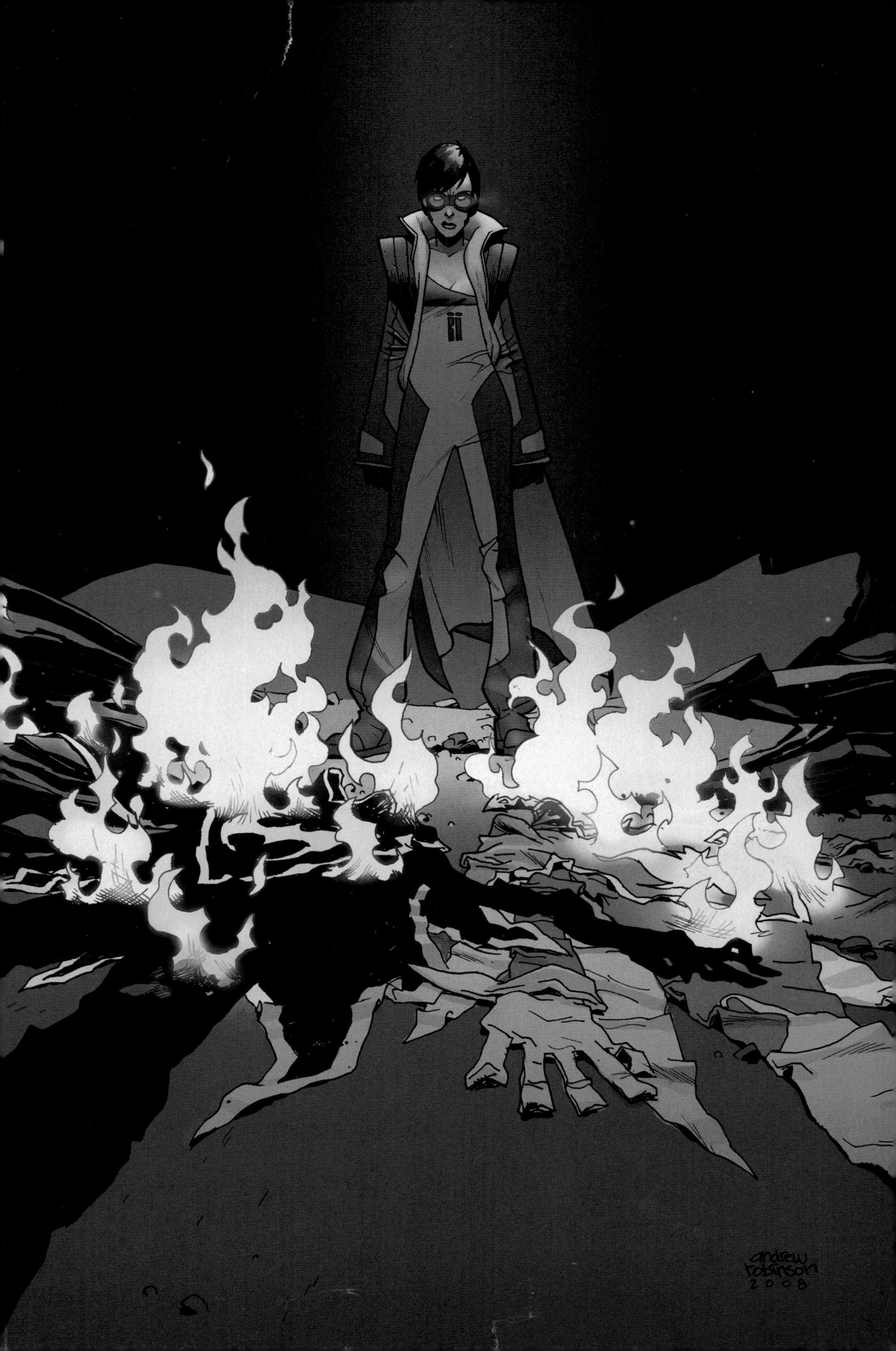
andrew robinson 2008

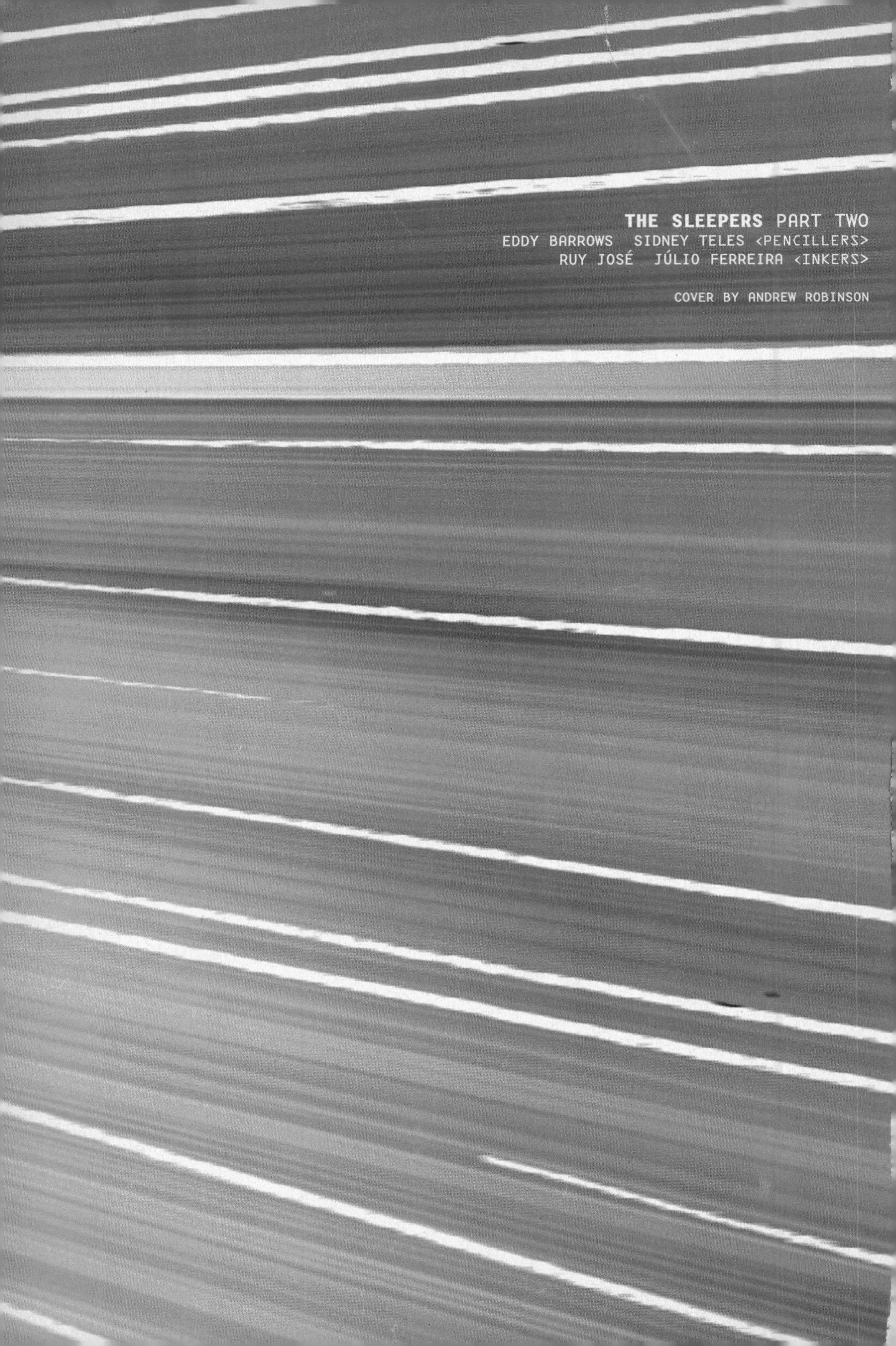

THE SLEEPERS PART TWO

EDDY BARROWS SIDNEY TELES <PENCILLERS>
RUY JOSÉ JÚLIO FERREIRA <INKERS>

COVER BY ANDREW ROBINSON

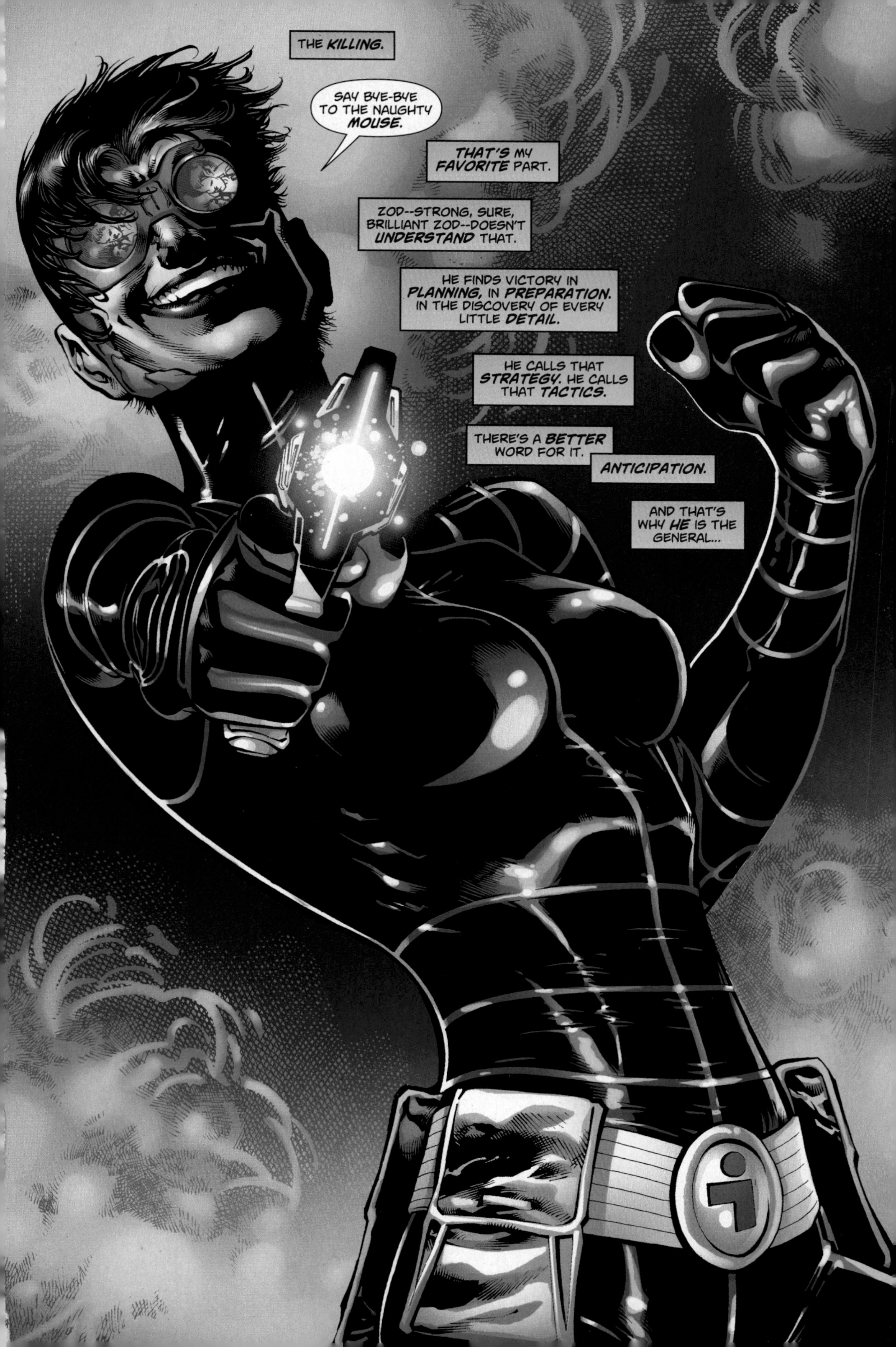
THE KILLING.
SAY BYE-BYE TO THE NAUGHTY MOUSE.
THAT'S MY FAVORITE PART.
ZOD--STRONG, SURE, BRILLIANT ZOD--DOESN'T UNDERSTAND THAT.
HE FINDS VICTORY IN PLANNING, IN PREPARATION. IN THE DISCOVERY OF EVERY LITTLE DETAIL.
HE CALLS THAT STRATEGY. HE CALLS THAT TACTICS.
THERE'S A BETTER WORD FOR IT.
ANTICIPATION.
AND THAT'S WHY HE IS THE GENERAL...

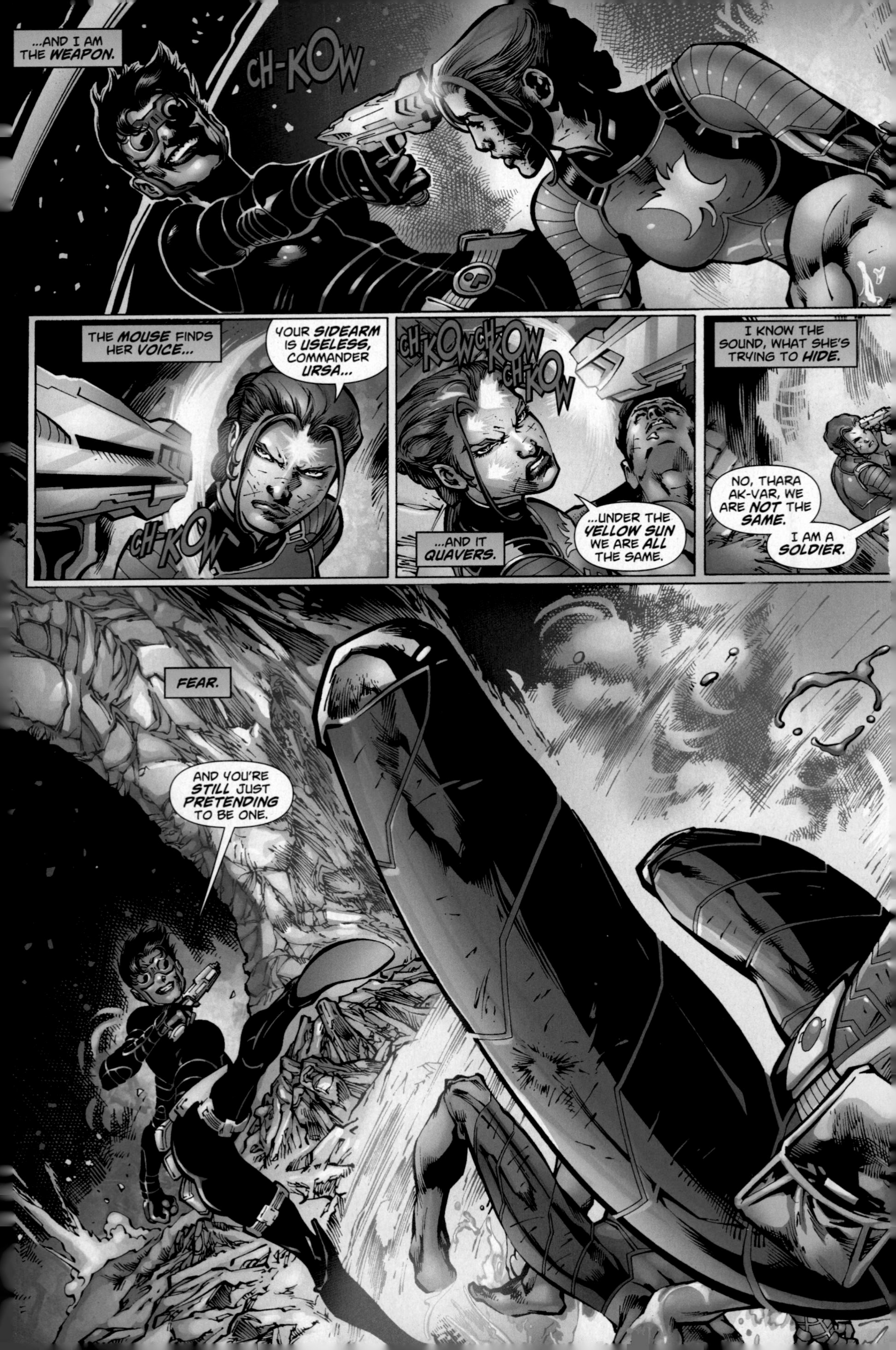
...AND I AM THE WEAPON.
CH-KOW
THE MOUSE FINDS HER VOICE...
YOUR SIDEARM IS USELESS, COMMANDER URSA...
CH-KOW
CH-KOW CH-KOW CH-KOW
...AND IT QUAVERS.
...UNDER THE YELLOW SUN WE ARE ALL THE SAME.
I KNOW THE SOUND, WHAT SHE'S TRYING TO HIDE.
NO, THARA AK-VAR, WE ARE NOT THE SAME.
I AM A SOLDIER.
FEAR.
AND YOU'RE STILL JUST PRETENDING TO BE ONE.

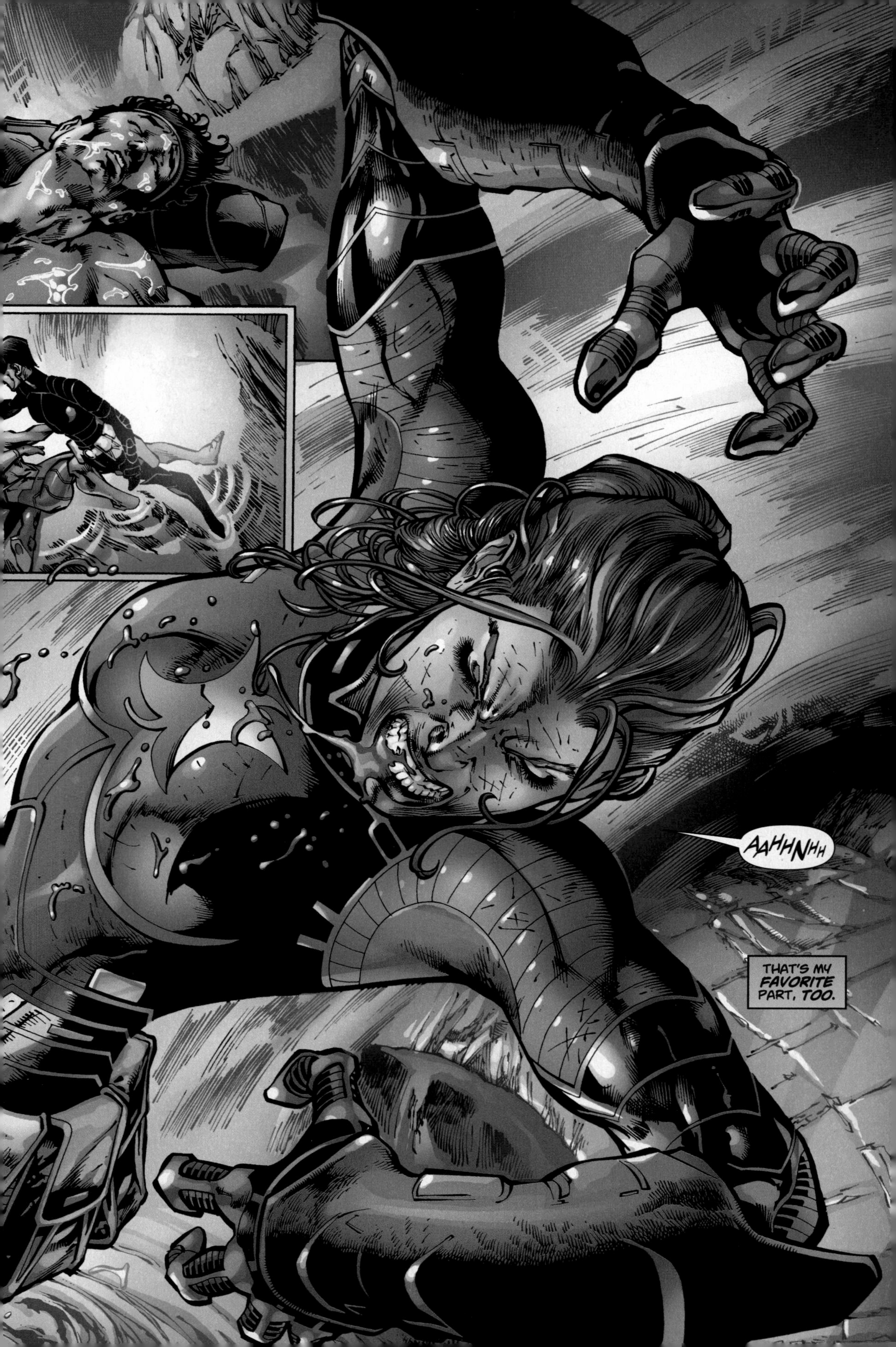
AAHHNHH
THAT'S MY FAVORITE PART, TOO.

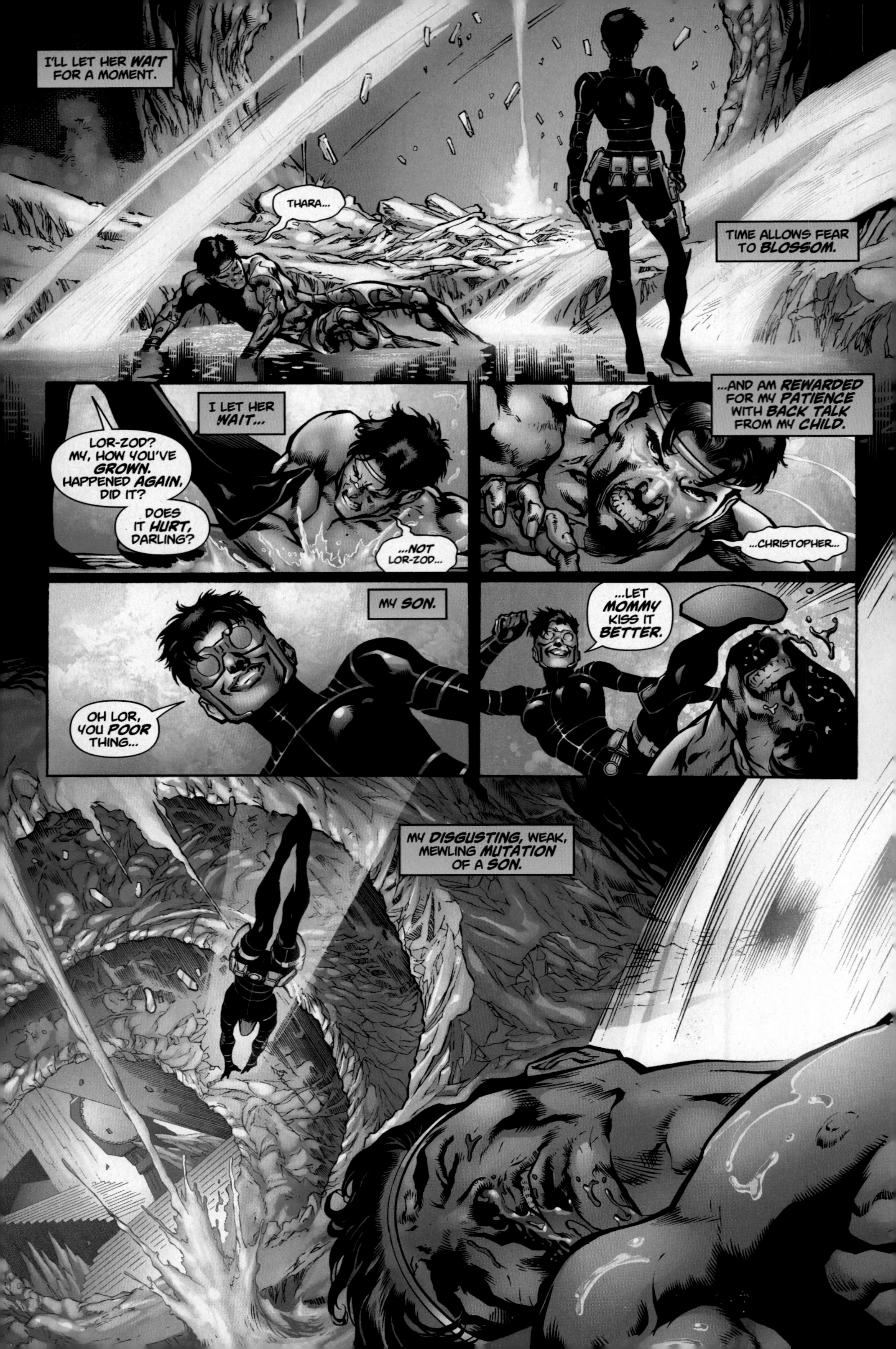
I'LL LET HER WAIT FOR A MOMENT.
THARA...
TIME ALLOWS FEAR TO BLOSSOM.
I LET HER WAIT...
LOR-ZOD? MY, HOW YOU'VE GROWN. HAPPENED AGAIN, DID IT?
DOES IT HURT, DARLING?
...NOT LOR-ZOD...
...AND AM REWARDED FOR MY PATIENCE WITH BACK TALK FROM MY CHILD.
...CHRISTOPHER...
MY SON.
OH LOR, YOU POOR THING...
...LET MOMMY KISS IT BETTER.
MY DISGUSTING, WEAK, MEWLING MUTATION OF A SON.

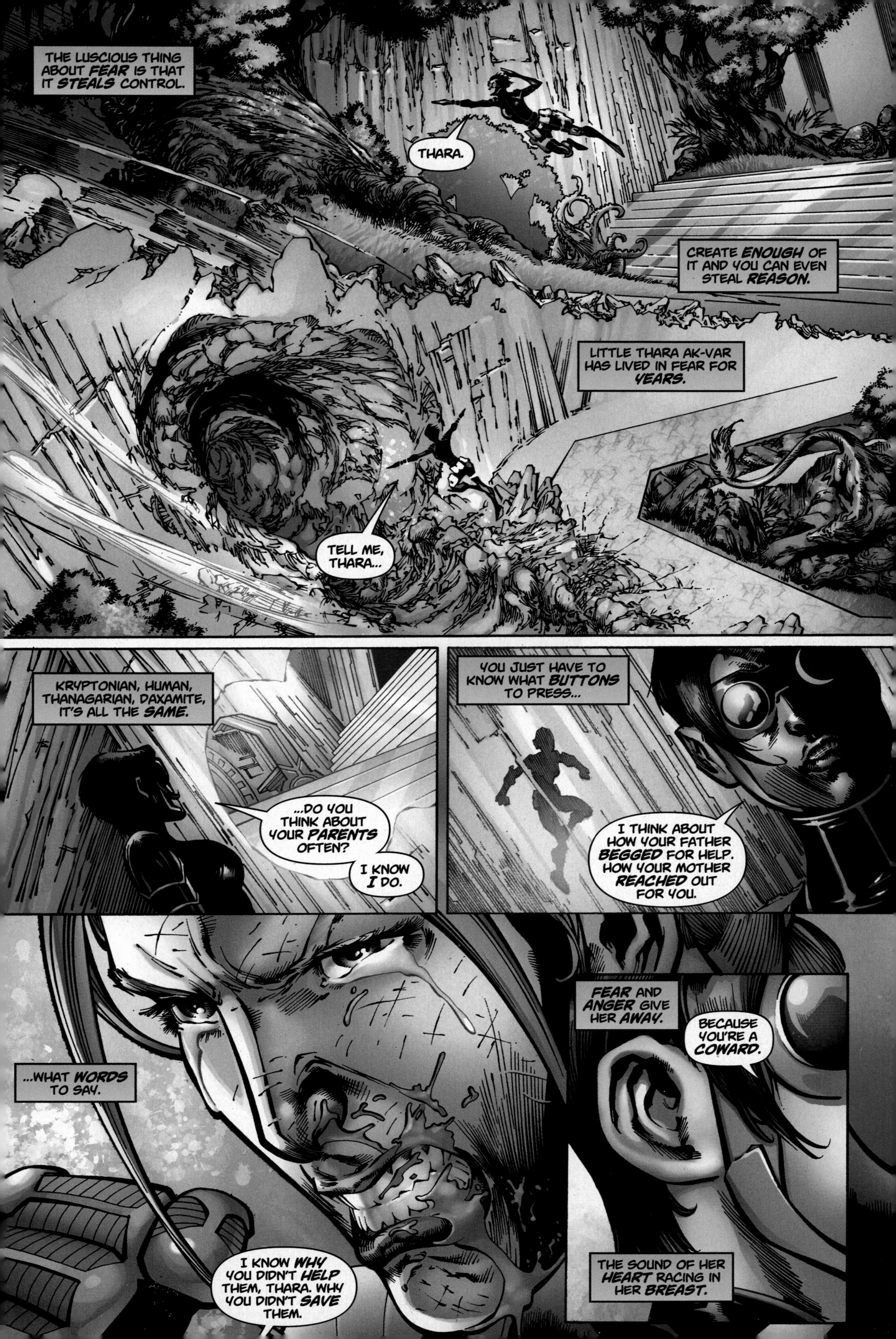
THE LUSCIOUS THING ABOUT FEAR IS THAT IT STEALS CONTROL.
THARA.
CREATE ENOUGH OF IT AND YOU CAN EVEN STEAL REASON.
LITTLE THARA AK-VAR HAS LIVED IN FEAR FOR YEARS.
TELL ME, THARA...
KRYPTONIAN, HUMAN, THANAGARIAN, DAXAMITE, IT'S ALL THE SAME.
...DO YOU THINK ABOUT YOUR PARENTS OFTEN?
I KNOW I DO.
YOU JUST HAVE TO KNOW WHAT BUTTONS TO PRESS...
I THINK ABOUT HOW YOUR FATHER BEGGED FOR HELP. HOW YOUR MOTHER REACHED OUT FOR YOU.
...WHAT WORDS TO SAY.
I KNOW WHY YOU DIDN'T HELP THEM, THARA. WHY YOU DIDN'T SAVE THEM.
FEAR AND ANGER GIVE HER AWAY.
BECAUSE YOU'RE A COWARD.
THE SOUND OF HER HEART RACING IN HER BREAST.

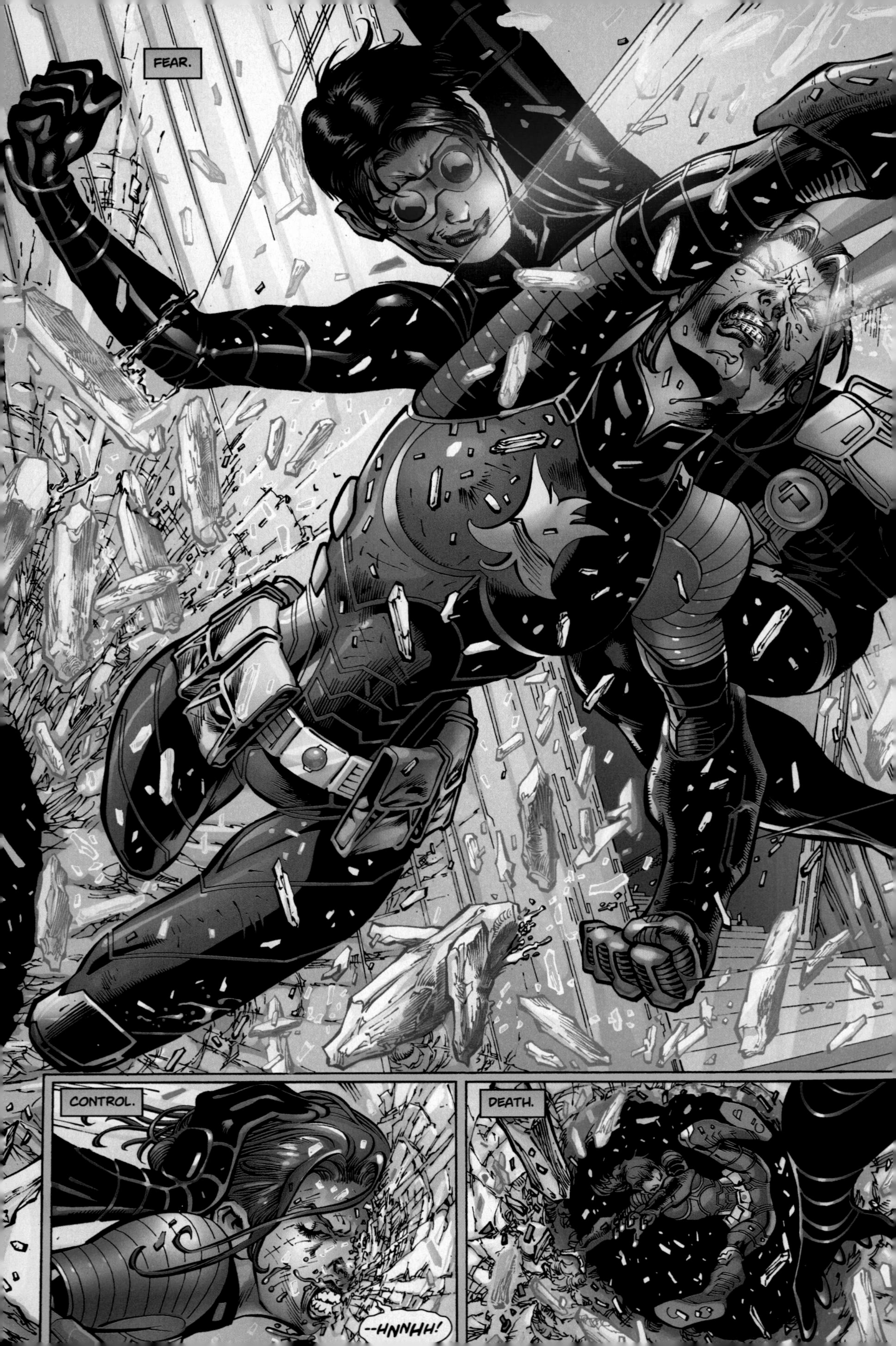
FEAR.
CONTROL.
--HNNHH!
DEATH.

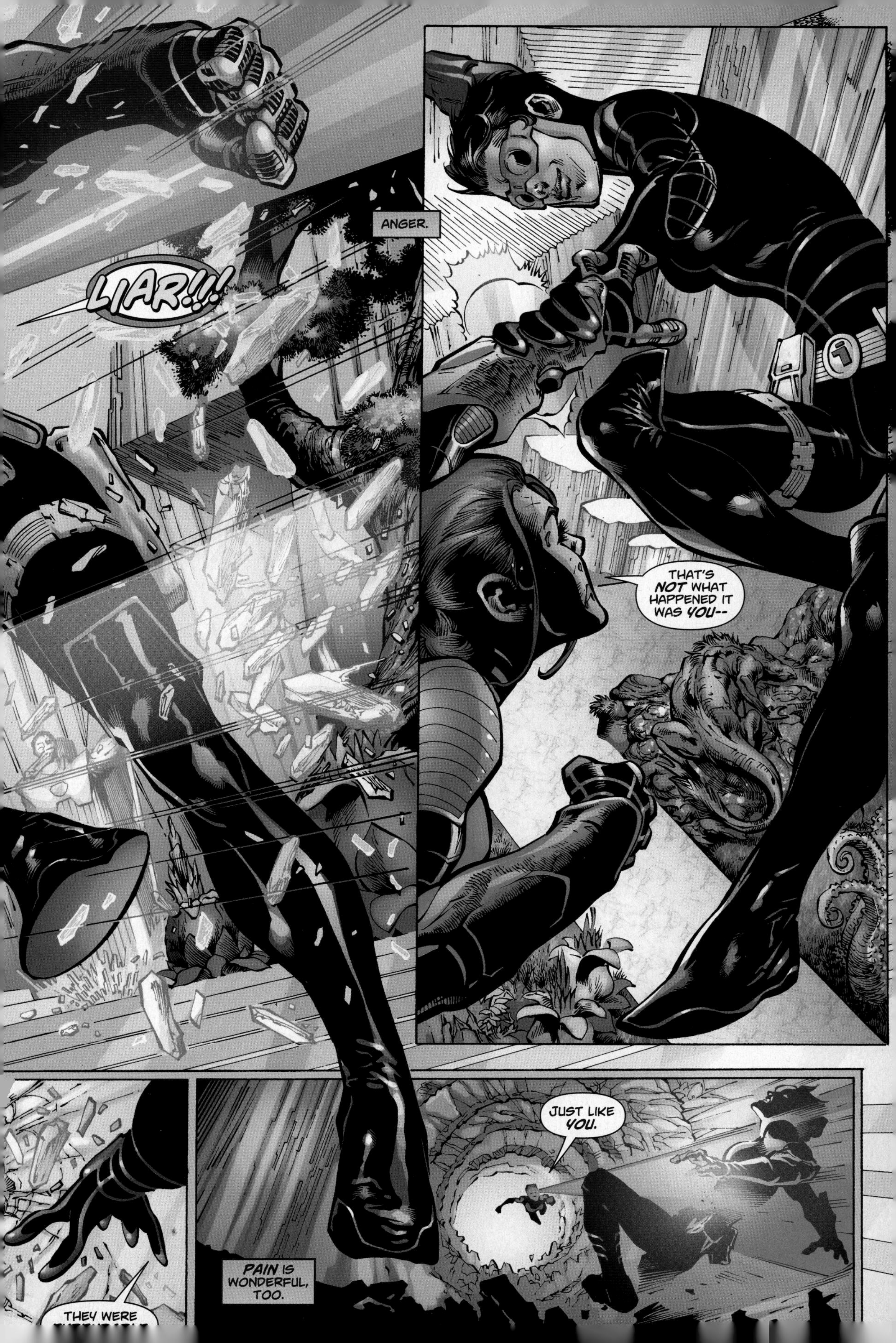
ANGER.
LIAR!!!
THAT'S NOT WHAT HAPPENED IT WAS YOU--
THEY WERE
PAIN IS WONDERFUL, TOO.
JUST LIKE YOU.

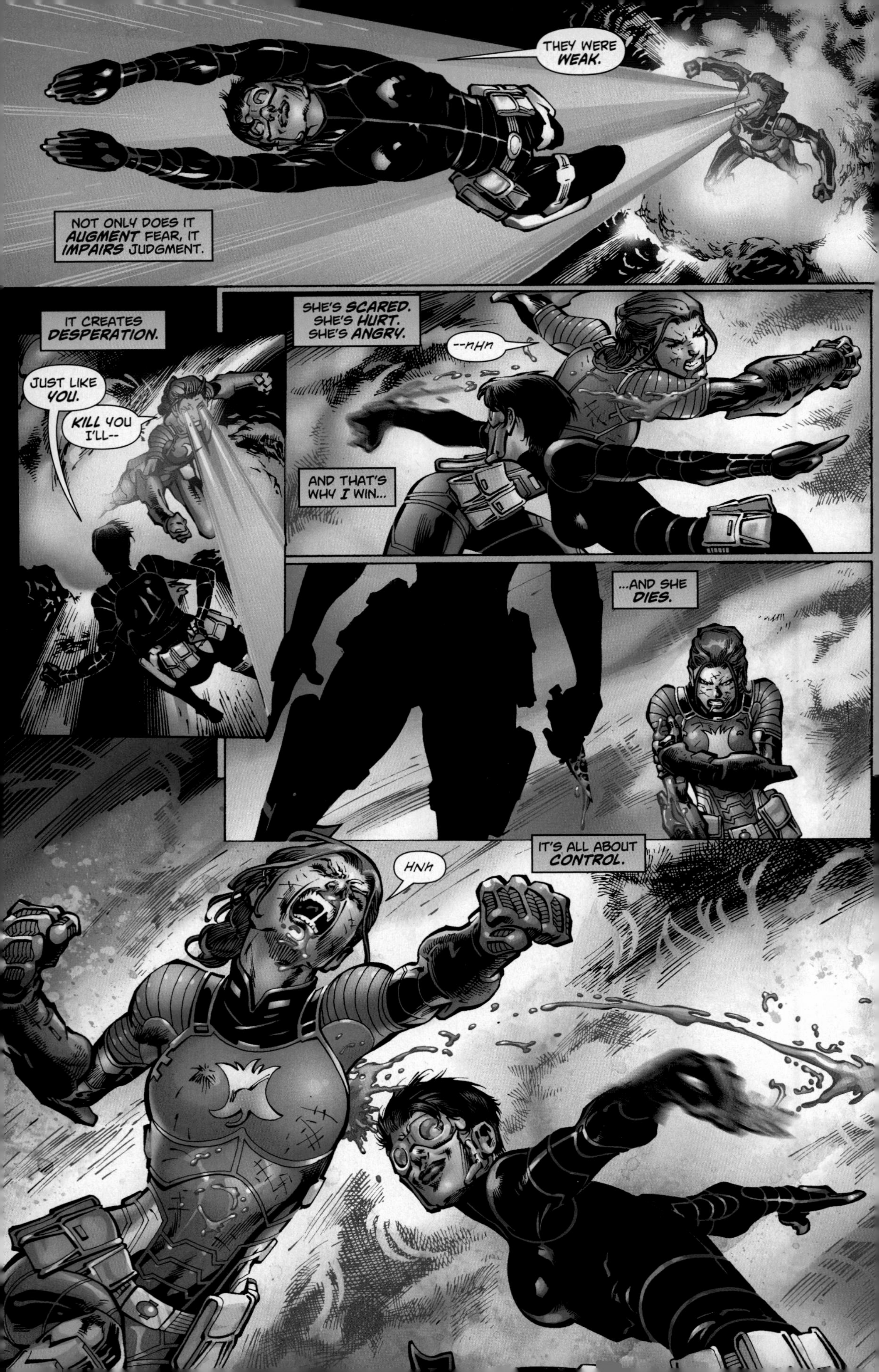
THEY WERE WEAK.
NOT ONLY DOES IT AUGMENT FEAR, IT IMPAIRS JUDGMENT.
IT CREATES DESPERATION.
JUST LIKE YOU.
KILL YOU I'LL--
SHE'S SCARED. SHE'S HURT. SHE'S ANGRY.
--nHn
AND THAT'S WHY I WIN...
...AND SHE DIES.
IT'S ALL ABOUT CONTROL.
HNh

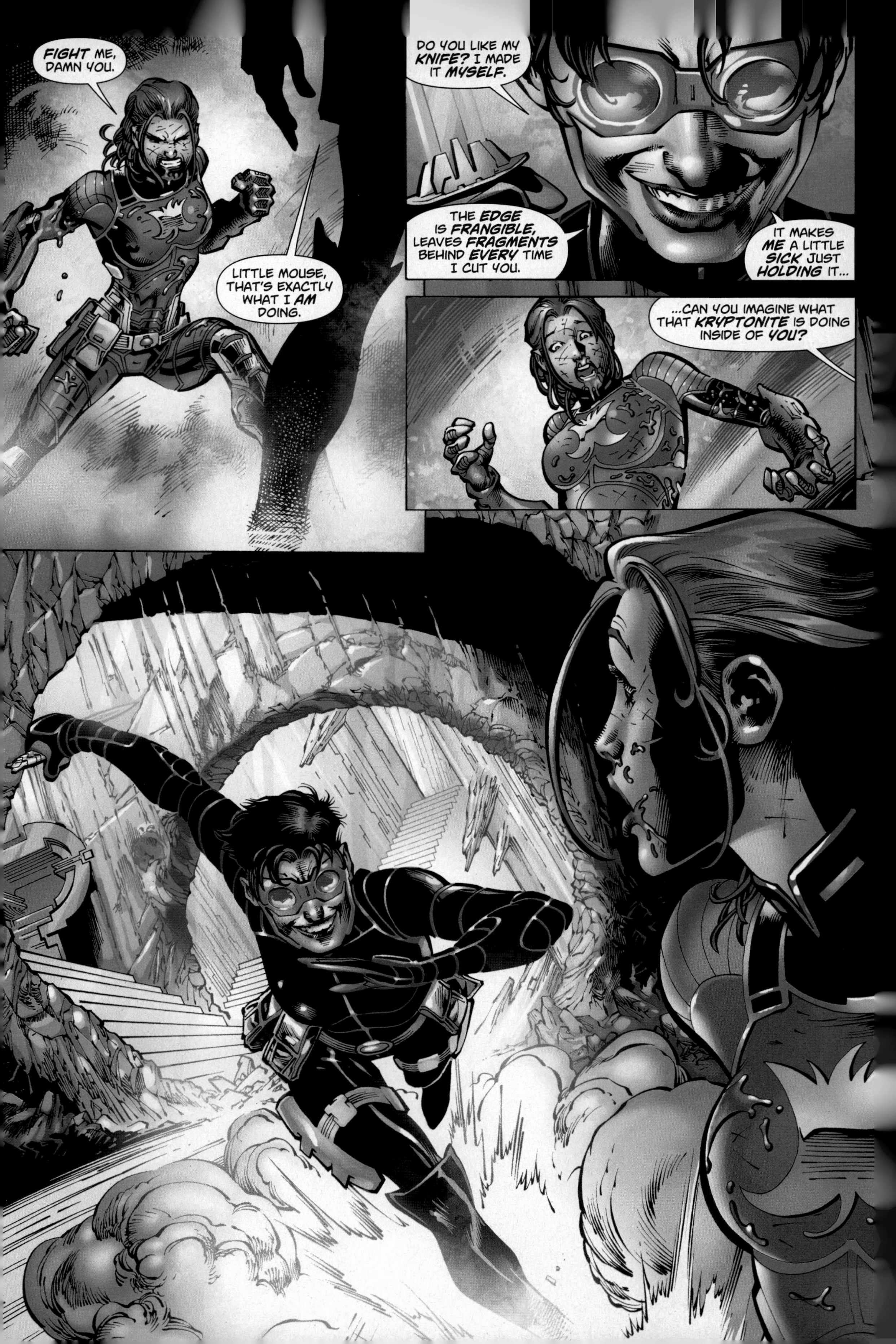
FIGHT ME, DAMN YOU.
LITTLE MOUSE, THAT'S EXACTLY WHAT I AM DOING.
DO YOU LIKE MY KNIFE? I MADE IT MYSELF.
THE EDGE IS FRANGIBLE, LEAVES FRAGMENTS BEHIND EVERY TIME I CUT YOU.
IT MAKES ME A LITTLE SICK JUST HOLDING IT...
...CAN YOU IMAGINE WHAT THAT KRYPTONITE IS DOING INSIDE OF YOU?

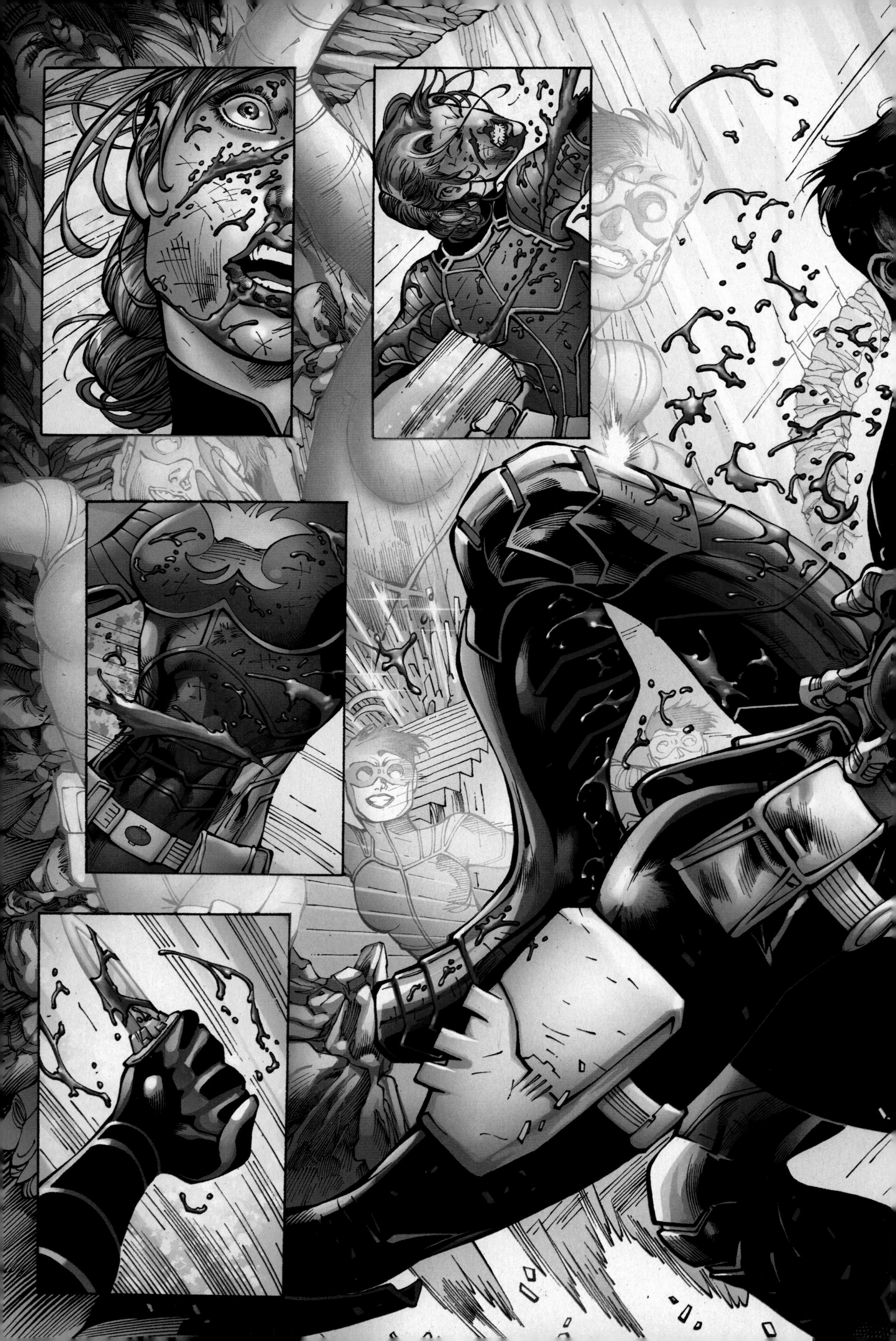

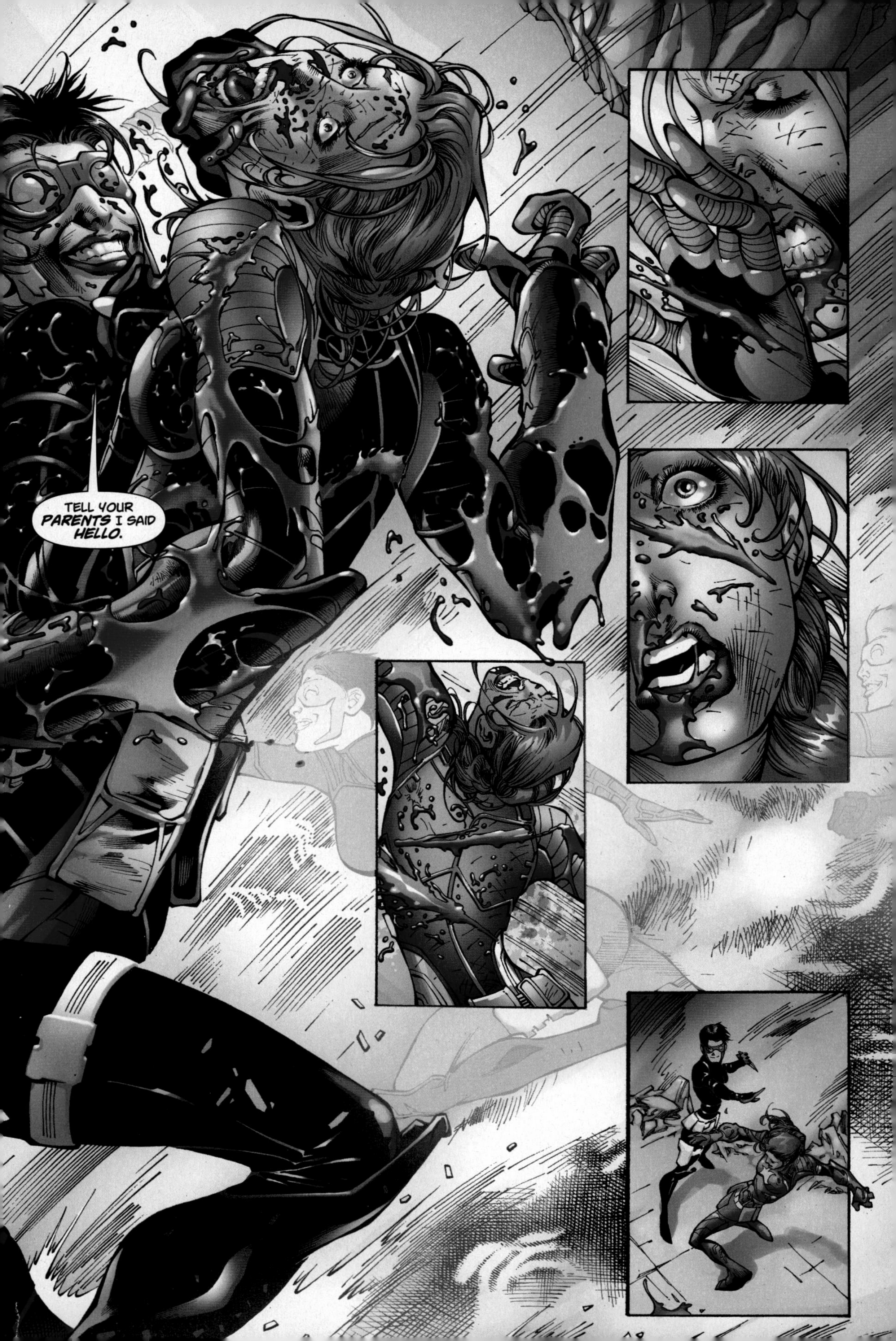
TELL YOUR PARENTS I SAID HELLO.

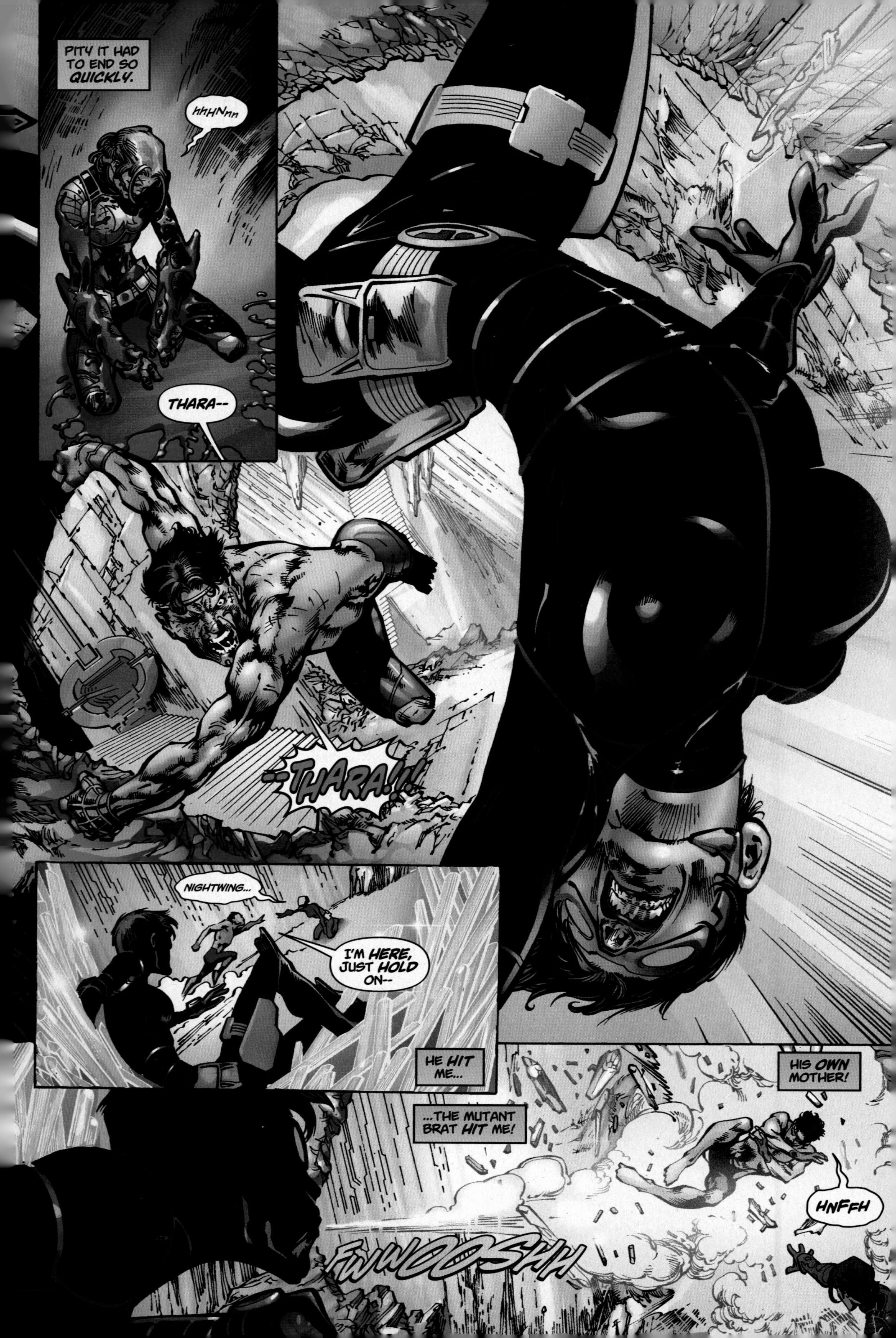
PITY IT HAD TO END SO QUICKLY.
hhHNnn
THARA--
--THARA!!!
NIGHTWING...
I'M HERE, JUST HOLD ON--
HE HIT ME...
...THE MUTANT BRAT HIT ME!
HIS OWN MOTHER!
HNFFH
FWWOOSHH

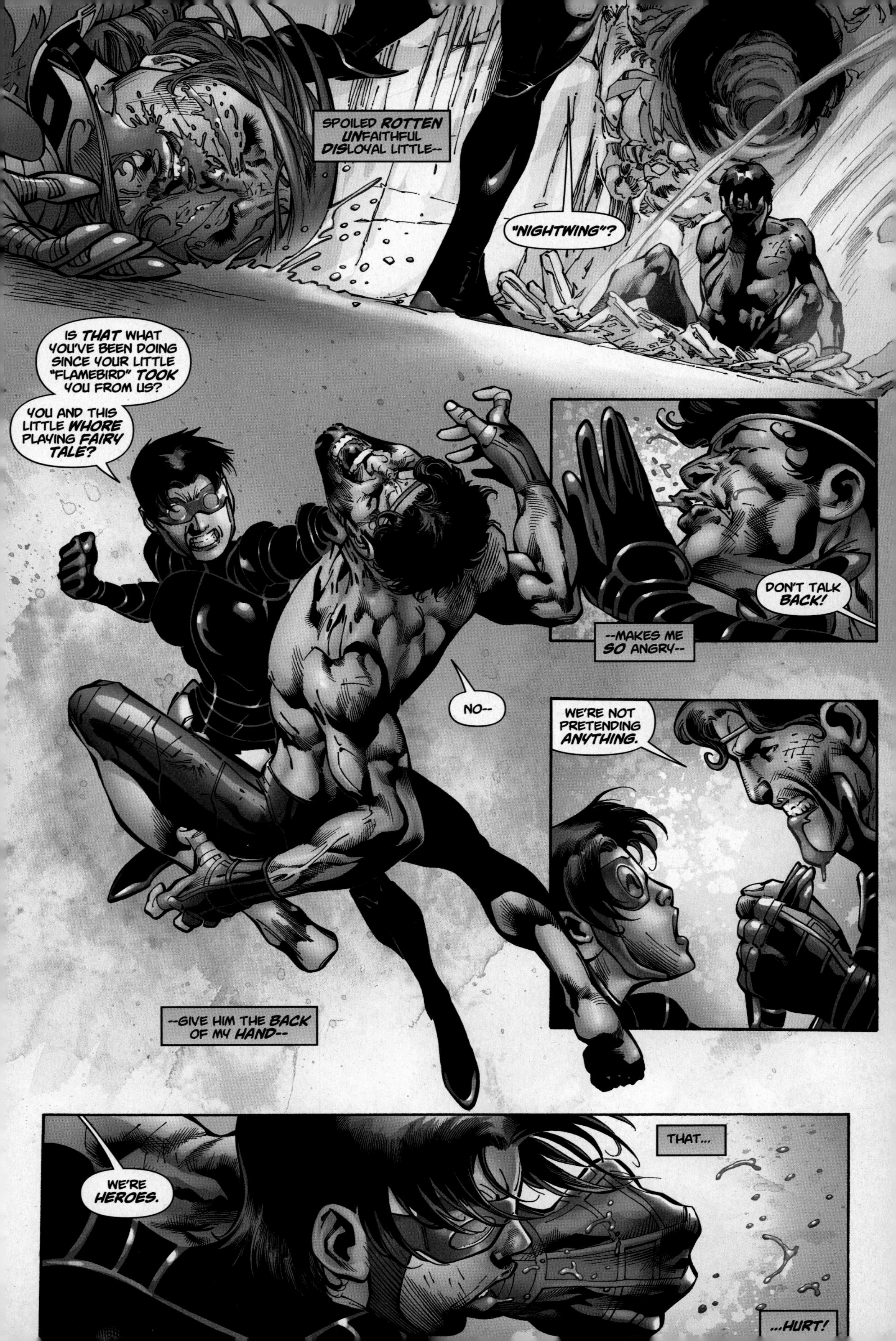
SPOILED ROTTEN UNFAITHFUL DISLOYAL LITTLE--
"NIGHTWING"?
IS THAT WHAT YOU'VE BEEN DOING SINCE YOUR LITTLE "FLAMEBIRD" TOOK YOU FROM US?
YOU AND THIS LITTLE WHORE PLAYING FAIRY TALE?
DON'T TALK BACK!
--MAKES ME SO ANGRY--
NO--
WE'RE NOT PRETENDING ANYTHING.
--GIVE HIM THE BACK OF MY HAND--
WE'RE HEROES.
THAT...
...HURT!

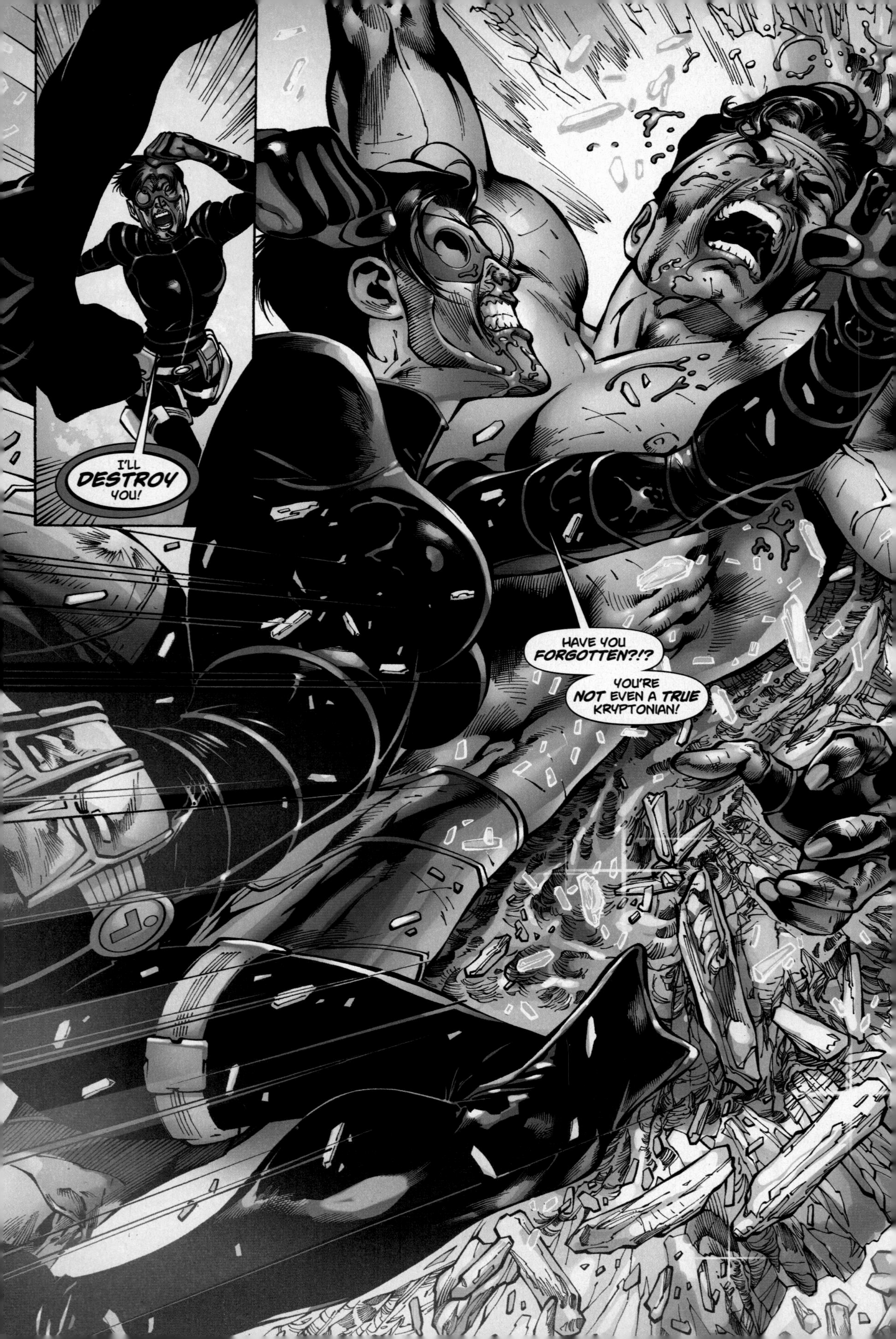
I'LL DESTROY YOU!
HAVE YOU FORGOTTEN?!?
YOU'RE NOT EVEN A TRUE KRYPTONIAN!

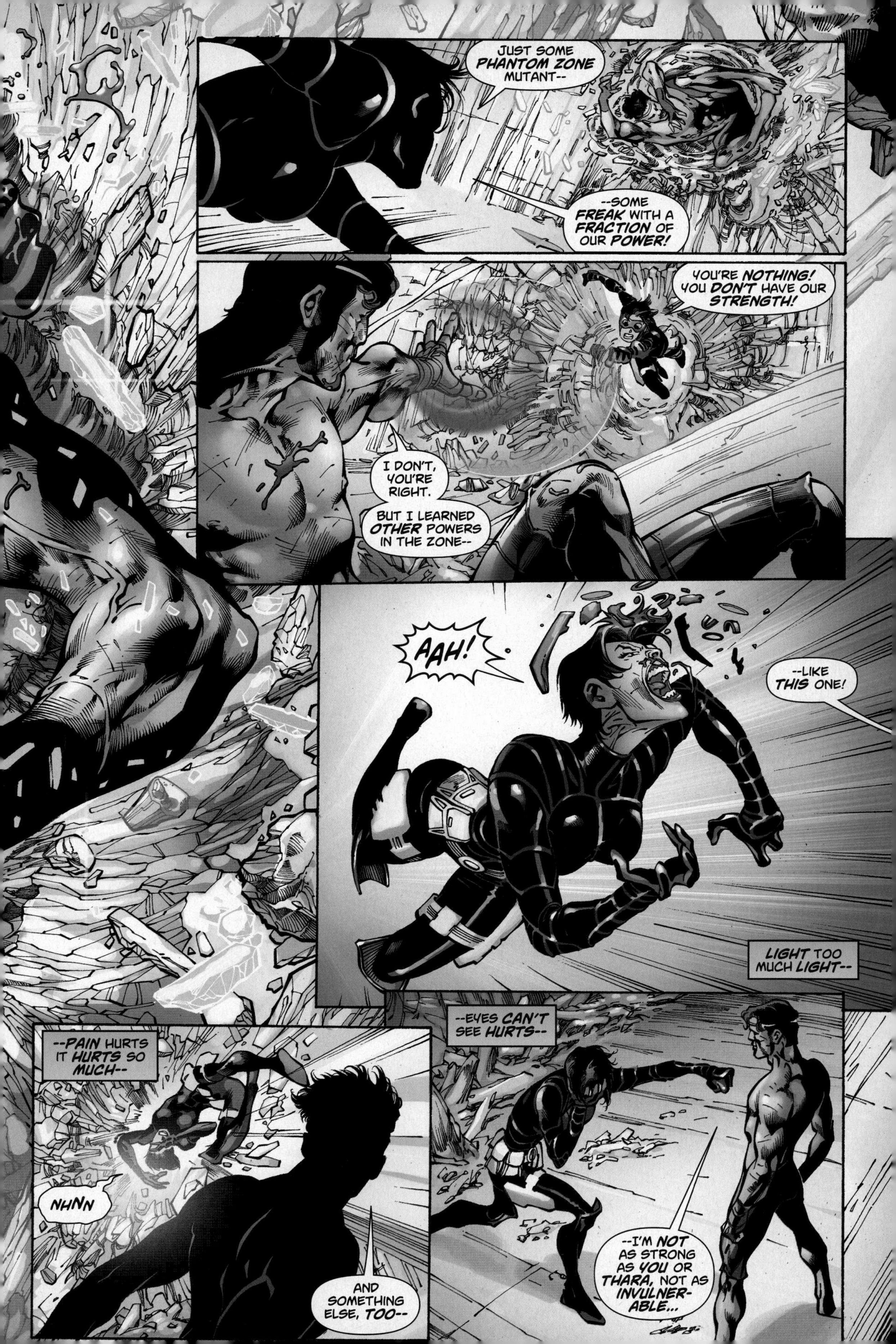
JUST SOME PHANTOM ZONE MUTANT--
--SOME FREAK WITH A FRACTION OF OUR POWER!
YOU'RE NOTHING! YOU DON'T HAVE OUR STRENGTH!
I DON'T, YOU'RE RIGHT.
BUT I LEARNED OTHER POWERS IN THE ZONE--
AAH!
--LIKE THIS ONE!
LIGHT TOO MUCH LIGHT--
--PAIN HURTS IT HURTS SO MUCH--
NHNN
AND SOMETHING ELSE, TOO--
--EYES CAN'T SEE HURTS--
--I'M NOT AS STRONG AS YOU OR THARA, NOT AS INVULNER-ABLE...

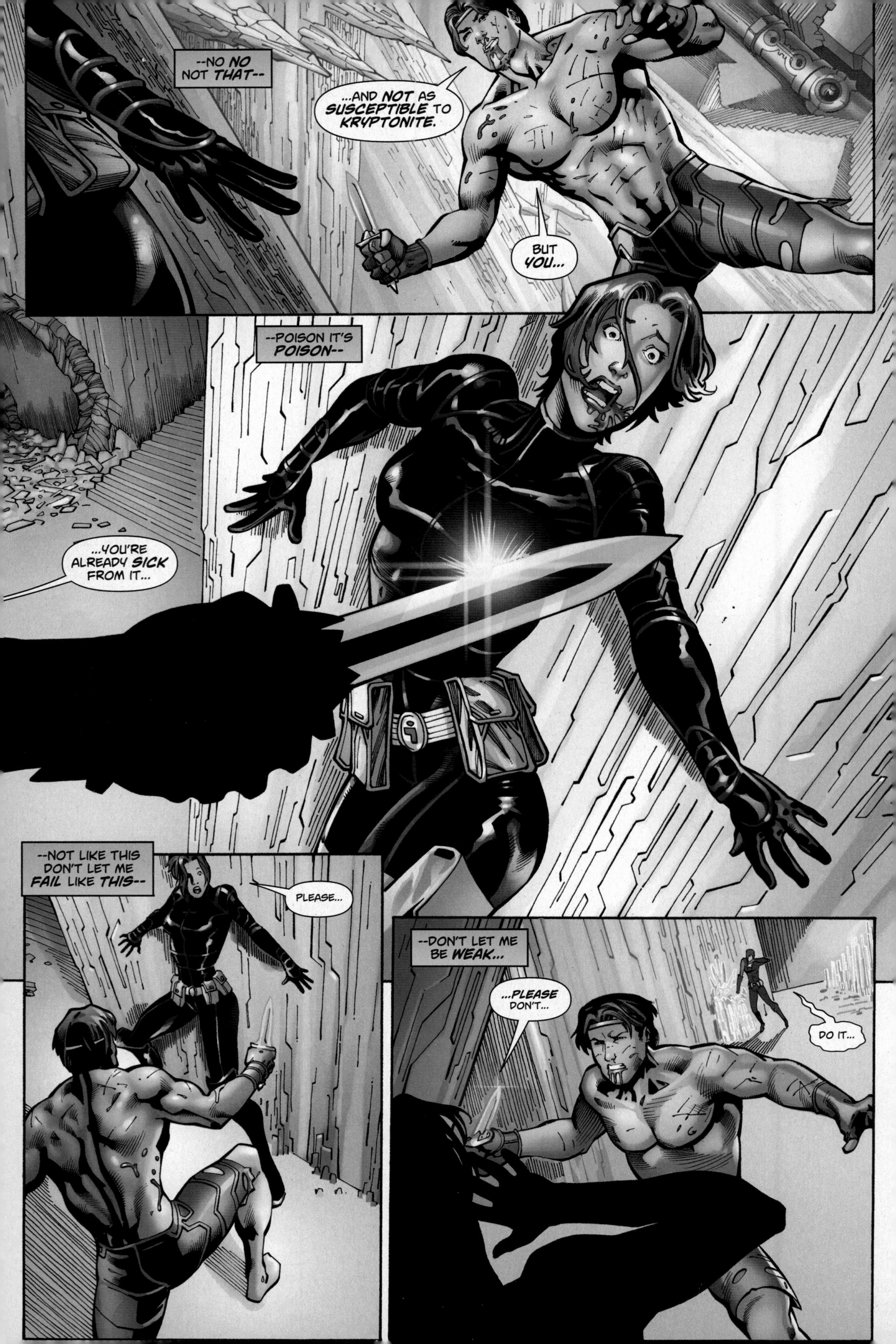
--NO NO NOT THAT--
...AND NOT AS SUSCEPTIBLE TO KRYPTONITE.
BUT YOU...
--POISON IT'S POISON--
...YOU'RE ALREADY SICK FROM IT...
--NOT LIKE THIS DON'T LET ME FAIL LIKE THIS--
PLEASE...
--DON'T LET ME BE WEAK...
...PLEASE DON'T...
DO IT...

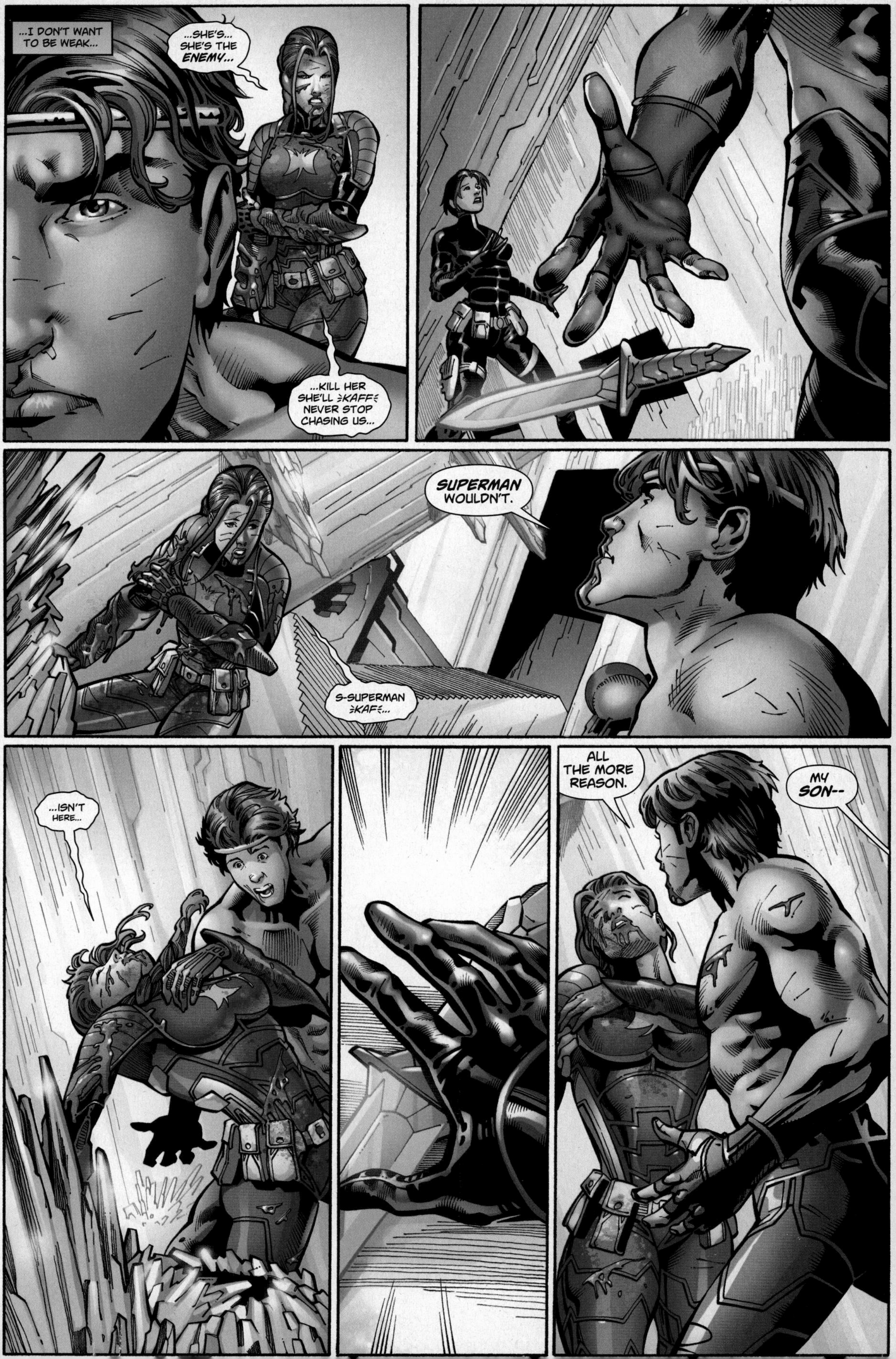
...I DON'T WANT TO BE WEAK...
...SHE'S... SHE'S THE ENEMY...
...KILL HER SHE'LL ≷KAFF≶ NEVER STOP CHASING US...
SUPERMAN WOULDN'T.
S-SUPERMAN ≷KAF≶...
...ISN'T HERE...
ALL THE MORE REASON.
MY SON--

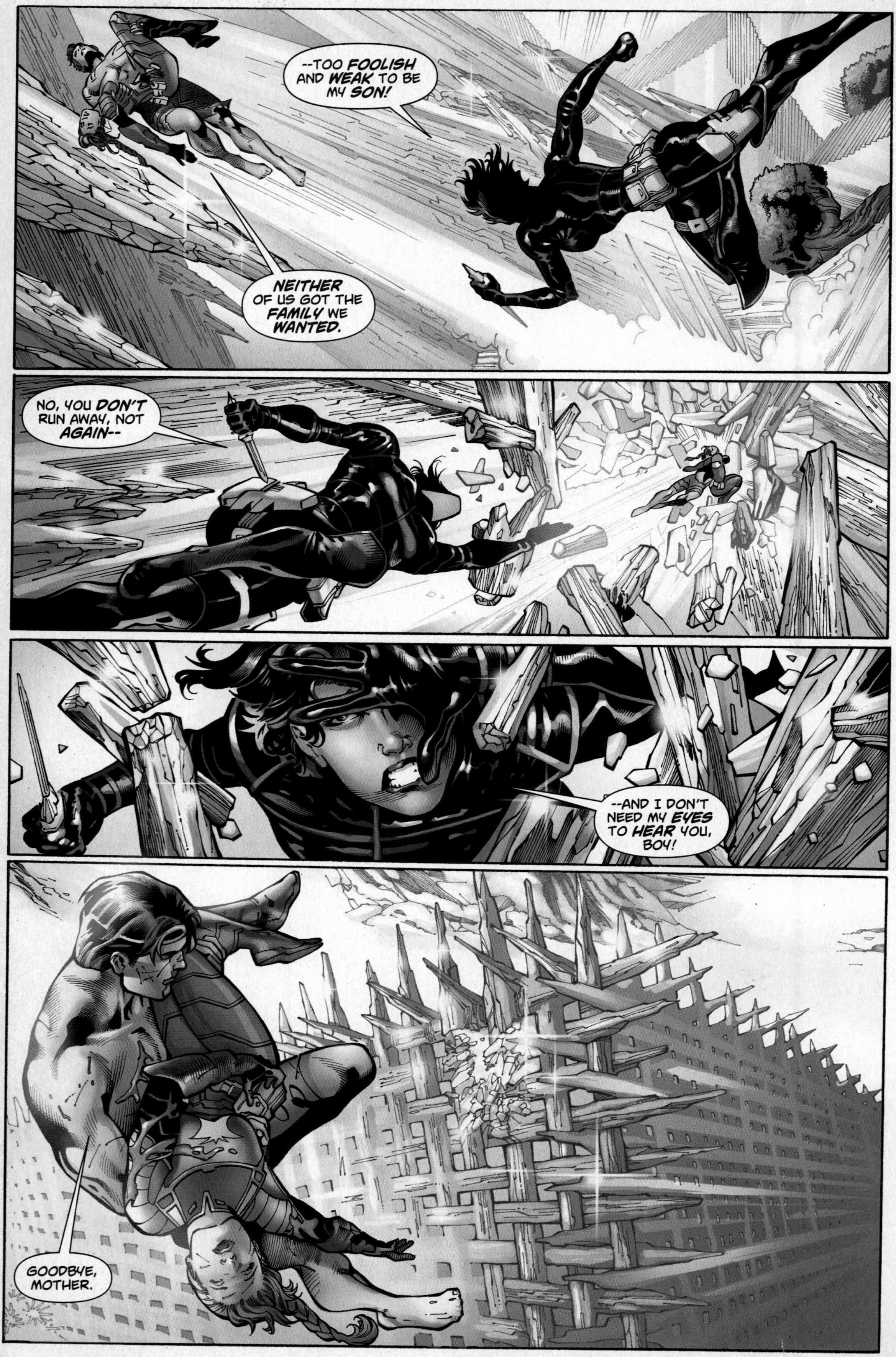
--TOO FOOLISH AND WEAK TO BE MY SON!
NEITHER OF US GOT THE FAMILY WE WANTED.
NO, YOU DON'T RUN AWAY, NOT AGAIN--
--AND I DON'T NEED MY EYES TO HEAR YOU, BOY!
GOODBYE, MOTHER.

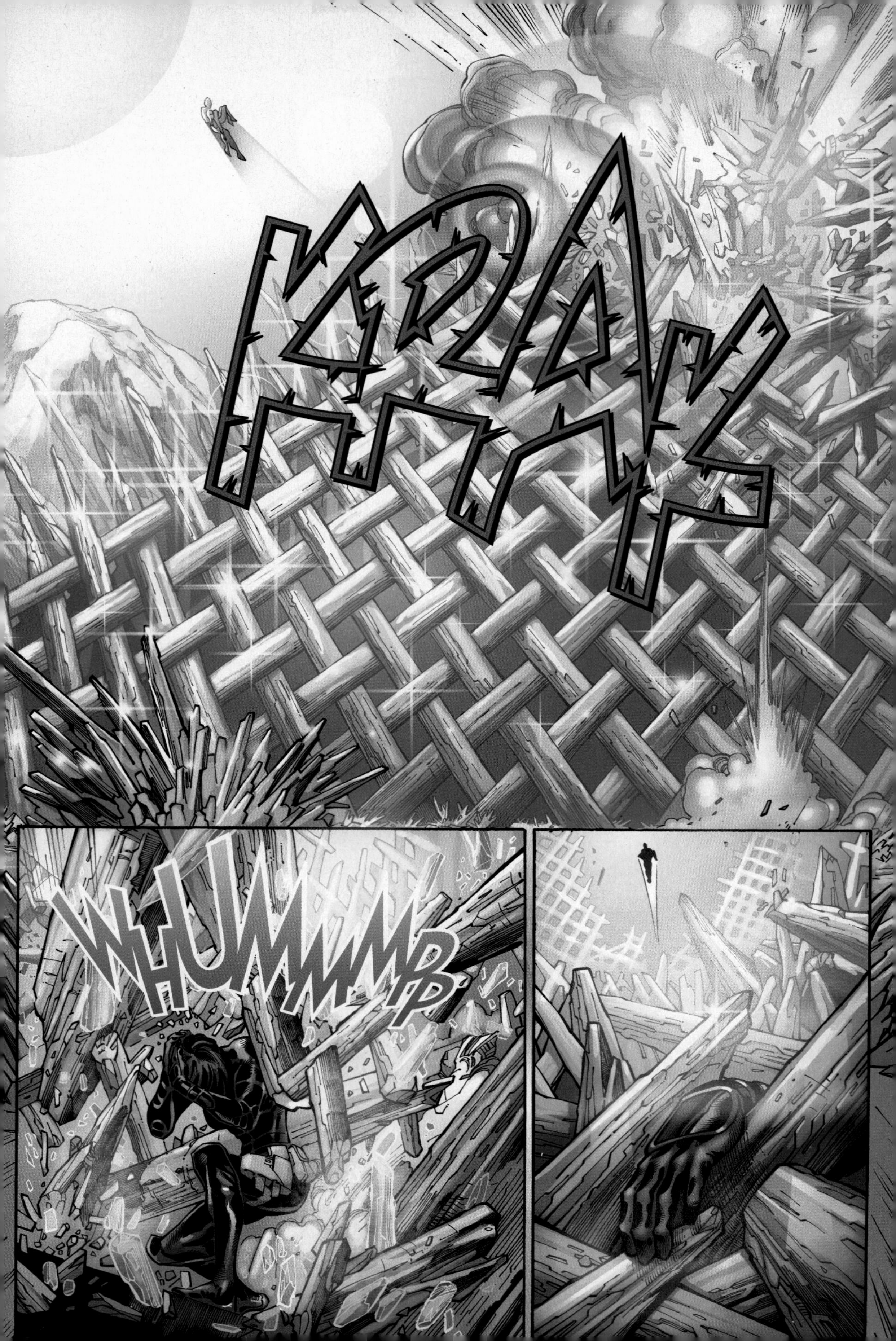

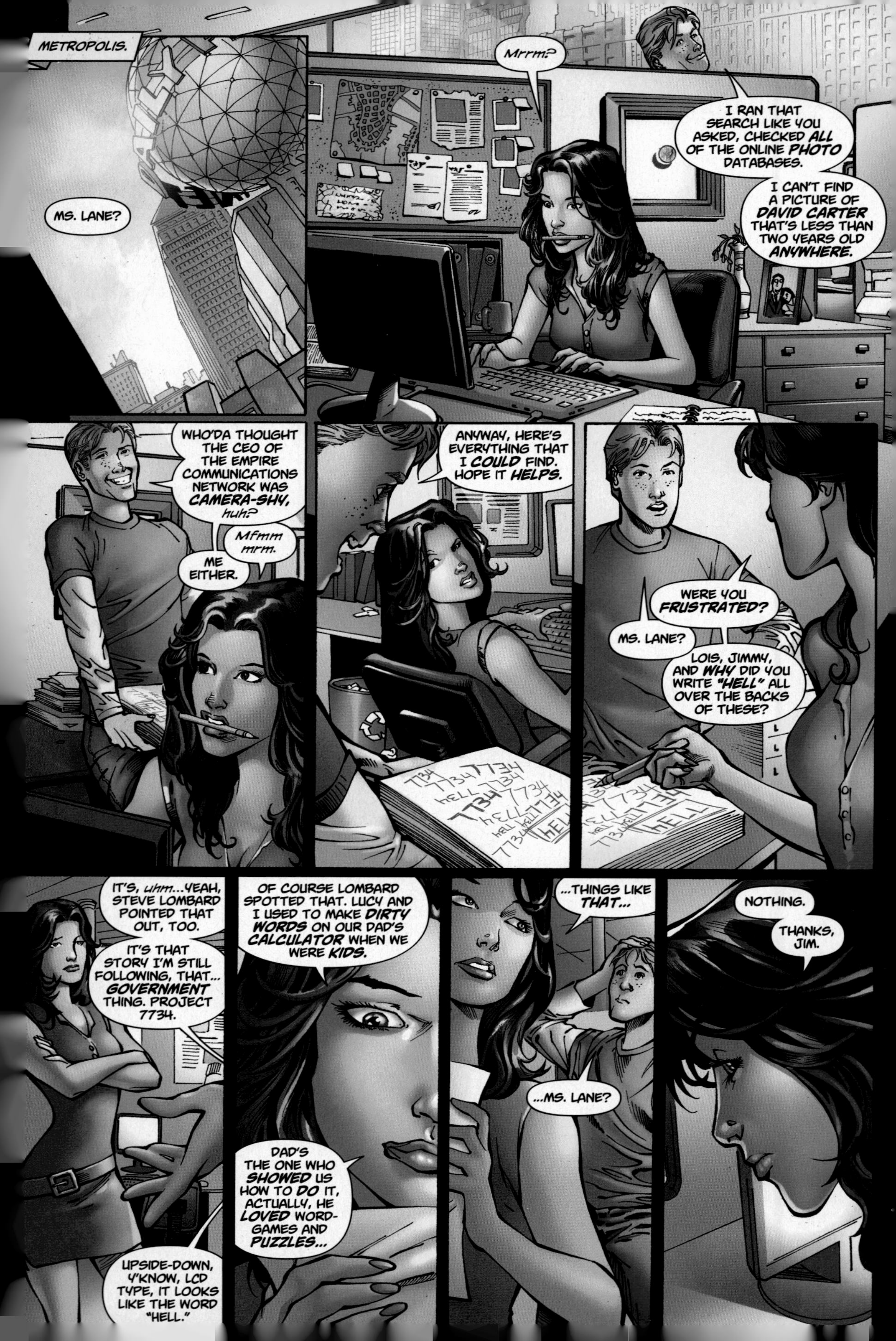
METROPOLIS.
MS. LANE?
Mrrm?
I RAN THAT SEARCH LIKE YOU ASKED, CHECKED ALL OF THE ONLINE PHOTO DATABASES.
I CAN'T FIND A PICTURE OF DAVID CARTER THAT'S LESS THAN TWO YEARS OLD ANYWHERE.
WHO'DA THOUGHT THE CEO OF THE EMPIRE COMMUNICATIONS NETWORK WAS CAMERA-SHY, huh?
Mfmm mrm.
ME EITHER.
ANYWAY, HERE'S EVERYTHING THAT I COULD FIND. HOPE IT HELPS.
WERE YOU FRUSTRATED?
MS. LANE?
LOIS, JIMMY, AND WHY DID YOU WRITE "HELL" ALL OVER THE BACKS OF THESE?
IT'S, uhm...YEAH, STEVE LOMBARD POINTED THAT OUT, TOO.
IT'S THAT STORY I'M STILL FOLLOWING, THAT... GOVERNMENT THING. PROJECT 7734.
UPSIDE-DOWN, Y'KNOW, LCD TYPE, IT LOOKS LIKE THE WORD "HELL."
OF COURSE LOMBARD SPOTTED THAT. LUCY AND I USED TO MAKE DIRTY WORDS ON OUR DAD'S CALCULATOR WHEN WE WERE KIDS.
DAD'S THE ONE WHO SHOWED US HOW TO DO IT, ACTUALLY, HE LOVED WORD-GAMES AND PUZZLES...
...THINGS LIKE THAT...
...MS. LANE?
NOTHING.
THANKS, JIM.

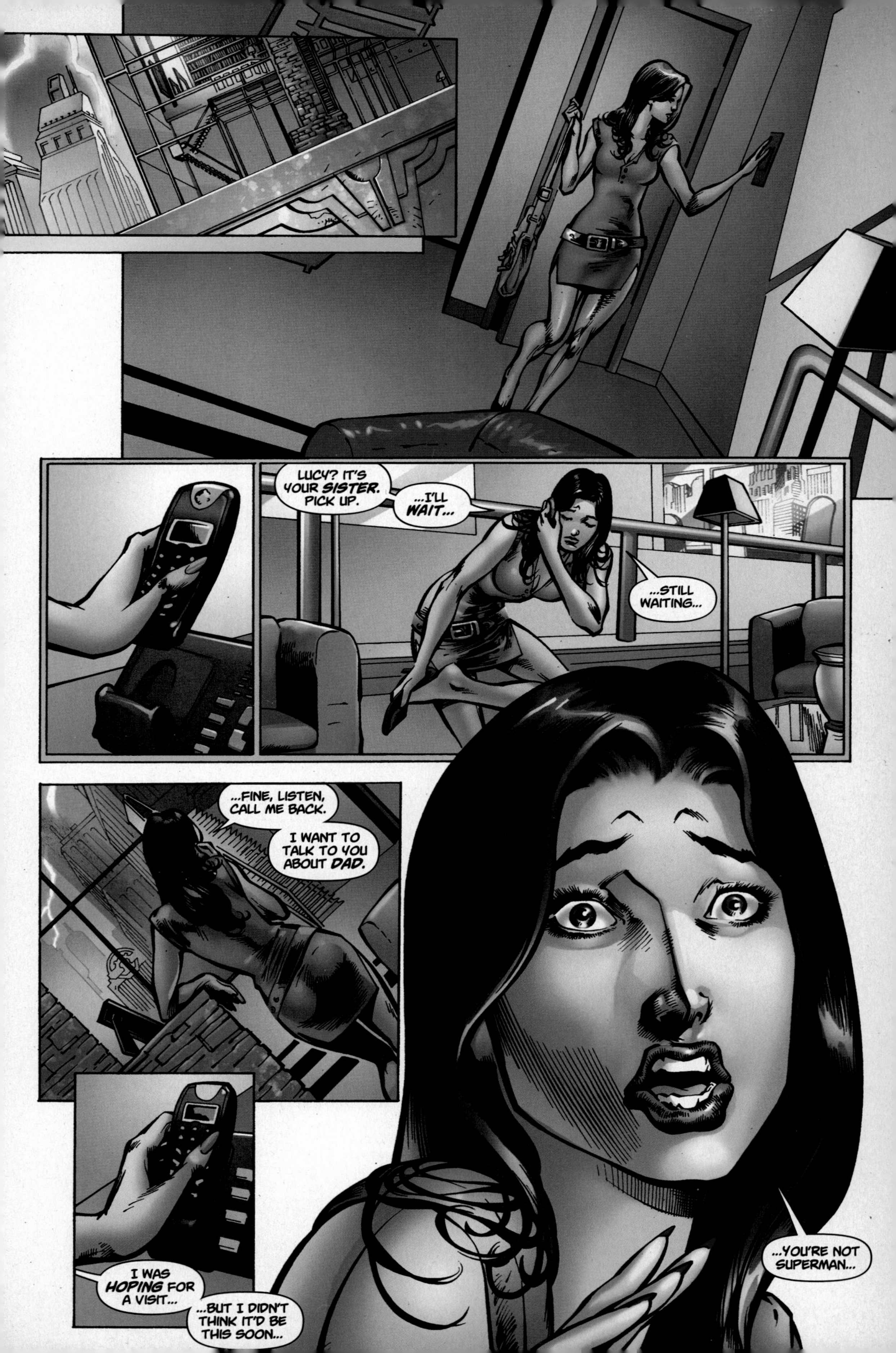
LUCY? IT'S YOUR SISTER. PICK UP.
...I'LL WAIT...
...STILL WAITING...
...FINE, LISTEN, CALL ME BACK.
I WANT TO TALK TO YOU ABOUT DAD.
I WAS HOPING FOR A VISIT...
...BUT I DIDN'T THINK IT'D BE THIS SOON...
...YOU'RE NOT SUPERMAN...

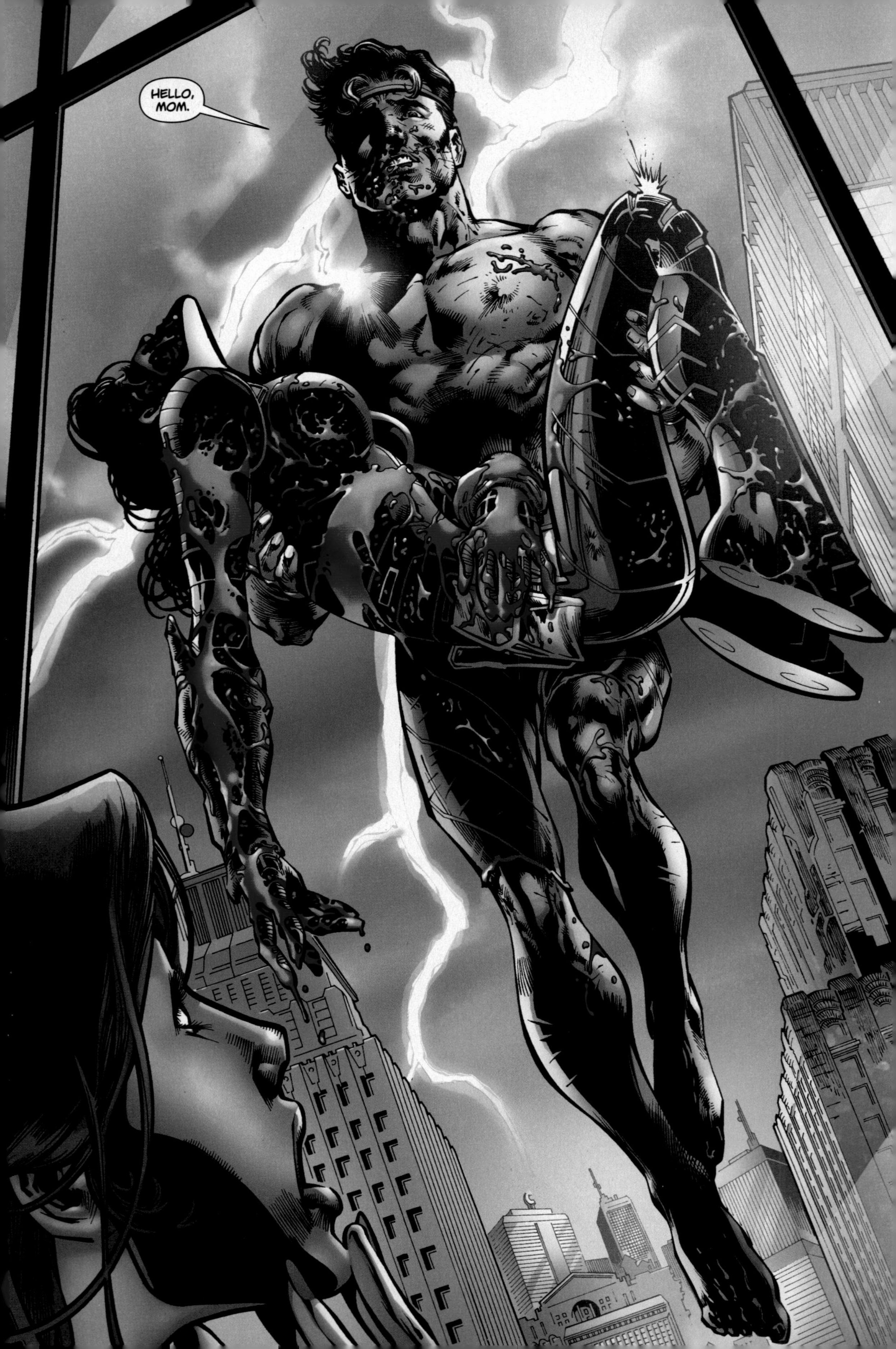
HELLO, MOM.

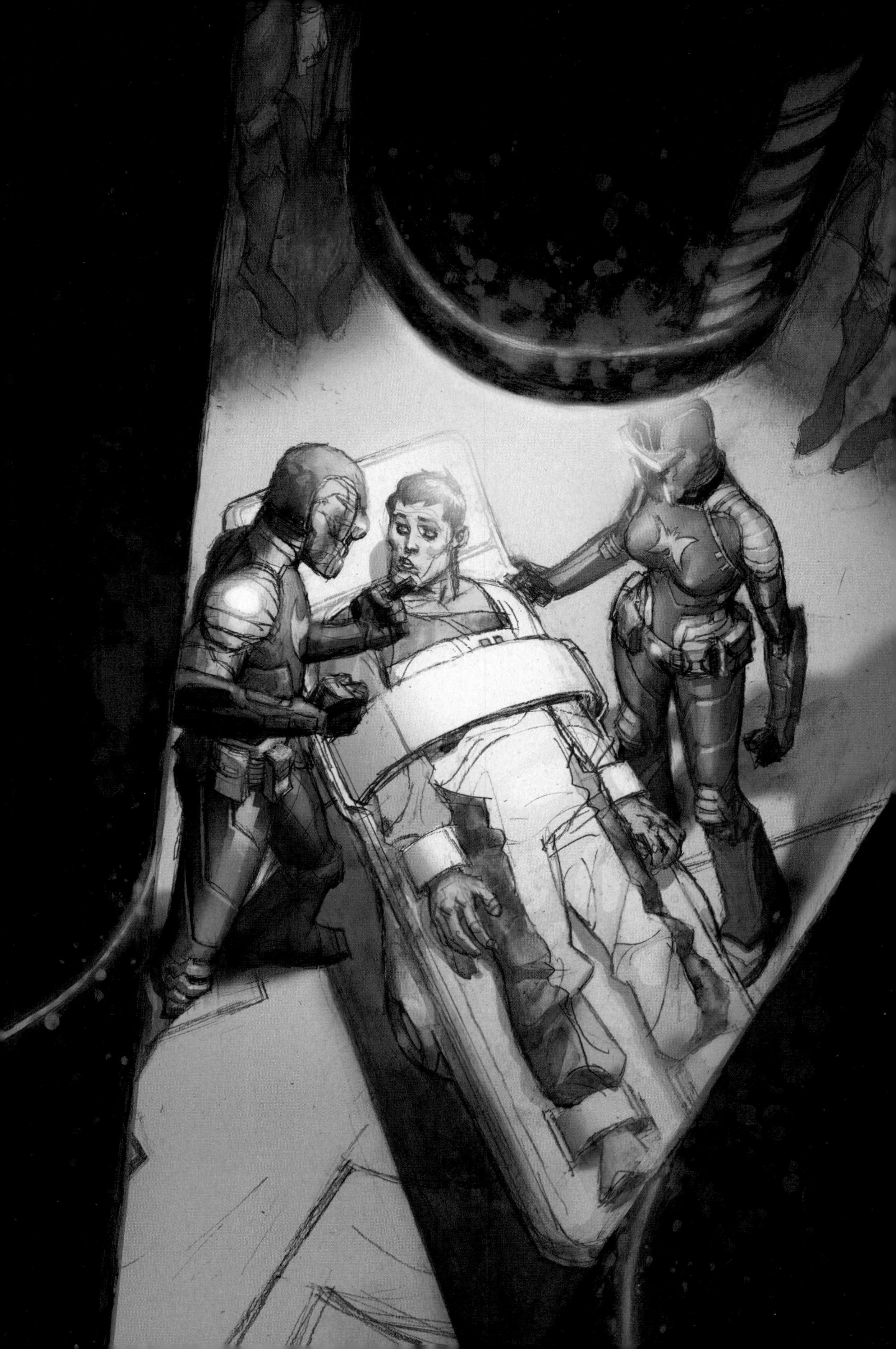

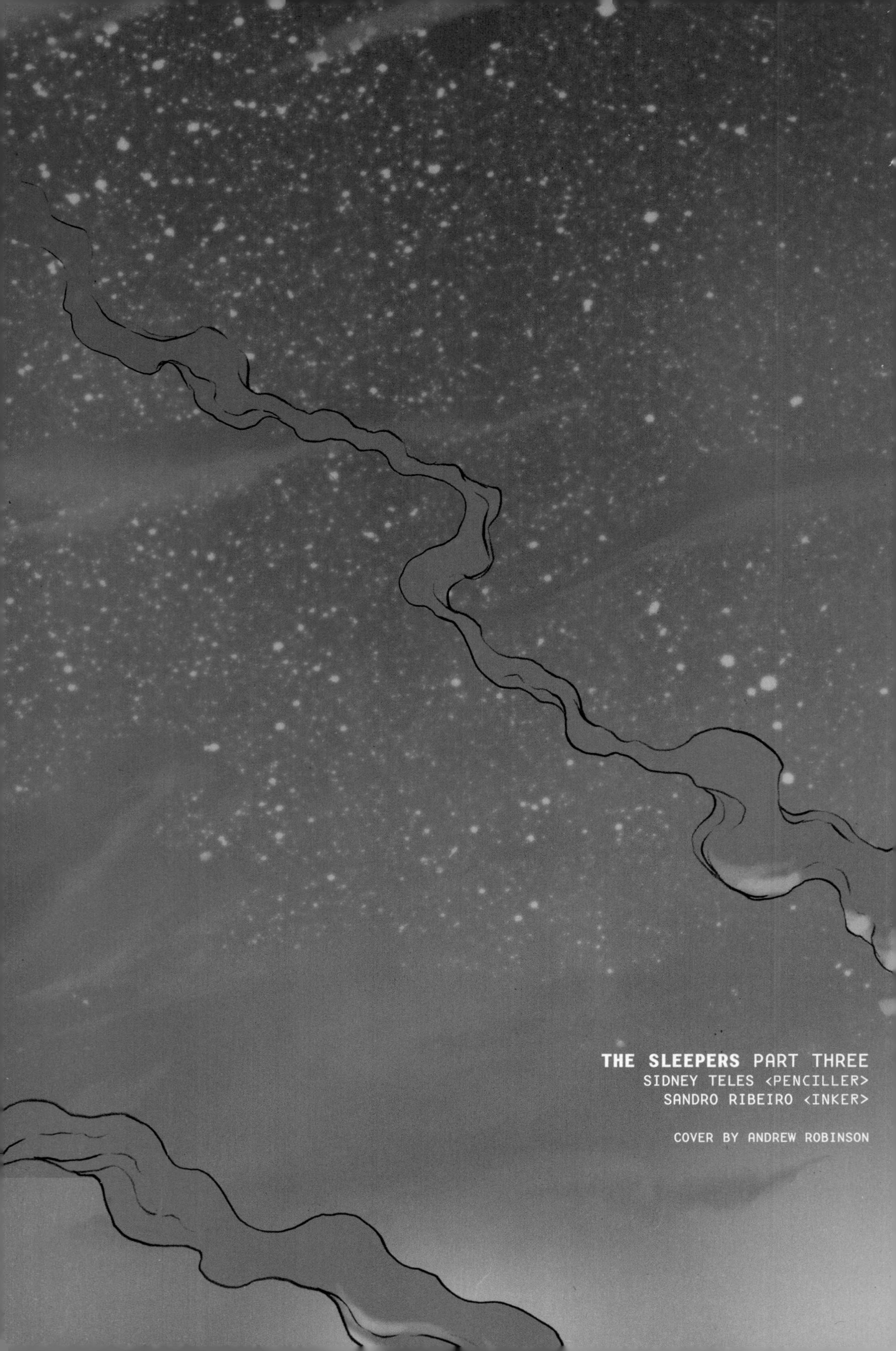
THE SLEEPERS PART THREE
SIDNEY TELES <PENCILLER>
SANDRO RIBEIRO <INKER>
COVER BY ANDREW ROBINSON

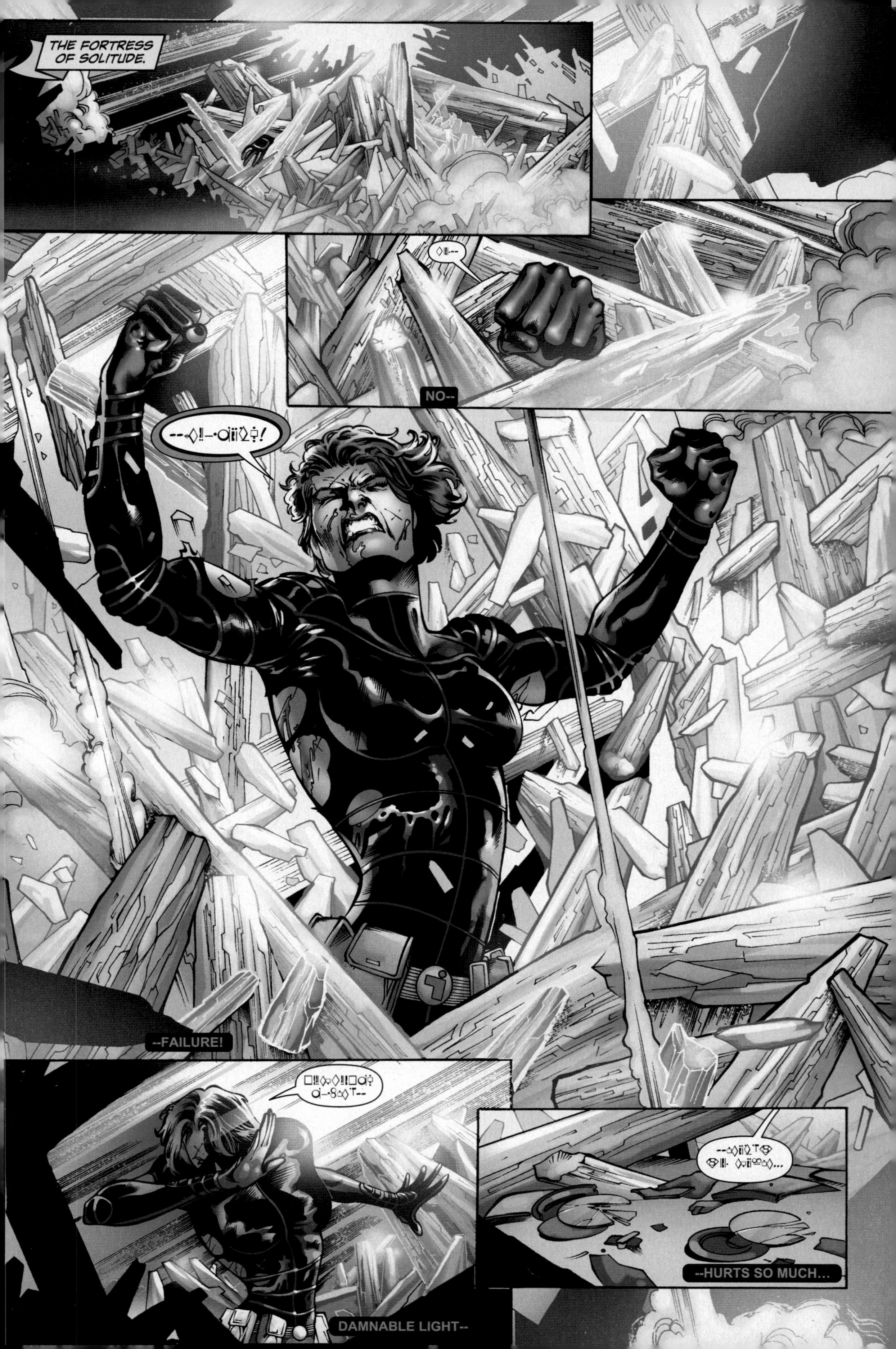
THE FORTRESS OF SOLITUDE.
NO--
--FAILURE!
DAMNABLE LIGHT--
--HURTS SO MUCH...

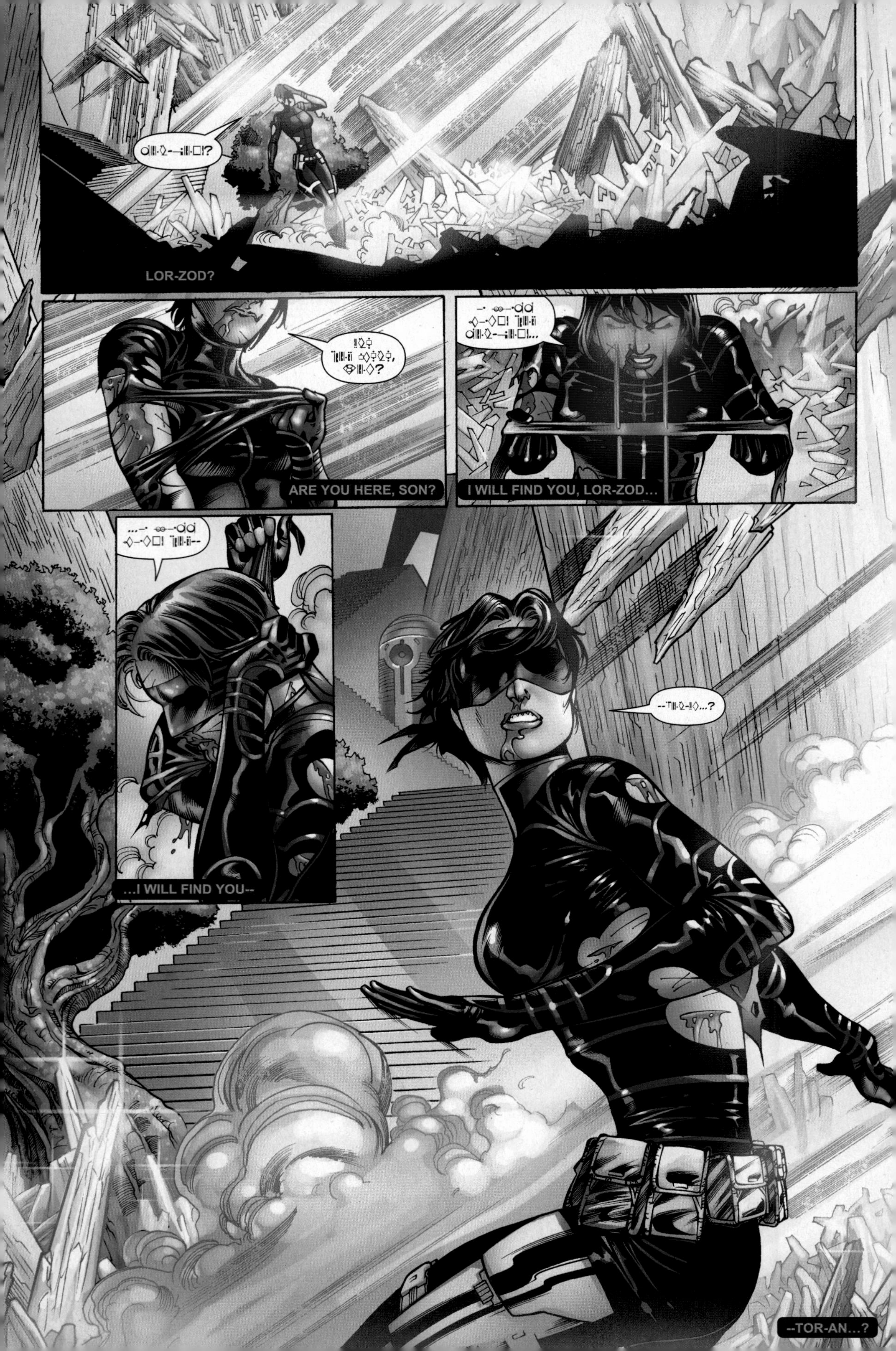
LOR-ZOD?
ARE YOU HERE, SON?
I WILL FIND YOU, LOR-ZOD...
...I WILL FIND YOU--
--TOR-AN...?

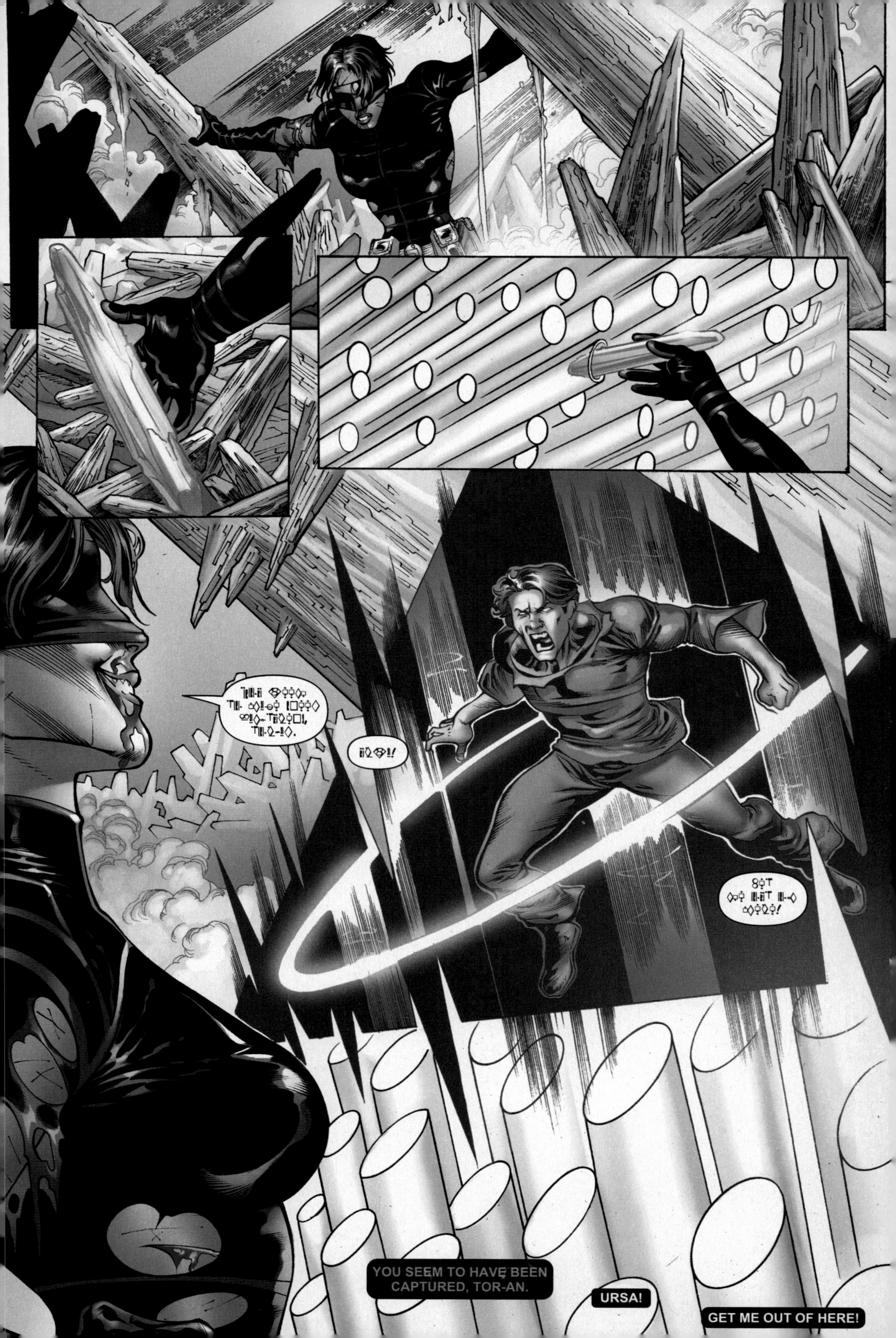
YOU SEEM TO HAVE BEEN CAPTURED, TOR-AN.
URSA!
GET ME OUT OF HERE!

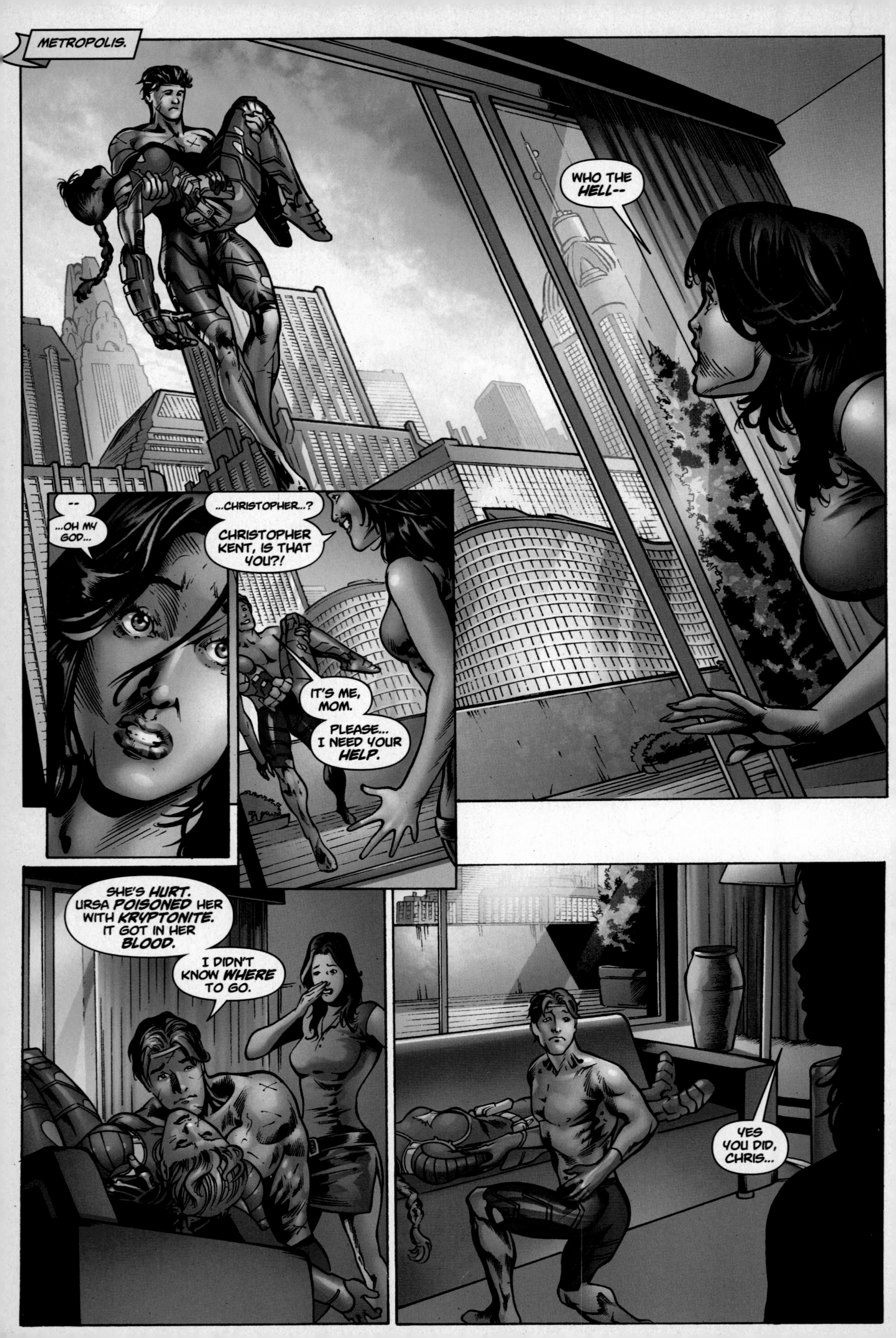
METROPOLIS.
WHO THE HELL--
--
...OH MY GOD...
...CHRISTOPHER...?
CHRISTOPHER KENT, IS THAT YOU?!
IT'S ME, MOM.
PLEASE... I NEED YOUR HELP.
SHE'S HURT. URSA POISONED HER WITH KRYPTONITE. IT GOT IN HER BLOOD.
I DIDN'T KNOW WHERE TO GO.
YES YOU DID, CHRIS...

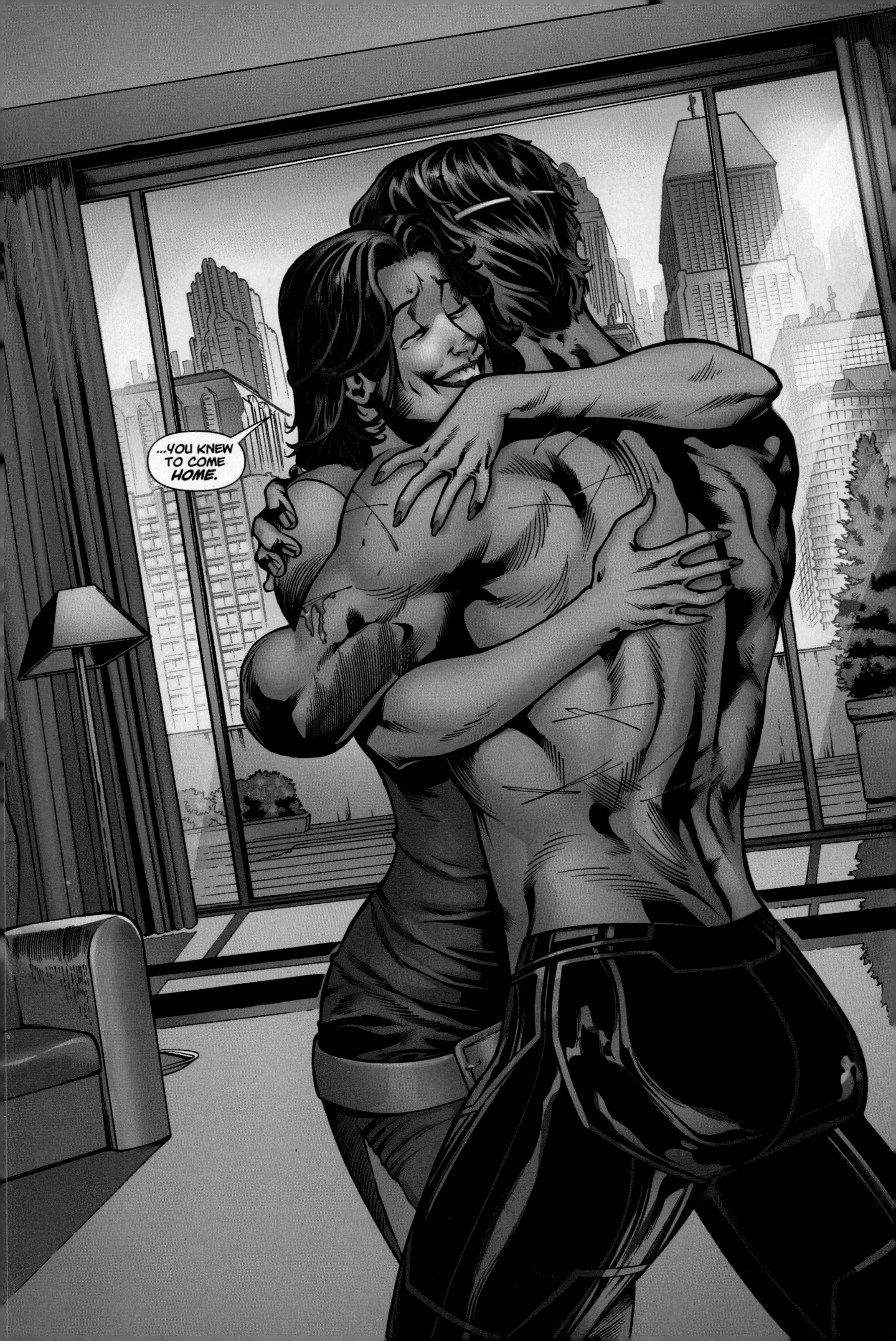
...YOU KNEW TO COME HOME.

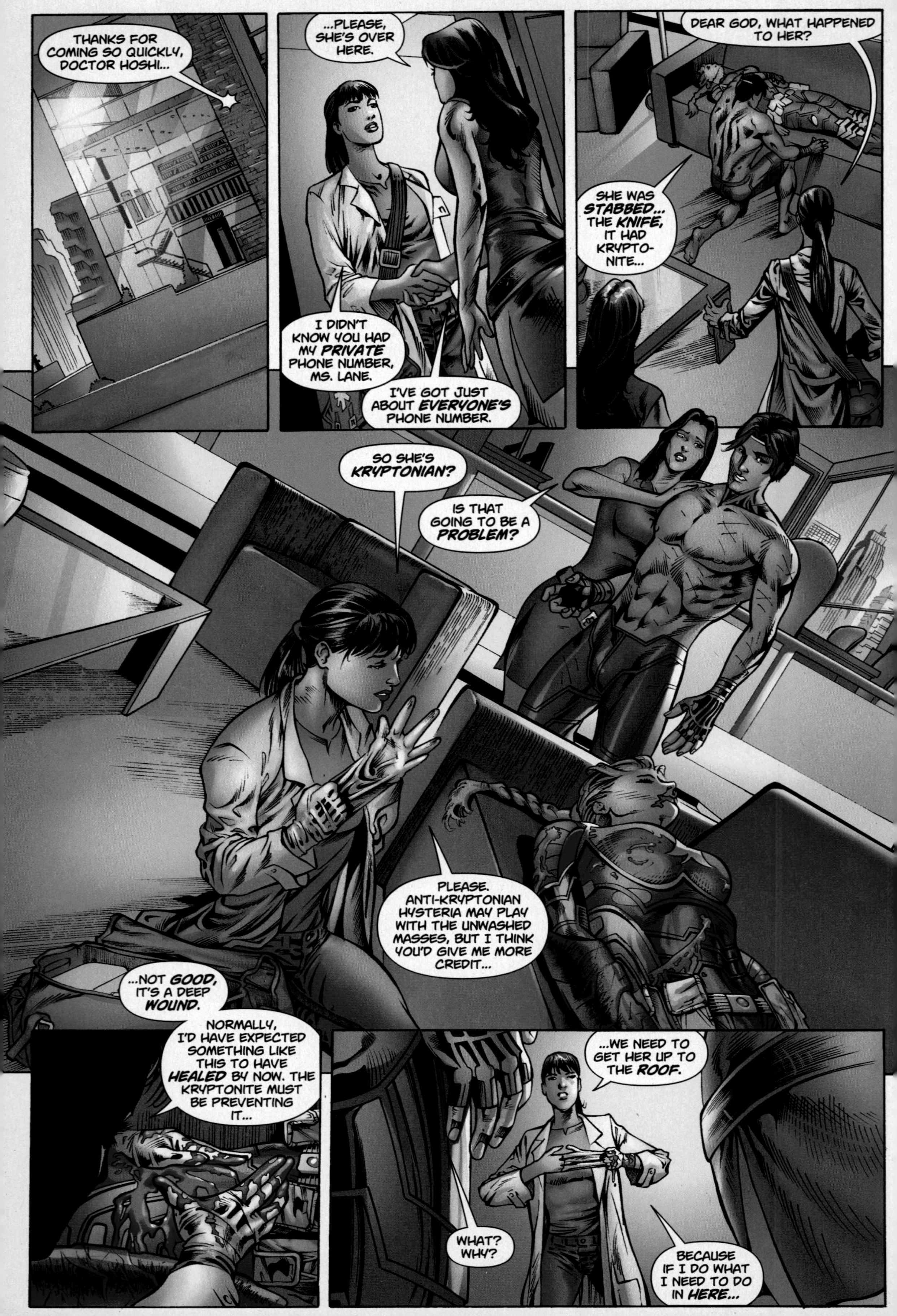
THANKS FOR COMING SO QUICKLY, DOCTOR HOSHI...
...PLEASE, SHE'S OVER HERE.
I DIDN'T KNOW YOU HAD MY PRIVATE PHONE NUMBER, MS. LANE.
I'VE GOT JUST ABOUT EVERYONE'S PHONE NUMBER.
DEAR GOD, WHAT HAPPENED TO HER?
SHE WAS STABBED... THE KNIFE, IT HAD KRYPTO- NITE...
SO SHE'S KRYPTONIAN?
IS THAT GOING TO BE A PROBLEM?
PLEASE. ANTI-KRYPTONIAN HYSTERIA MAY PLAY WITH THE UNWASHED MASSES, BUT I THINK YOU'D GIVE ME MORE CREDIT...
...NOT GOOD, IT'S A DEEP WOUND.
NORMALLY, I'D HAVE EXPECTED SOMETHING LIKE THIS TO HAVE HEALED BY NOW. THE KRYPTONITE MUST BE PREVENTING IT...
...WE NEED TO GET HER UP TO THE ROOF.
WHAT? WHY?
BECAUSE IF I DO WHAT I NEED TO DO IN HERE...

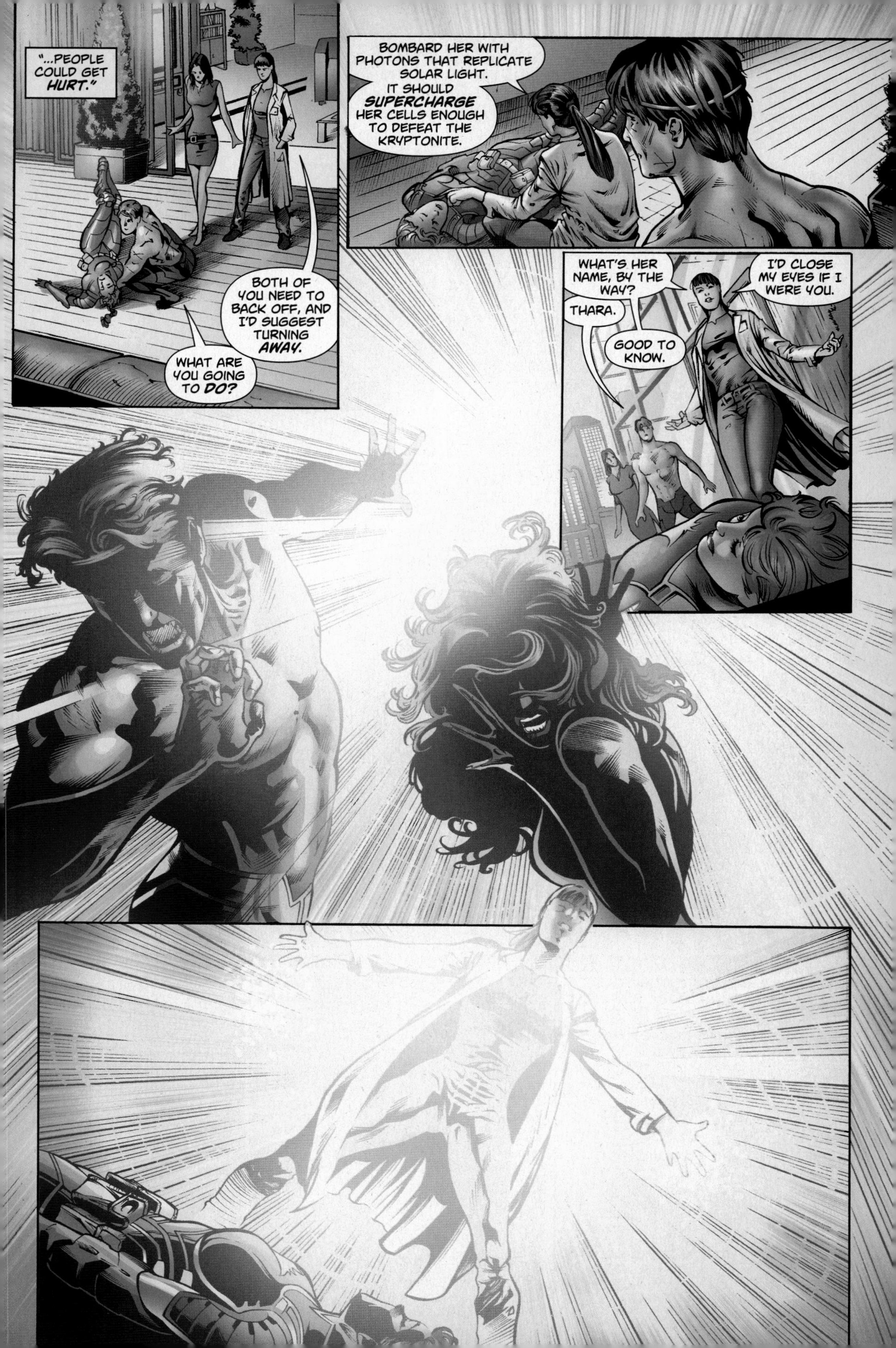
"...PEOPLE COULD GET *HURT*."
BOTH OF YOU NEED TO BACK OFF, AND I'D SUGGEST TURNING *AWAY*.
WHAT ARE YOU GOING TO *DO*?
BOMBARD HER WITH PHOTONS THAT REPLICATE SOLAR LIGHT.
IT SHOULD *SUPERCHARGE* HER CELLS ENOUGH TO DEFEAT THE KRYPTONITE.
WHAT'S HER NAME, BY THE WAY?
I'D CLOSE MY EYES IF I WERE YOU.
THARA.
GOOD TO KNOW.

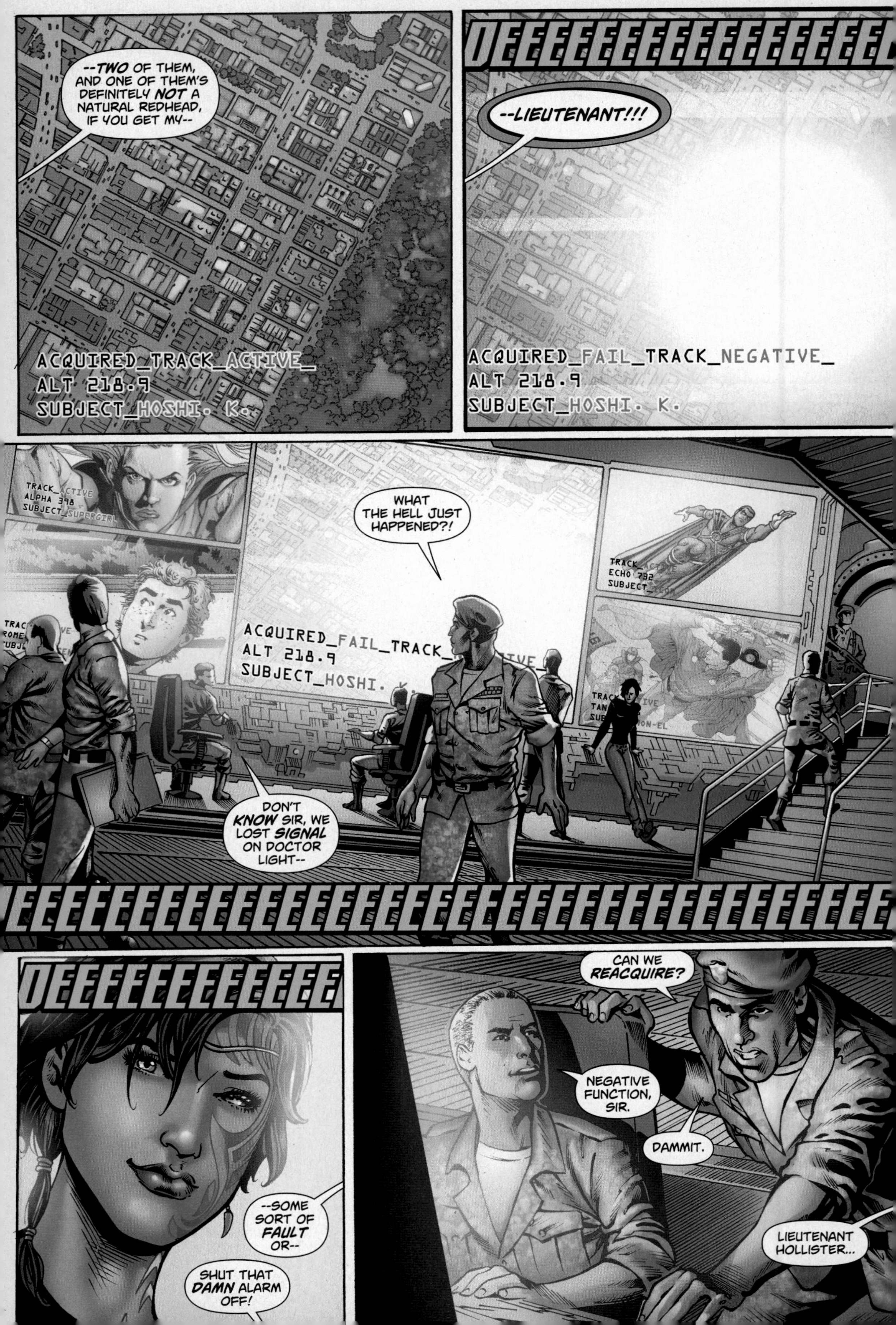

--TWO OF THEM, AND ONE OF THEM'S DEFINITELY NOT A NATURAL REDHEAD, IF YOU GET MY--
ACQUIRED_TRACK_ACTIVE_
ALT 218.9
SUBJECT_HOSHI. K.
DEEEEEEEEEEEEEEEE
--LIEUTENANT!!!
ACQUIRED_FAIL_TRACK_NEGATIVE_
ALT 218.9
SUBJECT_HOSHI. K.
TRACK_ACTIVE
ALPHA 398
SUBJECT_SUPERGIRL
WHAT THE HELL JUST HAPPENED?!
TRACK_ACTIVE
ECHO 732
ACQUIRED_FAIL_TRACK_
ALT 218.9
SUBJECT_HOSHI.
DON'T KNOW SIR, WE LOST SIGNAL ON DOCTOR LIGHT--
EEEEEEEEEEEEEEEEEEEEEEEEEEEEEEEEEE
DEEEEEEEEEEE
--SOME SORT OF FAULT OR--
SHUT THAT DAMN ALARM OFF!
CAN WE REACQUIRE?
NEGATIVE FUNCTION, SIR.
DAMMIT.
LIEUTENANT HOLLISTER...

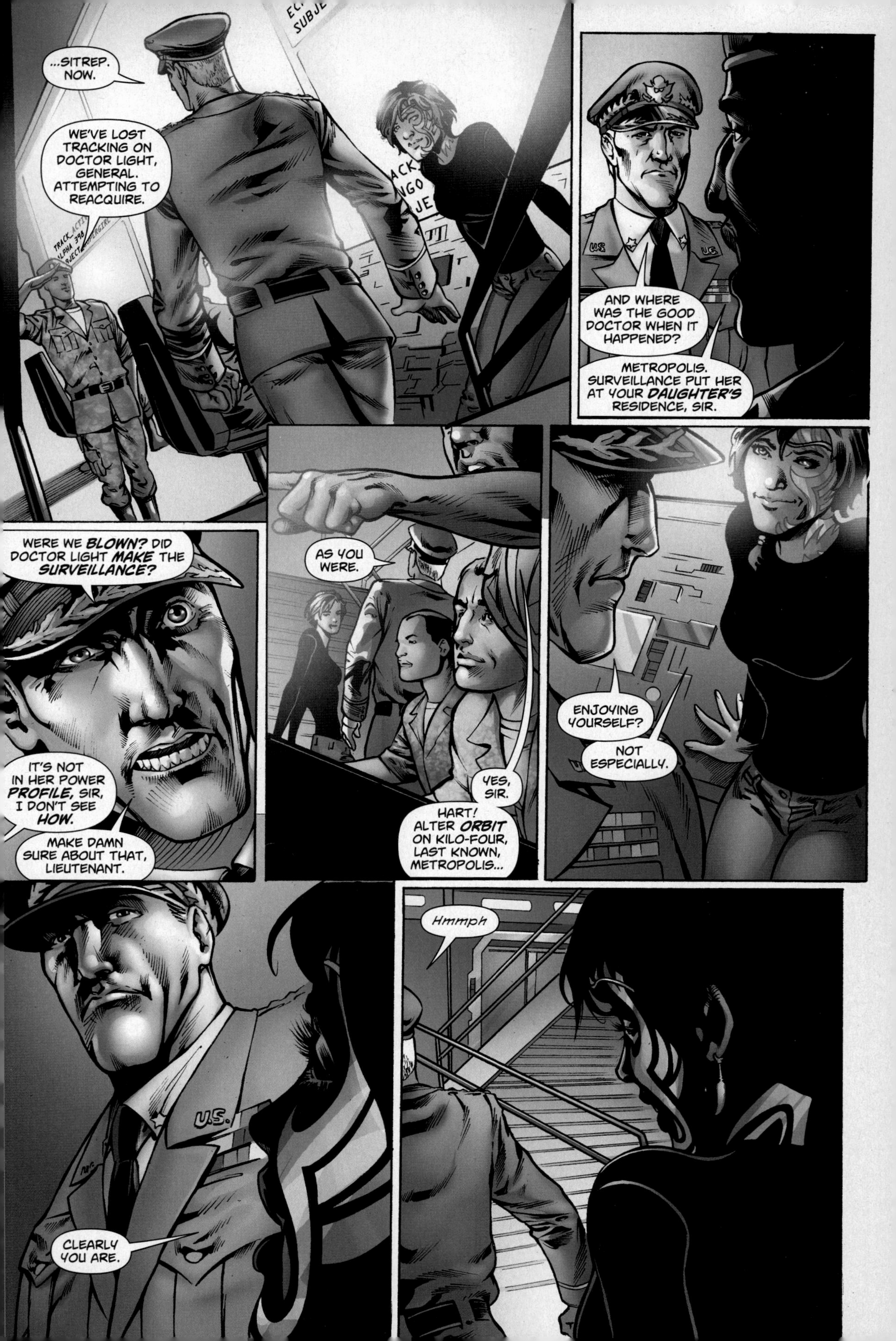
...SITREP. NOW.
WE'VE LOST TRACKING ON DOCTOR LIGHT, GENERAL. ATTEMPTING TO REACQUIRE.
AND WHERE WAS THE GOOD DOCTOR WHEN IT HAPPENED?
METROPOLIS. SURVEILLANCE PUT HER AT YOUR *DAUGHTER'S* RESIDENCE, SIR.
WERE WE *BLOWN?* DID DOCTOR LIGHT *MAKE* THE *SURVEILLANCE?*
IT'S NOT IN HER POWER *PROFILE,* SIR, I DON'T SEE *HOW.*
MAKE DAMN SURE ABOUT THAT, LIEUTENANT.
AS YOU WERE.
YES, SIR.
HART! ALTER *ORBIT* ON KILO-FOUR, LAST KNOWN, METROPOLIS...
ENJOYING YOURSELF?
NOT ESPECIALLY.
CLEARLY YOU ARE.
Hmmph

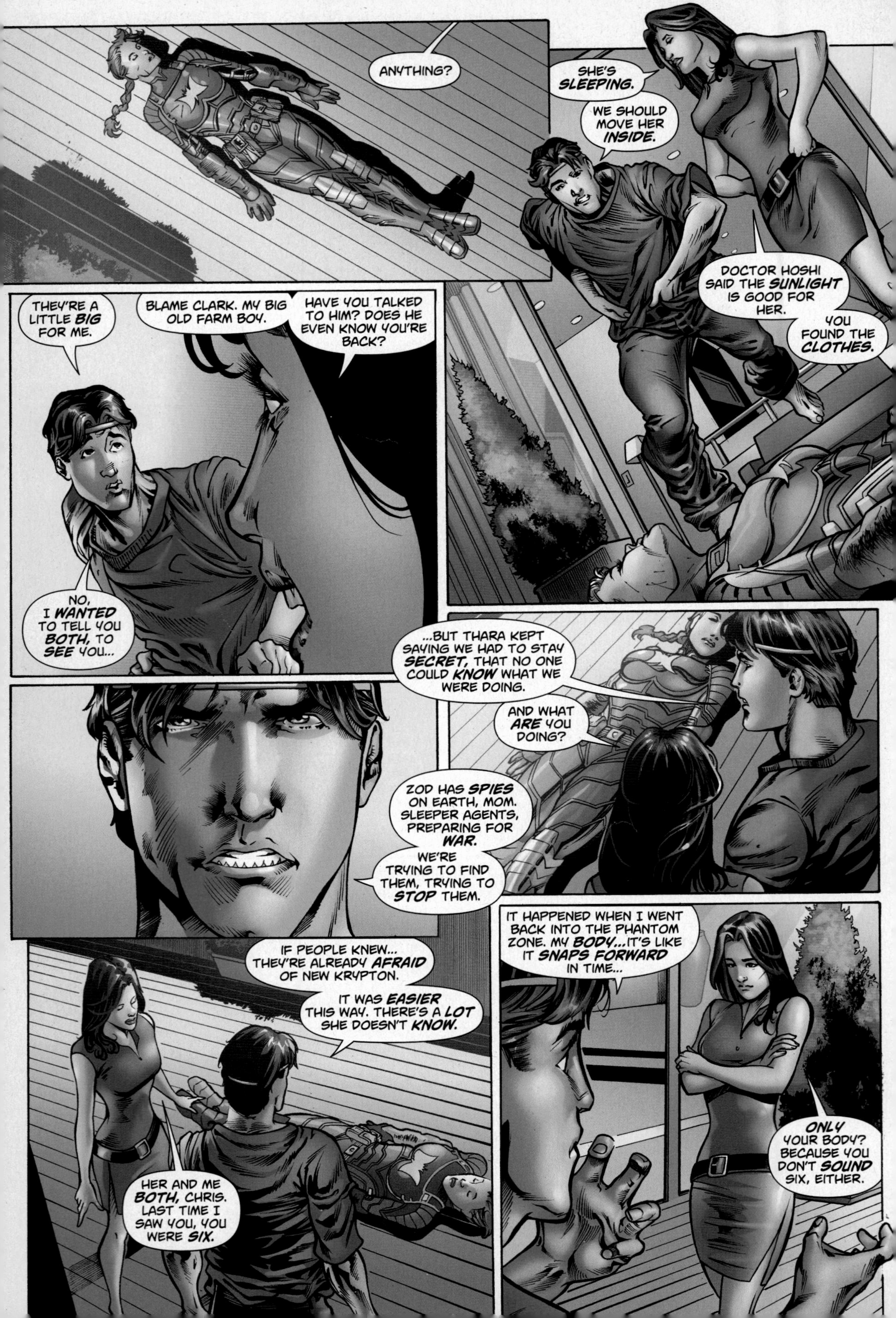

ANYTHING?
SHE'S SLEEPING.
WE SHOULD MOVE HER INSIDE.
DOCTOR HOSHI SAID THE SUNLIGHT IS GOOD FOR HER.
YOU FOUND THE CLOTHES.
THEY'RE A LITTLE BIG FOR ME.
BLAME CLARK. MY BIG OLD FARM BOY.
HAVE YOU TALKED TO HIM? DOES HE EVEN KNOW YOU'RE BACK?
NO, I WANTED TO TELL YOU BOTH, TO SEE YOU...
...BUT THARA KEPT SAYING WE HAD TO STAY SECRET, THAT NO ONE COULD KNOW WHAT WE WERE DOING.
AND WHAT ARE YOU DOING?
ZOD HAS SPIES ON EARTH, MOM. SLEEPER AGENTS, PREPARING FOR WAR.
WE'RE TRYING TO FIND THEM, TRYING TO STOP THEM.
IF PEOPLE KNEW... THEY'RE ALREADY AFRAID OF NEW KRYPTON.
IT WAS EASIER THIS WAY. THERE'S A LOT SHE DOESN'T KNOW.
HER AND ME BOTH, CHRIS. LAST TIME I SAW YOU, YOU WERE SIX.
IT HAPPENED WHEN I WENT BACK INTO THE PHANTOM ZONE. MY BODY...IT'S LIKE IT SNAPS FORWARD IN TIME...
ONLY YOUR BODY? BECAUSE YOU DON'T SOUND SIX, EITHER.

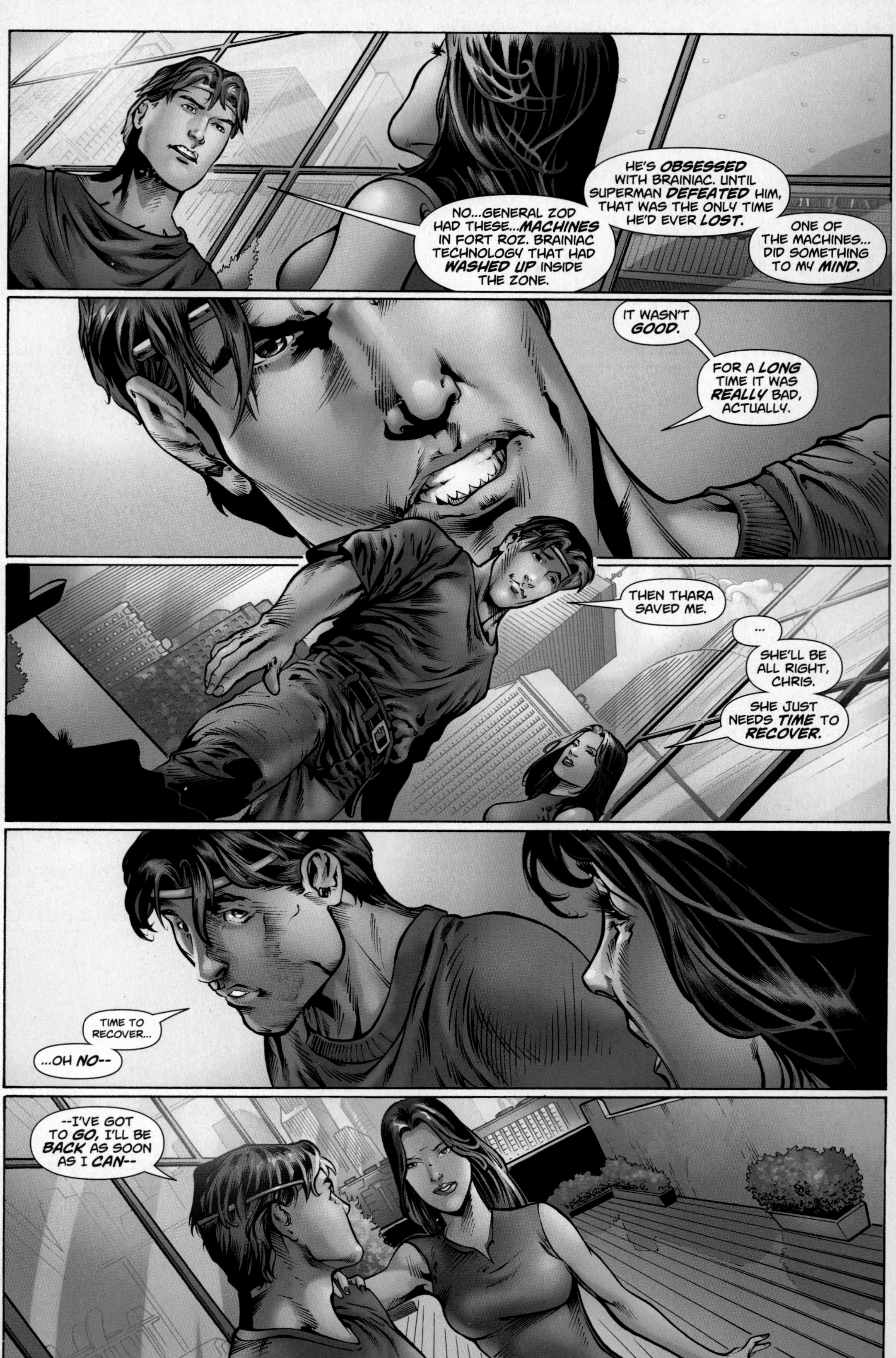

NO...GENERAL ZOD HAD THESE...MACHINES IN FORT ROZ. BRAINIAC TECHNOLOGY THAT HAD WASHED UP INSIDE THE ZONE.
HE'S OBSESSED WITH BRAINIAC. UNTIL SUPERMAN DEFEATED HIM, THAT WAS THE ONLY TIME HE'D EVER LOST.
ONE OF THE MACHINES... DID SOMETHING TO MY MIND.
IT WASN'T GOOD.
FOR A LONG TIME IT WAS REALLY BAD, ACTUALLY.
THEN THARA SAVED ME.
...
SHE'LL BE ALL RIGHT, CHRIS.
SHE JUST NEEDS TIME TO RECOVER.
TIME TO RECOVER...
...OH NO--
--I'VE GOT TO GO, I'LL BE BACK AS SOON AS I CAN--

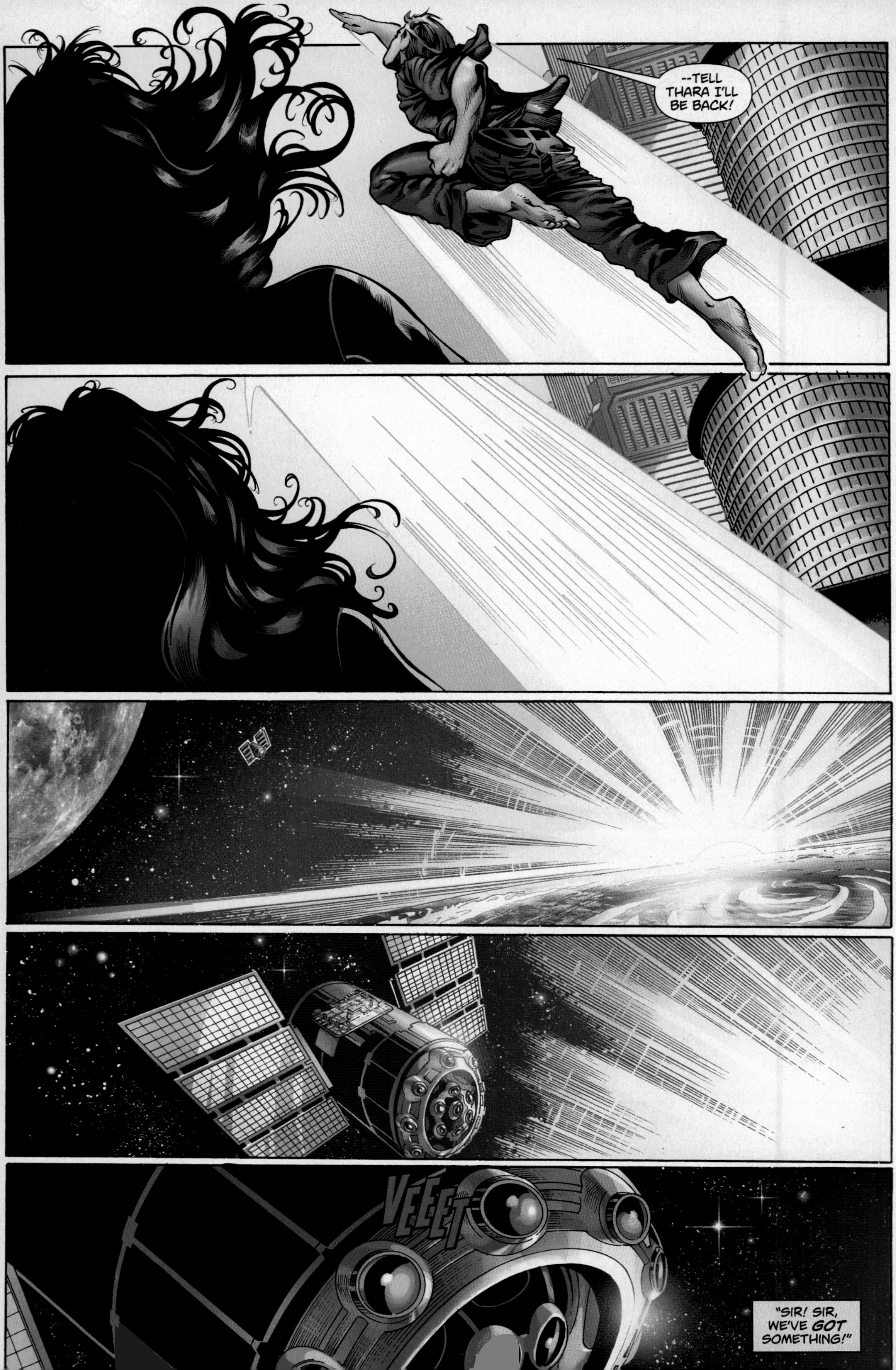
--TELL THARA I'LL BE BACK!
VEEET
"SIR! SIR, WE'VE GOT SOMETHING!"

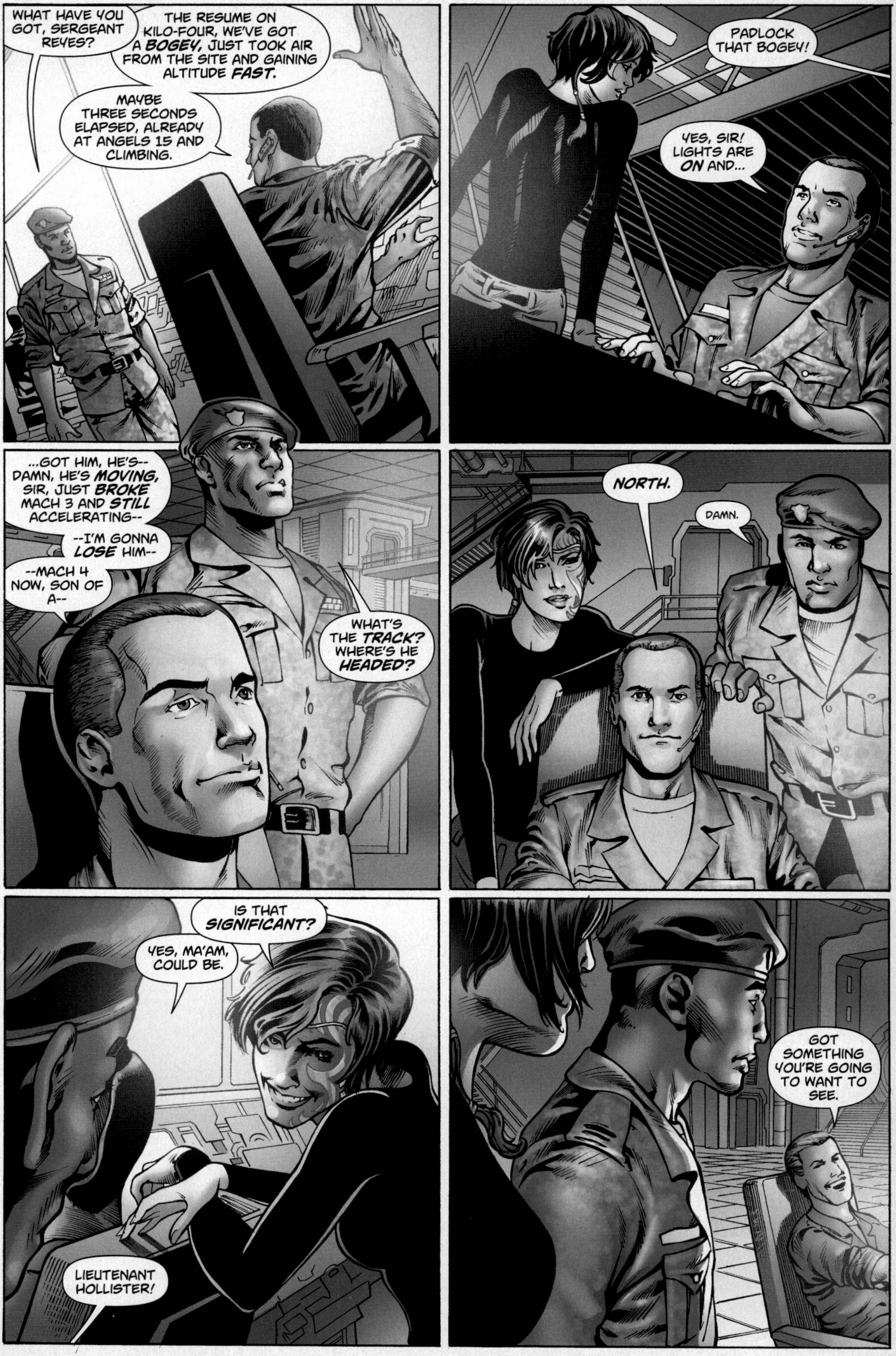
WHAT HAVE YOU GOT, SERGEANT REYES?
THE RESUME ON KILO-FOUR, WE'VE GOT A BOGEY, JUST TOOK AIR FROM THE SITE AND GAINING ALTITUDE FAST.
MAYBE THREE SECONDS ELAPSED, ALREADY AT ANGELS 15 AND CLIMBING.
PADLOCK THAT BOGEY!
YES, SIR! LIGHTS ARE ON AND...
...GOT HIM, HE'S-- DAMN, HE'S MOVING, SIR, JUST BROKE MACH 3 AND STILL ACCELERATING--
--I'M GONNA LOSE HIM--
--MACH 4 NOW, SON OF A--
WHAT'S THE TRACK? WHERE'S HE HEADED?
NORTH.
DAMN.
IS THAT SIGNIFICANT?
YES, MA'AM, COULD BE.
LIEUTENANT HOLLISTER!
GOT SOMETHING YOU'RE GOING TO WANT TO SEE.

...RESUMED SATELLITE SURVEILLANCE AS YOU ORDERED.

FOUR MINUTES AGO, KILO-FOUR PINGED ON A *BOGEY* TAKING OFF FROM THE ROOFTOP OF THE RESIDENCE.

HEADING WAS DUE NORTH, ACCELERATION AND CLIMB RATE *CONSISTENT* WITH THE KRYPTONIAN FLIGHT PROFILE.

IF YOU'RE ABOUT TO TELL ME *SUPERMAN* HAS COME *BACK* TO EARTH, LIEUTENANT, I'M GOING TO WANT A *DAMN* GOOD REASON AS TO HOW WE *MISSED* THAT.

NO, SIR. THIS IS SOMETHING *ELSE*.

RIGHT AFTER TAKEOFF, SERGEANT HART RECONNED THE KILO-FOUR FOR A *CLOSER* LOOK.

DEET

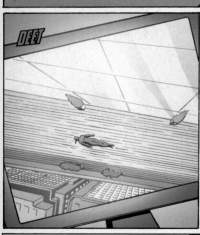

DEET

DEET

DEET

THE *ARMOR* MATCHES THAT WORN BY ONE OF THE TWO *FLYERS* SPOTTED IN *SYDNEY* BEFORE CARTER'S DISAPPEARANCE.

DEET

WE *MATCHED* HER FACE TO FOOTAGE TAKEN WHEN THE KRYPTONIAN DELEGATION MET WITH THE PRESIDENT.**

WE'VE *ID*'ED HER AS THARA AK-VAR.

HEAD OF SECURITY FOR ALURA ZOR-EL, THE *RULER* OF NEW KRYPTON.

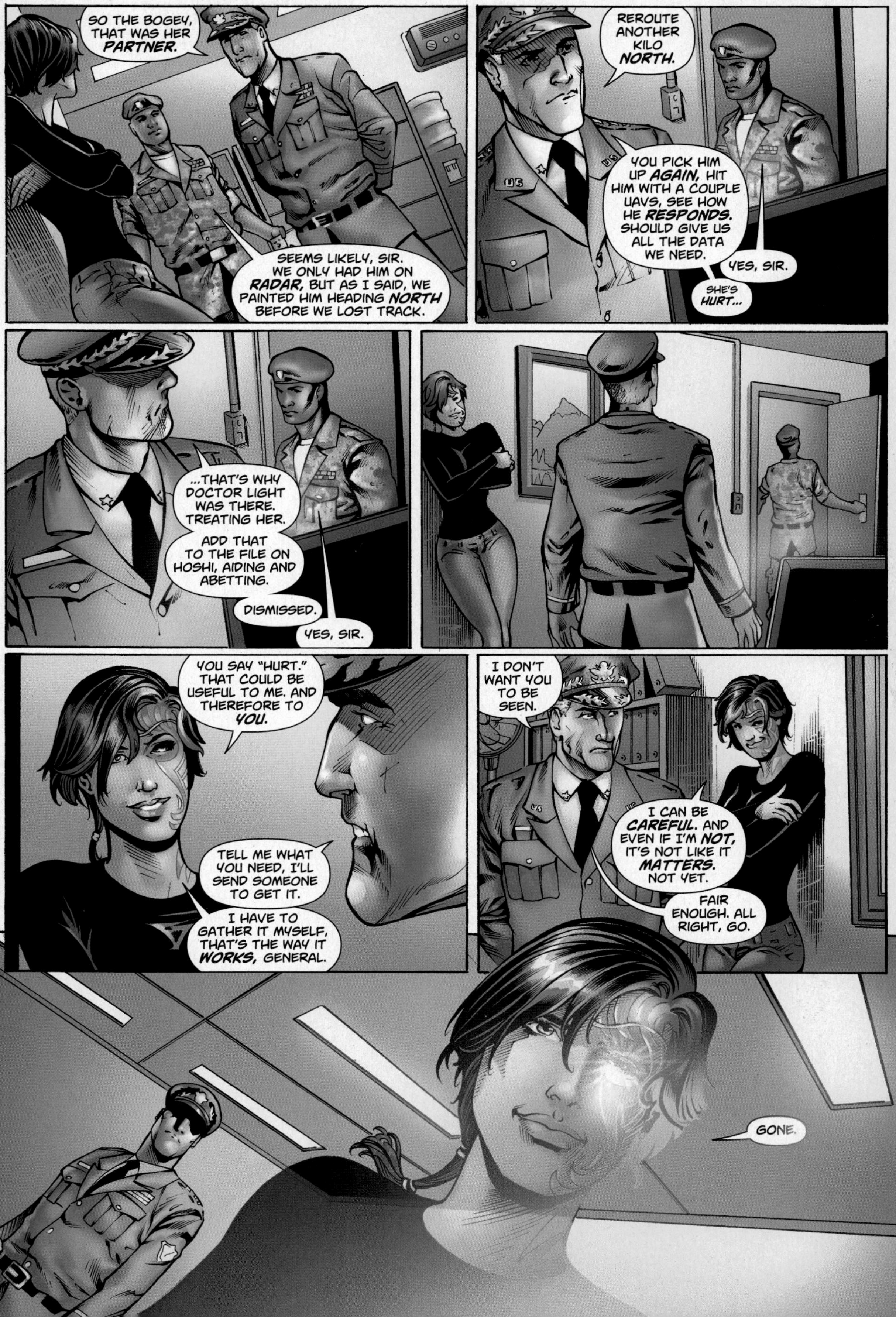
SO THE BOGEY, THAT WAS HER PARTNER.
SEEMS LIKELY, SIR. WE ONLY HAD HIM ON RADAR, BUT AS I SAID, WE PAINTED HIM HEADING NORTH BEFORE WE LOST TRACK.
REROUTE ANOTHER KILO NORTH.
YOU PICK HIM UP AGAIN, HIT HIM WITH A COUPLE UAVS, SEE HOW HE RESPONDS. SHOULD GIVE US ALL THE DATA WE NEED.
YES, SIR.
SHE'S HURT...
...THAT'S WHY DOCTOR LIGHT WAS THERE. TREATING HER.
ADD THAT TO THE FILE ON HOSHI, AIDING AND ABETTING.
DISMISSED.
YES, SIR.
YOU SAY "HURT." THAT COULD BE USEFUL TO ME. AND THEREFORE TO YOU.
TELL ME WHAT YOU NEED, I'LL SEND SOMEONE TO GET IT.
I HAVE TO GATHER IT MYSELF, THAT'S THE WAY IT WORKS, GENERAL.
I DON'T WANT YOU TO BE SEEN.
I CAN BE CAREFUL. AND EVEN IF I'M NOT, IT'S NOT LIKE IT MATTERS. NOT YET.
FAIR ENOUGH. ALL RIGHT, GO.
GONE.

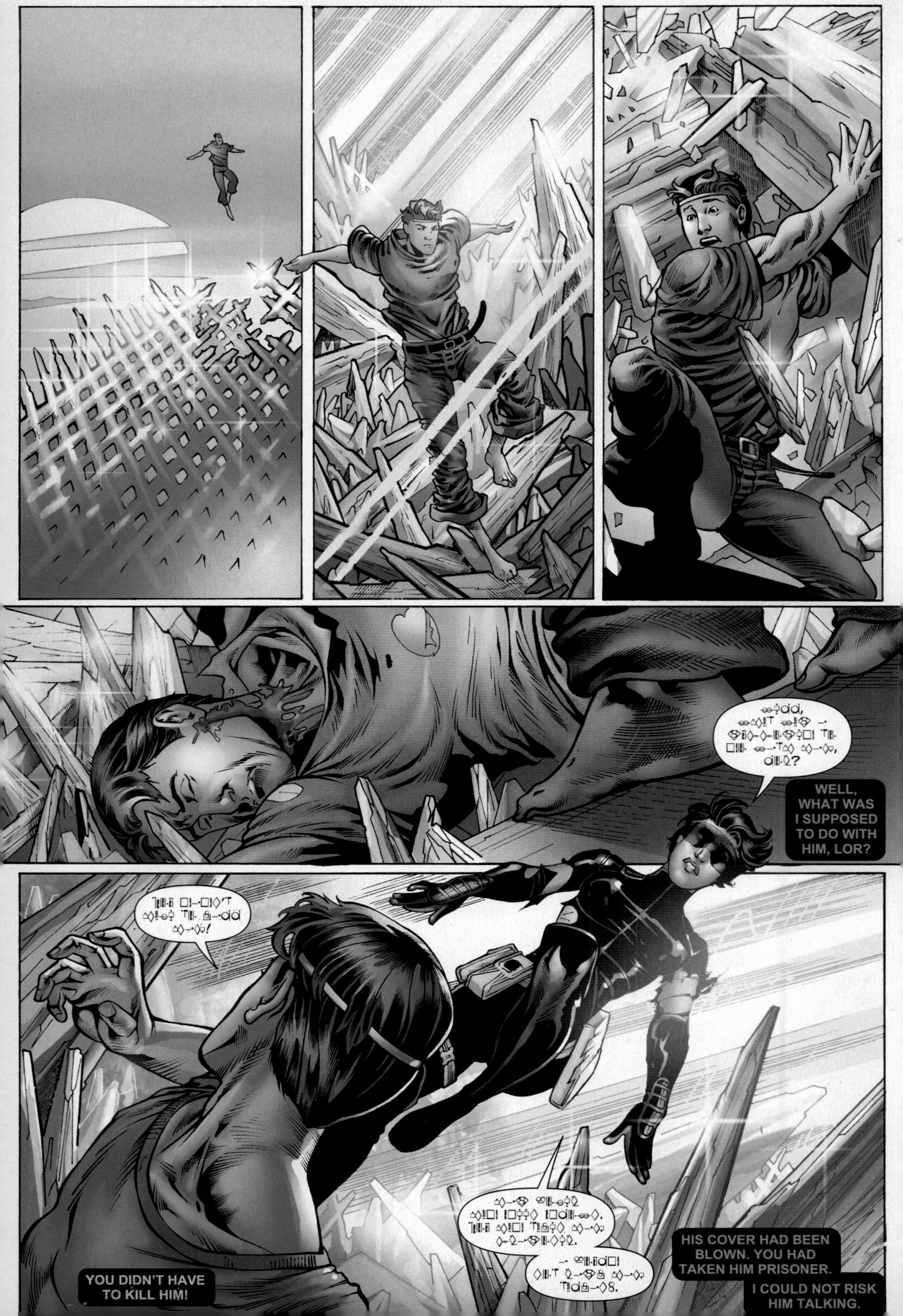

WELL, WHAT WAS I SUPPOSED TO DO WITH HIM, LOR?
YOU DIDN'T HAVE TO KILL HIM!
HIS COVER HAD BEEN BLOWN. YOU HAD TAKEN HIM PRISONER.
I COULD NOT RISK HIM TALKING.

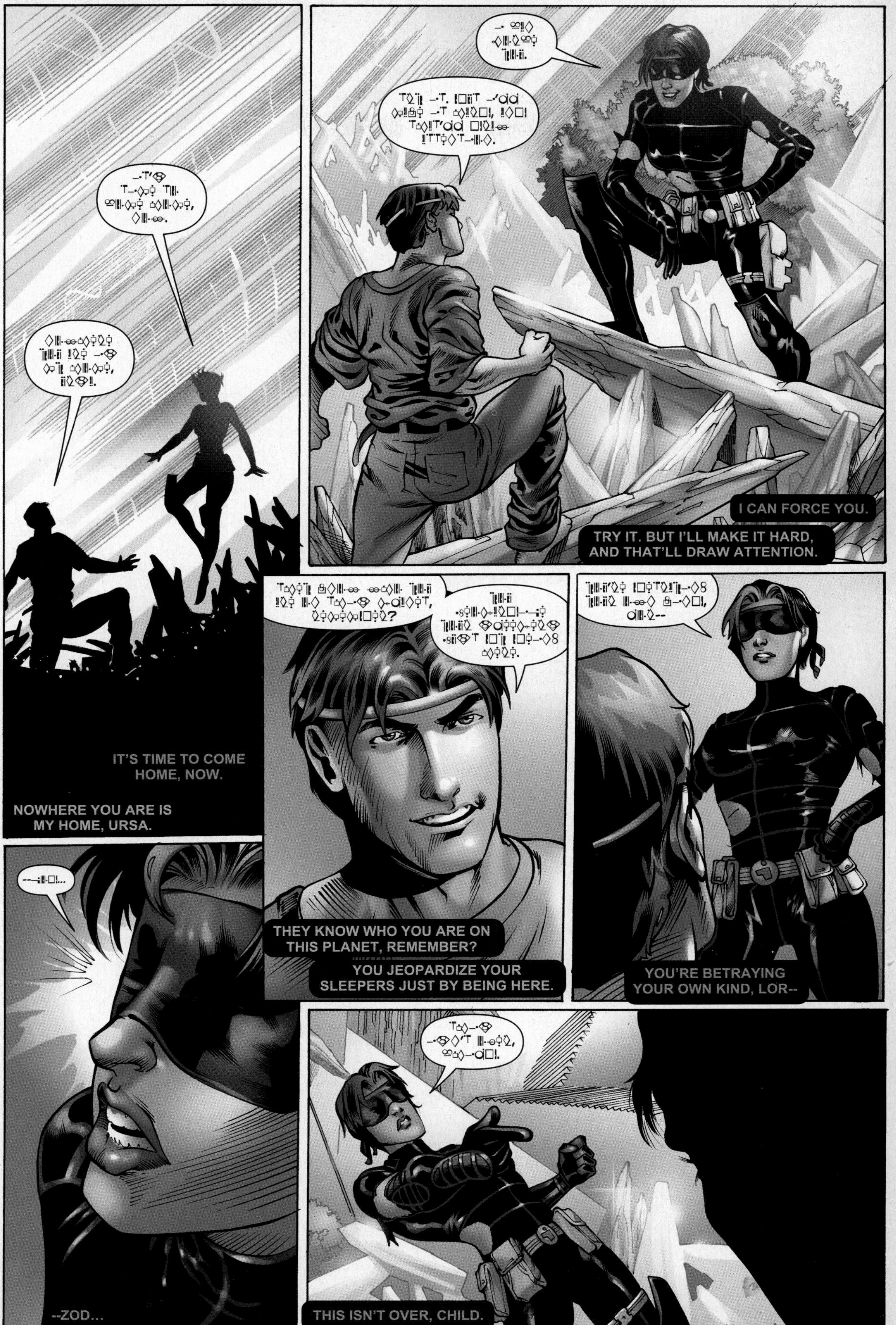
IT'S TIME TO COME HOME, NOW.
NOWHERE YOU ARE IS MY HOME, URSA.
I CAN FORCE YOU.
TRY IT. BUT I'LL MAKE IT HARD, AND THAT'LL DRAW ATTENTION.
THEY KNOW WHO YOU ARE ON THIS PLANET, REMEMBER?
YOU JEOPARDIZE YOUR SLEEPERS JUST BY BEING HERE.
YOU'RE BETRAYING YOUR OWN KIND, LOR--
--ZOD...
THIS ISN'T OVER, CHILD.

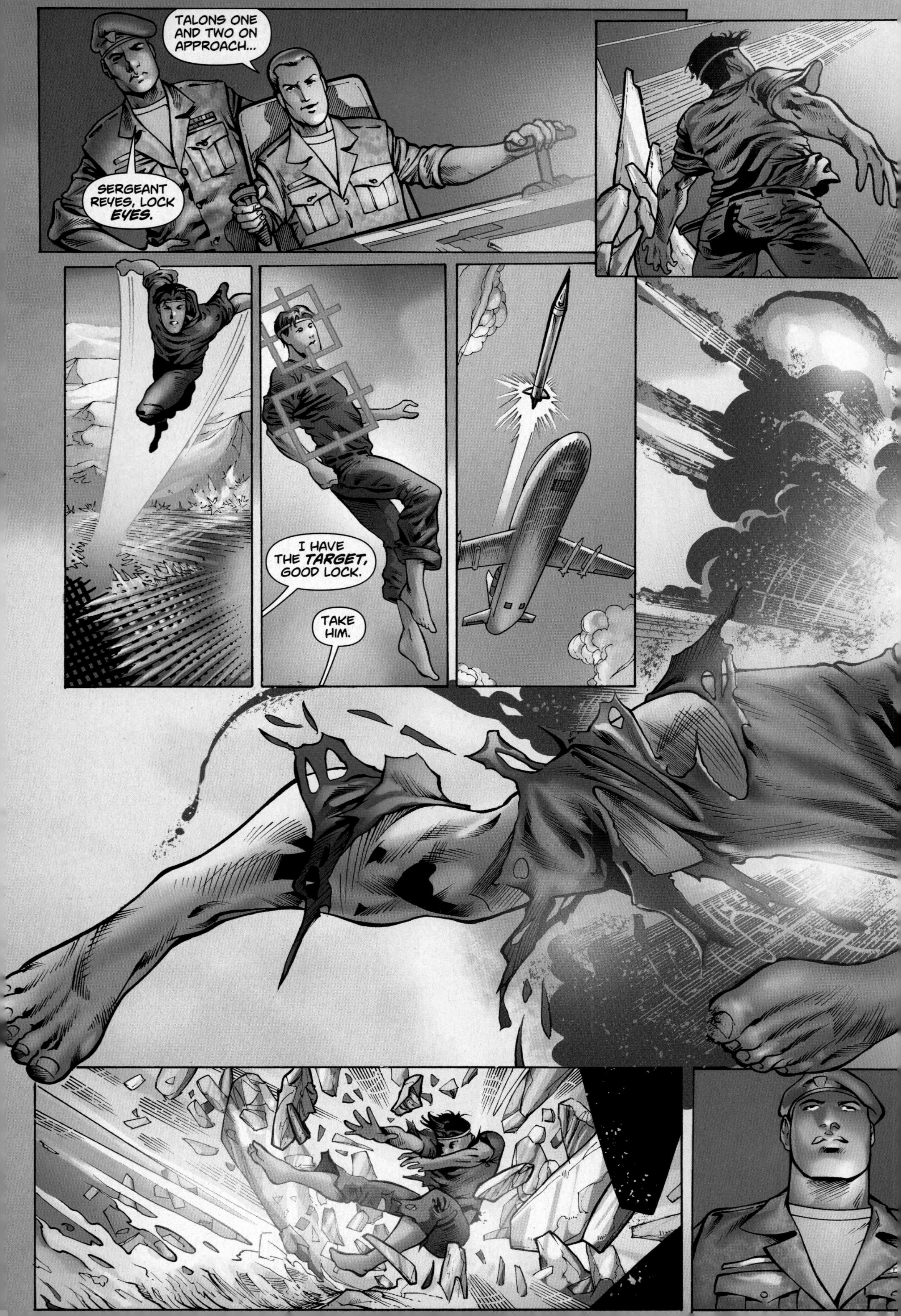
TALONS ONE AND TWO ON APPROACH...
SERGEANT REYES, LOCK EYES.
I HAVE THE TARGET, GOOD LOCK.
TAKE HIM.

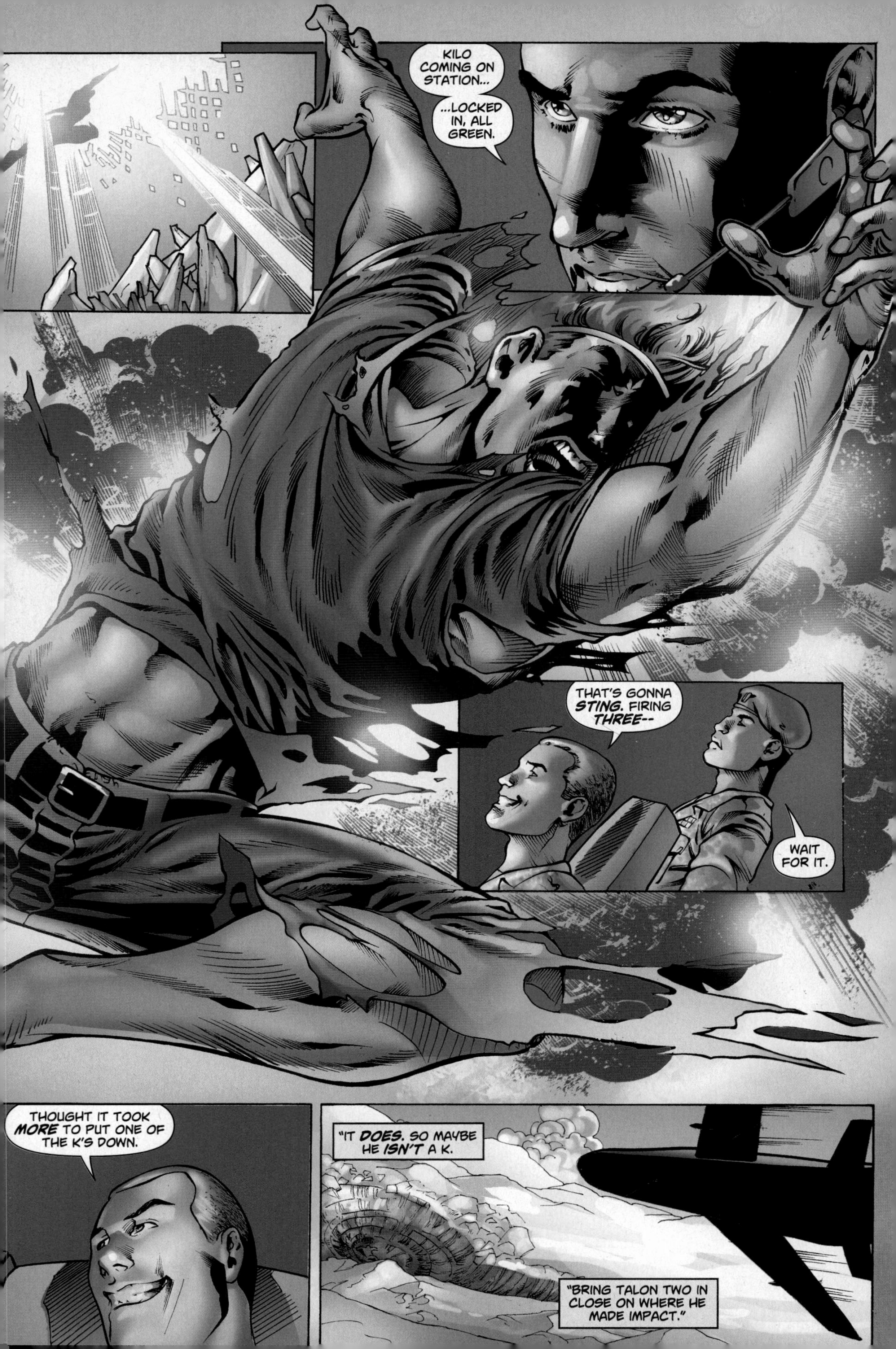
KILO COMING ON STATION...
...LOCKED IN, ALL GREEN.
THAT'S GONNA STING. FIRING THREE--
WAIT FOR IT.
THOUGHT IT TOOK MORE TO PUT ONE OF THE K'S DOWN.
"IT DOES. SO MAYBE HE ISN'T A K.
"BRING TALON TWO IN CLOSE ON WHERE HE MADE IMPACT."

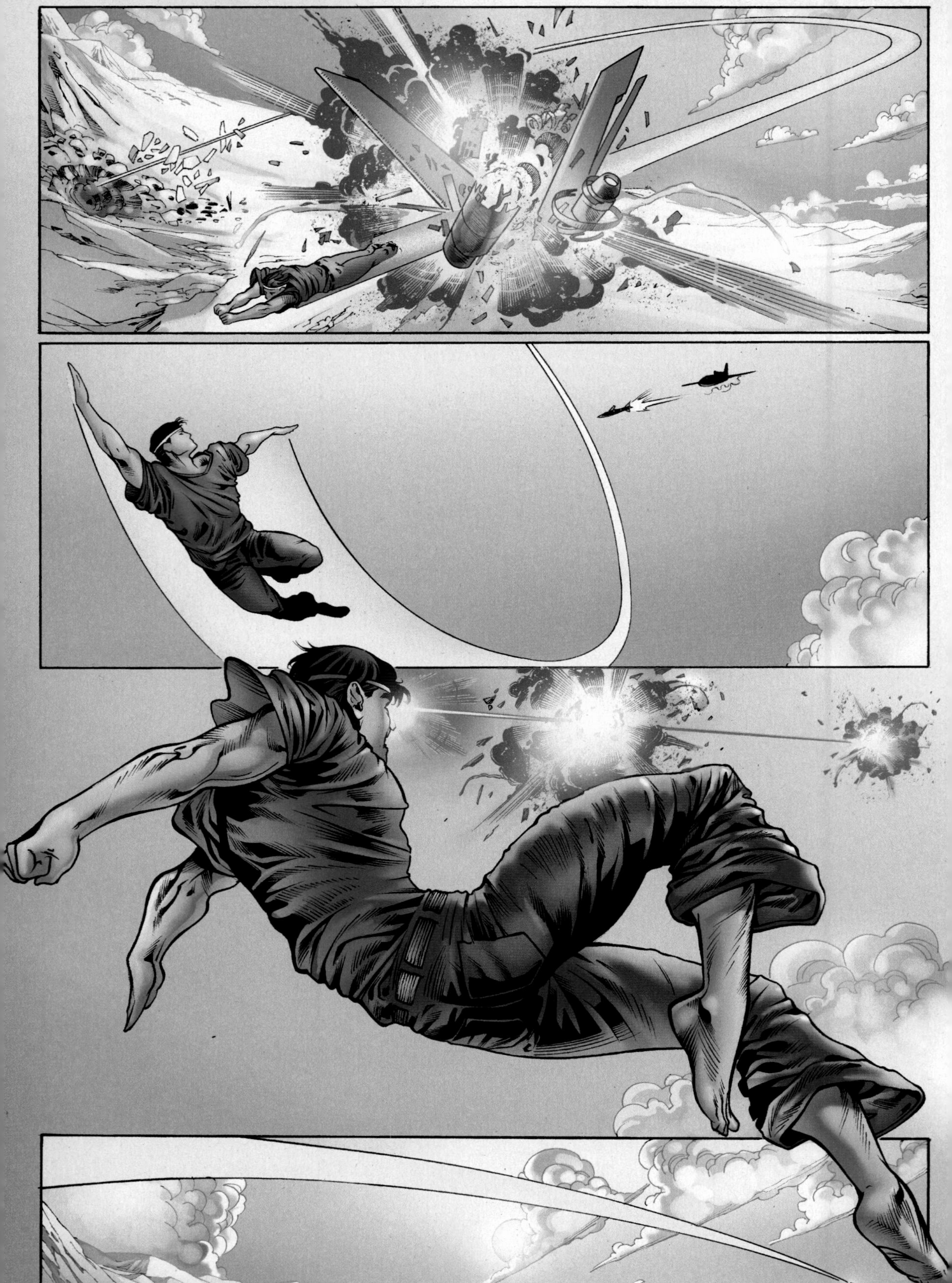

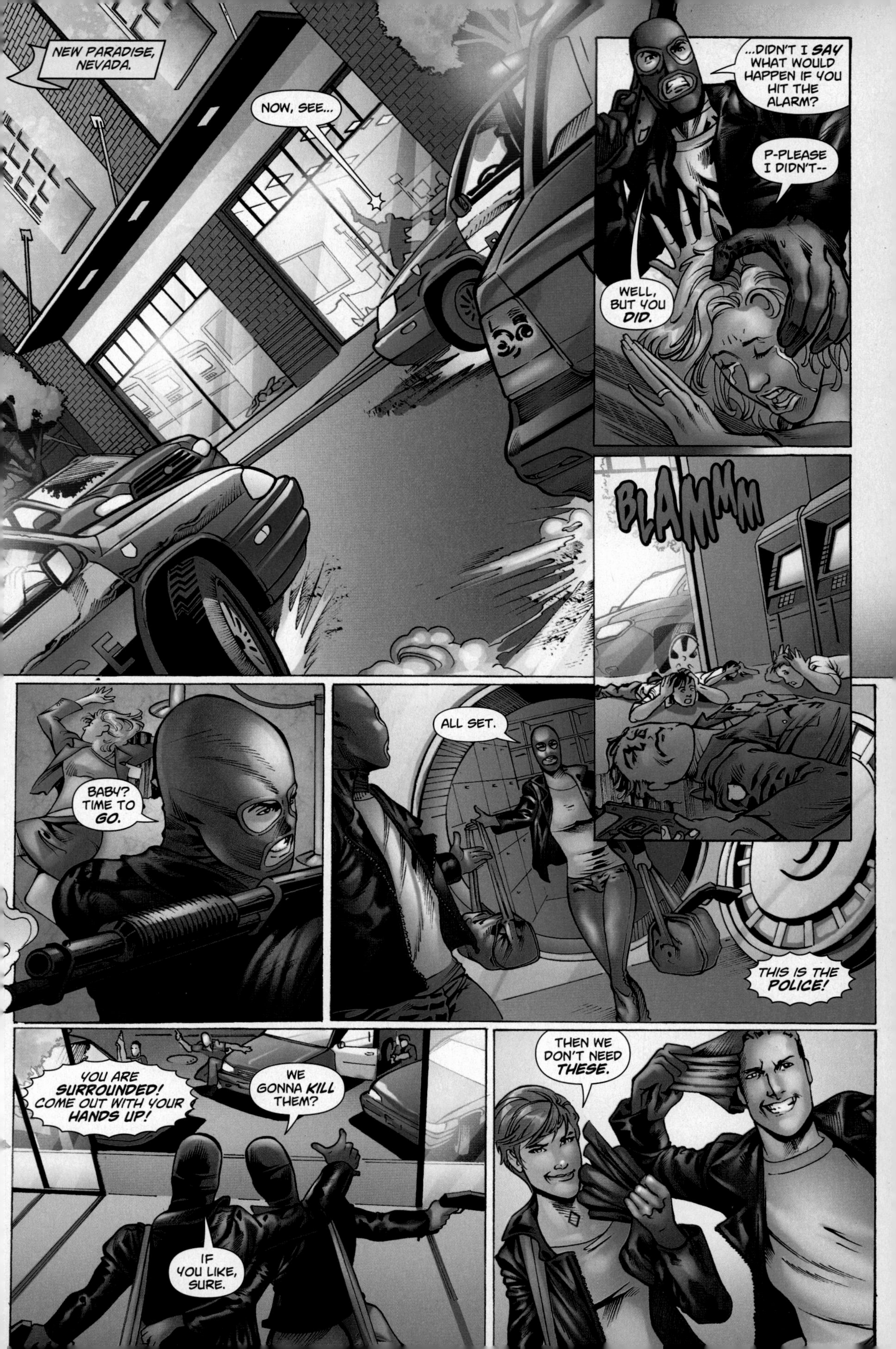
NEW PARADISE, NEVADA.
NOW, SEE...
...DIDN'T I SAY WHAT WOULD HAPPEN IF YOU HIT THE ALARM?
P-PLEASE I DIDN'T--
WELL, BUT YOU DID.
BLAMMM
BABY? TIME TO GO.
ALL SET.
THIS IS THE POLICE!
YOU ARE SURROUNDED! COME OUT WITH YOUR HANDS UP!
WE GONNA KILL THEM?
IF YOU LIKE, SURE.
THEN WE DON'T NEED THESE.

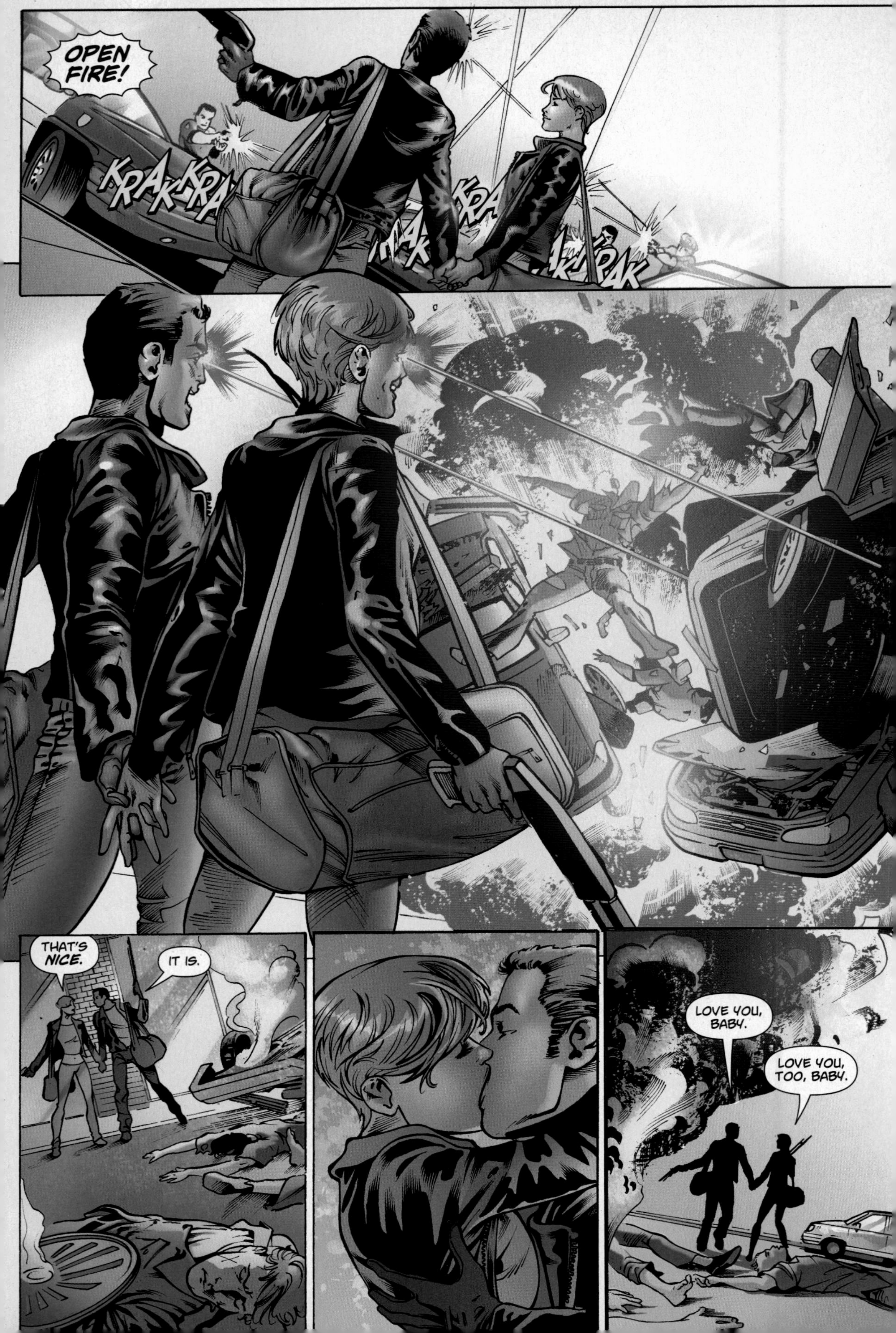
OPEN FIRE!
KRAK KRAK KRA
KRAK KRA
KRAK KRAK
THAT'S NICE.
IT IS.
LOVE YOU, BABY.
LOVE YOU, TOO, BABY.

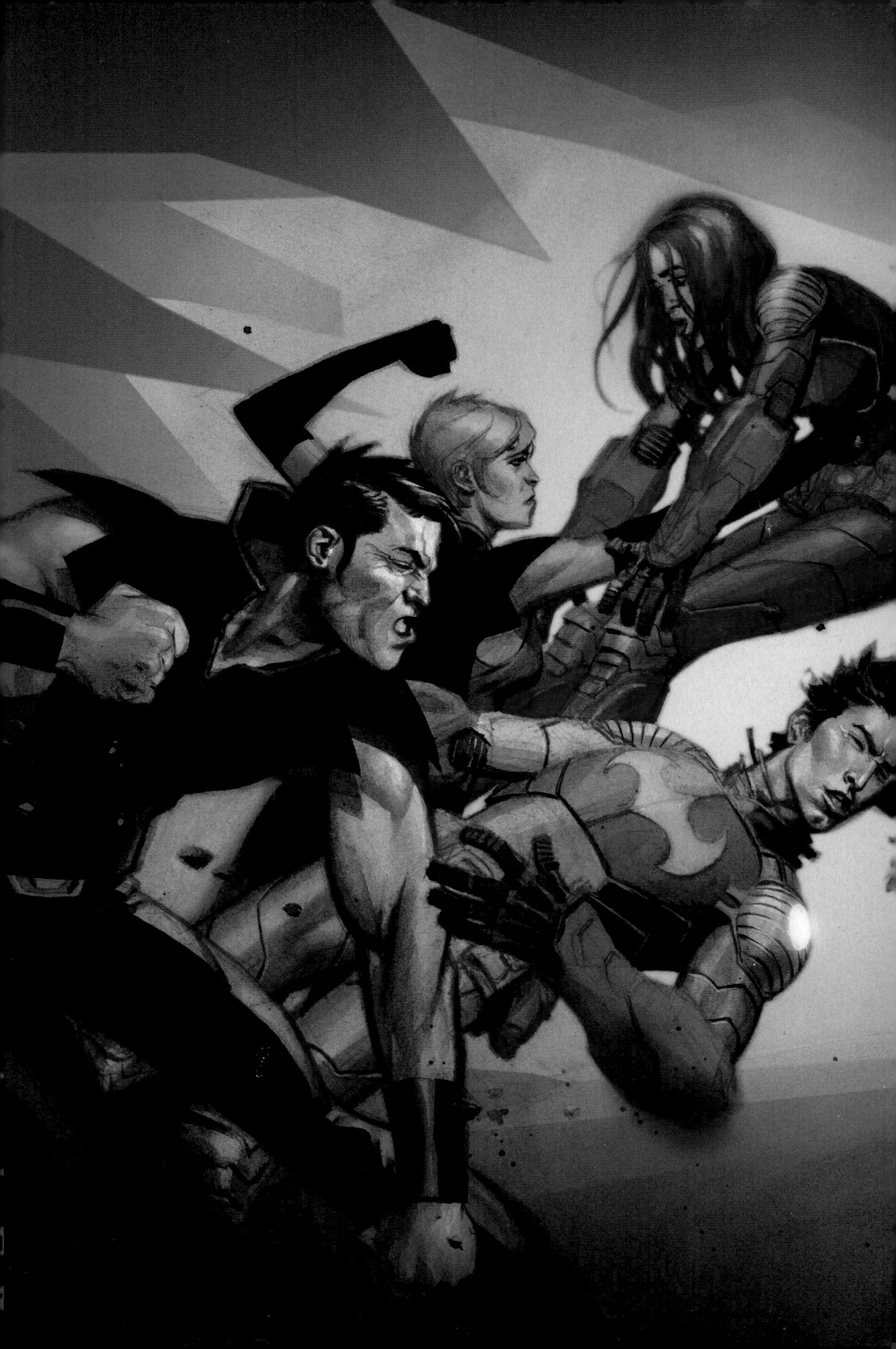

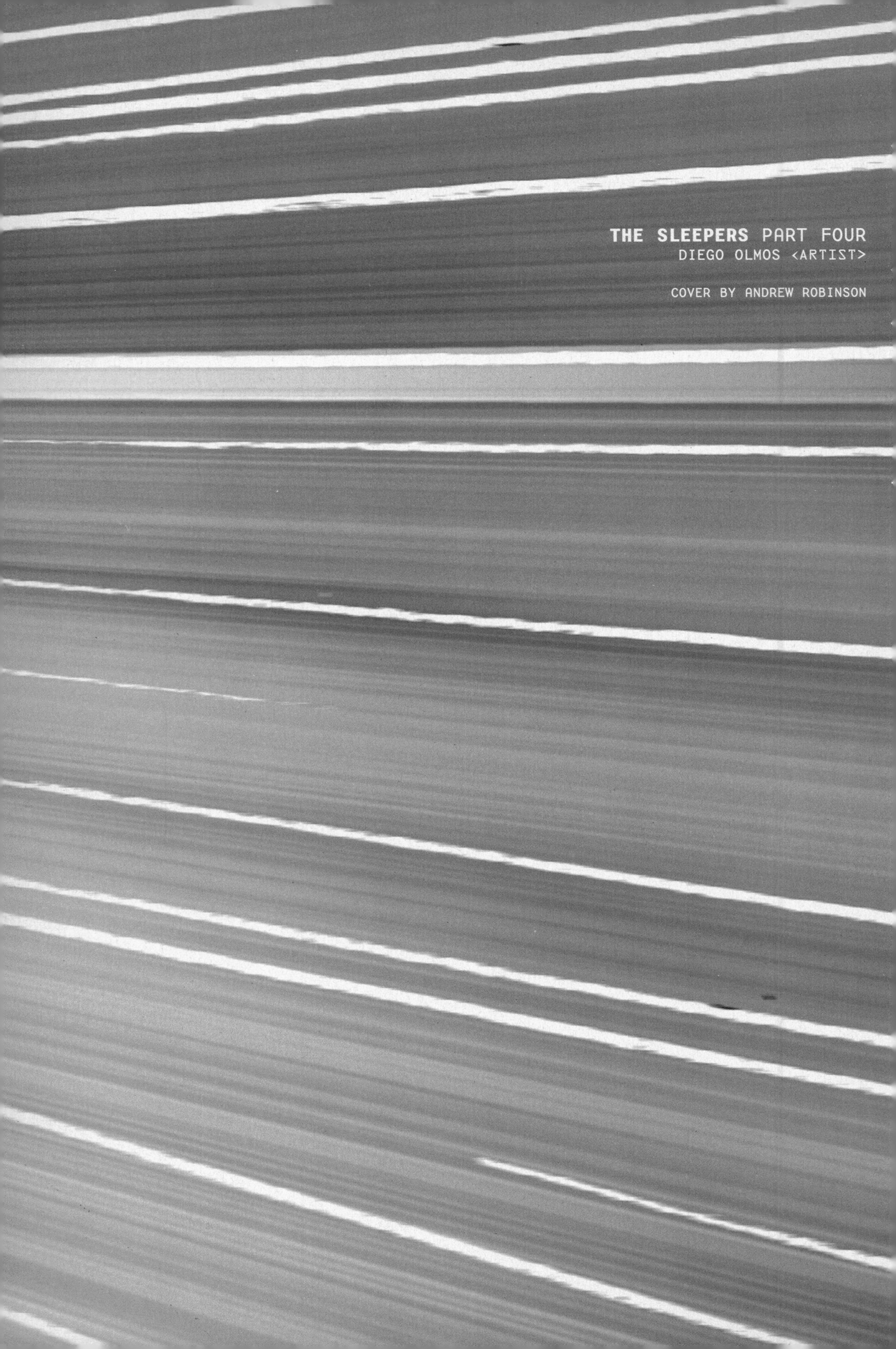

THE SLEEPERS PART FOUR

DIEGO OLMOS <ARTIST>

COVER BY ANDREW ROBINSON

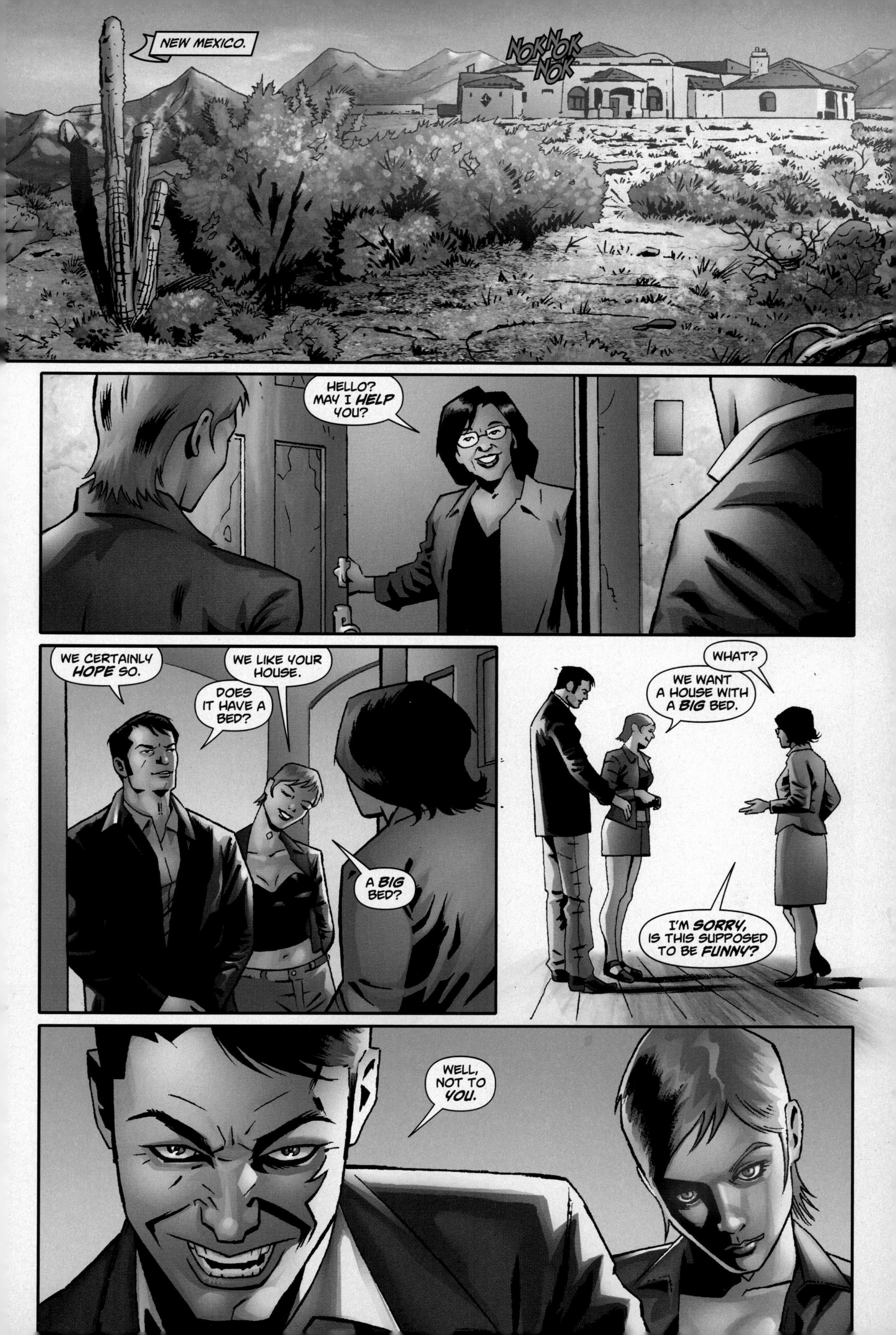
NEW MEXICO.
NOK NOK NOK
HELLO? MAY I HELP YOU?
WE CERTAINLY HOPE SO.
WE LIKE YOUR HOUSE.
DOES IT HAVE A BED?
A BIG BED?
WHAT?
WE WANT A HOUSE WITH A BIG BED.
I'M SORRY, IS THIS SUPPOSED TO BE FUNNY?
WELL, NOT TO YOU.

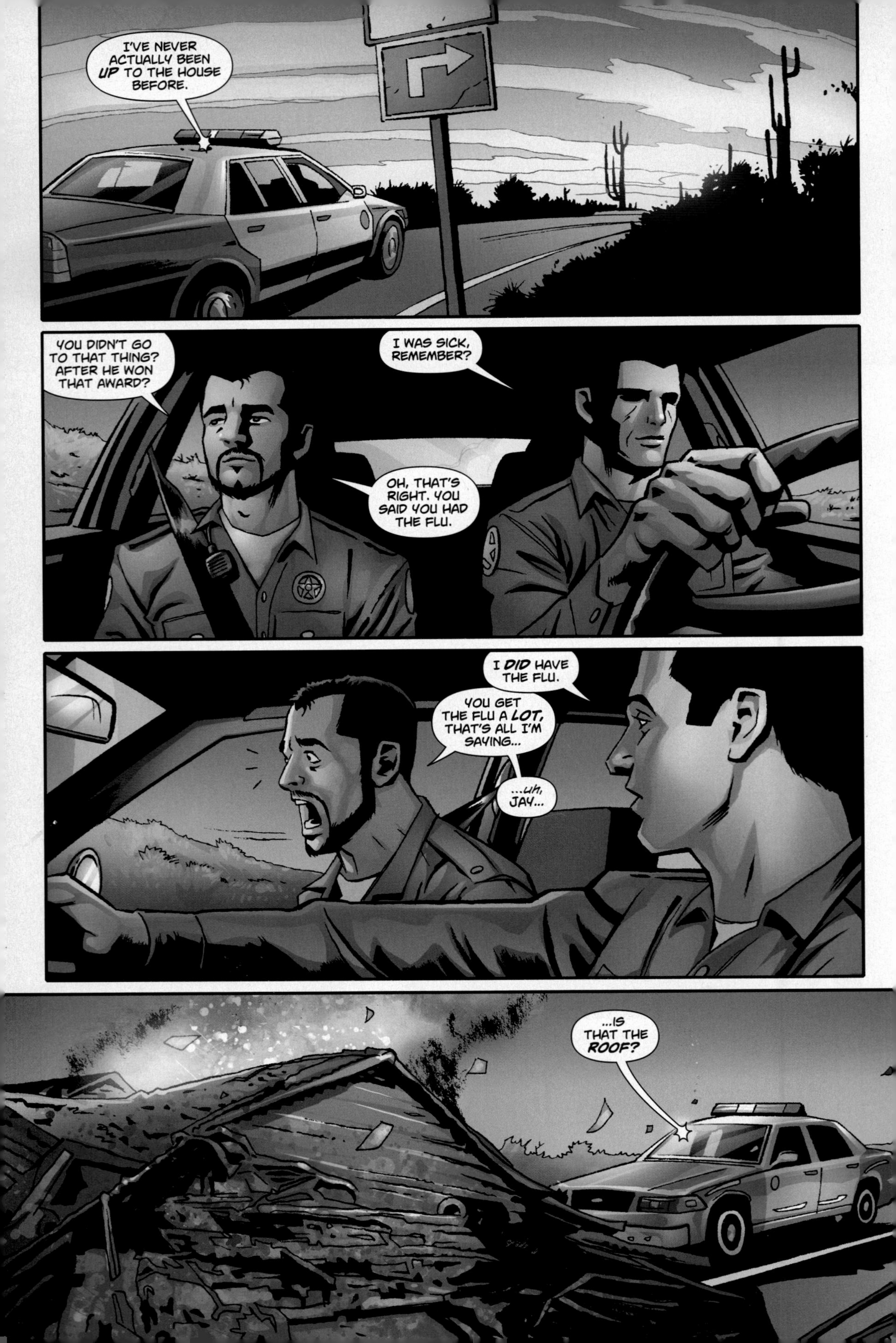

I'VE NEVER ACTUALLY BEEN UP TO THE HOUSE BEFORE.
YOU DIDN'T GO TO THAT THING? AFTER HE WON THAT AWARD?
I WAS SICK, REMEMBER?
OH, THAT'S RIGHT. YOU SAID YOU HAD THE FLU.
I DID HAVE THE FLU.
YOU GET THE FLU A LOT, THAT'S ALL I'M SAYING...
...uh, JAY...
...IS THAT THE ROOF?

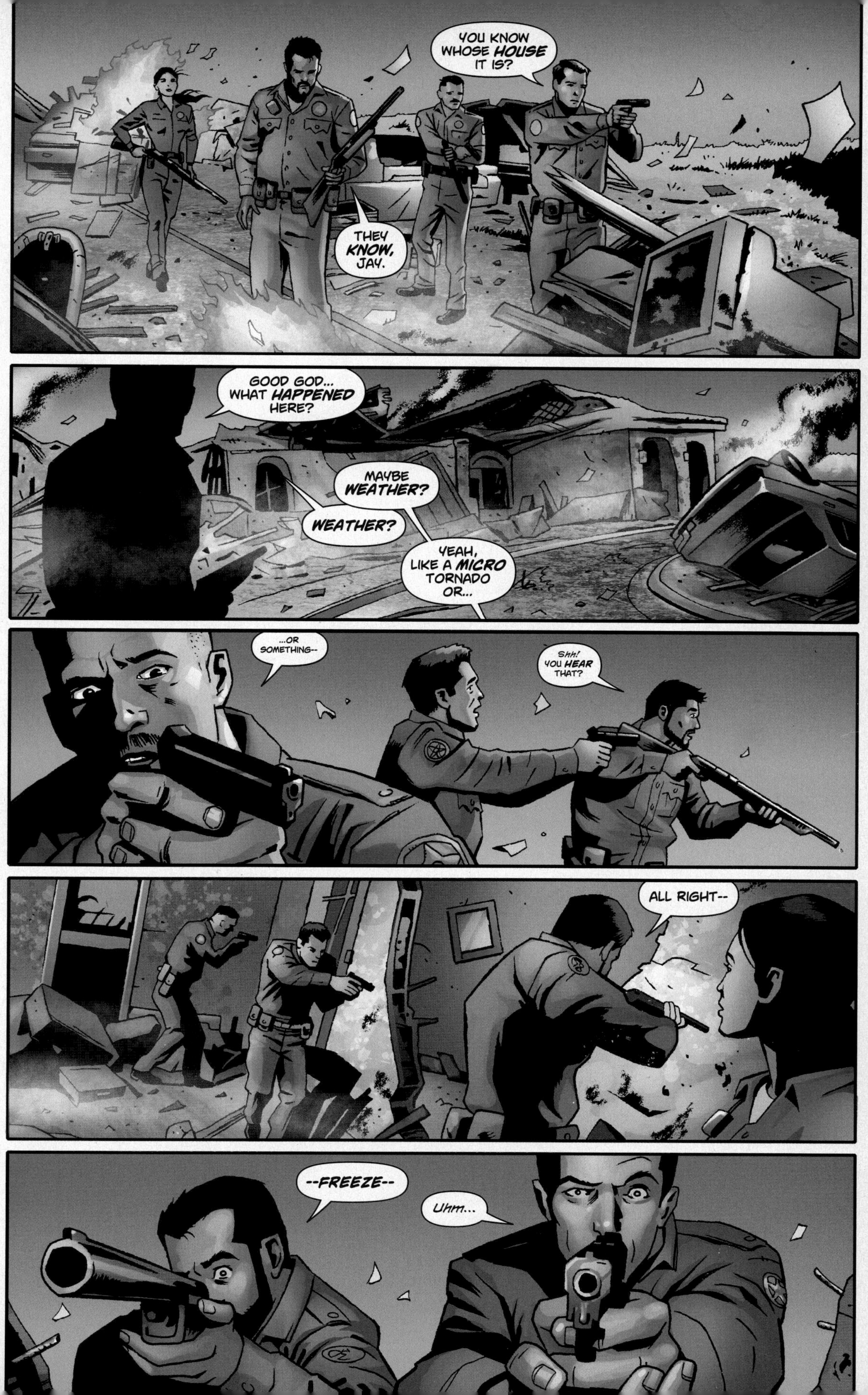
YOU KNOW WHOSE HOUSE IT IS?
THEY KNOW, JAY.
GOOD GOD... WHAT HAPPENED HERE?
MAYBE WEATHER?
WEATHER?
YEAH, LIKE A MICRO TORNADO OR...
...OR SOMETHING--
Shh! YOU HEAR THAT?
ALL RIGHT--
--FREEZE--
Uhm...

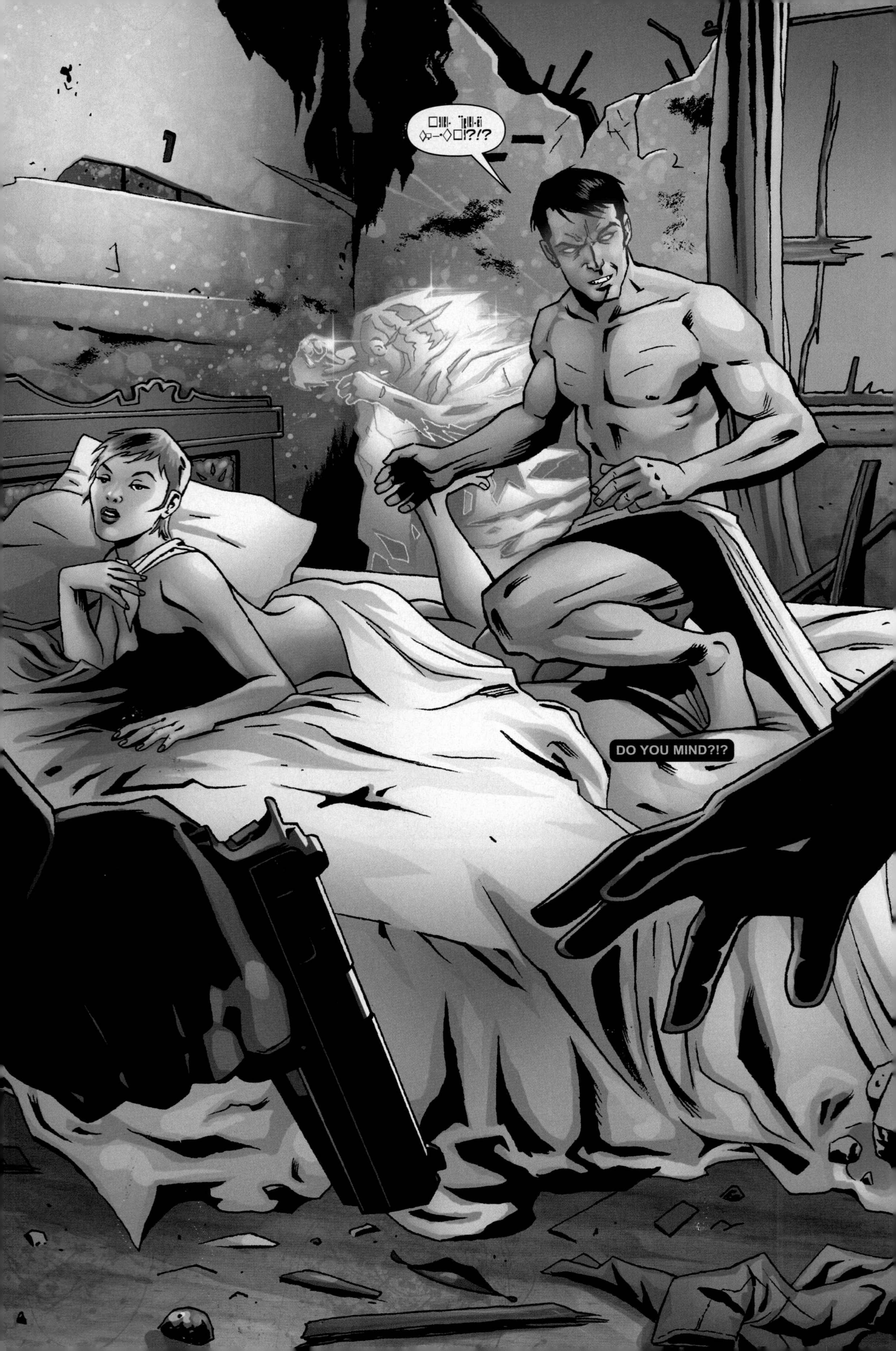
DO YOU MIND?!?

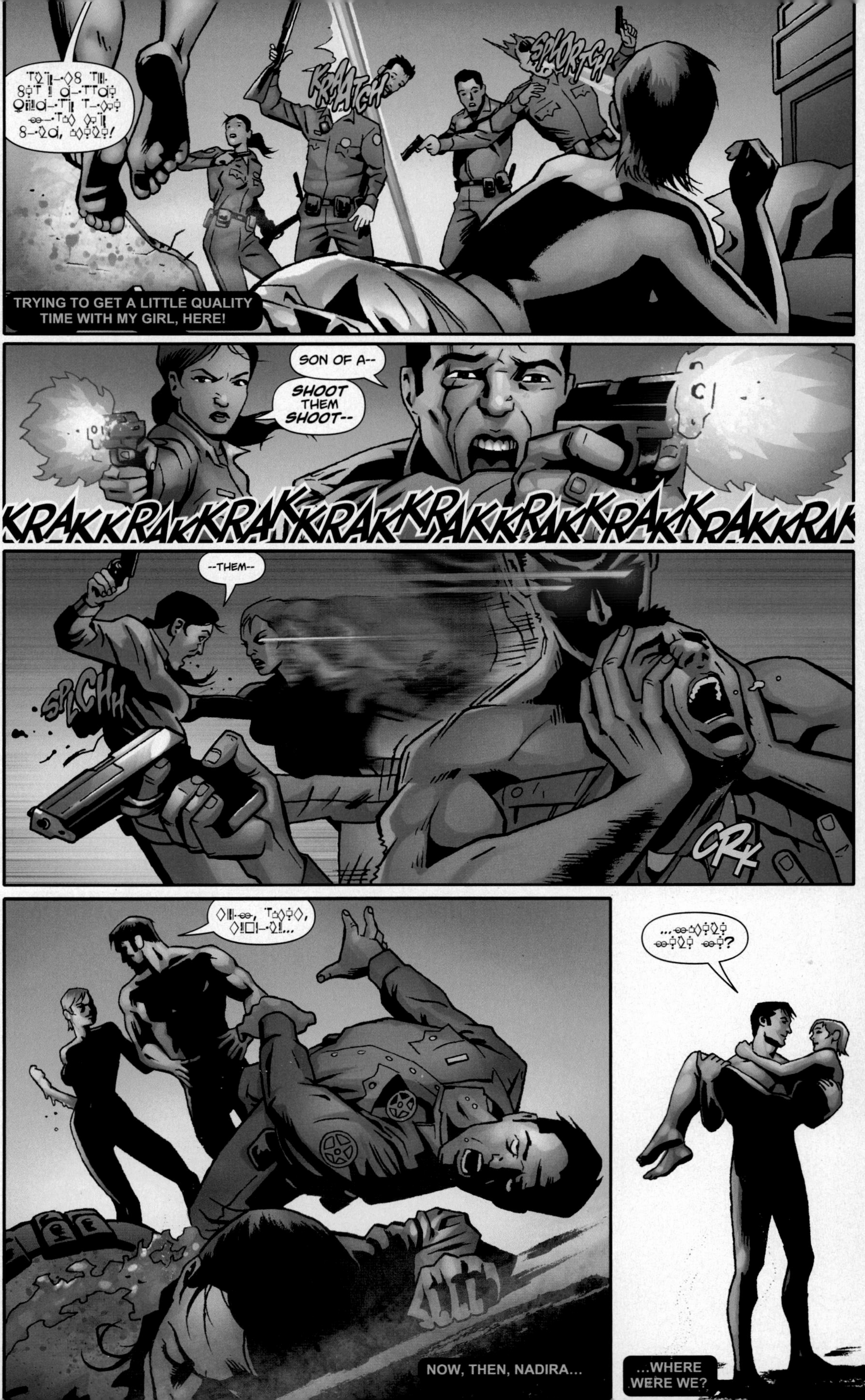
KRAATCH
SPLORTCH
TRYING TO GET A LITTLE QUALITY TIME WITH MY GIRL, HERE!
SON OF A--
SHOOT THEM SHOOT--
KRAKKRAKKRAKKRAKKRAKKRAKKRAKKRAKKRAK
--THEM--
SPLCHH
CRK
NOW, THEN, NADIRA...
...WHERE WERE WE?

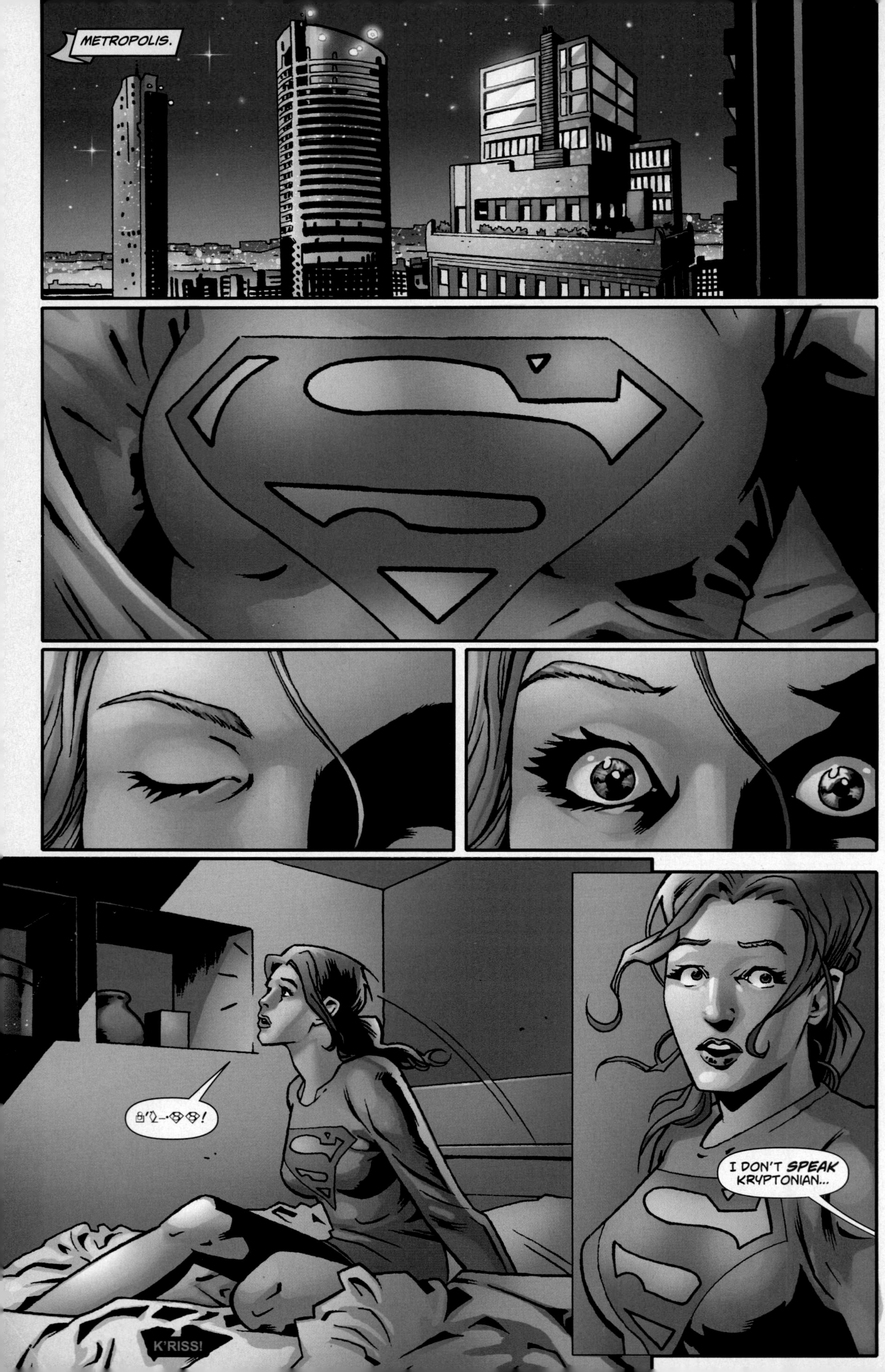
METROPOLIS.
K'RISS!
I DON'T SPEAK KRYPTONIAN...

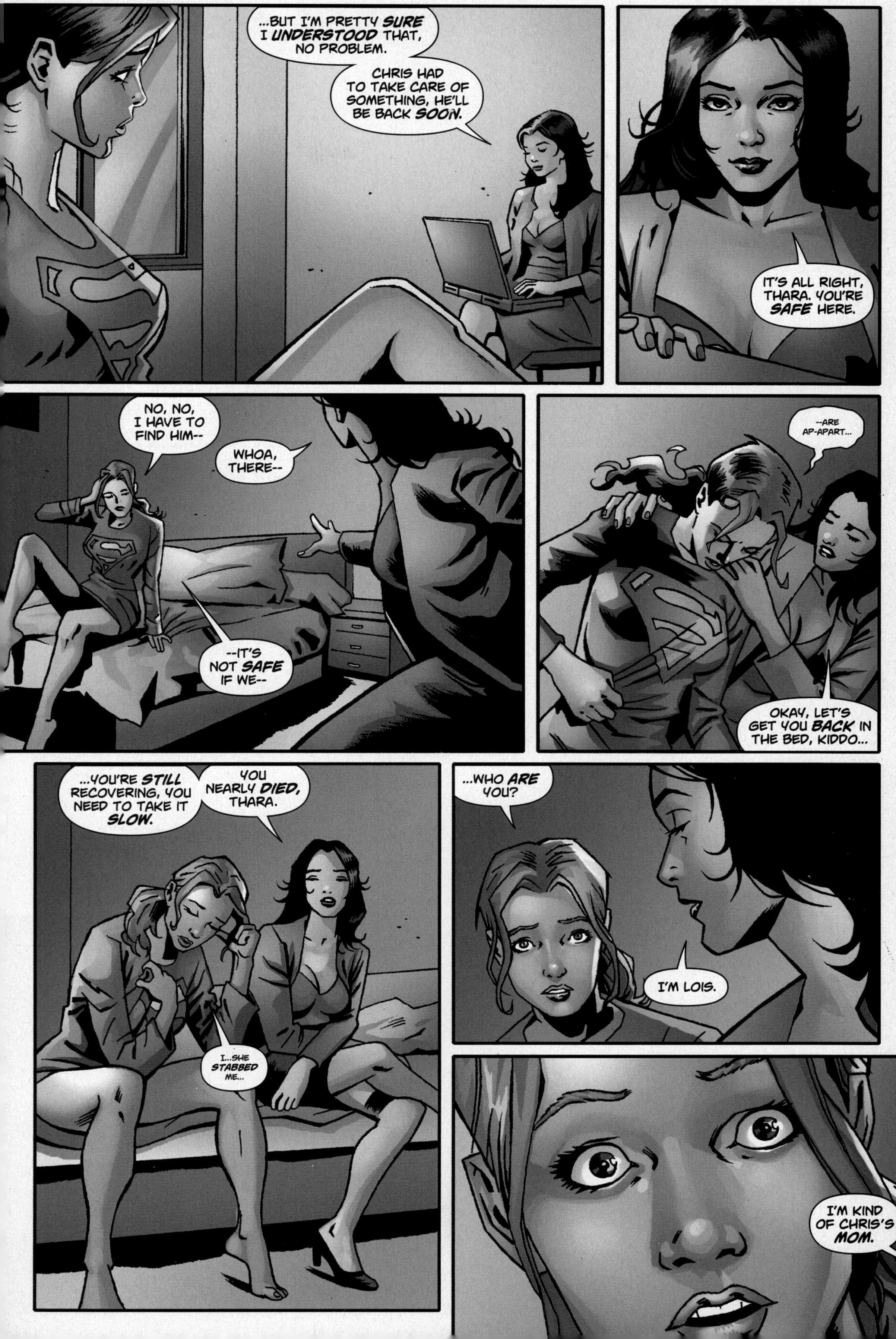
...BUT I'M PRETTY SURE I UNDERSTOOD THAT, NO PROBLEM.
CHRIS HAD TO TAKE CARE OF SOMETHING, HE'LL BE BACK SOON.
IT'S ALL RIGHT, THARA. YOU'RE SAFE HERE.
NO, NO, I HAVE TO FIND HIM--
WHOA, THERE--
--IT'S NOT SAFE IF WE--
--ARE AP-APART...
OKAY, LET'S GET YOU BACK IN THE BED, KIDDO...
...YOU'RE STILL RECOVERING, YOU NEED TO TAKE IT SLOW.
YOU NEARLY DIED, THARA.
I...SHE STABBED ME...
...WHO ARE YOU?
I'M LOIS.
I'M KIND OF CHRIS'S MOM.

YOU...THAT'S *NOT* POSSIBLE.

I HOPE THAT'S BECAUSE YOU THINK I LOOK TOO *YOUNG.*

YOU ARE *HUMAN.*

AND THERE'S *THAT,* YEAH.

I SAID "KIND OF," NOT THAT I *WAS...*

...AND IT *ISN'T* BIOLOGY *ALONE* THAT MAKES SOMEONE A *PARENT.*

BEING RAISED IN KANDOR, I'D THINK YOU'D HAVE *LEARNED* THAT.

HOW DO YOU KNOW I'M FROM KANDOR?

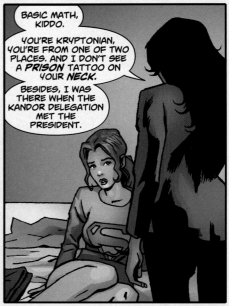

BASIC MATH, KIDDO.

YOU'RE KRYPTONIAN, YOU'RE FROM ONE OF TWO PLACES. AND I DON'T SEE A *PRISON* TATTOO ON YOUR *NECK.*

BESIDES, I WAS THERE WHEN THE KANDOR DELEGATION MET THE PRESIDENT.

YOU LOOK LIKE YOU'RE FEELING BETTER.

YOU SHOULD GET CLEANED UP, PUT THESE ON...

...THEN YOU CAN TELL ME ALL ABOUT WHAT YOU'VE BEEN GETTING *UP* TO WITH MY *SON.*

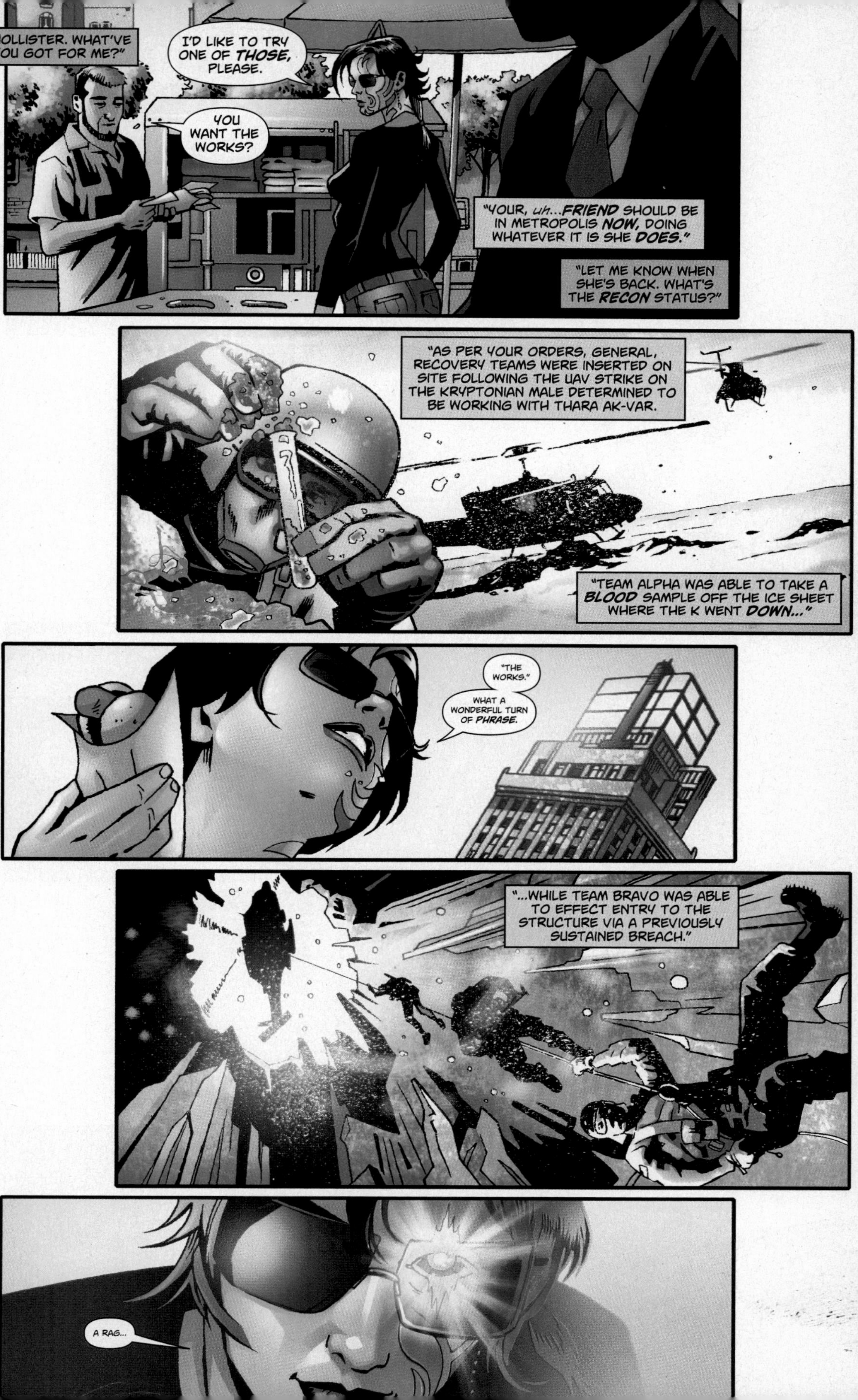
"HOLLISTER. WHAT'VE YOU GOT FOR ME?"
I'D LIKE TO TRY ONE OF *THOSE,* PLEASE.
YOU WANT THE WORKS?
"YOUR, *uh*...*FRIEND* SHOULD BE IN METROPOLIS *NOW,* DOING WHATEVER IT IS SHE *DOES.*"
"LET ME KNOW WHEN SHE'S BACK. WHAT'S THE *RECON* STATUS?"
"AS PER YOUR ORDERS, GENERAL, RECOVERY TEAMS WERE INSERTED ON SITE FOLLOWING THE UAV STRIKE ON THE KRYPTONIAN MALE DETERMINED TO BE WORKING WITH THARA AK-VAR.
"TEAM ALPHA WAS ABLE TO TAKE A *BLOOD* SAMPLE OFF THE ICE SHEET WHERE THE K WENT *DOWN*..."
"THE WORKS."
WHAT A WONDERFUL TURN OF *PHRASE.*
"...WHILE TEAM BRAVO WAS ABLE TO EFFECT ENTRY TO THE STRUCTURE VIA A PREVIOUSLY SUSTAINED BREACH."
A RAG...

"...AT WHICH TIME THEY DISCOVERED THE **BODY** OF THE MISSING EMPIRE COMMUNICATIONS CEO, DAVID CARTER."

WARNING.

...A BONE...

"BRAVO MANAGED TO RECOVER THE BODY BEFORE LOCAL DEFENSES WENT **ACTIVE**."

YOU ARE **TRESPASSING** ON PRIVATE PROPERTY. **WARNING**.

SECURITY COUNTERMEASURES ARE IN EFFECT.

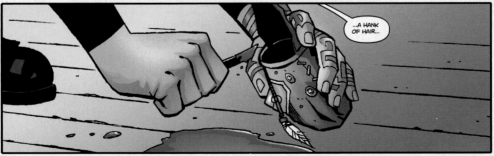

...A HANK OF HAIR...

"THE TEAM MADE **IMMEDIATE** EXFIL, COMPLETE TO SAFE **RECOVERY**."

"YOU HAVE THE **ANALYSIS?**"

YES, SIR, RIGHT HERE.

I THINK THE RESULTS MAY *SURPRISE* YOU.

DAVID CARTER WAS *KRYPTONIAN*?

THAT'S THE *PRELIMINARY* ON THE *AUTOPSY*, YES, SIR.

THERE'S *MORE*.

DNA FROM THE *BLOOD* SAMPLE ALPHA TEAM TOOK OFF THE ICE--THE ONE LEFT BY AK-VAR'S *PARTNER*--MATCHED A SEQUENCE IN THE DEPARTMENT OF METAHUMAN AFFAIRS *DATABASE*.

THIS BOY. THE KRYPTONIAN KID THAT SUPERMAN *KIDNAPPED* FROM DMA CUSTODY A WHILE BACK.

WE CAN'T EXPLAIN THE APPARENT DISCREPANCY IN *AGE*, BUT IT'S A 100% *MATCH*.

YOU HAVE CAUSE OF *DEATH* ON "DAVID CARTER"?

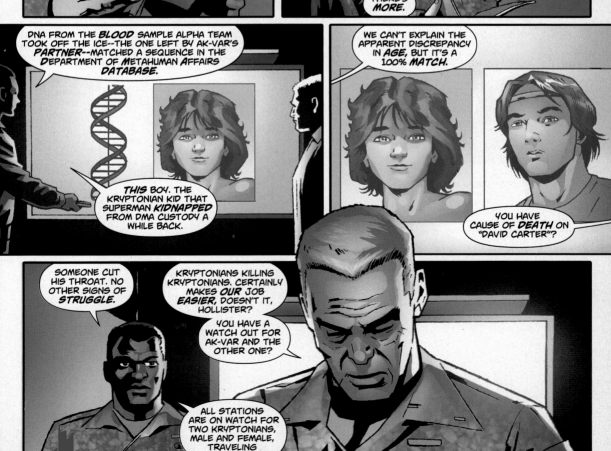

SOMEONE CUT HIS THROAT. NO OTHER SIGNS OF *STRUGGLE*.

KRYPTONIANS KILLING *KRYPTONIANS.* CERTAINLY MAKES *OUR* JOB *EASIER*, DOESN'T IT, HOLLISTER?

YOU HAVE A WATCH OUT FOR AK-VAR AND THE OTHER ONE?

ALL STATIONS ARE ON WATCH FOR TWO KRYPTONIANS, MALE AND FEMALE, TRAVELING TOGETHER.

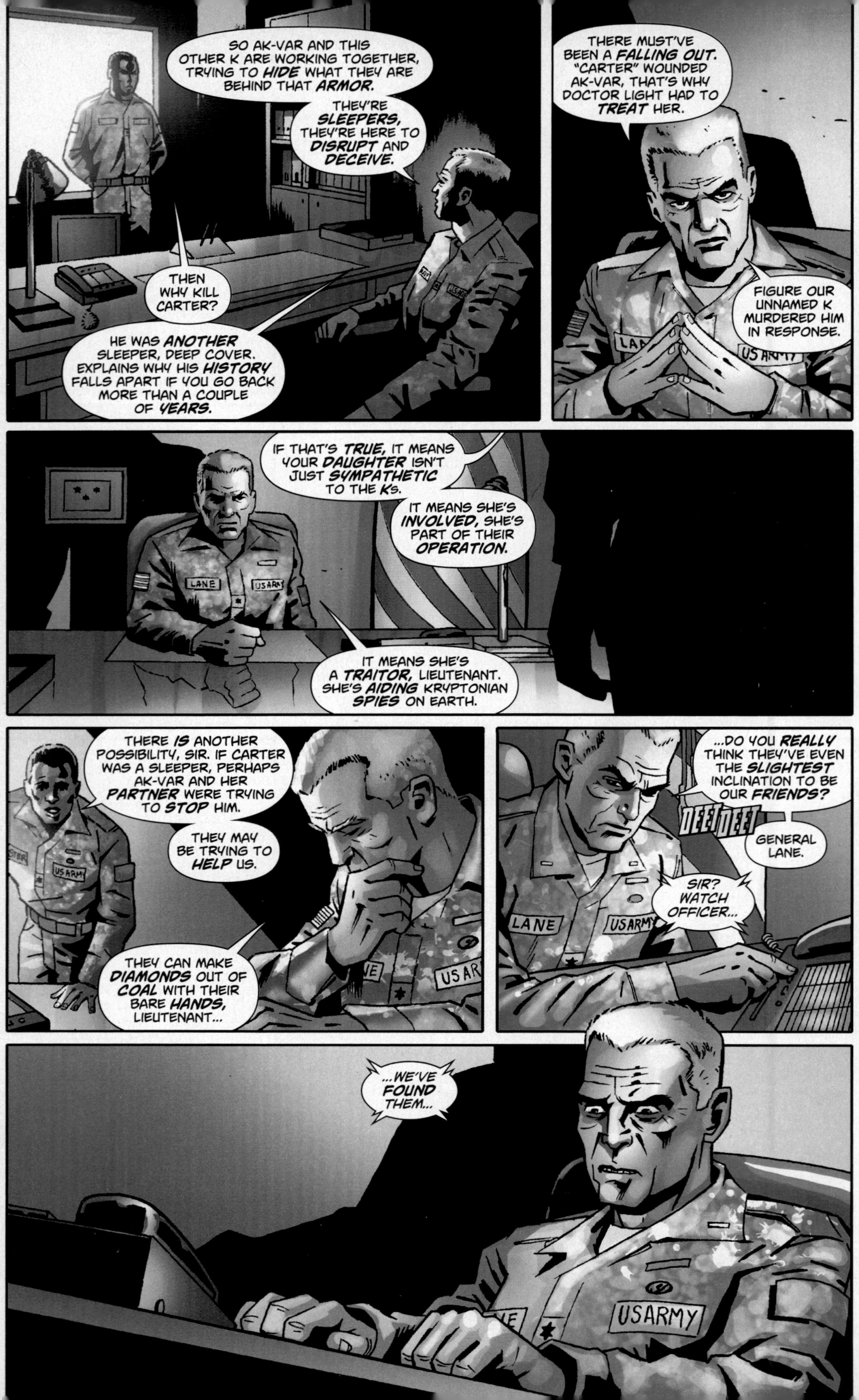

SO AK-VAR AND THIS OTHER K ARE WORKING TOGETHER, TRYING TO HIDE WHAT THEY ARE BEHIND THAT ARMOR.
THEY'RE SLEEPERS, THEY'RE HERE TO DISRUPT AND DECEIVE.
THEN WHY KILL CARTER?
HE WAS ANOTHER SLEEPER, DEEP COVER. EXPLAINS WHY HIS HISTORY FALLS APART IF YOU GO BACK MORE THAN A COUPLE OF YEARS.
THERE MUST'VE BEEN A FALLING OUT. "CARTER" WOUNDED AK-VAR, THAT'S WHY DOCTOR LIGHT HAD TO TREAT HER.
FIGURE OUR UNNAMED K MURDERED HIM IN RESPONSE.
IF THAT'S TRUE, IT MEANS YOUR DAUGHTER ISN'T JUST SYMPATHETIC TO THE Ks.
IT MEANS SHE'S INVOLVED, SHE'S PART OF THEIR OPERATION.
IT MEANS SHE'S A TRAITOR, LIEUTENANT. SHE'S AIDING KRYPTONIAN SPIES ON EARTH.
THERE IS ANOTHER POSSIBILITY, SIR. IF CARTER WAS A SLEEPER, PERHAPS AK-VAR AND HER PARTNER WERE TRYING TO STOP HIM.
THEY MAY BE TRYING TO HELP US.
THEY CAN MAKE DIAMONDS OUT OF COAL WITH THEIR BARE HANDS, LIEUTENANT...
...DO YOU REALLY THINK THEY'VE EVEN THE SLIGHTEST INCLINATION TO BE OUR FRIENDS?
DEET DEET
GENERAL LANE.
SIR? WATCH OFFICER...
...WE'VE FOUND THEM...

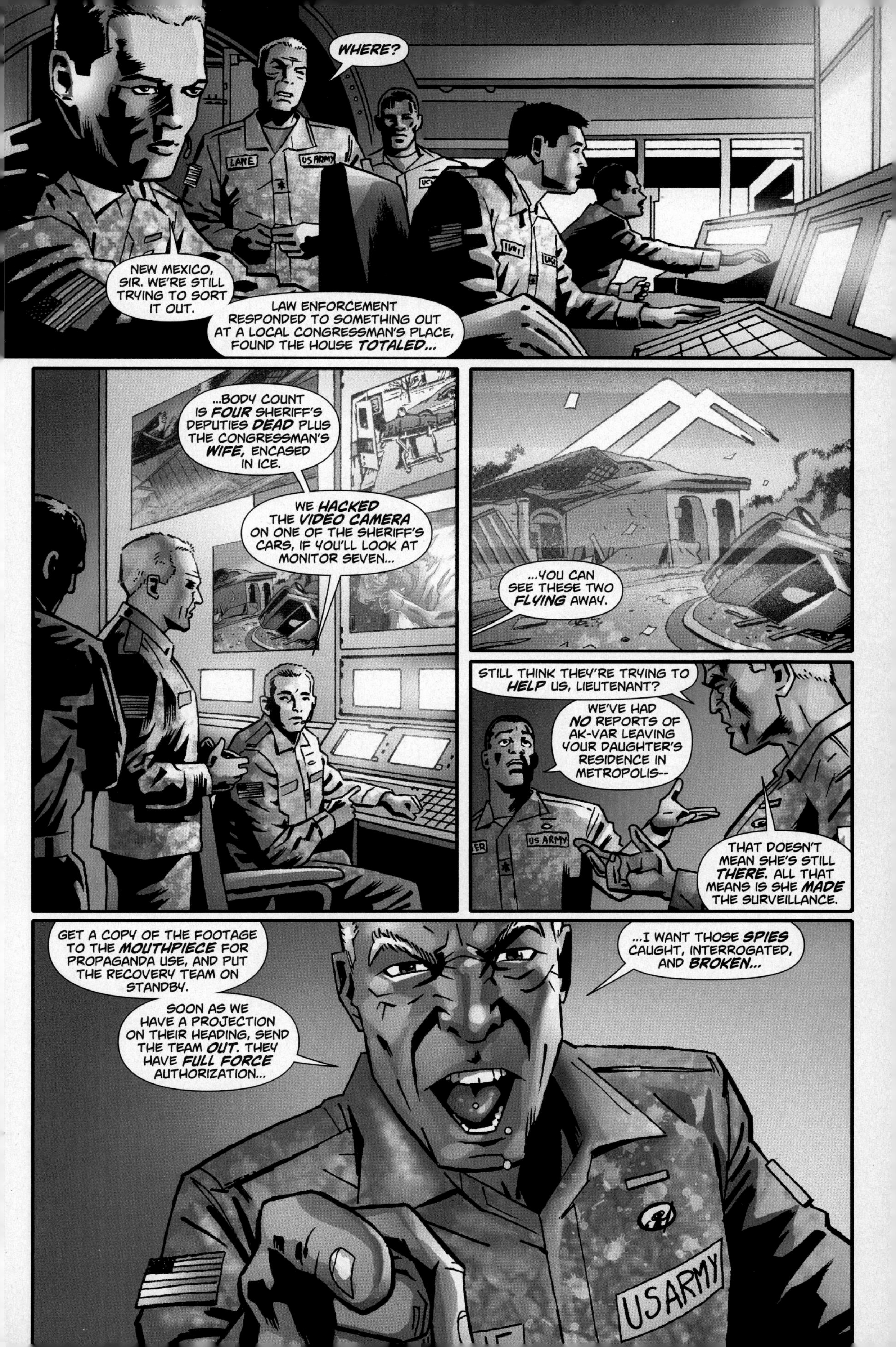
WHERE?
NEW MEXICO, SIR. WE'RE STILL TRYING TO SORT IT OUT.
LAW ENFORCEMENT RESPONDED TO SOMETHING OUT AT A LOCAL CONGRESSMAN'S PLACE, FOUND THE HOUSE TOTALED...
...BODY COUNT IS FOUR SHERIFF'S DEPUTIES DEAD PLUS THE CONGRESSMAN'S WIFE, ENCASED IN ICE.
WE HACKED THE VIDEO CAMERA ON ONE OF THE SHERIFF'S CARS, IF YOU'LL LOOK AT MONITOR SEVEN...
...YOU CAN SEE THESE TWO FLYING AWAY.
STILL THINK THEY'RE TRYING TO HELP US, LIEUTENANT?
WE'VE HAD NO REPORTS OF AK-VAR LEAVING YOUR DAUGHTER'S RESIDENCE IN METROPOLIS--
THAT DOESN'T MEAN SHE'S STILL THERE. ALL THAT MEANS IS SHE MADE THE SURVEILLANCE.
GET A COPY OF THE FOOTAGE TO THE MOUTHPIECE FOR PROPAGANDA USE, AND PUT THE RECOVERY TEAM ON STANDBY.
SOON AS WE HAVE A PROJECTION ON THEIR HEADING, SEND THE TEAM OUT. THEY HAVE FULL FORCE AUTHORIZATION...
...I WANT THOSE SPIES CAUGHT, INTERROGATED, AND BROKEN...

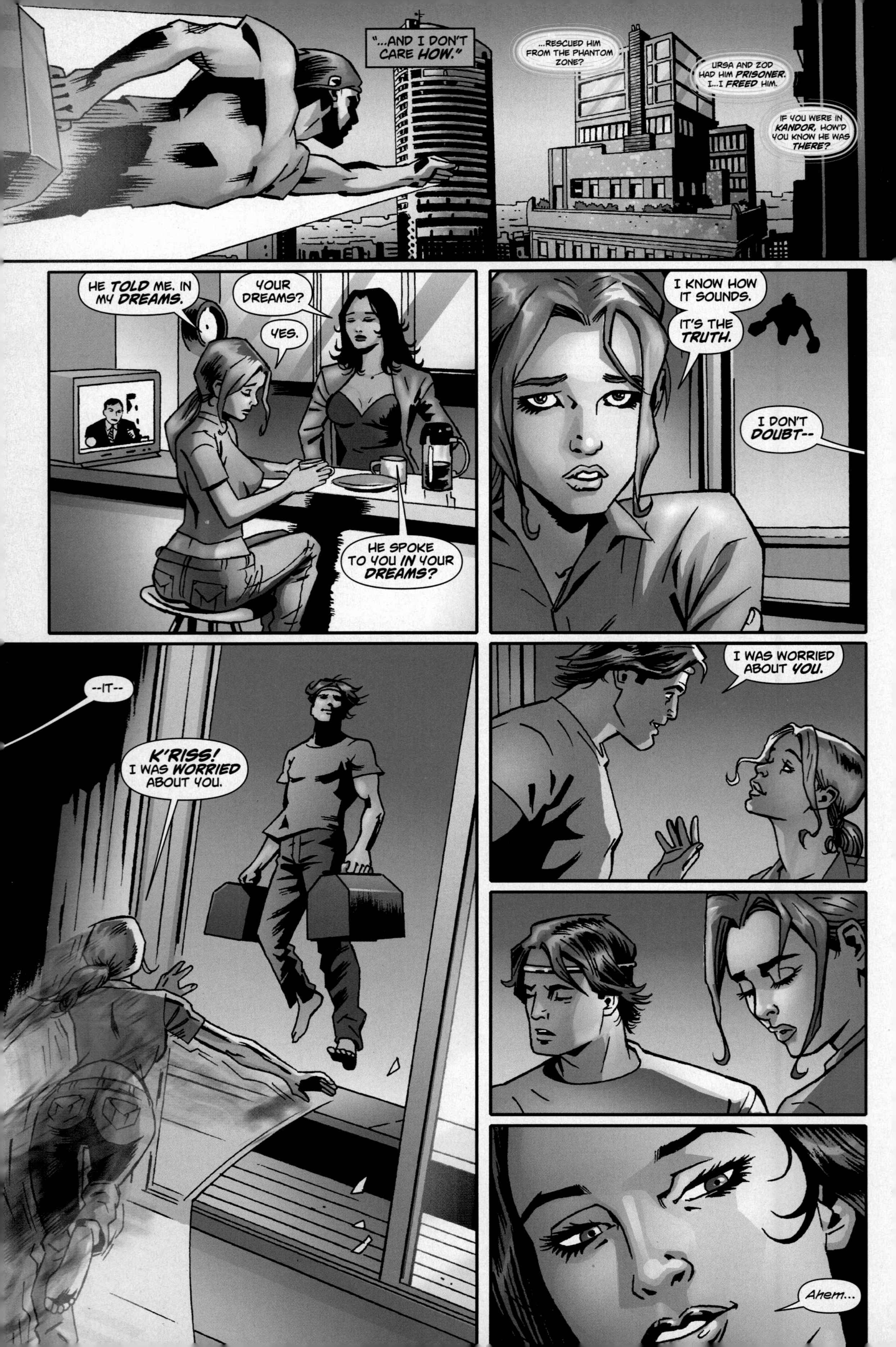
"...AND I DON'T CARE HOW."
...RESCUED HIM FROM THE PHANTOM ZONE?
URSA AND ZOD HAD HIM PRISONER. I...I FREED HIM.
IF YOU WERE IN KANDOR, HOW'D YOU KNOW HE WAS THERE?
HE TOLD ME. IN MY DREAMS.
YOUR DREAMS?
YES.
HE SPOKE TO YOU IN YOUR DREAMS?
I KNOW HOW IT SOUNDS.
IT'S THE TRUTH.
I DON'T DOUBT--
--IT--
K'RISS! I WAS WORRIED ABOUT YOU.
I WAS WORRIED ABOUT YOU.
Ahem...

...WHAT KEPT YOU?

I'M SORRY, MOM, I GOT BACK AS SOON AS I COULD. I GOT ATTACKED, AND THEN I HAD TO--

ATTACKED? AT THE FORTRESS--

URSA WAS *STILL* THERE? SHE WAS--

NO, I MEAN *YES*, BUT...

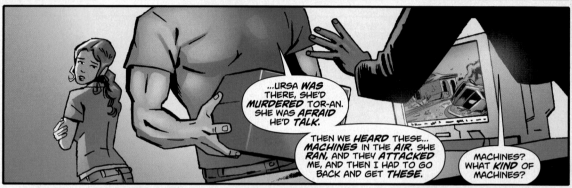

...URSA *WAS* THERE, SHE'D *MURDERED* TOR-AN. SHE WAS *AFRAID* HE'D *TALK*.

THEN WE *HEARD* THESE... *MACHINES* IN THE *AIR*. SHE *RAN*, AND THEY *ATTACKED* ME, AND THEN I HAD TO GO BACK AND GET *THESE*.

MACHINES? WHAT *KIND* OF MACHINES?

LIKE LITTLE JET PLANES. TWO OF THEM.

SOMEONE SENT UAVs AFTER YOU?

UAVs? WHAT'S THAT?

UNMANNED AERIAL VEHICLES...

...BUT THAT'S *MILITARY* TECHNOLOGY...

LOOK!

⸱ᴵᵀ'ˢ [alien text in speech bubble]

WHAT? WHERE?

HOLD ON--

IT'S AZ-REL AND NADIRA!

--OF THE CONGRESSMAN'S NEW MEXICO HOME WITH FREEZE BREATH AND TOTAL DESTRUCTION?!?

THIS COUPLE IS LOOSE ON EARTH, RIGHT NOW! AND IF THEY ARE KRYPTONIANS, THEN THE ONLY QUESTION IS...

...WHERE WILL THEY STRIKE NEXT? THIS IS MORGAN EDGE...

WHO--

WE'LL BE BACK.

I'LL BE HERE.

...HELLO, COMMANDER HARPER? THIS IS LOIS LANE, FROM THE DAILY PLANET...

...OH, I HAVE EVERYONE'S NUMBER. LISTEN, I'M WONDERING IF YOU COULD HELP ME WITH A FAVOR...

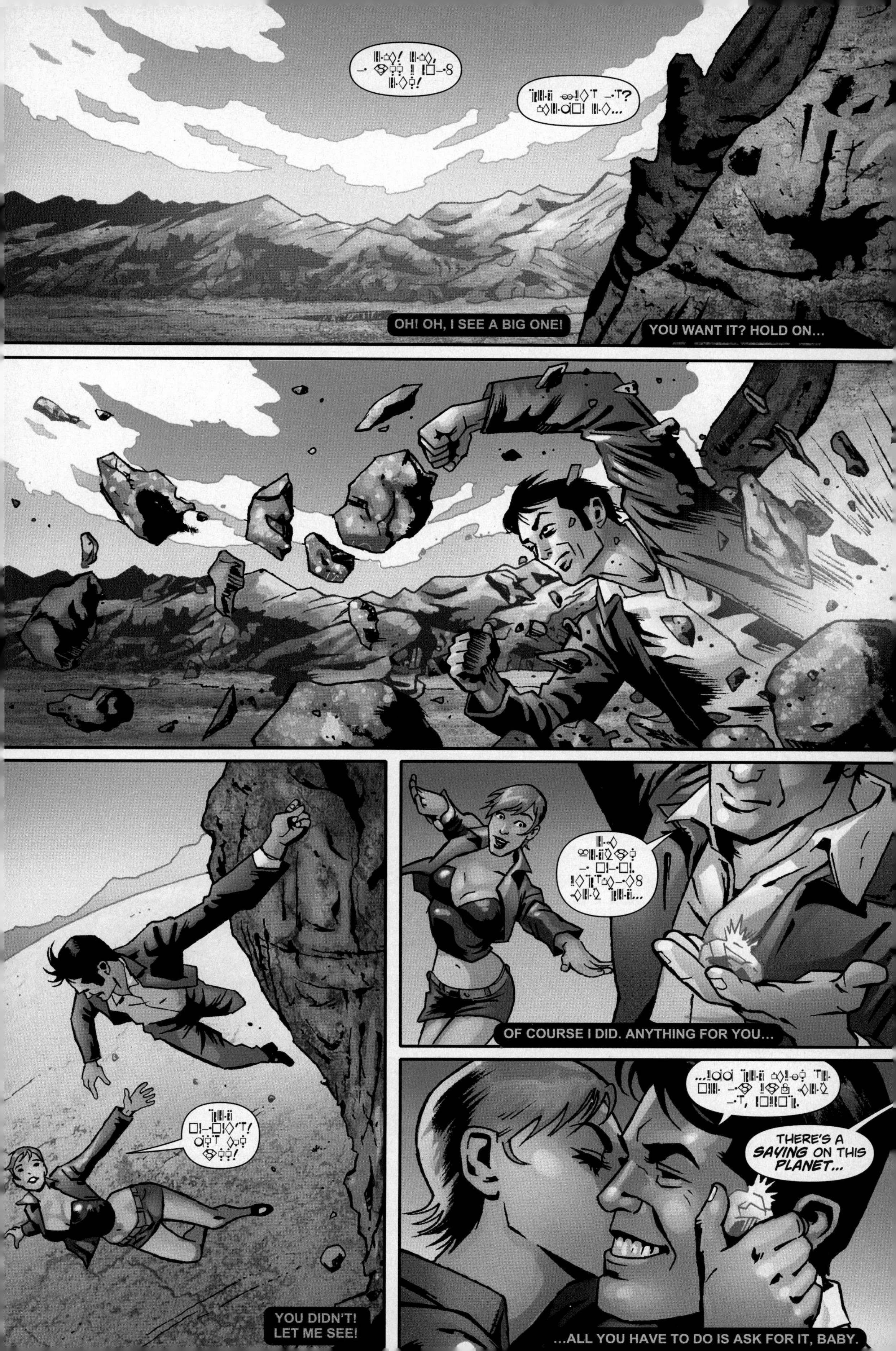
OH! OH, I SEE A BIG ONE!
YOU WANT IT? HOLD ON…
YOU DIDN'T! LET ME SEE!
OF COURSE I DID. ANYTHING FOR YOU…
THERE'S A *SAYING* ON THIS *PLANET*...
…ALL YOU HAVE TO DO IS ASK FOR IT, BABY.

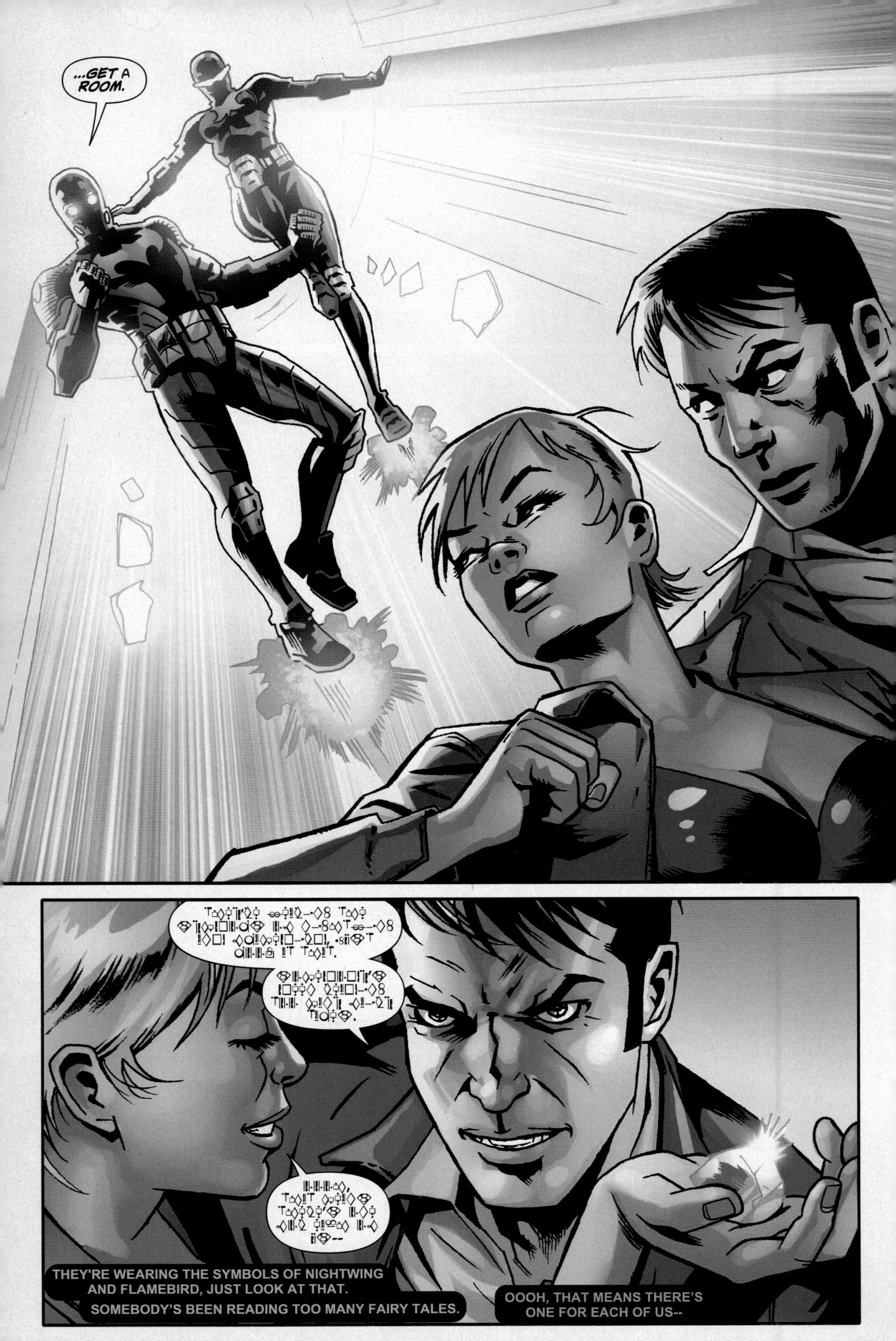
...GET A ROOM.
THEY'RE WEARING THE SYMBOLS OF NIGHTWING AND FLAMEBIRD, JUST LOOK AT THAT.
SOMEBODY'S BEEN READING TOO MANY FAIRY TALES.
OOOH, THAT MEANS THERE'S ONE FOR EACH OF US--

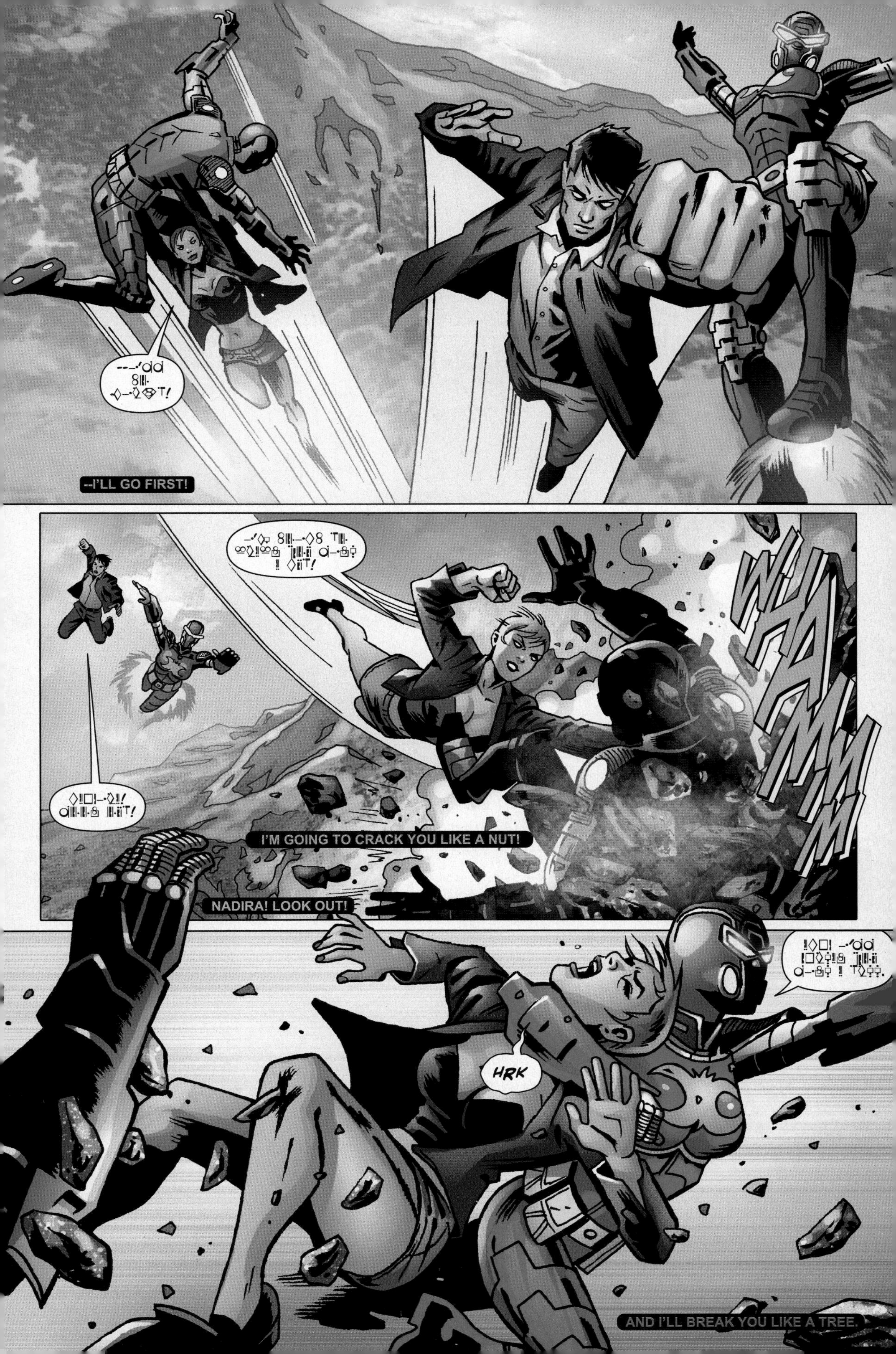
--I'LL GO FIRST!
WHAMMM
I'M GOING TO CRACK YOU LIKE A NUT!
NADIRA! LOOK OUT!
HRK
AND I'LL BREAK YOU LIKE A TREE.

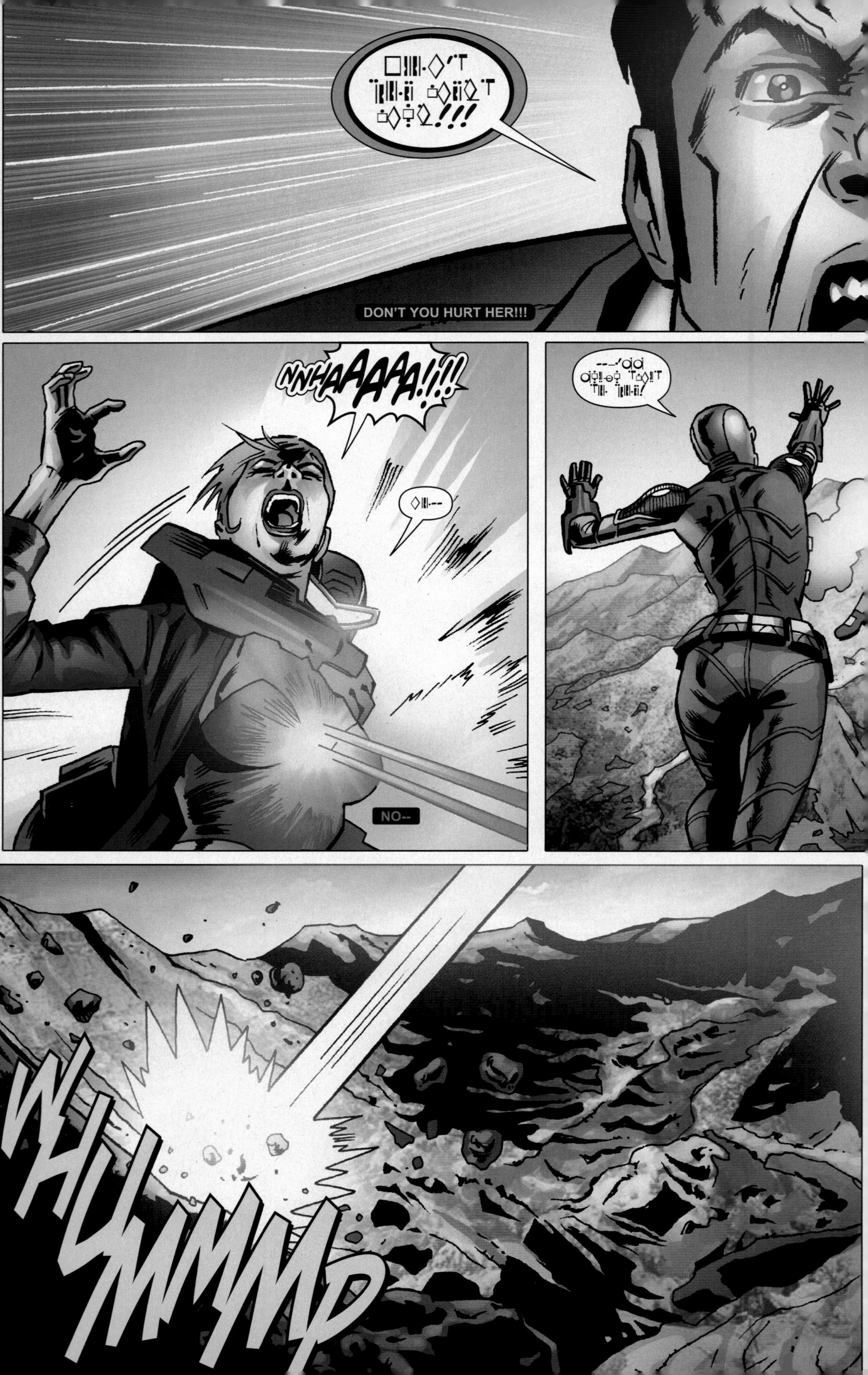
DON'T YOU HURT HER!!!
NNHAAAAA!!!!
NO--
WHUMMMP

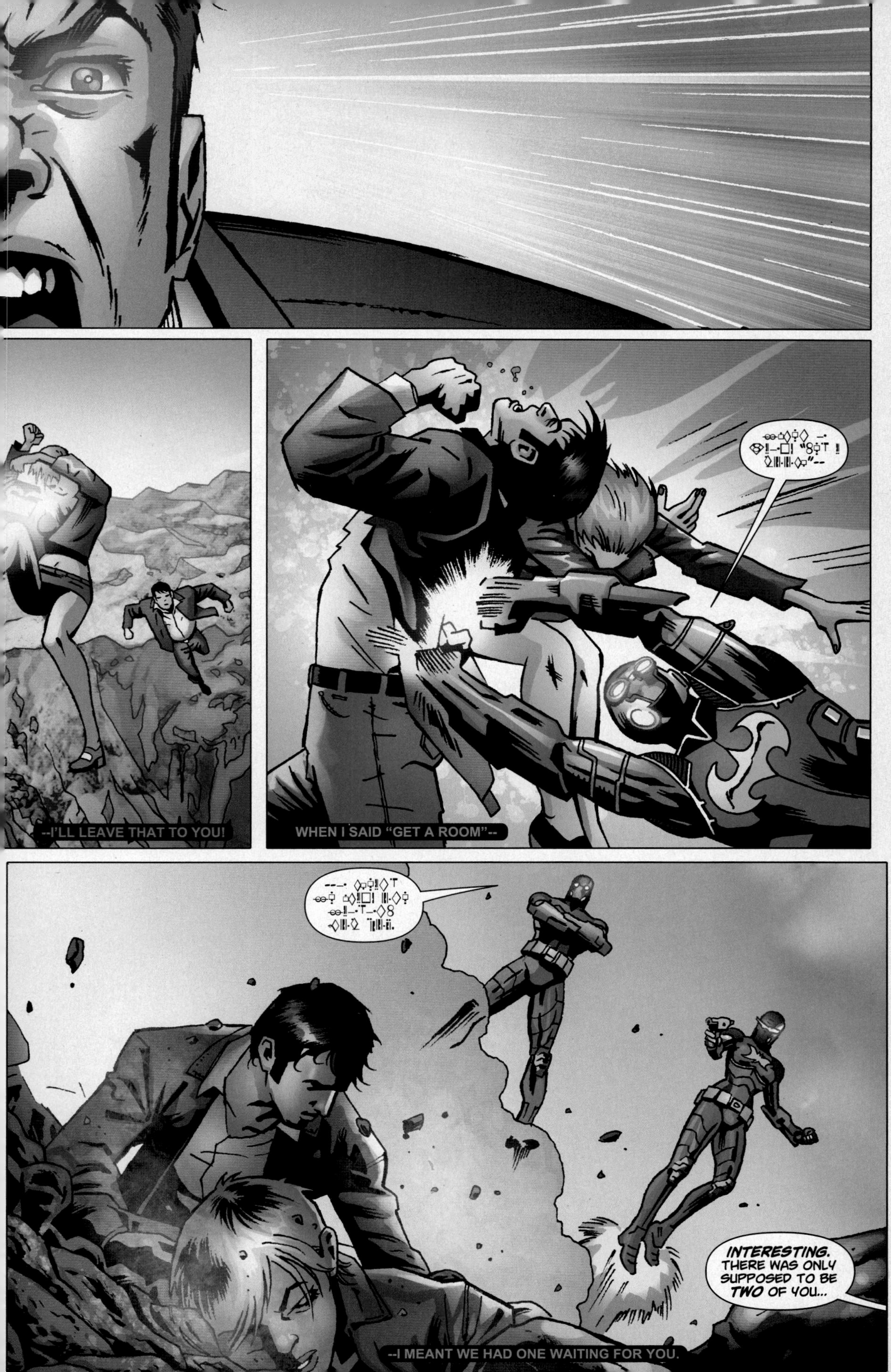
--I'LL LEAVE THAT TO YOU!
WHEN I SAID "GET A ROOM"--
INTERESTING. THERE WAS ONLY SUPPOSED TO BE TWO OF YOU...
--I MEANT WE HAD ONE WAITING FOR YOU.

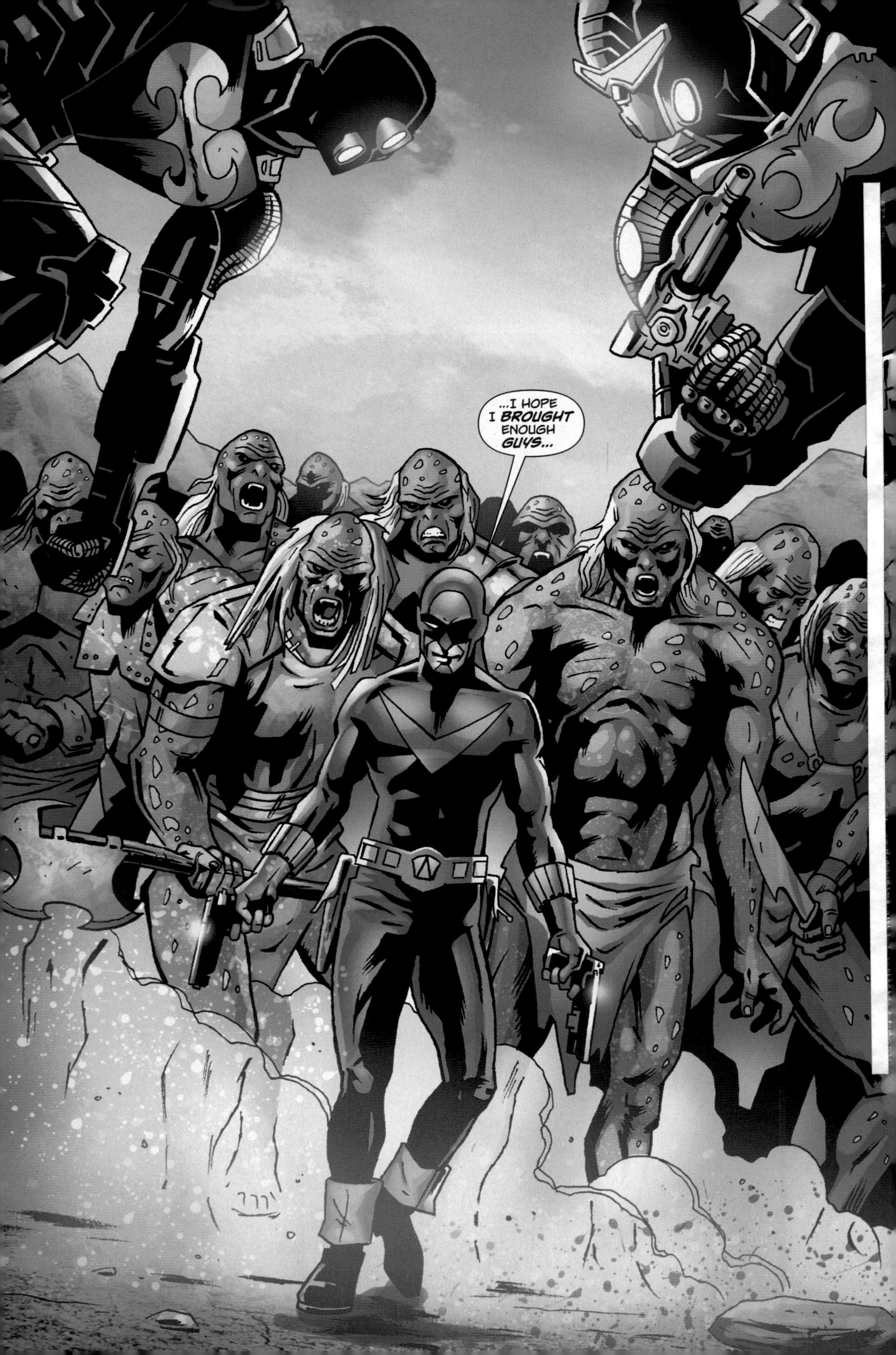
...I HOPE I BROUGHT ENOUGH GUYS...

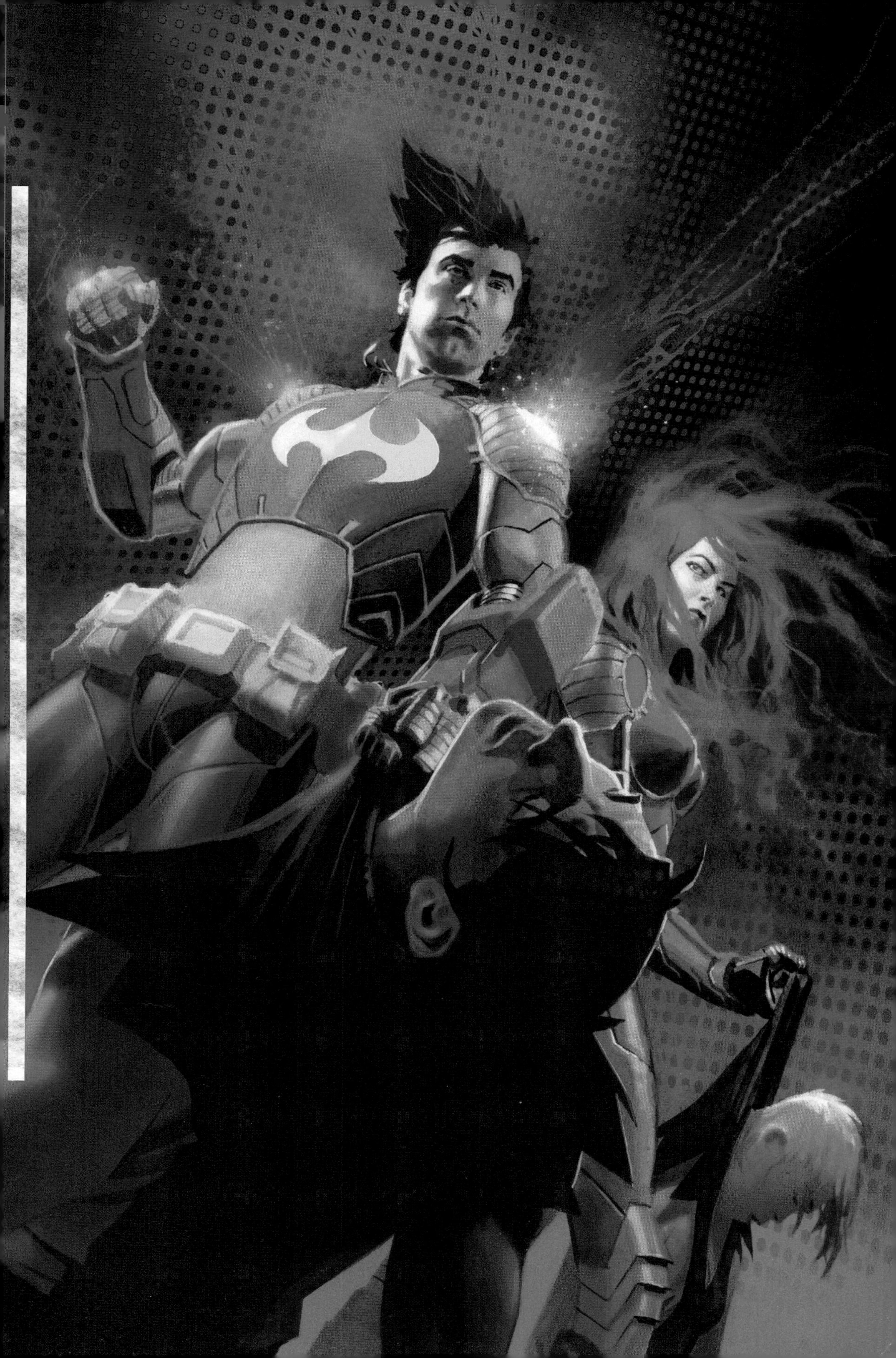

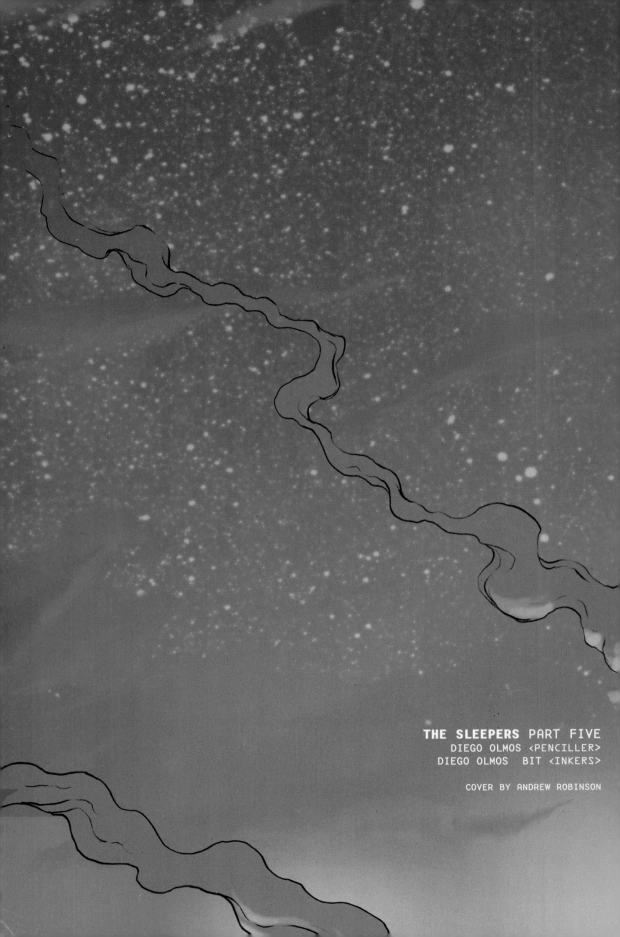

THE SLEEPERS PART FIVE
DIEGO OLMOS <PENCILLER>
DIEGO OLMOS   BIT <INKERS>

COVER BY ANDREW ROBINSON

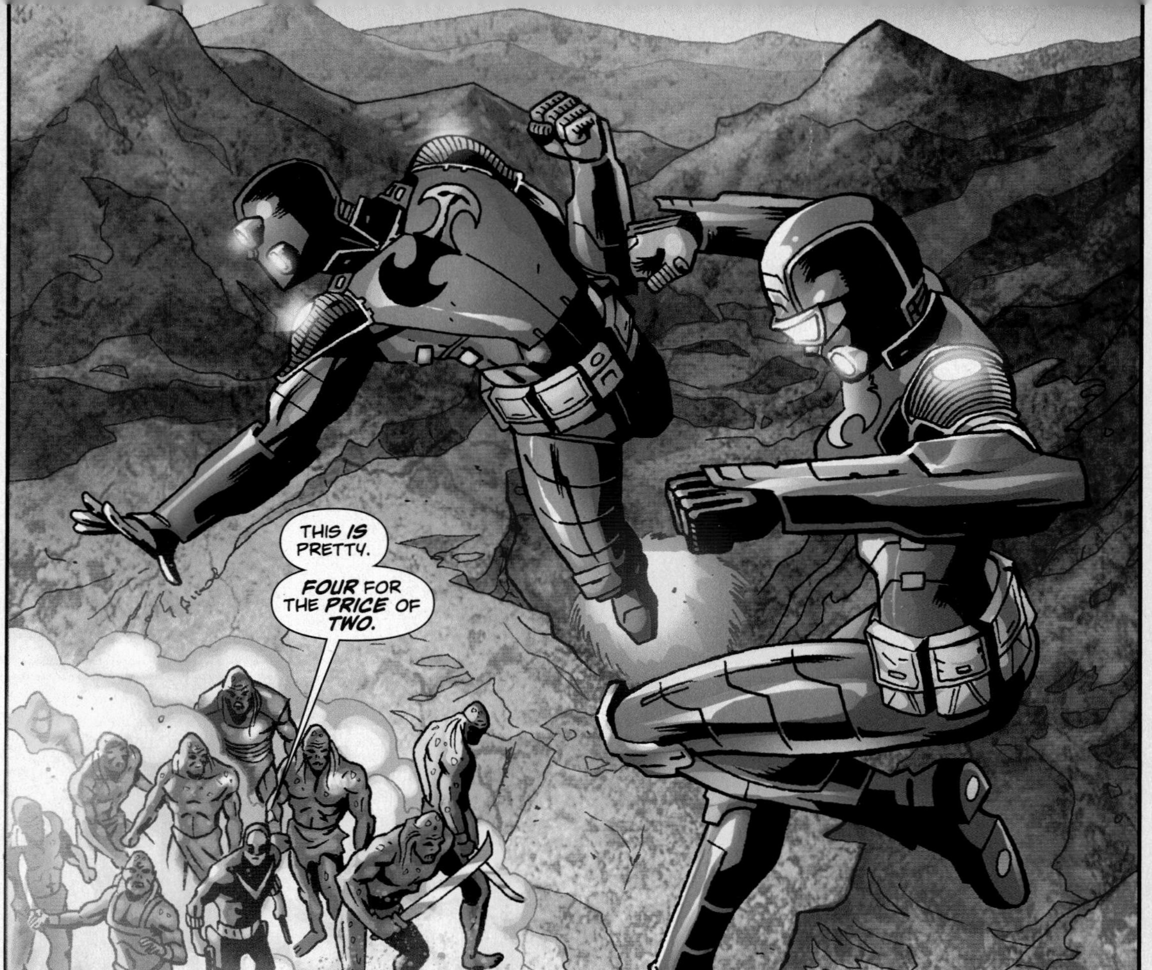
THIS IS PRETTY.
FOUR FOR THE PRICE OF TWO.

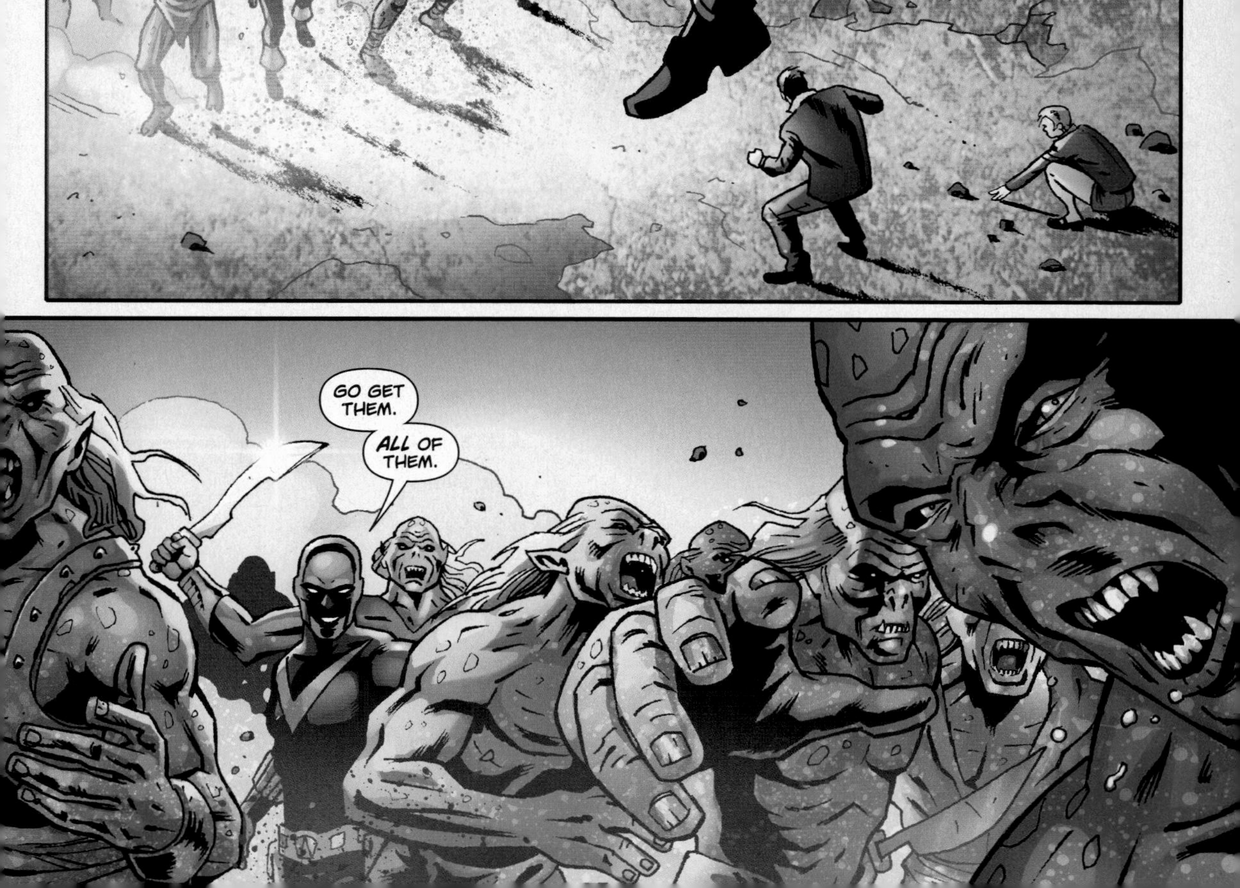
GO GET THEM.
ALL OF THEM.

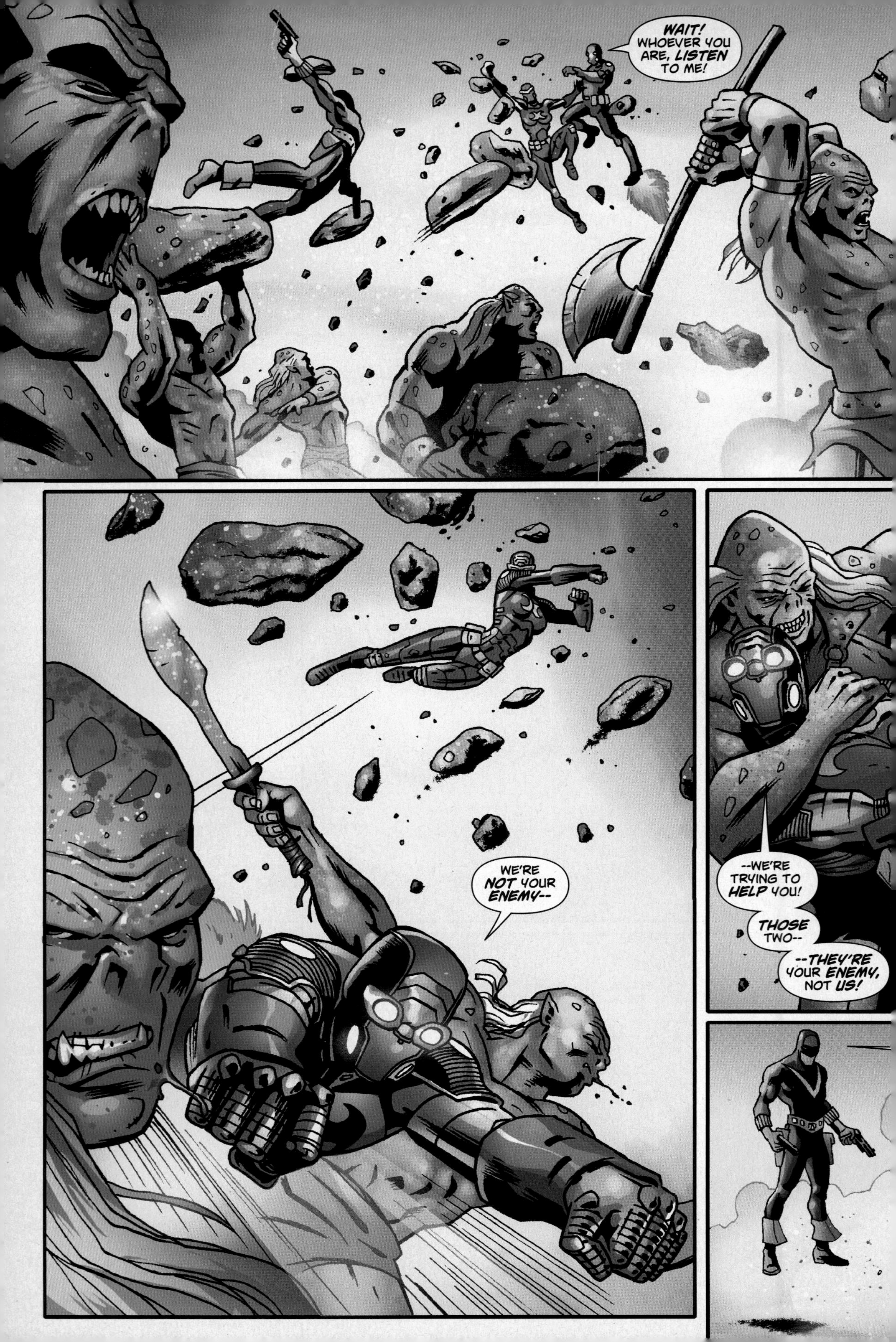
WAIT! WHOEVER YOU ARE, LISTEN TO ME!
WE'RE NOT YOUR ENEMY--
--WE'RE TRYING TO HELP YOU!
THOSE TWO--
--THEY'RE YOUR ENEMY, NOT US!

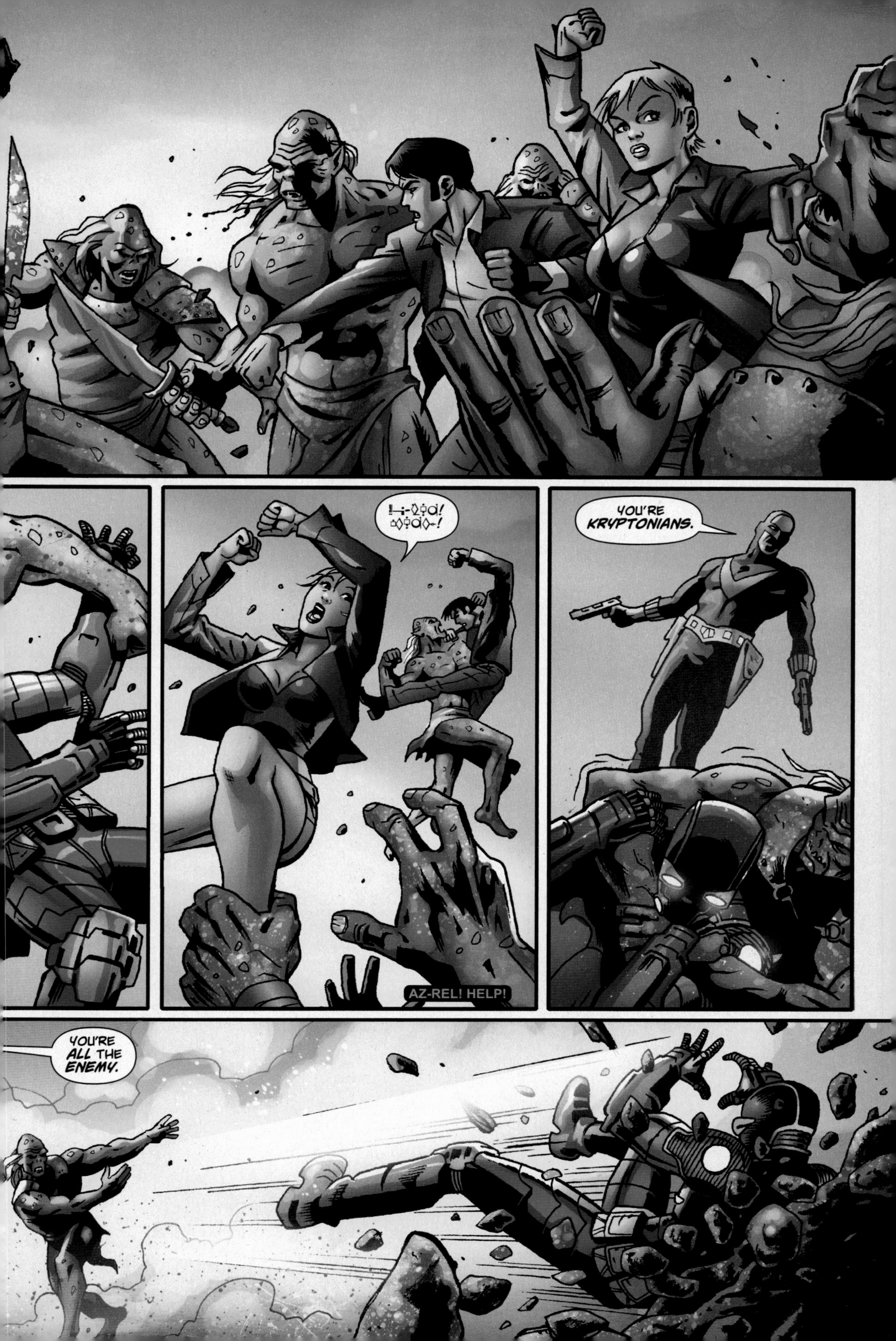
AZ-REL! HELP!
YOU'RE KRYPTONIANS.
YOU'RE ALL THE ENEMY.

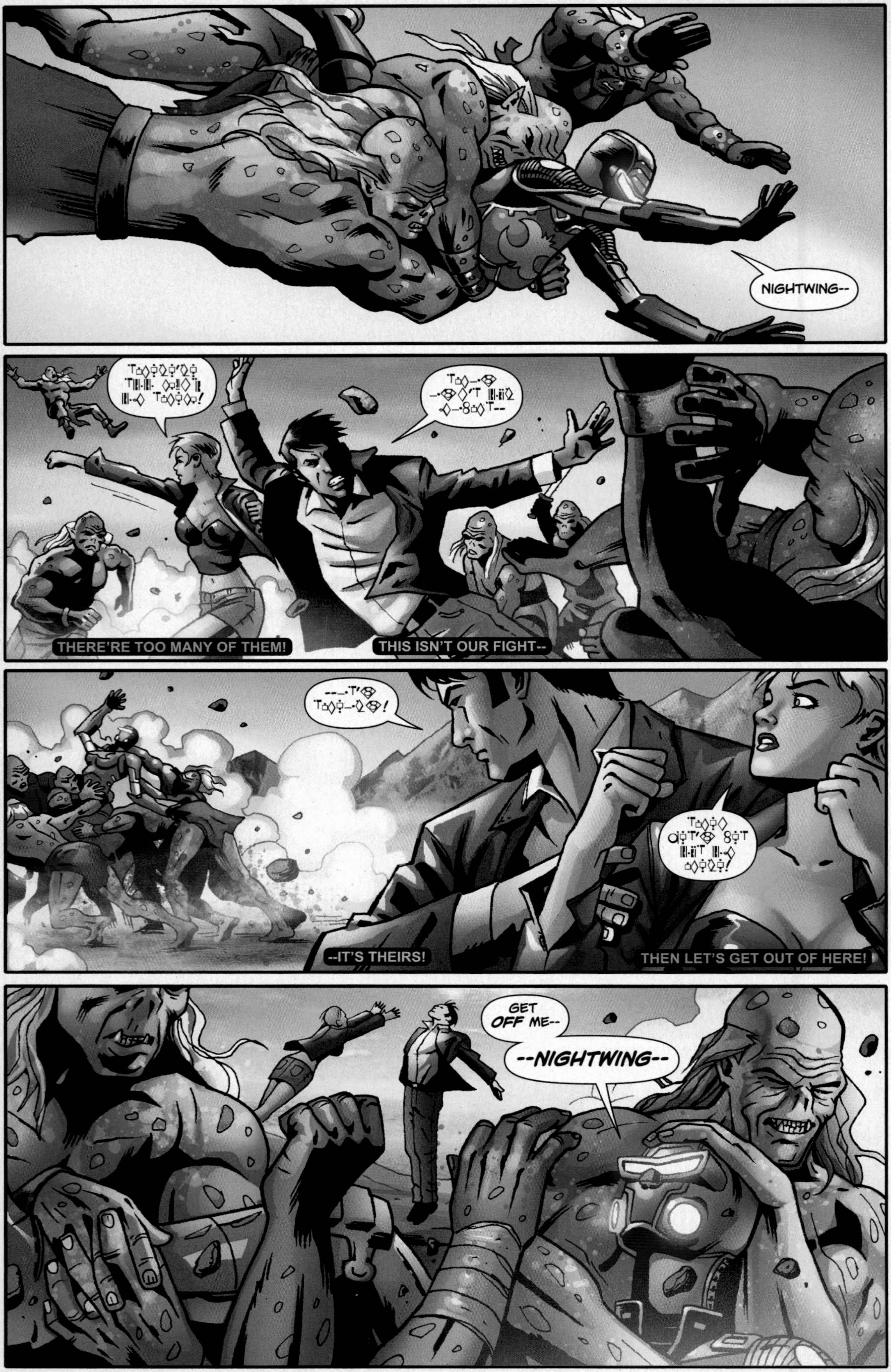
NIGHTWING--
THERE'RE TOO MANY OF THEM!
THIS ISN'T OUR FIGHT--
--IT'S THEIRS!
THEN LET'S GET OUT OF HERE!
GET OFF ME--
--NIGHTWING--

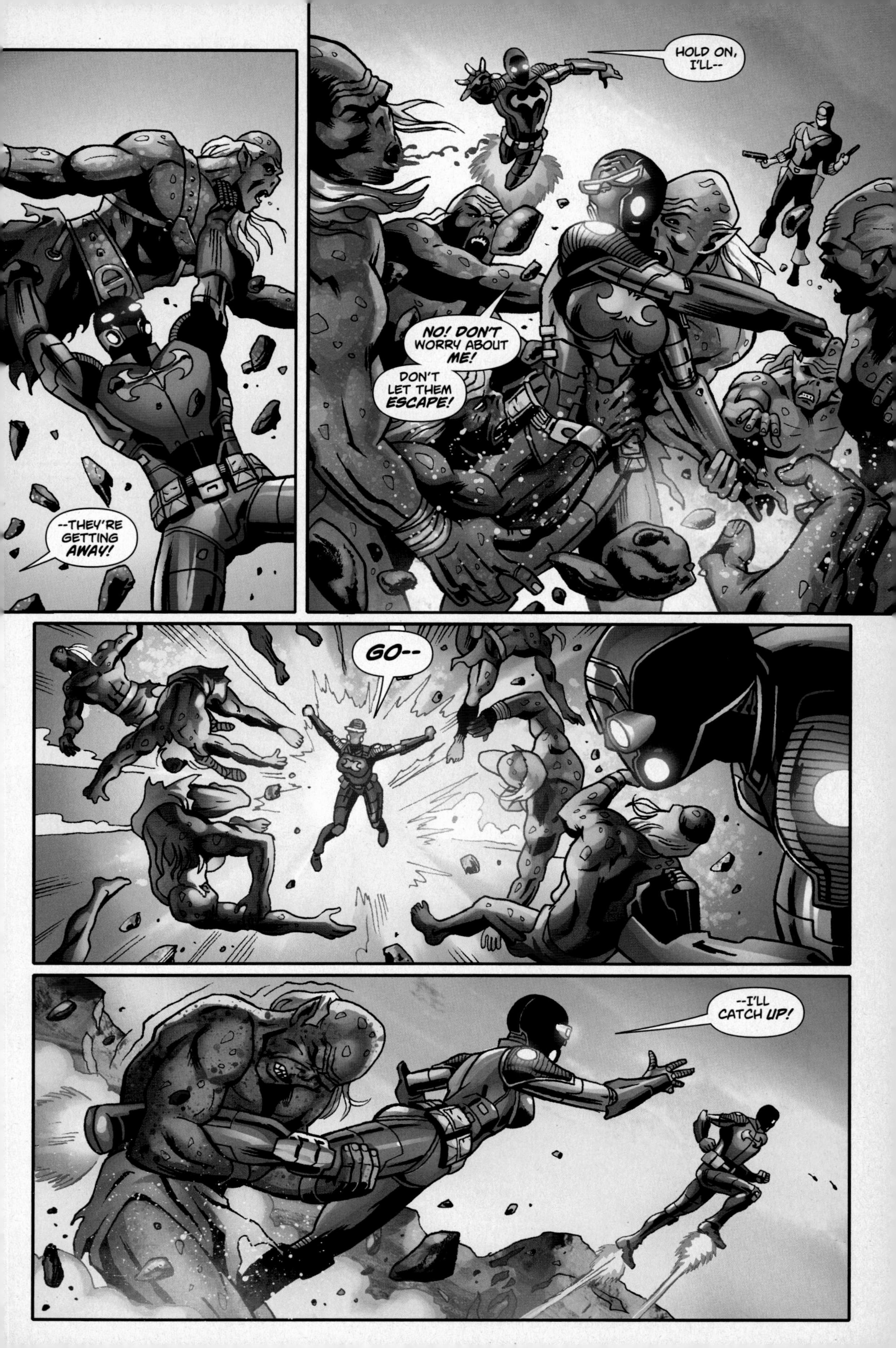
--THEY'RE GETTING AWAY!
HOLD ON, I'LL--
NO! DON'T WORRY ABOUT ME!
DON'T LET THEM ESCAPE!
GO--
--I'LL CATCH UP!

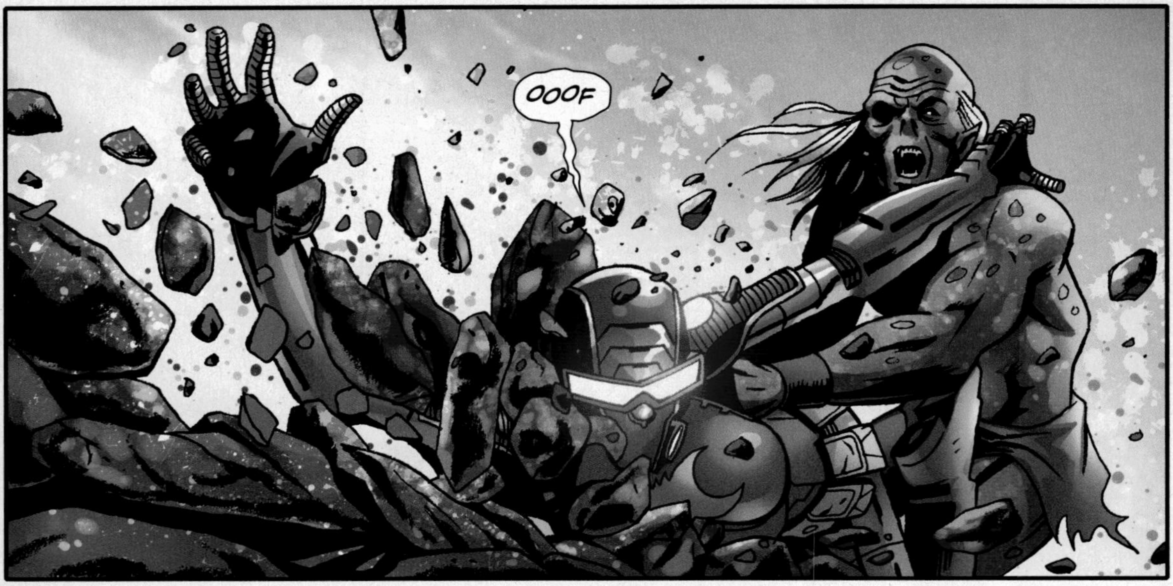
OOOF

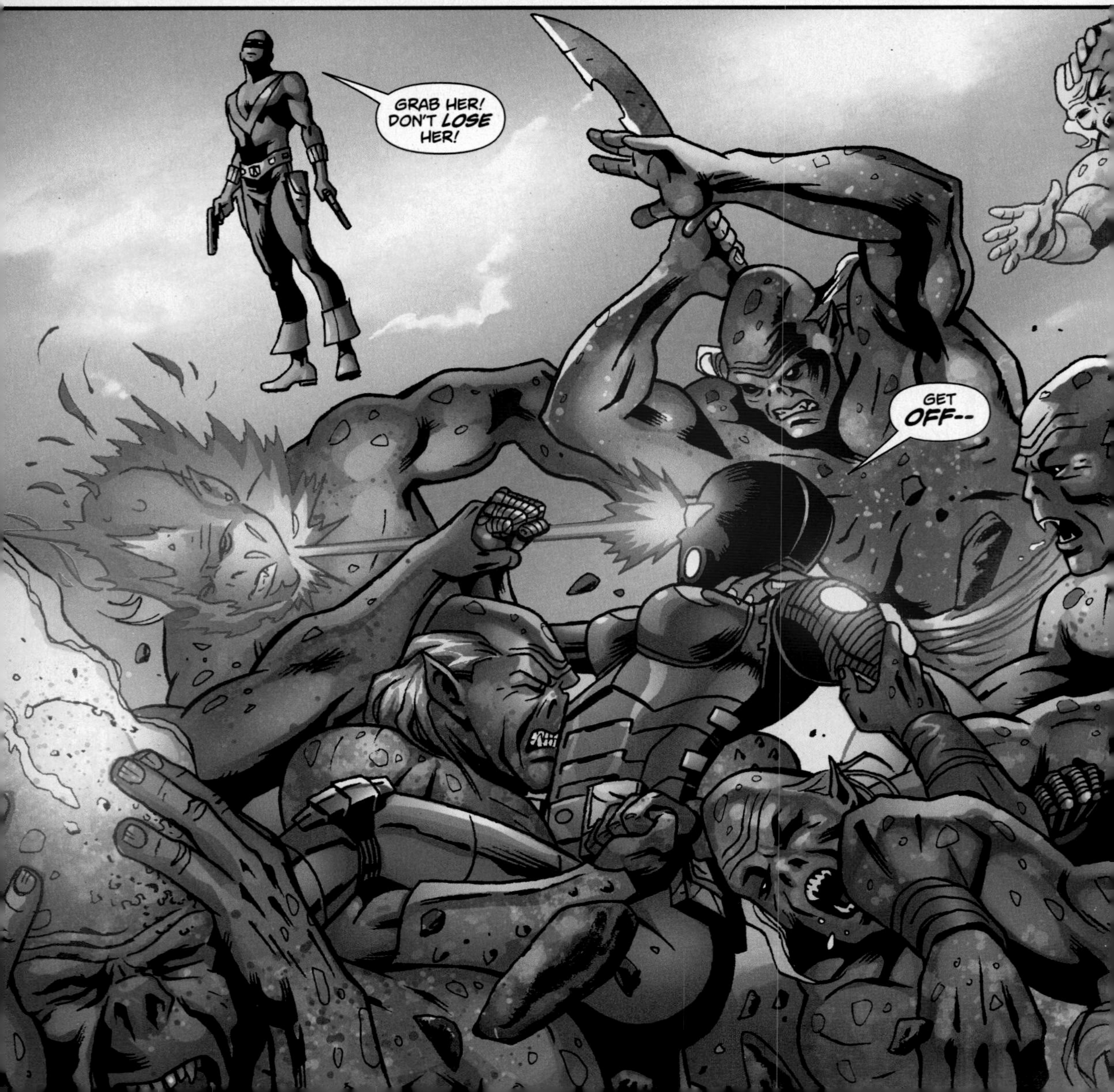
GRAB HER! DON'T LOSE HER!
GET OFF--

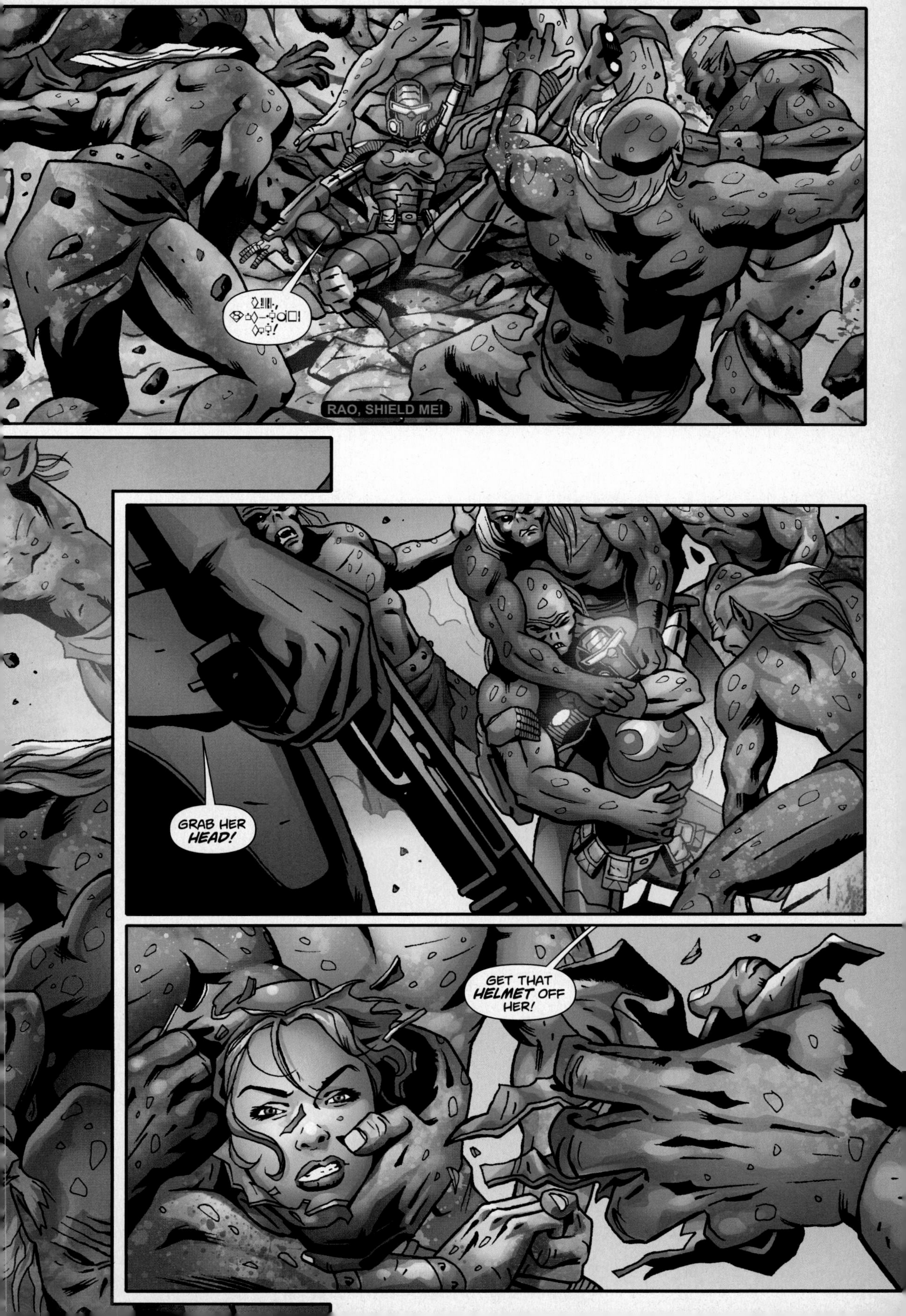
RAO, SHIELD ME!
GRAB HER HEAD!
GET THAT HELMET OFF HER!

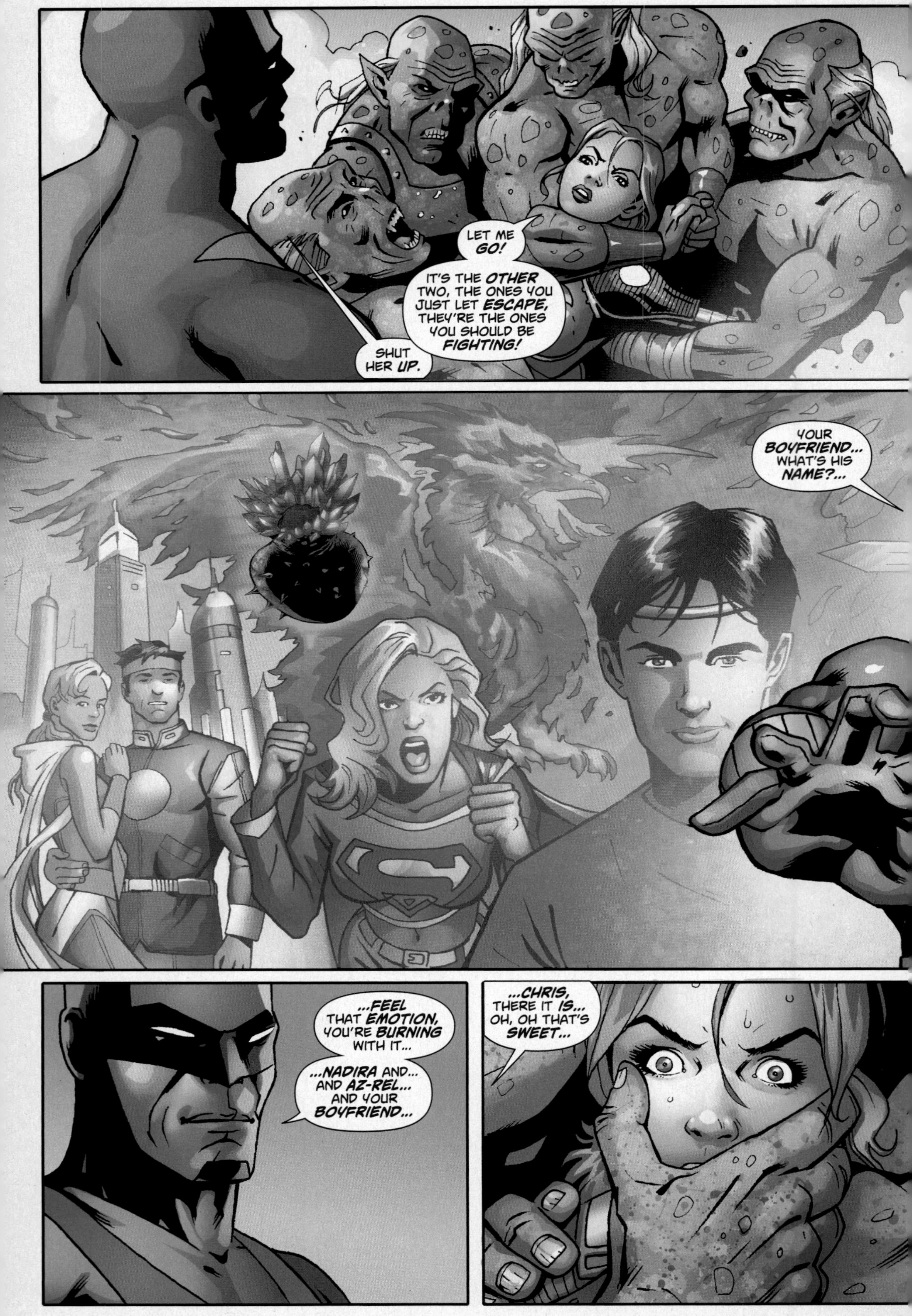
LET ME GO!
IT'S THE OTHER TWO, THE ONES YOU JUST LET ESCAPE, THEY'RE THE ONES YOU SHOULD BE FIGHTING!
SHUT HER UP.
YOUR BOYFRIEND... WHAT'S HIS NAME?...
...FEEL THAT EMOTION, YOU'RE BURNING WITH IT...
...NADIRA AND... AND AZ-REL... AND YOUR BOYFRIEND...
...CHRIS, THERE IT IS... OH, OH THAT'S SWEET...

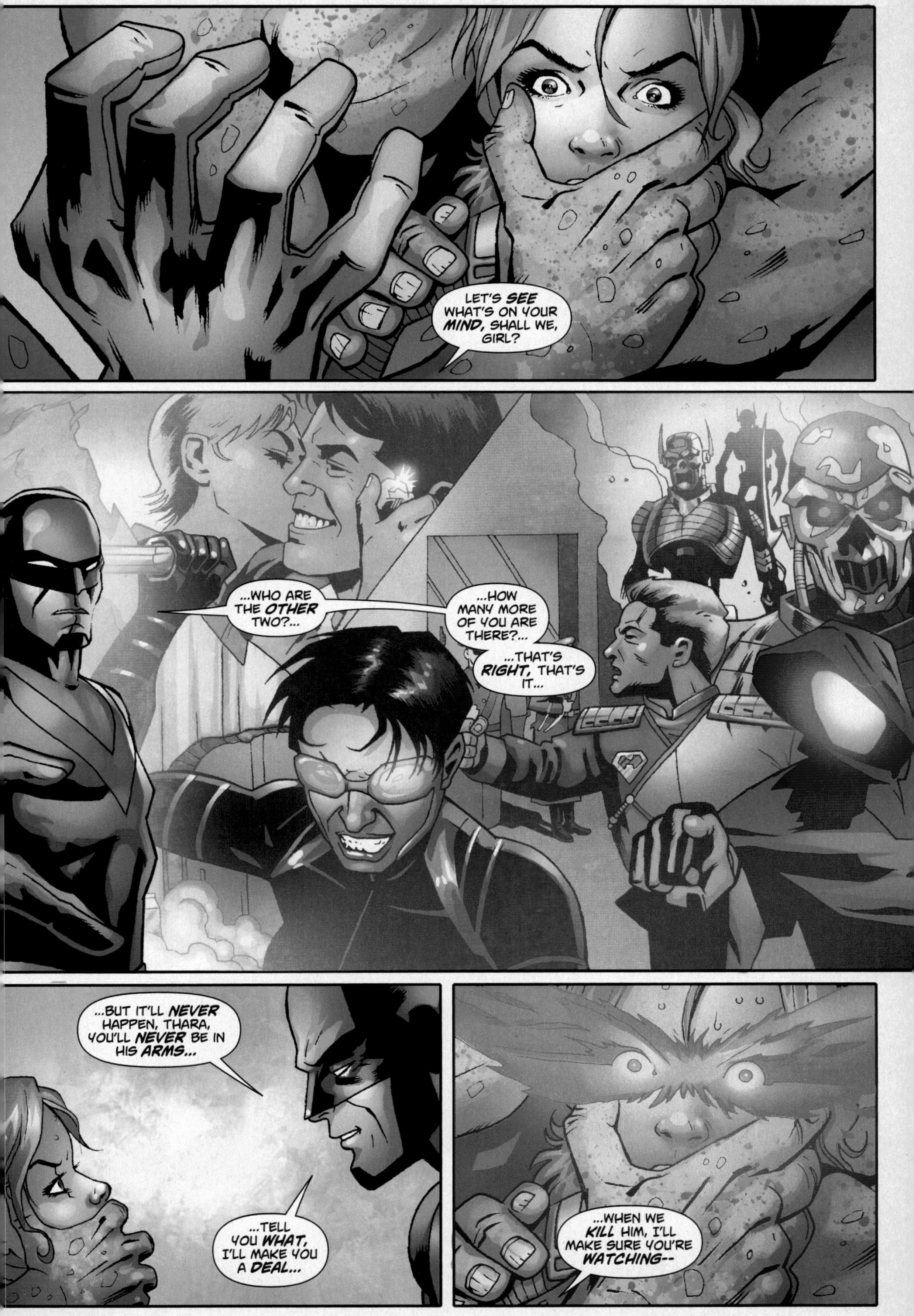
LET'S SEE WHAT'S ON YOUR MIND, SHALL WE, GIRL?
...WHO ARE THE OTHER TWO?...
...HOW MANY MORE OF YOU ARE THERE?...
...THAT'S RIGHT, THAT'S IT...
...BUT IT'LL NEVER HAPPEN, THARA, YOU'LL NEVER BE IN HIS ARMS...
...TELL YOU WHAT, I'LL MAKE YOU A DEAL...
...WHEN WE KILL HIM, I'LL MAKE SURE YOU'RE WATCHING--

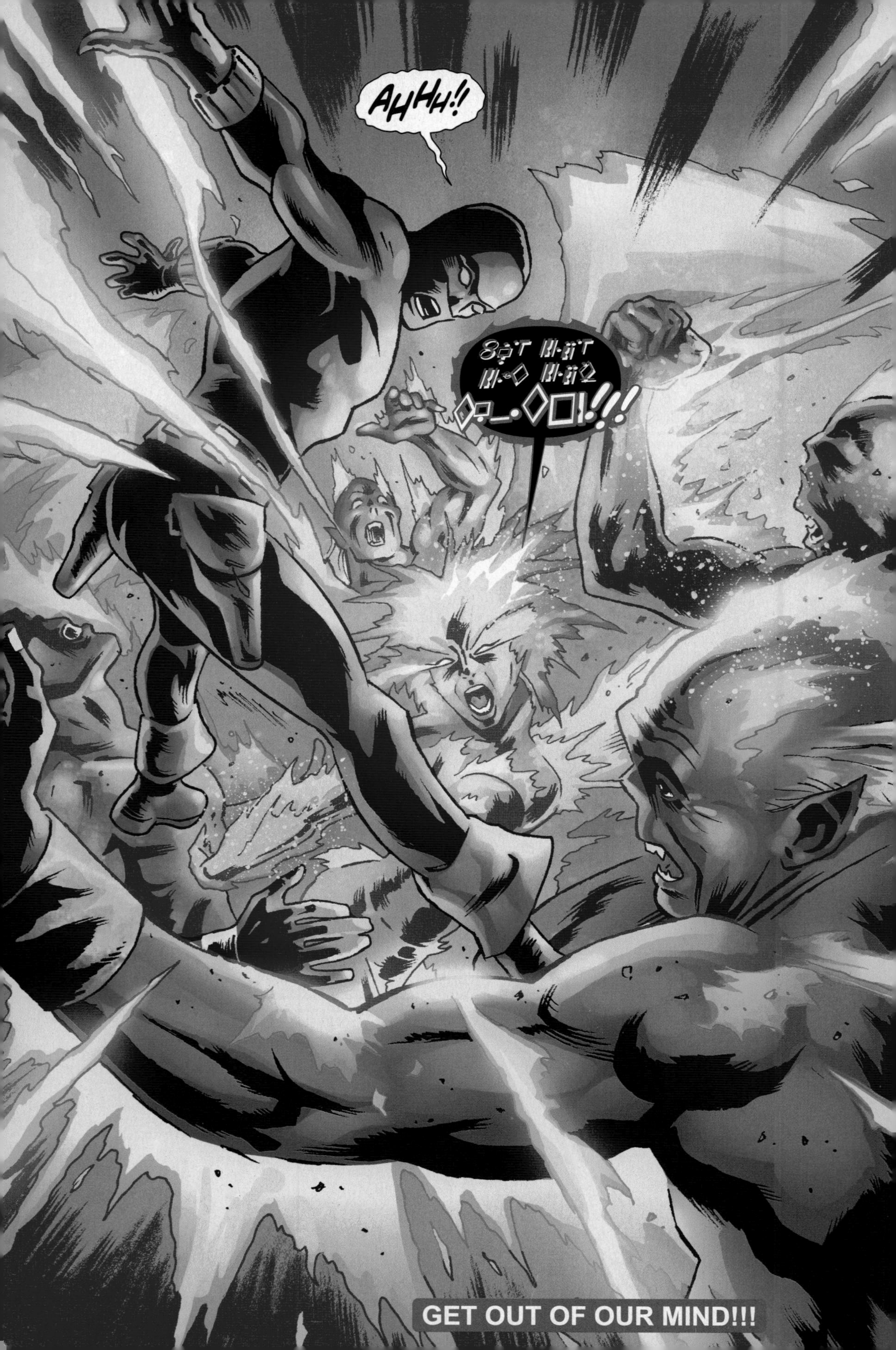
AHHH!!
GET OUT OF OUR MIND!!!

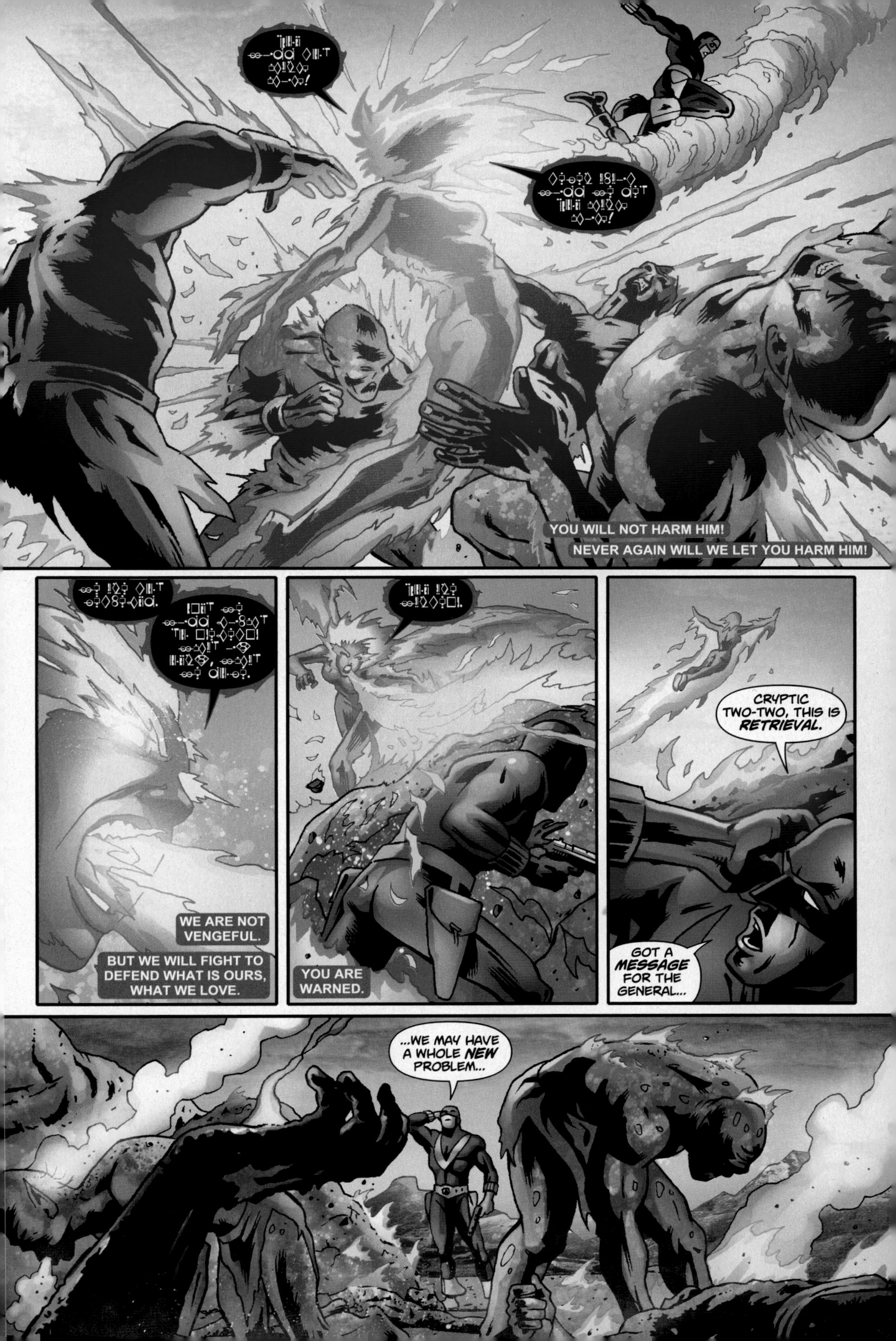
YOU WILL NOT HARM HIM!
NEVER AGAIN WILL WE LET YOU HARM HIM!
WE ARE NOT VENGEFUL.
BUT WE WILL FIGHT TO DEFEND WHAT IS OURS, WHAT WE LOVE.
YOU ARE WARNED.
CRYPTIC TWO-TWO, THIS IS RETRIEVAL.
GOT A MESSAGE FOR THE GENERAL...
...WE MAY HAVE A WHOLE NEW PROBLEM...

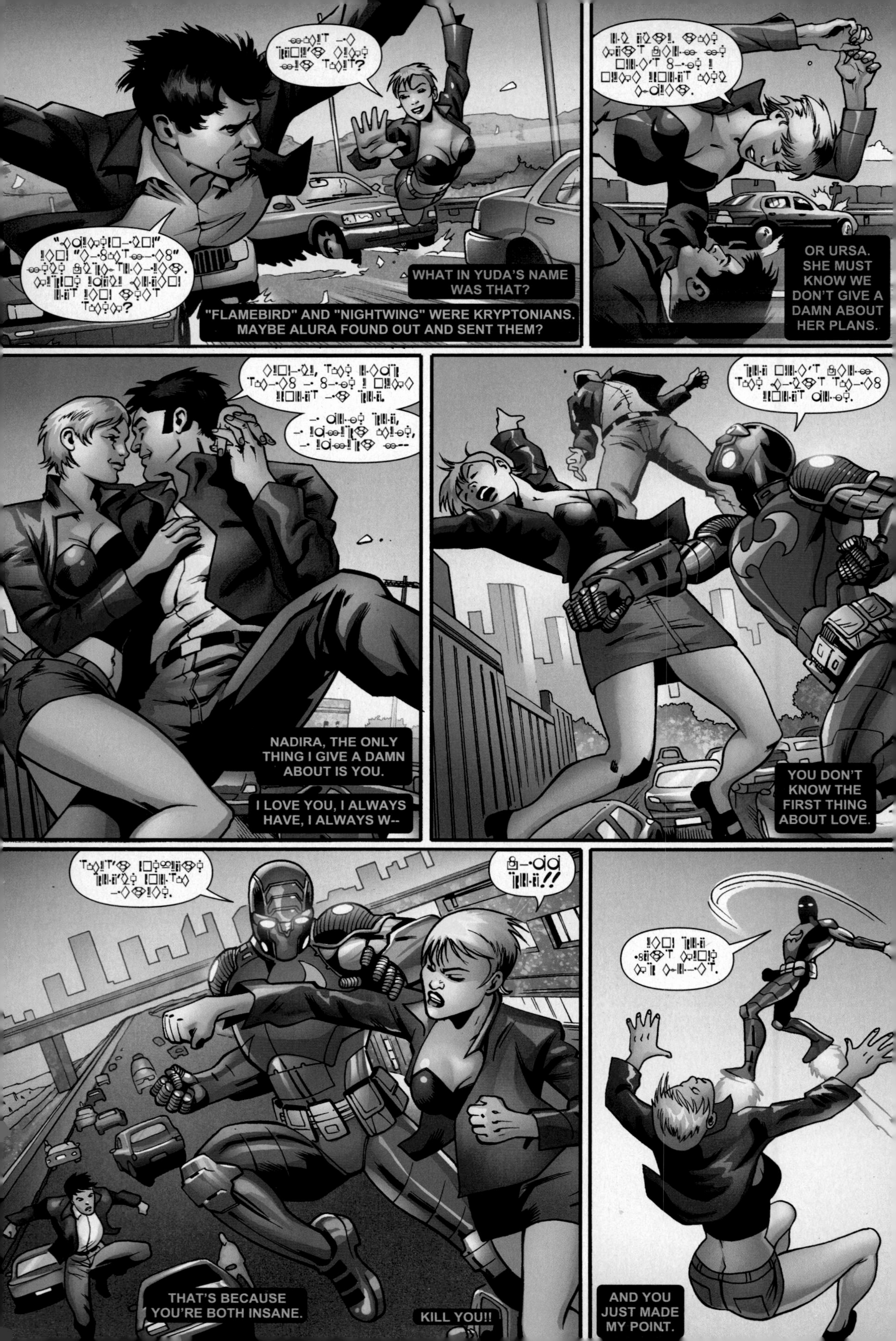
WHAT IN YUDA'S NAME WAS THAT?
"FLAMEBIRD" AND "NIGHTWING" WERE KRYPTONIANS. MAYBE ALURA FOUND OUT AND SENT THEM?
OR URSA. SHE MUST KNOW WE DON'T GIVE A DAMN ABOUT HER PLANS.
NADIRA, THE ONLY THING I GIVE A DAMN ABOUT IS YOU.
I LOVE YOU, I ALWAYS HAVE, I ALWAYS W--
YOU DON'T KNOW THE FIRST THING ABOUT LOVE.
THAT'S BECAUSE YOU'RE BOTH INSANE.
KILL YOU!!
AND YOU JUST MADE MY POINT.

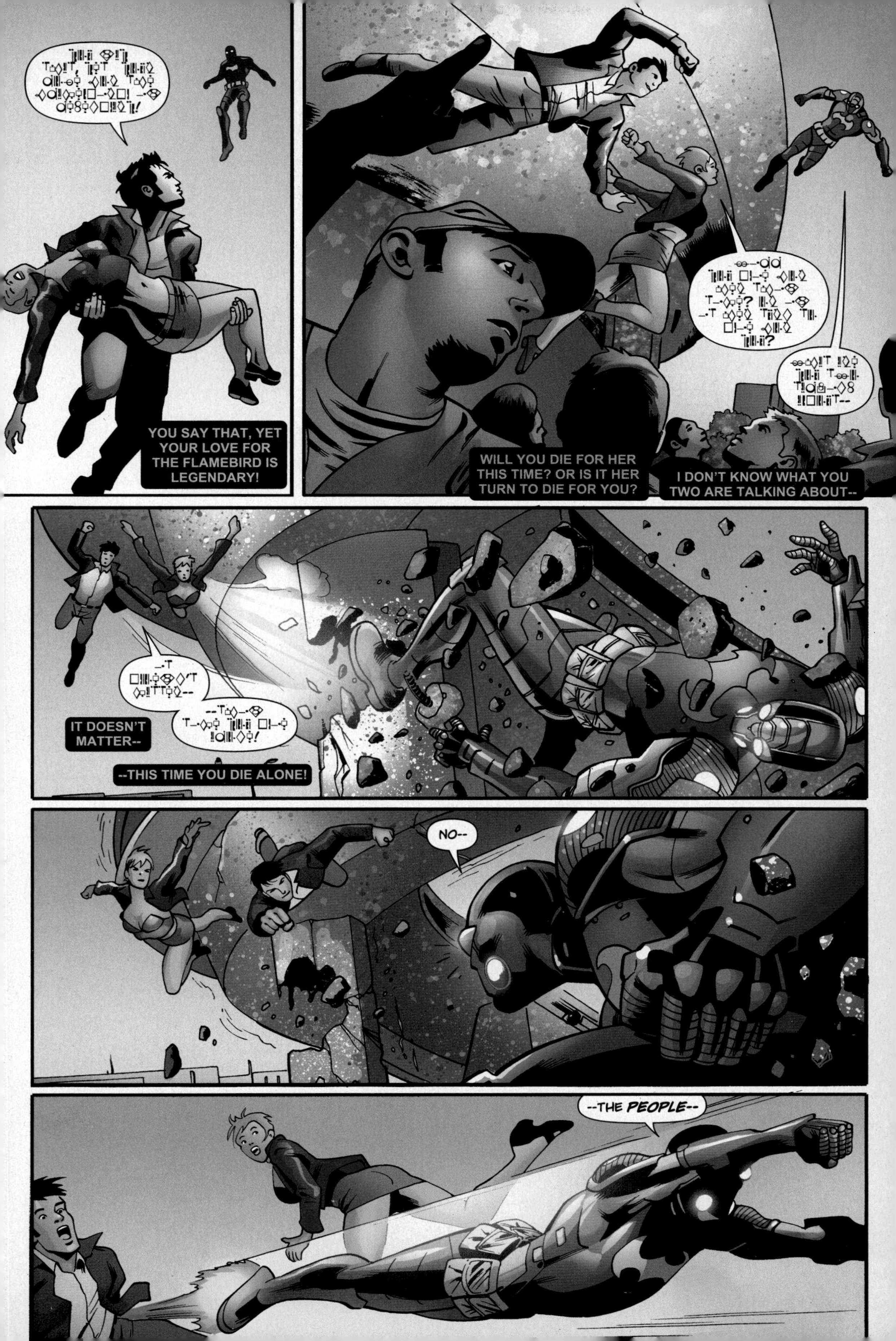
YOU SAY THAT, YET YOUR LOVE FOR THE FLAMEBIRD IS LEGENDARY!
WILL YOU DIE FOR HER THIS TIME? OR IS IT HER TURN TO DIE FOR YOU?
I DON'T KNOW WHAT YOU TWO ARE TALKING ABOUT--
IT DOESN'T MATTER--
--THIS TIME YOU DIE ALONE!
NO--
--THE PEOPLE--

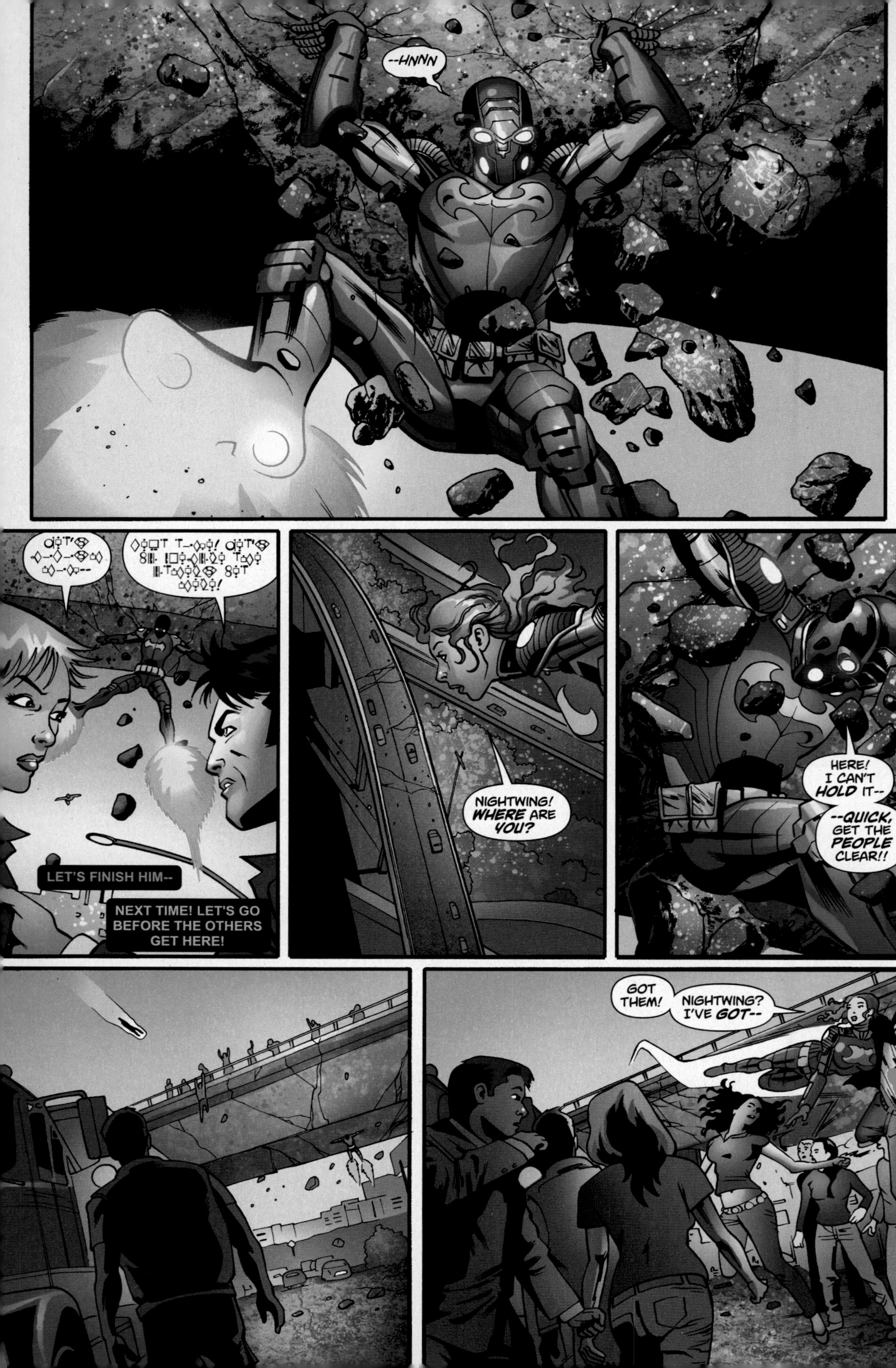
--HNNN
LET'S FINISH HIM--
NEXT TIME! LET'S GO BEFORE THE OTHERS GET HERE!
NIGHTWING! WHERE ARE YOU?
HERE! I CAN'T HOLD IT--
--QUICK, GET THE PEOPLE CLEAR!!
GOT THEM!
NIGHTWING? I'VE GOT--

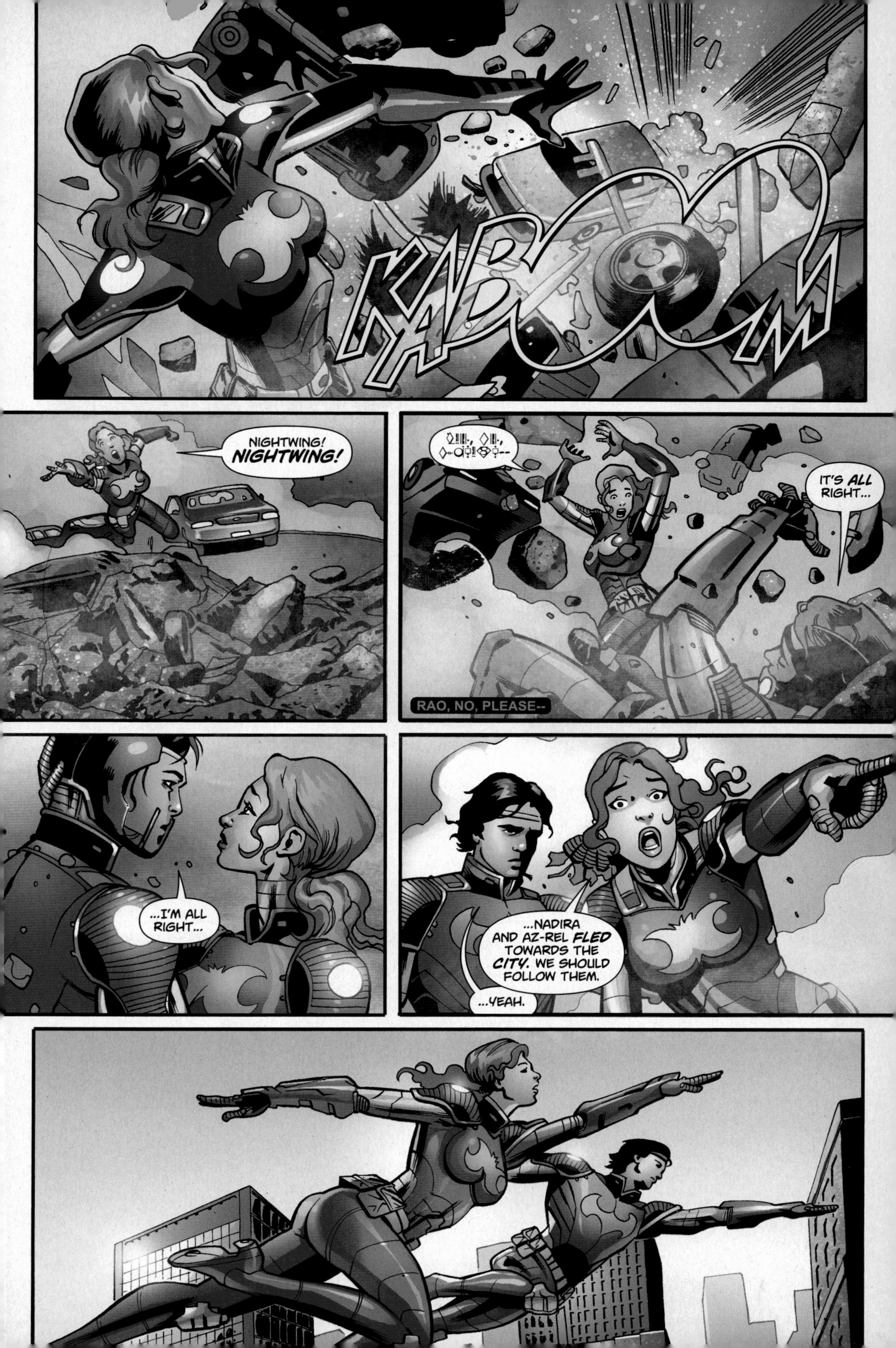
KABOOM
NIGHTWING! NIGHTWING!
IT'S ALL RIGHT...
RAO, NO, PLEASE--
...I'M ALL RIGHT...
...NADIRA AND AZ-REL FLED TOWARDS THE CITY. WE SHOULD FOLLOW THEM.
...YEAH.

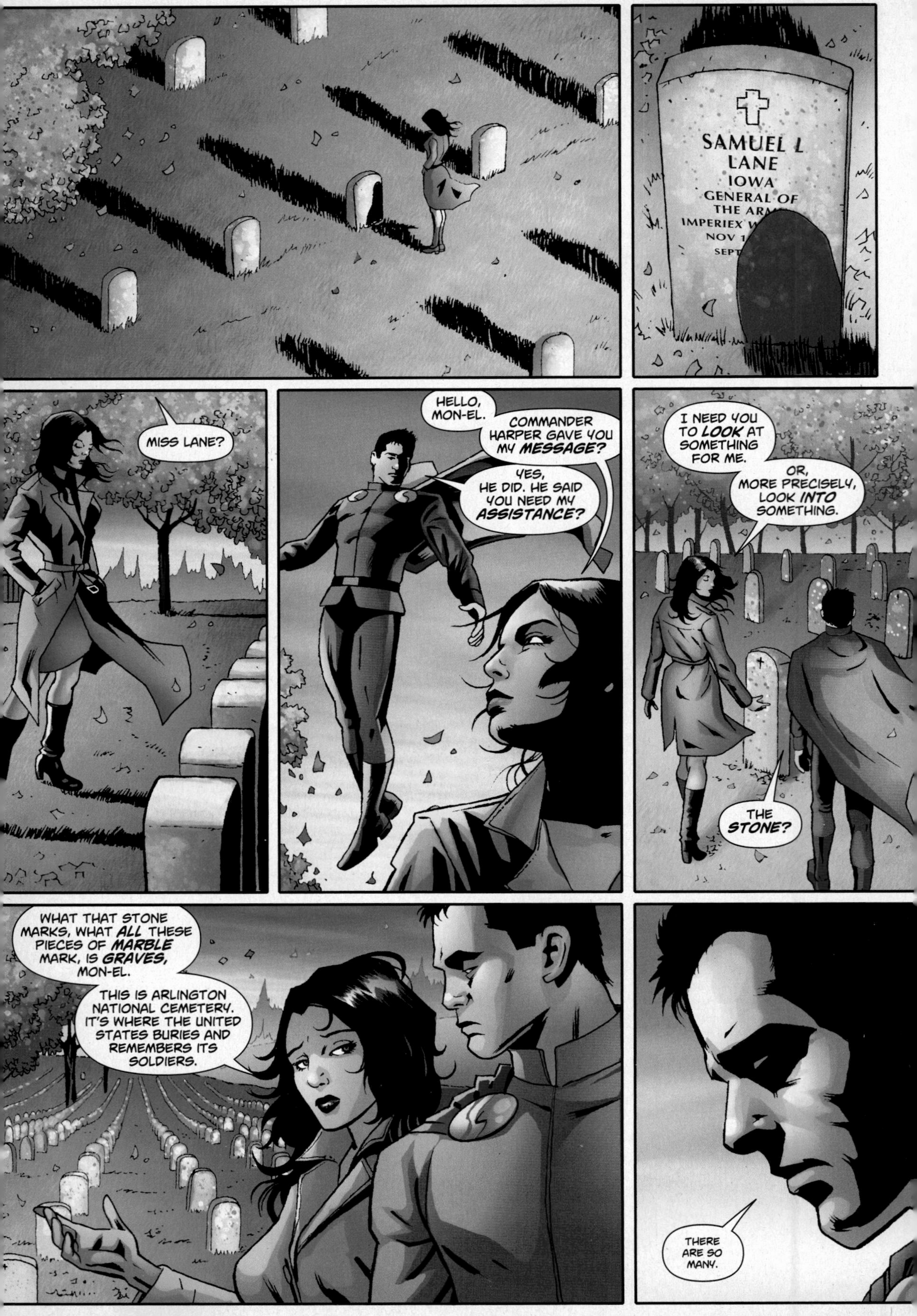
SAMUEL L
LANE
IOWA
GENERAL OF
THE ARM
IMPERIEX W
NOV 1
SEPT
MISS LANE?
HELLO, MON-EL.
COMMANDER HARPER GAVE YOU MY MESSAGE?
YES, HE DID. HE SAID YOU NEED MY ASSISTANCE?
I NEED YOU TO LOOK AT SOMETHING FOR ME.
OR, MORE PRECISELY, LOOK INTO SOMETHING.
THE STONE?
WHAT THAT STONE MARKS, WHAT ALL THESE PIECES OF MARBLE MARK, IS GRAVES, MON-EL.
THIS IS ARLINGTON NATIONAL CEMETERY. IT'S WHERE THE UNITED STATES BURIES AND REMEMBERS ITS SOLDIERS.
THERE ARE SO MANY.

THIS IS MY **FATHER'S** GRAVE.

YOU HAVE MY CONDOLENCES.

I MAY NOT **NEED** THEM.

TELL ME WHAT YOU **SEE.**

THERE IS A BOX OF SOME SORT, SEVERAL FEET DOWN... BONES IN IT, THOSE OF AN ADULT HUMAN MALE.

LOOK AT THE LEFT WRIST, THERE SHOULD BE--

A SMALL PIECE OF **METAL.** A **SCREW,** I BELIEVE, HOLDING ONE OF THE BONES TO **ANOTHER.**

YEAH, YOU'D **BE** THAT THOROUGH, WOULDN'T YOU, DAD?

CAN YOU SEE THE **TEETH?**

YES.

COUNT THEM.

...THIRTY-TWO.

HOW MANY?

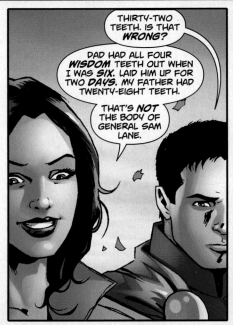

THIRTY-TWO TEETH. IS THAT **WRONG?**

DAD HAD ALL FOUR **WISDOM** TEETH OUT WHEN I WAS **SIX.** LAID HIM UP FOR TWO **DAYS.** MY FATHER HAD TWENTY-EIGHT TEETH.

THAT'S **NOT** THE BODY OF GENERAL SAM LANE.

MY FATHER IS **ALIVE.**

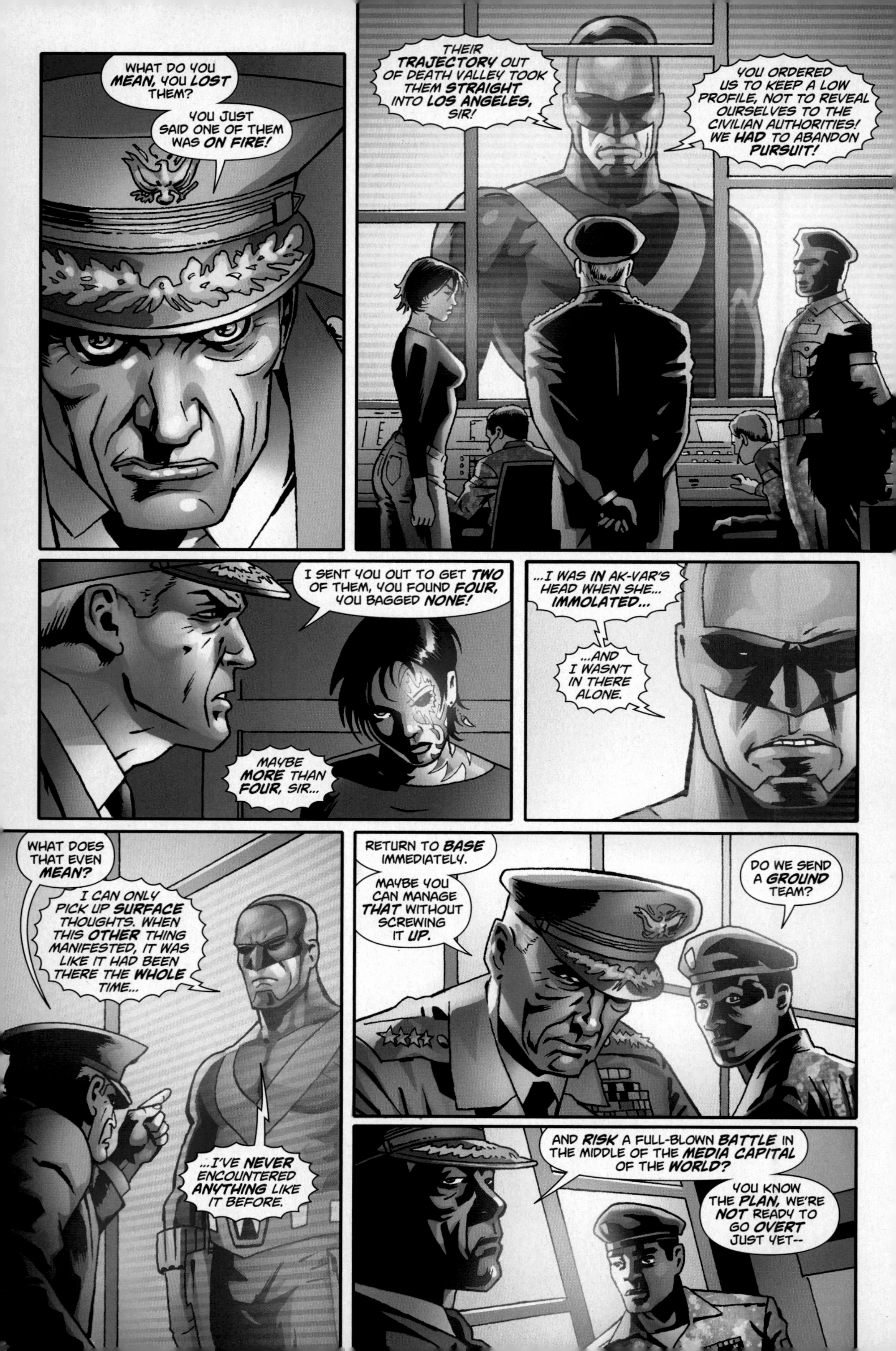
WHAT DO YOU MEAN, YOU LOST THEM?
YOU JUST SAID ONE OF THEM WAS ON FIRE!
THEIR TRAJECTORY OUT OF DEATH VALLEY TOOK THEM STRAIGHT INTO LOS ANGELES, SIR!
YOU ORDERED US TO KEEP A LOW PROFILE, NOT TO REVEAL OURSELVES TO THE CIVILIAN AUTHORITIES! WE HAD TO ABANDON PURSUIT!
I SENT YOU OUT TO GET TWO OF THEM, YOU FOUND FOUR, YOU BAGGED NONE!
MAYBE MORE THAN FOUR, SIR...
...I WAS IN AK-VAR'S HEAD WHEN SHE... IMMOLATED...
...AND I WASN'T IN THERE ALONE.
WHAT DOES THAT EVEN MEAN?
I CAN ONLY PICK UP SURFACE THOUGHTS. WHEN THIS OTHER THING MANIFESTED, IT WAS LIKE IT HAD BEEN THERE THE WHOLE TIME...
...I'VE NEVER ENCOUNTERED ANYTHING LIKE IT BEFORE.
RETURN TO BASE IMMEDIATELY.
MAYBE YOU CAN MANAGE THAT WITHOUT SCREWING IT UP.
DO WE SEND A GROUND TEAM?
AND RISK A FULL-BLOWN BATTLE IN THE MIDDLE OF THE MEDIA CAPITAL OF THE WORLD?
YOU KNOW THE PLAN, WE'RE NOT READY TO GO OVERT JUST YET--

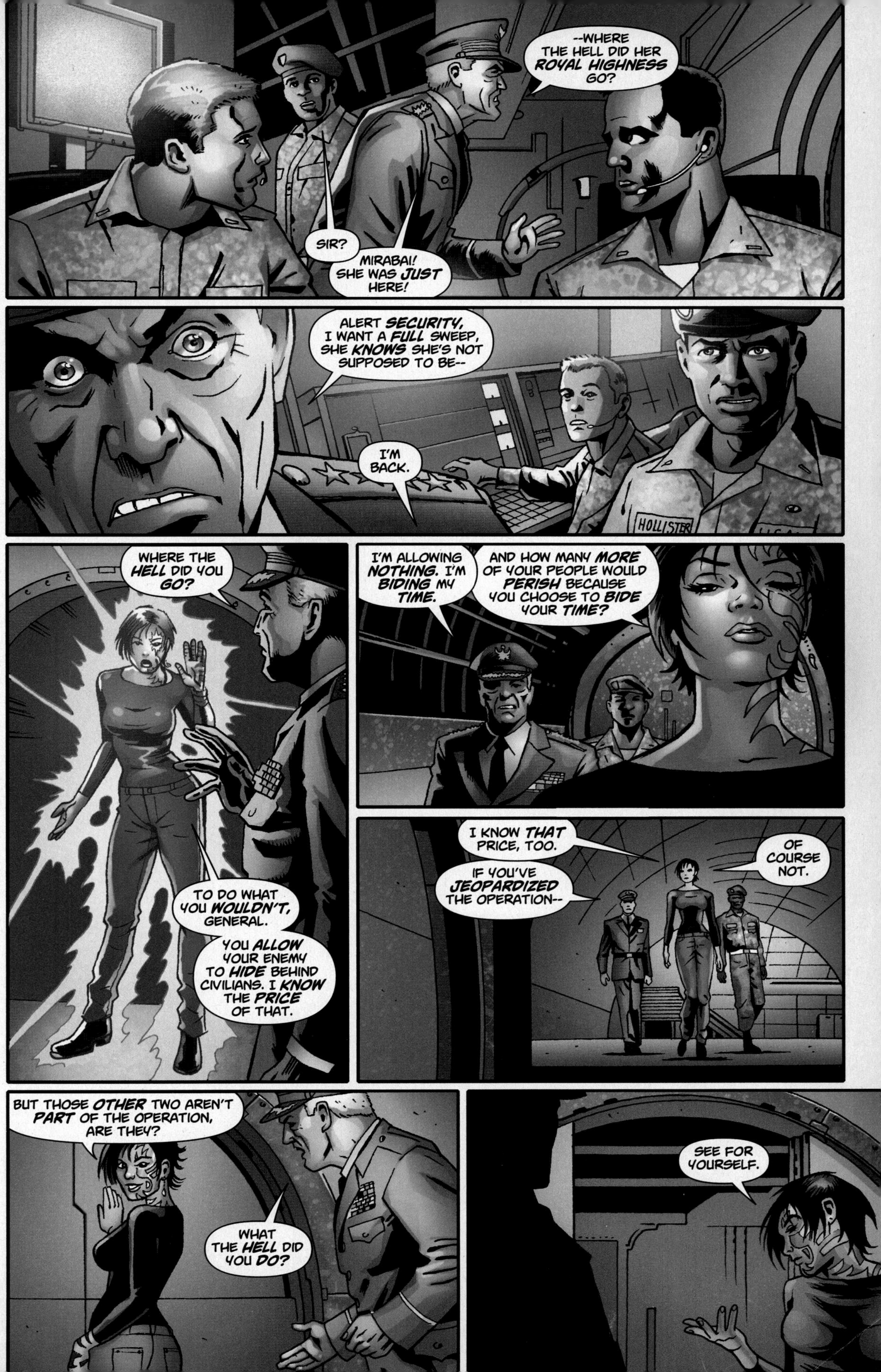
--WHERE THE HELL DID HER ROYAL HIGHNESS GO?
SIR?
MIRABAI! SHE WAS JUST HERE!
ALERT SECURITY, I WANT A FULL SWEEP, SHE KNOWS SHE'S NOT SUPPOSED TO BE--
I'M BACK.
HOLLISTER
WHERE THE HELL DID YOU GO?
TO DO WHAT YOU WOULDN'T, GENERAL.
YOU ALLOW YOUR ENEMY TO HIDE BEHIND CIVILIANS. I KNOW THE PRICE OF THAT.
I'M ALLOWING NOTHING. I'M BIDING MY TIME.
AND HOW MANY MORE OF YOUR PEOPLE WOULD PERISH BECAUSE YOU CHOOSE TO BIDE YOUR TIME?
I KNOW THAT PRICE, TOO.
IF YOU'VE JEOPARDIZED THE OPERATION--
OF COURSE NOT.
BUT THOSE OTHER TWO AREN'T PART OF THE OPERATION, ARE THEY?
WHAT THE HELL DID YOU DO?
SEE FOR YOURSELF.

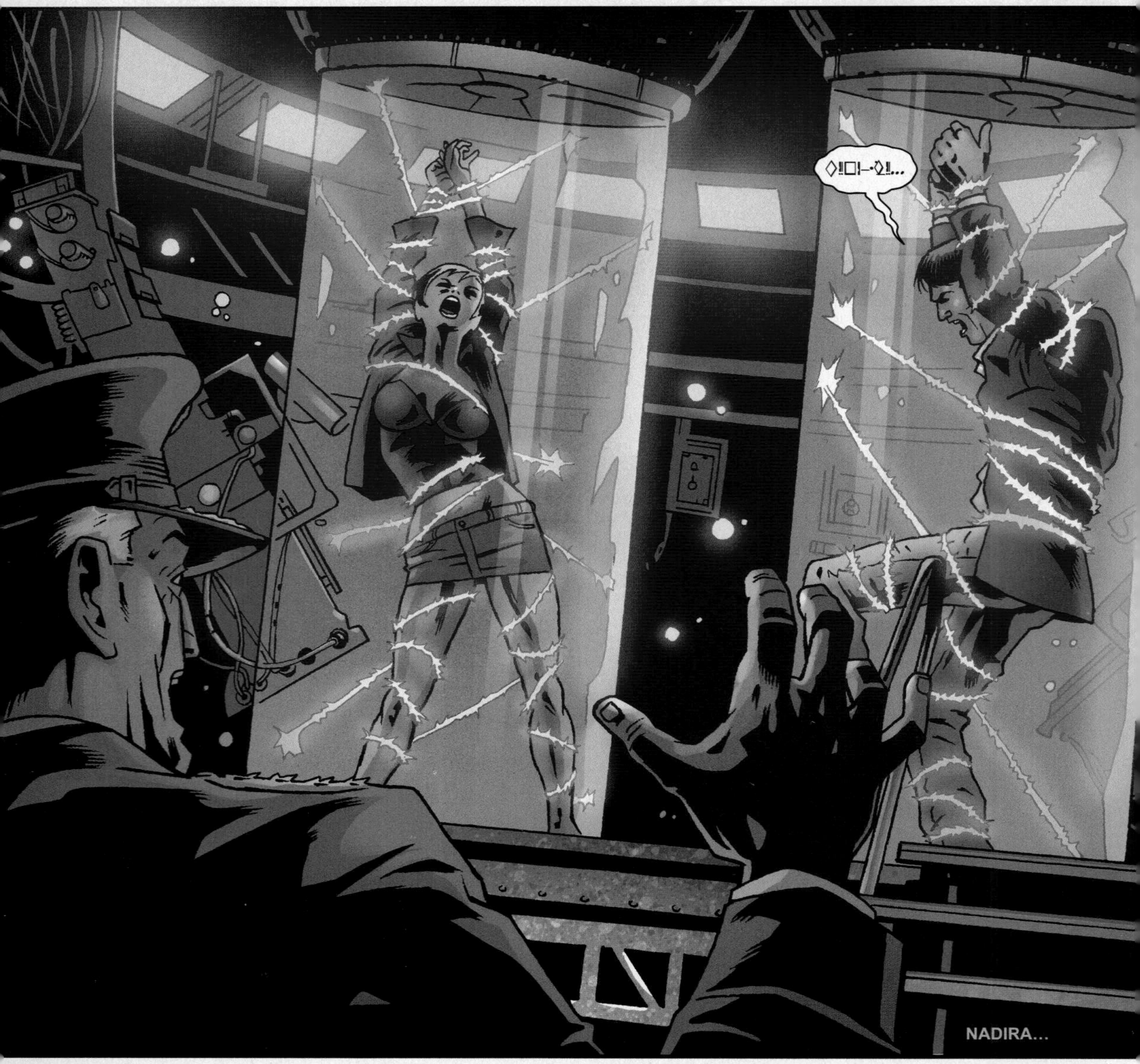
NADIRA...

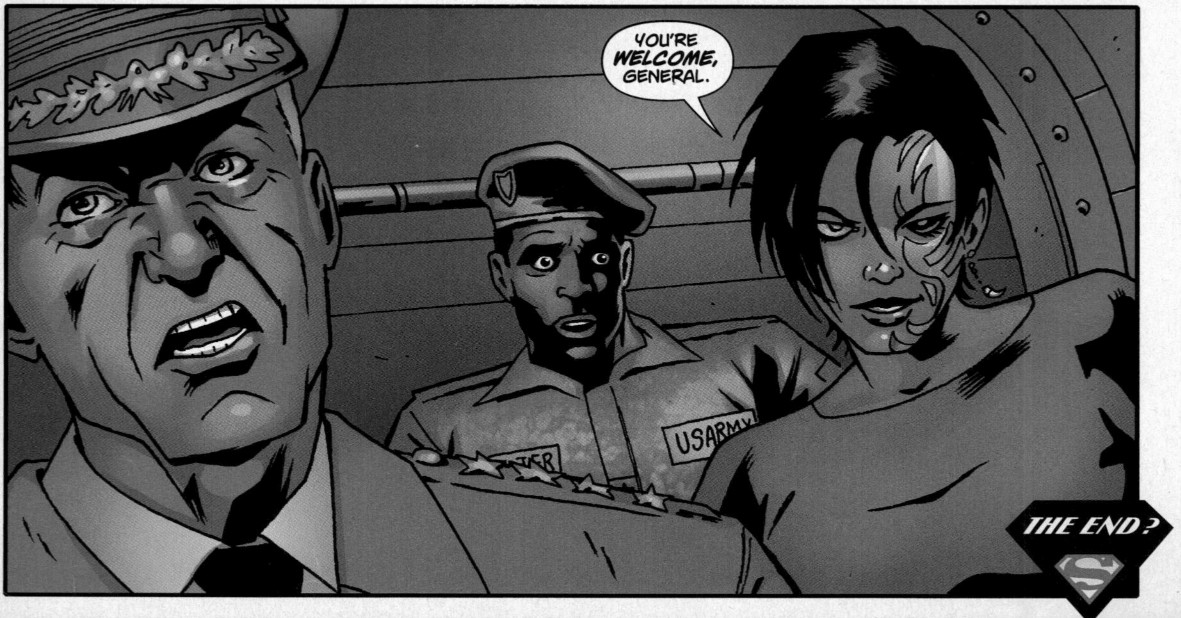
YOU'RE WELCOME, GENERAL.
USARMY
THE END?

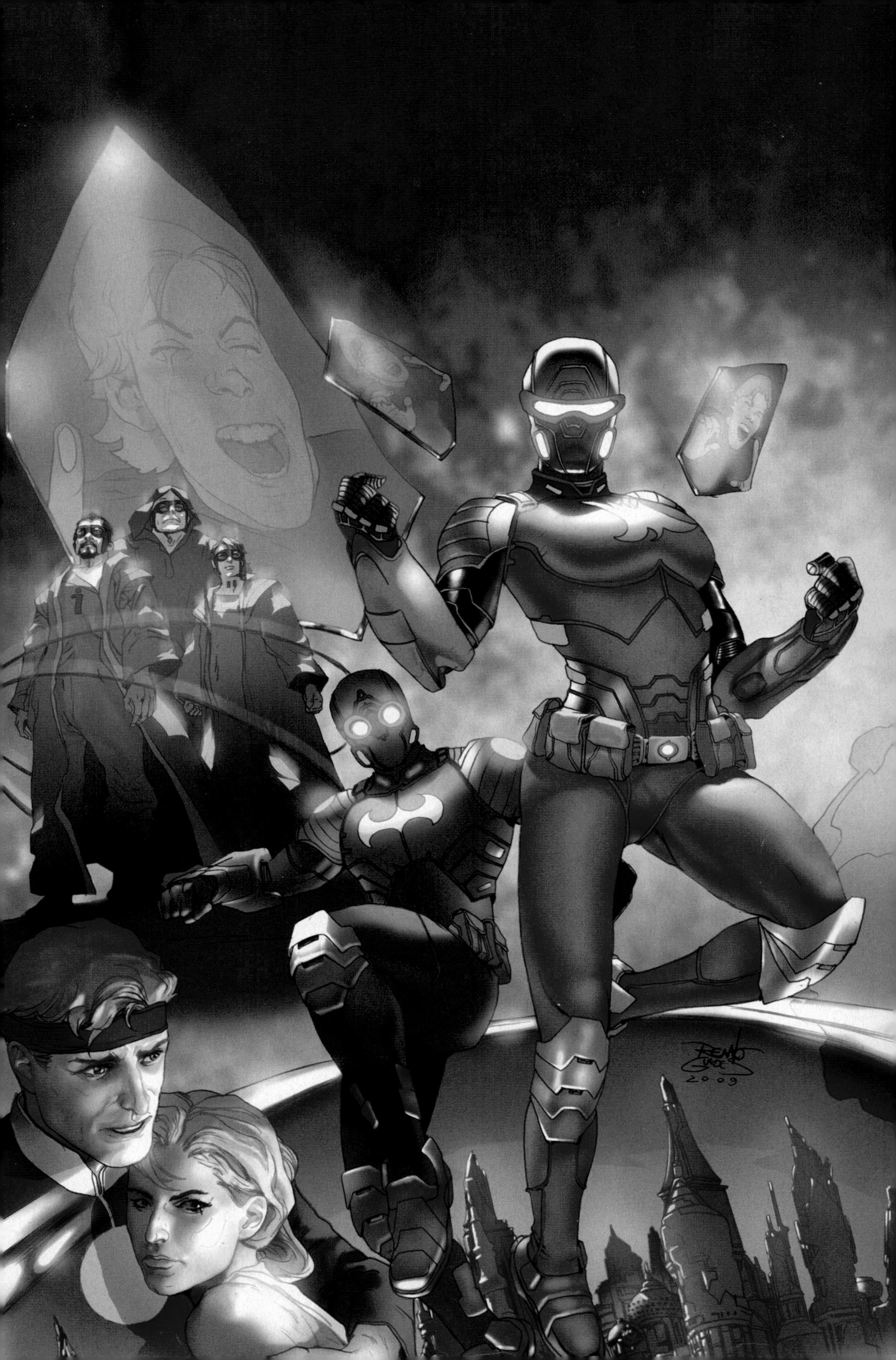

THE ORIGIN OF NIGHTWING AND FLAMEBIRD
PERE PÉREZ <ARTIST>

COVER BY RENATO GUEDES

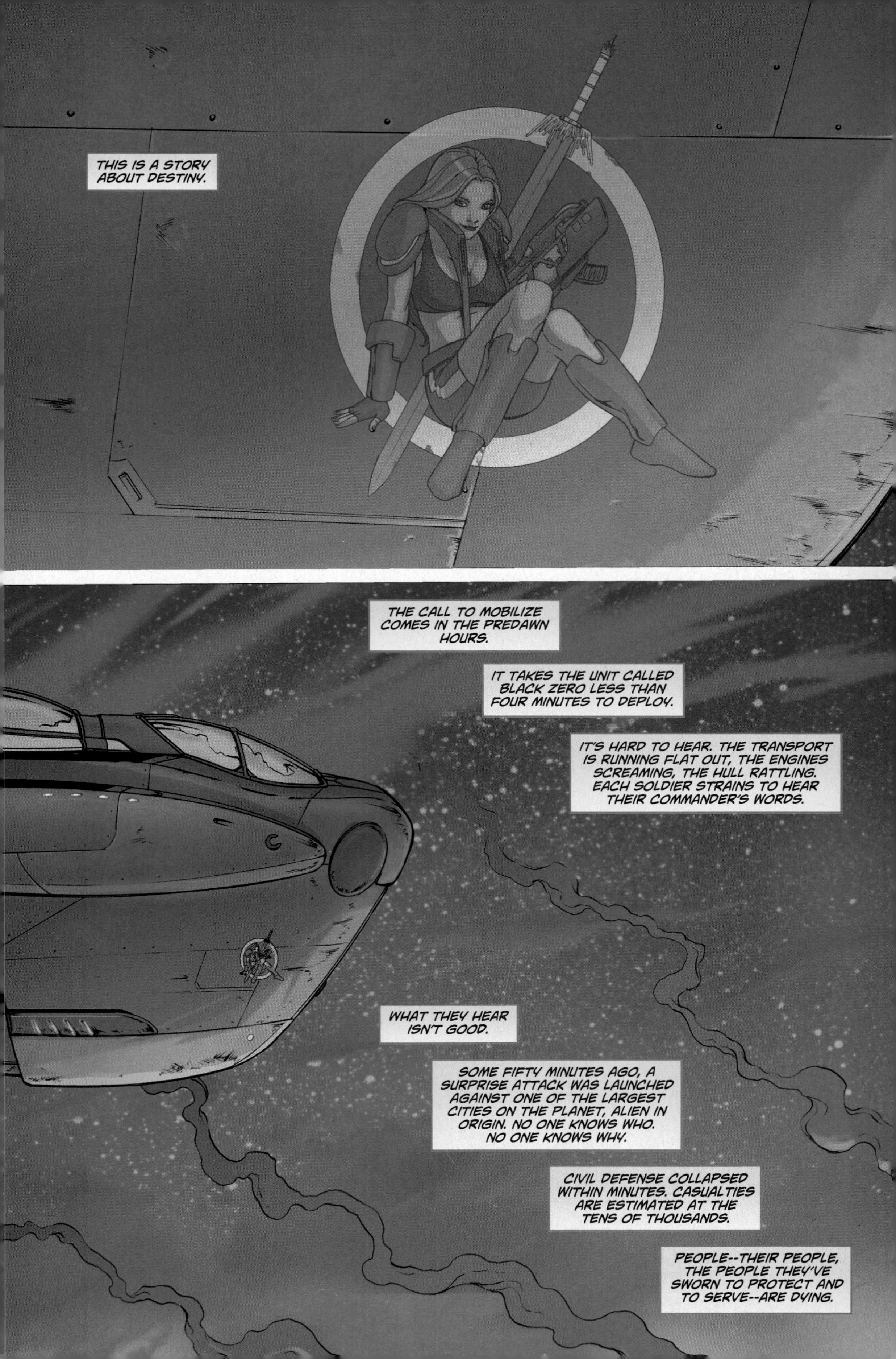
THIS IS A STORY ABOUT DESTINY.
THE CALL TO MOBILIZE COMES IN THE PREDAWN HOURS.
IT TAKES THE UNIT CALLED BLACK ZERO LESS THAN FOUR MINUTES TO DEPLOY.
IT'S HARD TO HEAR. THE TRANSPORT IS RUNNING FLAT OUT, THE ENGINES SCREAMING, THE HULL RATTLING. EACH SOLDIER STRAINS TO HEAR THEIR COMMANDER'S WORDS.
WHAT THEY HEAR ISN'T GOOD.
SOME FIFTY MINUTES AGO, A SURPRISE ATTACK WAS LAUNCHED AGAINST ONE OF THE LARGEST CITIES ON THE PLANET, ALIEN IN ORIGIN. NO ONE KNOWS WHO. NO ONE KNOWS WHY.
CIVIL DEFENSE COLLAPSED WITHIN MINUTES. CASUALTIES ARE ESTIMATED AT THE TENS OF THOUSANDS.
PEOPLE--THEIR PEOPLE, THE PEOPLE THEY'VE SWORN TO PROTECT AND TO SERVE--ARE DYING.

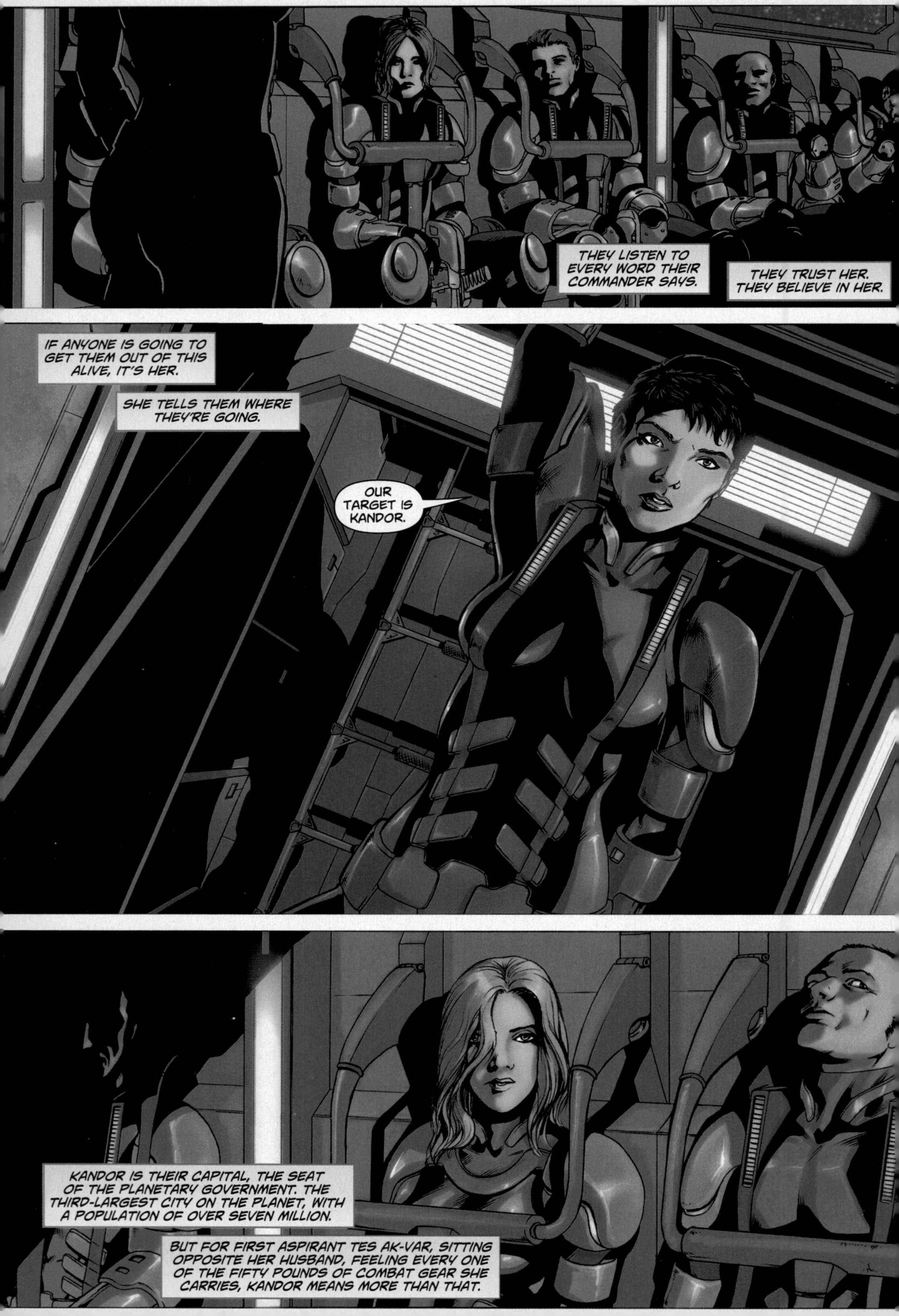
THEY LISTEN TO EVERY WORD THEIR COMMANDER SAYS.
THEY TRUST HER. THEY BELIEVE IN HER.
IF ANYONE IS GOING TO GET THEM OUT OF THIS ALIVE, IT'S HER.
SHE TELLS THEM WHERE THEY'RE GOING.
OUR TARGET IS KANDOR.
KANDOR IS THEIR CAPITAL, THE SEAT OF THE PLANETARY GOVERNMENT. THE THIRD-LARGEST CITY ON THE PLANET, WITH A POPULATION OF OVER SEVEN MILLION.
BUT FOR FIRST ASPIRANT TES AK-VAR, SITTING OPPOSITE HER HUSBAND, FEELING EVERY ONE OF THE FIFTY POUNDS OF COMBAT GEAR SHE CARRIES, KANDOR MEANS MORE THAN THAT.

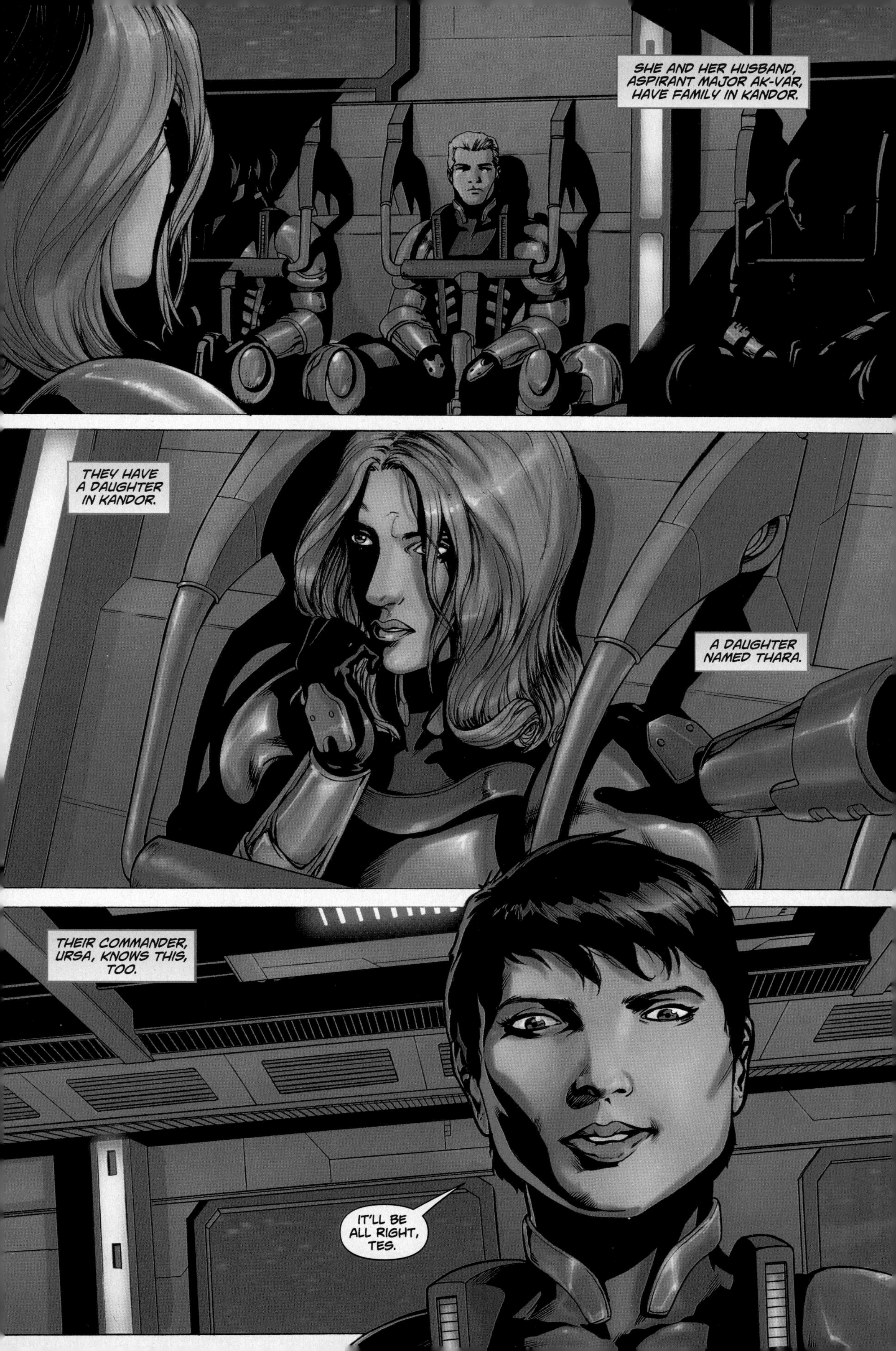
SHE AND HER HUSBAND, ASPIRANT MAJOR AK-VAR, HAVE FAMILY IN KANDOR.
THEY HAVE A DAUGHTER IN KANDOR.
A DAUGHTER NAMED THARA.
THEIR COMMANDER, URSA, KNOWS THIS, TOO.
IT'LL BE ALL RIGHT, TES.

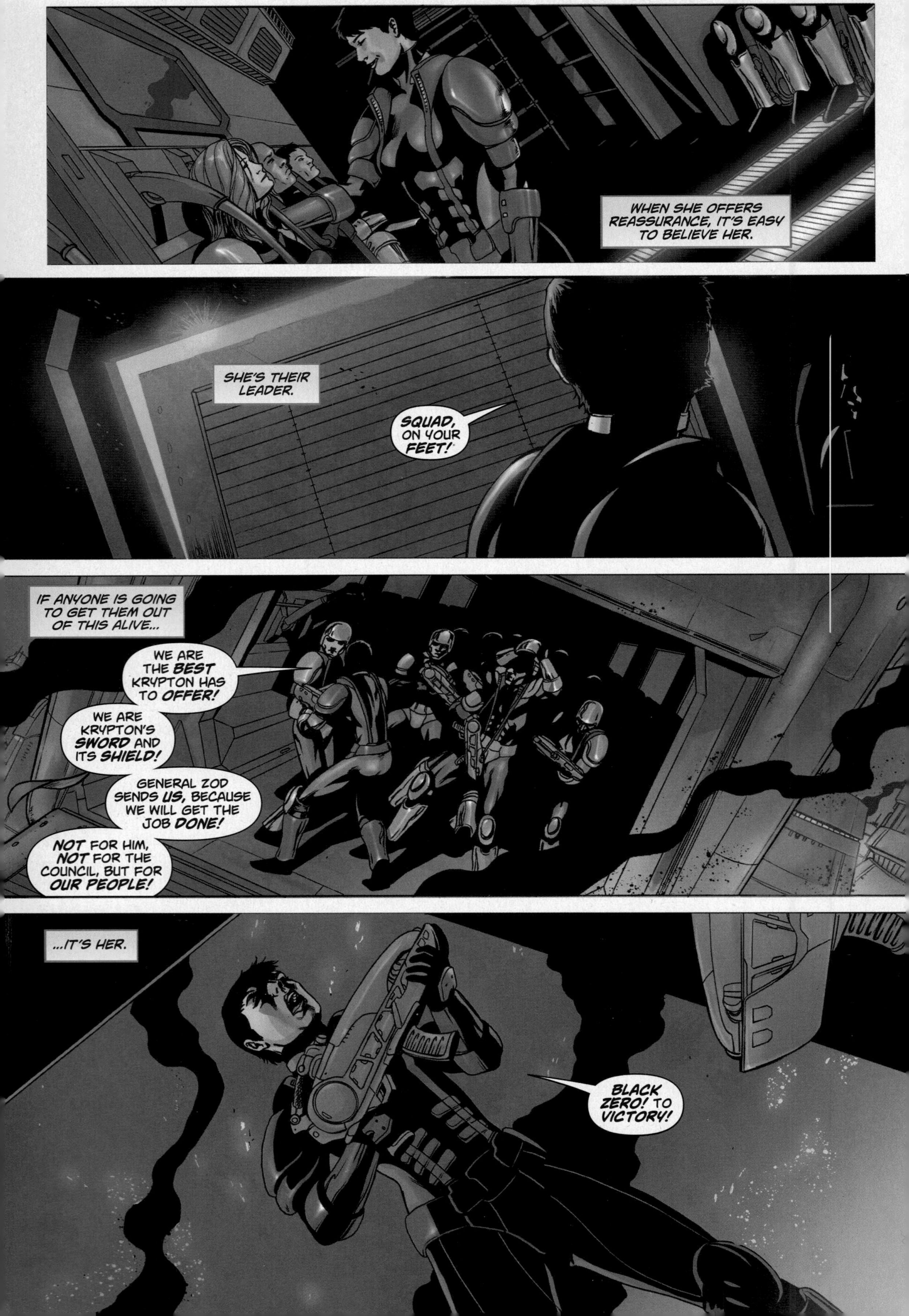

WHEN SHE OFFERS REASSURANCE, IT'S EASY TO BELIEVE HER.
SHE'S THEIR LEADER.
SQUAD, ON YOUR FEET!
IF ANYONE IS GOING TO GET THEM OUT OF THIS ALIVE...
WE ARE THE BEST KRYPTON HAS TO OFFER!
WE ARE KRYPTON'S SWORD AND ITS SHIELD!
GENERAL ZOD SENDS US, BECAUSE WE WILL GET THE JOB DONE!
NOT FOR HIM, NOT FOR THE COUNCIL, BUT FOR OUR PEOPLE!
...IT'S HER.
BLACK ZERO! TO VICTORY!

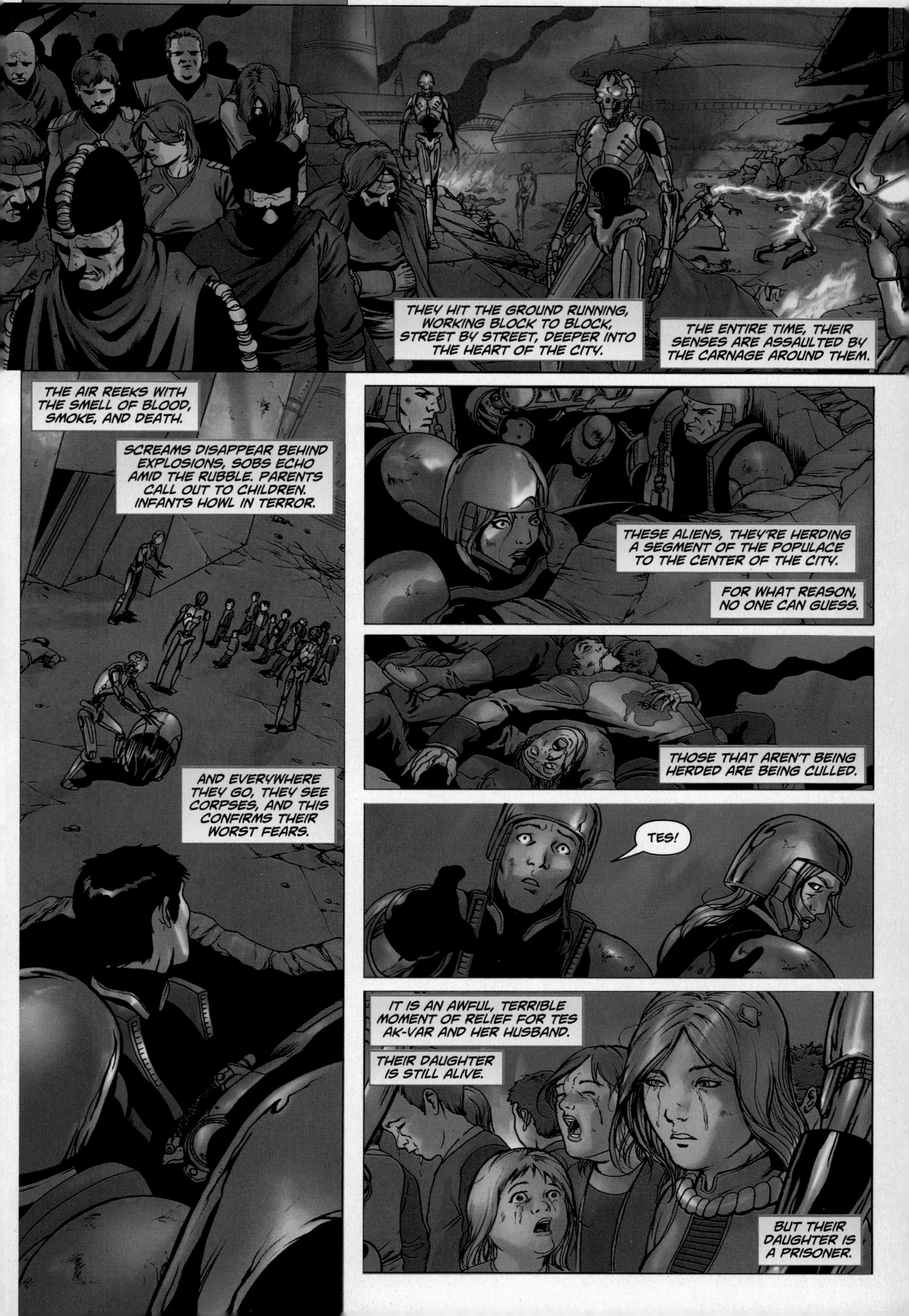
THEY HIT THE GROUND RUNNING, WORKING BLOCK TO BLOCK, STREET BY STREET, DEEPER INTO THE HEART OF THE CITY.
THE ENTIRE TIME, THEIR SENSES ARE ASSAULTED BY THE CARNAGE AROUND THEM.
THE AIR REEKS WITH THE SMELL OF BLOOD, SMOKE, AND DEATH.
SCREAMS DISAPPEAR BEHIND EXPLOSIONS, SOBS ECHO AMID THE RUBBLE. PARENTS CALL OUT TO CHILDREN. INFANTS HOWL IN TERROR.
AND EVERYWHERE THEY GO, THEY SEE CORPSES, AND THIS CONFIRMS THEIR WORST FEARS.
THESE ALIENS, THEY'RE HERDING A SEGMENT OF THE POPULACE TO THE CENTER OF THE CITY.
FOR WHAT REASON, NO ONE CAN GUESS.
THOSE THAT AREN'T BEING HERDED ARE BEING CULLED.
TES!
IT IS AN AWFUL, TERRIBLE MOMENT OF RELIEF FOR TES AK-VAR AND HER HUSBAND.
THEIR DAUGHTER IS STILL ALIVE.
BUT THEIR DAUGHTER IS A PRISONER.

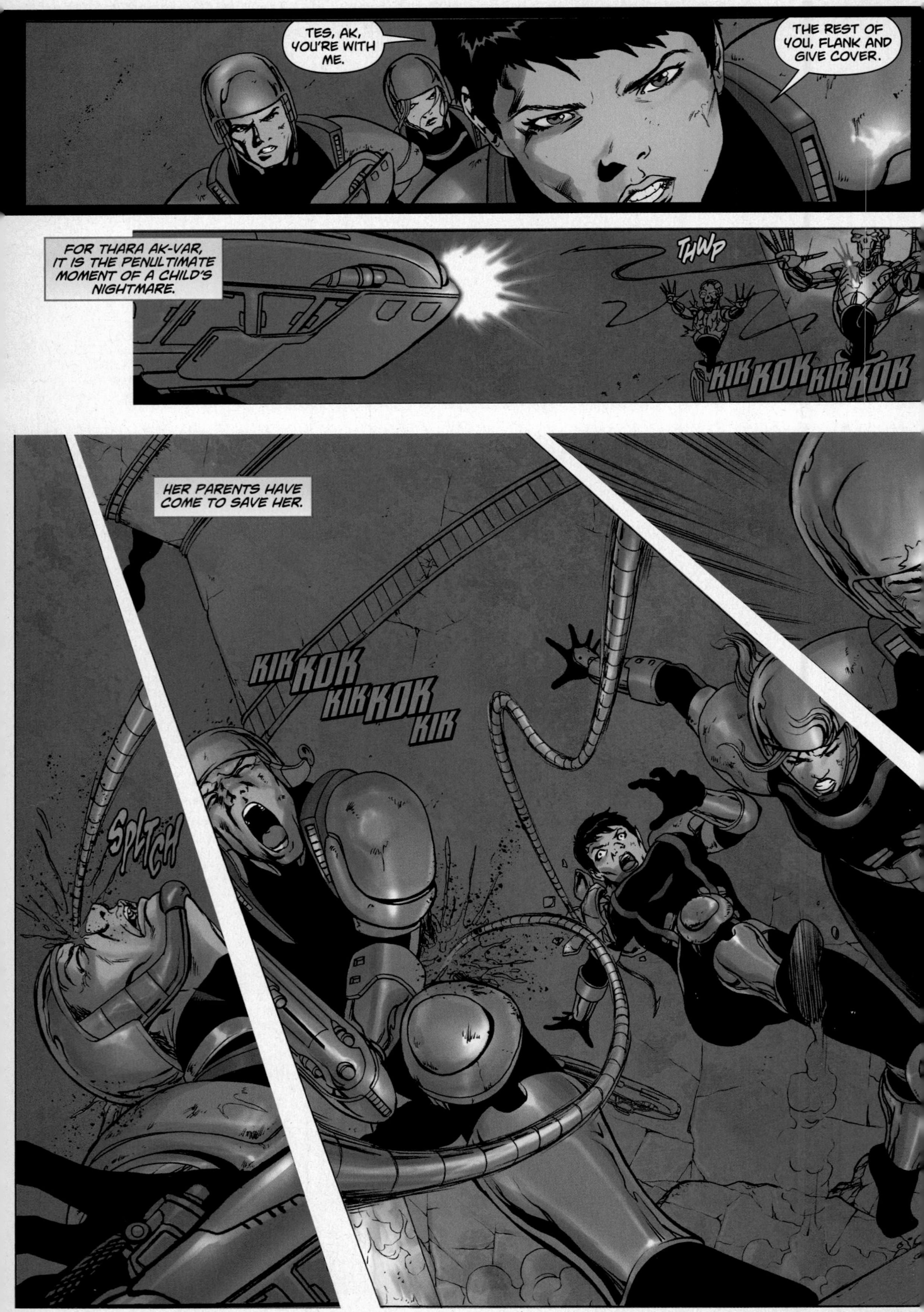
TES, AK, YOU'RE WITH ME.
THE REST OF YOU, FLANK AND GIVE COVER.
FOR THARA AK-VAR, IT IS THE PENULTIMATE MOMENT OF A CHILD'S NIGHTMARE.
THWP
KIK KOK KIK KOK
HER PARENTS HAVE COME TO SAVE HER.
KIK KOK KIK KOK KIK
SPLTCH

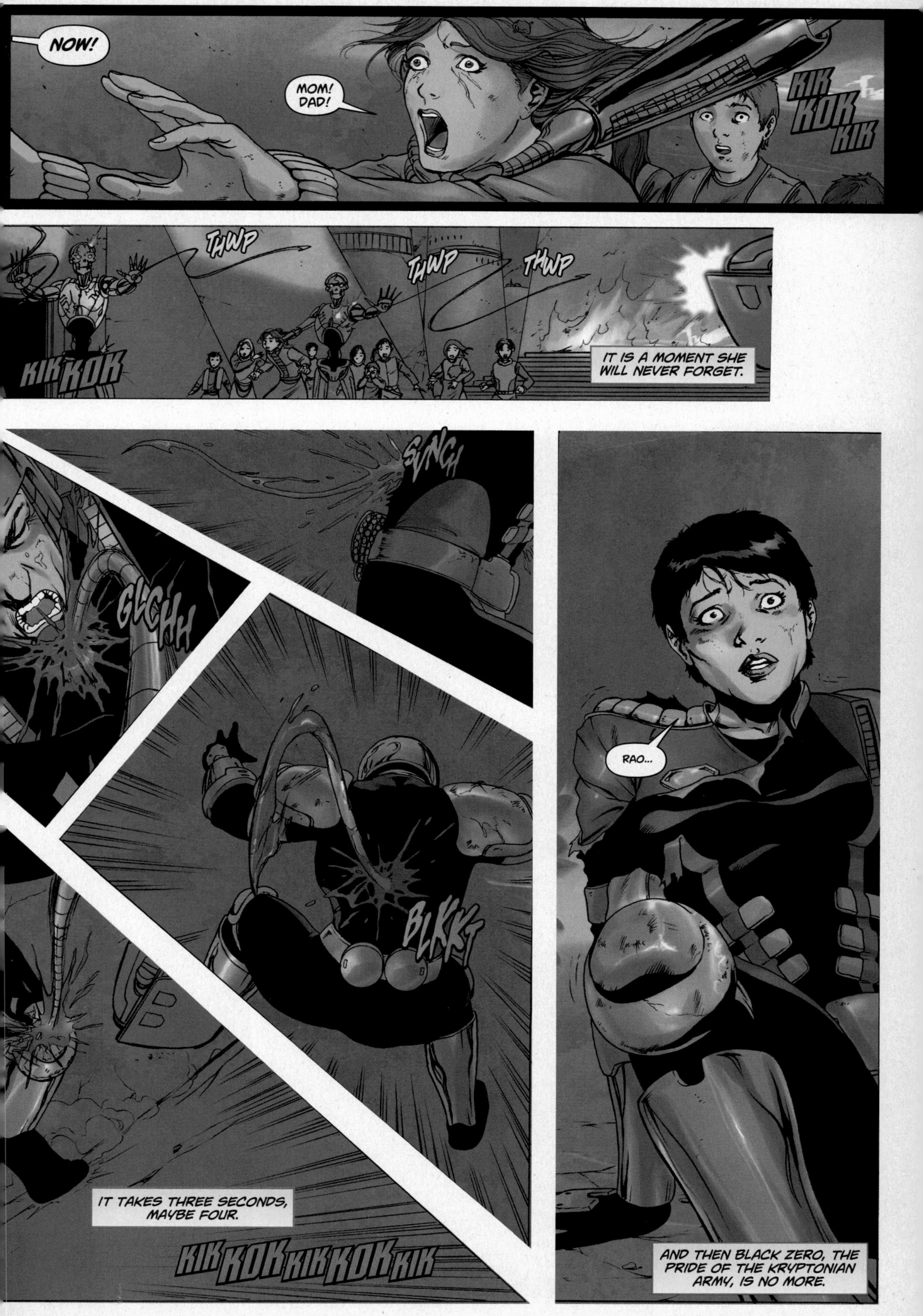
NOW!
MOM! DAD!
KIK KOK KIK
THWP
THWP
THWP
KIK KOK
IT IS A MOMENT SHE WILL NEVER FORGET.
SLNCH
GLCHH
BLKKT
IT TAKES THREE SECONDS, MAYBE FOUR.
KIK KOK KIK KOK KIK
RAO...
AND THEN BLACK ZERO, THE PRIDE OF THE KRYPTONIAN ARMY, IS NO MORE.

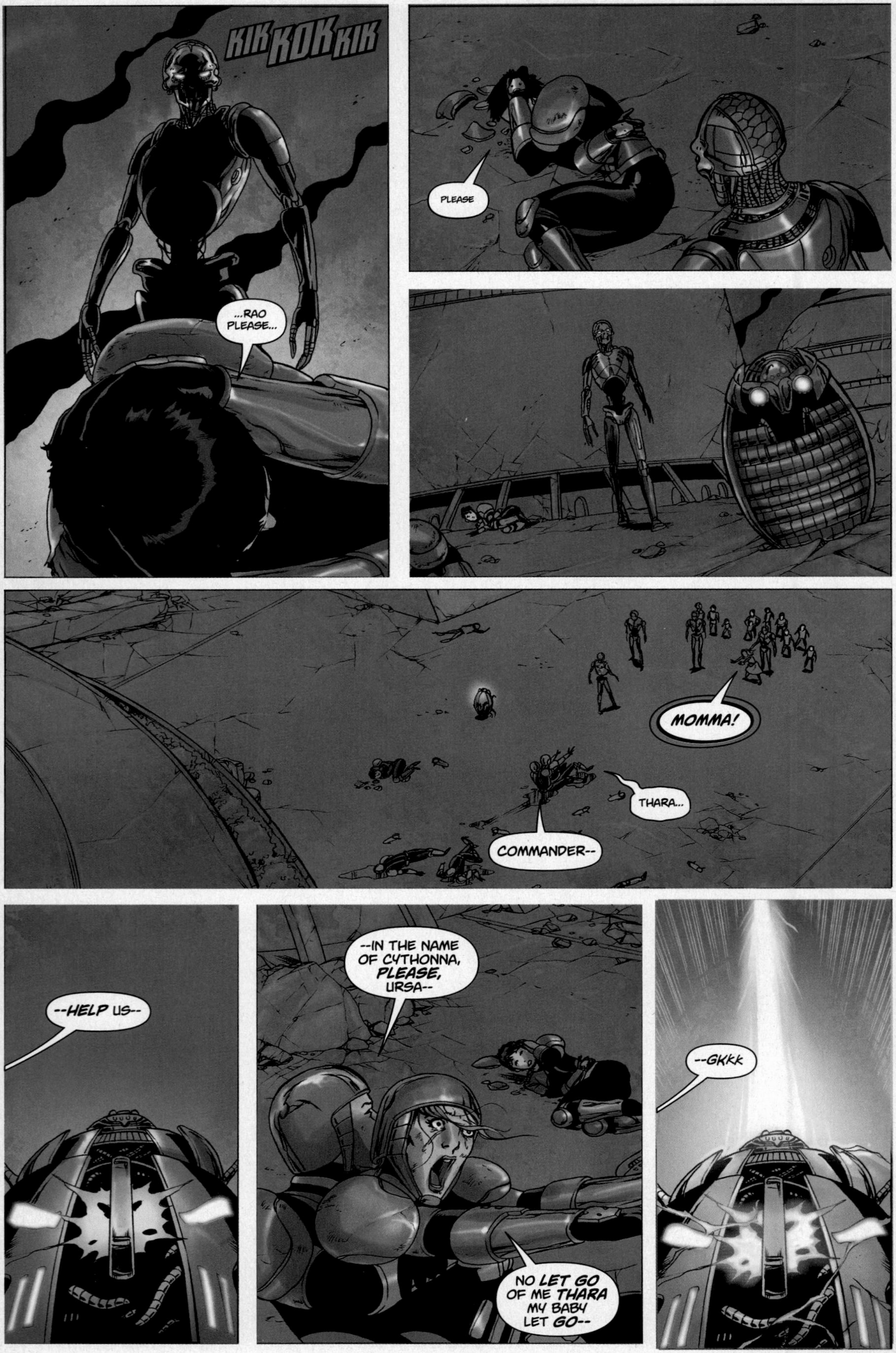
KIK KOK KIK
...RAO PLEASE...
PLEASE
MOMMA!
THARA...
COMMANDER--
--HELP US--
--IN THE NAME OF CYTHONNA, PLEASE, URSA--
NO LET GO OF ME THARA MY BABY LET GO--
--GKKK

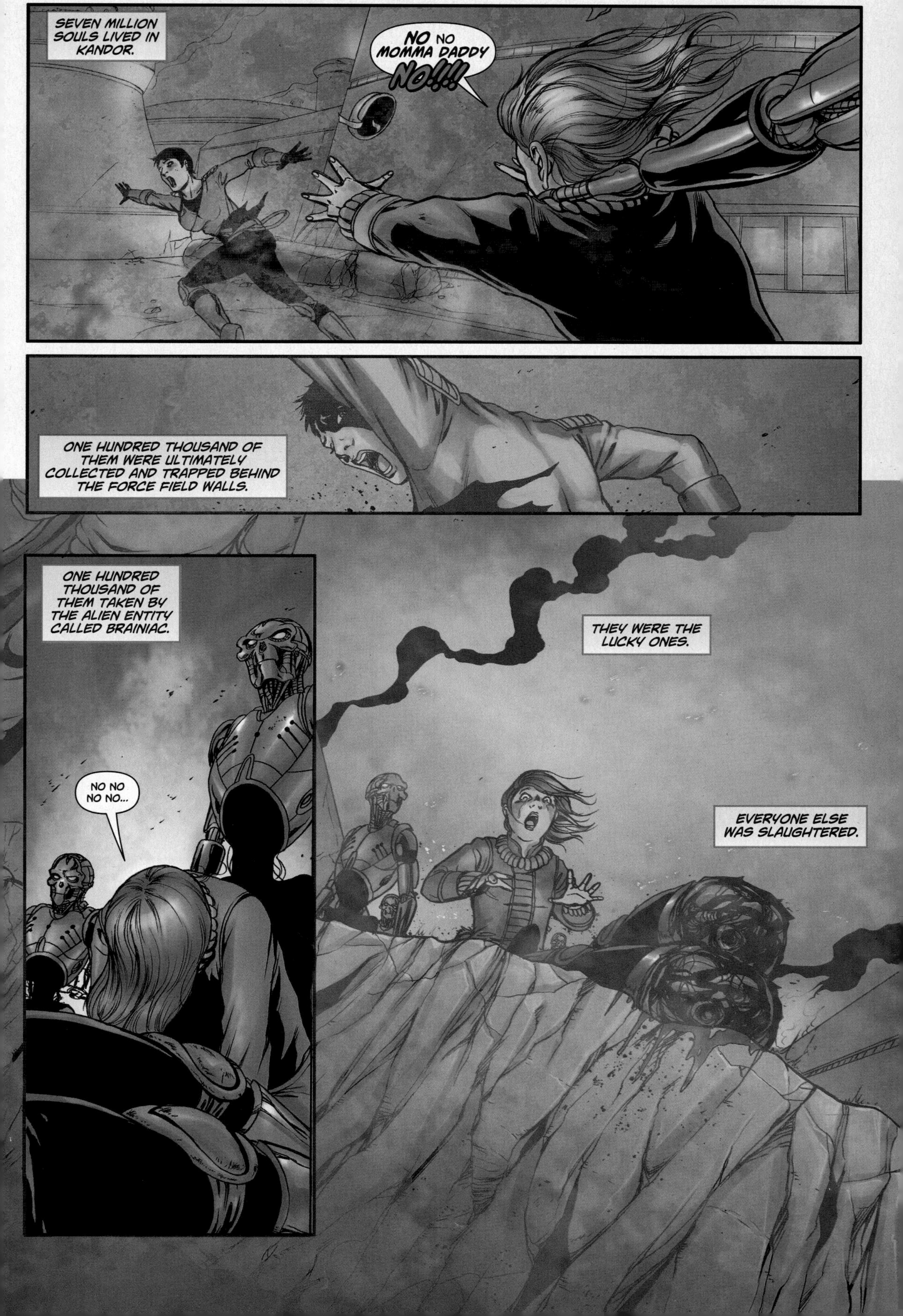
SEVEN MILLION SOULS LIVED IN KANDOR.
NO NO MOMMA DADDY NO!!!
ONE HUNDRED THOUSAND OF THEM WERE ULTIMATELY COLLECTED AND TRAPPED BEHIND THE FORCE FIELD WALLS.
ONE HUNDRED THOUSAND OF THEM TAKEN BY THE ALIEN ENTITY CALLED BRAINIAC.
NO NO NO NO...
THEY WERE THE LUCKY ONES.
EVERYONE ELSE WAS SLAUGHTERED.

IN THE TERRIFYING DAYS THAT FOLLOW THEIR ABDUCTION, KANDOR STRUGGLES TO RECOVER FROM WHAT HAS HAPPENED.

THE BODIES OF THE DEAD ARE BURNED, THE SOULS OF THE DEPARTED ESCORTED BACK TO RAO ON PRAYERS OF THE RELIGIOUS GUILD.

SLOWLY, THE REALIZATION DAWNS THAT THEIR JAILOR'S INTEREST IN THEM IS LIMITED.

TO BRAINIAC, THE ONE HUNDRED THOUSAND KRYPTONIANS TRAPPED IN THE BOTTLE CITY ARE ANTS IN A FARM, TO BE OBSERVED, NOTHING MORE.

A SMALL COMFORT WHEN FAMILIES HAVE BEEN TORN APART AND SLAUGHTERED, WHEN FRIENDS AND LOVERS HAVE BEEN LOST.

NOT ONE SURVIVOR FAILS TO EXHIBIT SYMPTOMS OF POST-TRAUMATIC STRESS. SLEEP IS PLAGUED WITH NIGHTMARES, DAYS AWASH IN DEPRESSION, IRRATIONAL ANGER, AND SORROW.

FACED WITH AN UNCERTAIN FUTURE, KANDOR STRUGGLES TO RE-ESTABLISH SOME OF WHAT HAS BEEN LOST, TO REBUILD SOME REPLICA OF KRYPTONIAN SOCIETY.

KANDOR'S ORPHANS ARE QUICKLY PLACED INTO DIFFERENT GUILDS.

LIKE HER PARENTS, AND THEIR PARENTS BEFORE THEM, THARA AK-VAR ENTERS SERVICE IN THE MILITARY GUILD.

THE HOPE IS THAT, ONE DAY, SHE AND THE REST OF HER GUILD WILL SEE COMBAT.

THE HOPE IS THAT, ONE DAY, THE PRISONERS OF KANDOR WILL SOMEHOW RISE UP, AND TAKE BACK THEIR FREEDOM.

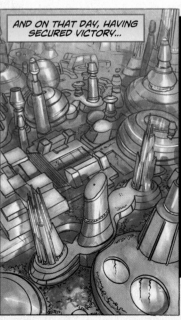

AND ON THAT DAY, HAVING SECURED VICTORY...

...THEY WILL BE ABLE TO RETURN HOME.

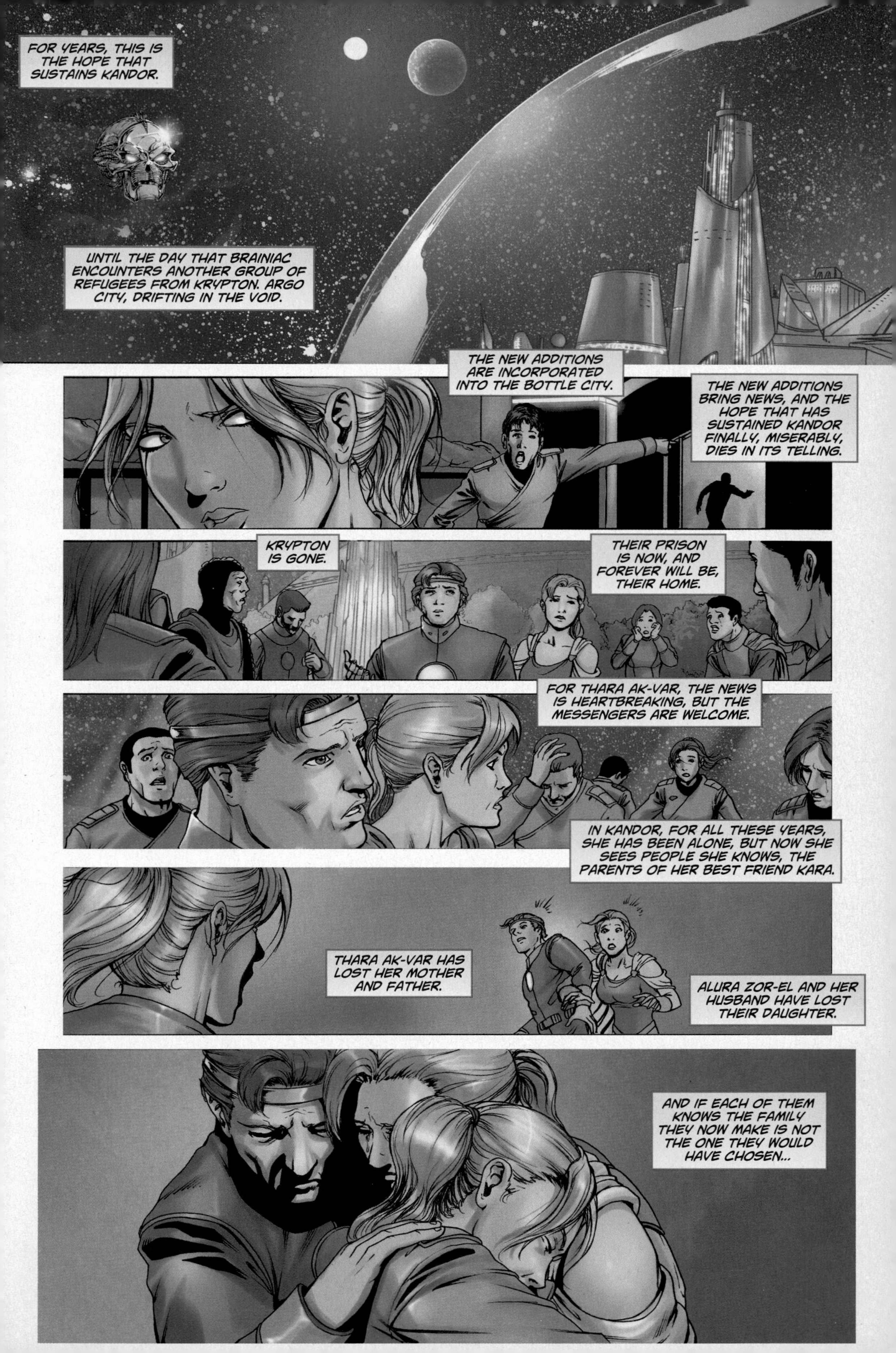
FOR YEARS, THIS IS THE HOPE THAT SUSTAINS KANDOR.
UNTIL THE DAY THAT BRAINIAC ENCOUNTERS ANOTHER GROUP OF REFUGEES FROM KRYPTON. ARGO CITY, DRIFTING IN THE VOID.
THE NEW ADDITIONS ARE INCORPORATED INTO THE BOTTLE CITY.
THE NEW ADDITIONS BRING NEWS, AND THE HOPE THAT HAS SUSTAINED KANDOR FINALLY, MISERABLY, DIES IN ITS TELLING.
KRYPTON IS GONE.
THEIR PRISON IS NOW, AND FOREVER WILL BE, THEIR HOME.
FOR THARA AK-VAR, THE NEWS IS HEARTBREAKING, BUT THE MESSENGERS ARE WELCOME.
IN KANDOR, FOR ALL THESE YEARS, SHE HAS BEEN ALONE, BUT NOW SHE SEES PEOPLE SHE KNOWS, THE PARENTS OF HER BEST FRIEND KARA.
THARA AK-VAR HAS LOST HER MOTHER AND FATHER.
ALURA ZOR-EL AND HER HUSBAND HAVE LOST THEIR DAUGHTER.
AND IF EACH OF THEM KNOWS THE FAMILY THEY NOW MAKE IS NOT THE ONE THEY WOULD HAVE CHOSEN...

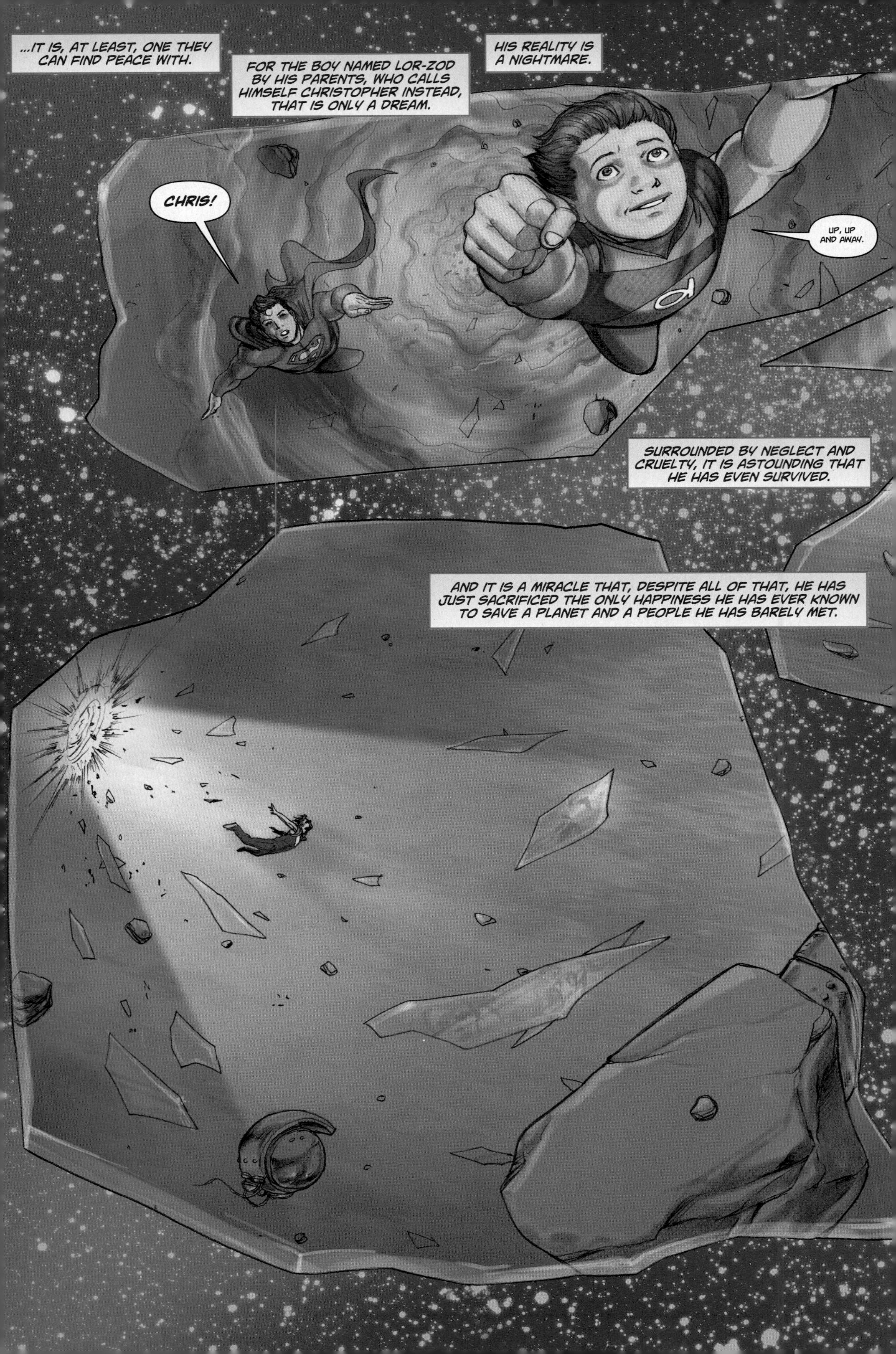
...IT IS, AT LEAST, ONE THEY CAN FIND PEACE WITH.
FOR THE BOY NAMED LOR-ZOD BY HIS PARENTS, WHO CALLS HIMSELF CHRISTOPHER INSTEAD, THAT IS ONLY A DREAM.
HIS REALITY IS A NIGHTMARE.
CHRIS!
UP, UP AND AWAY.
SURROUNDED BY NEGLECT AND CRUELTY, IT IS ASTOUNDING THAT HE HAS EVEN SURVIVED.
AND IT IS A MIRACLE THAT, DESPITE ALL OF THAT, HE HAS JUST SACRIFICED THE ONLY HAPPINESS HE HAS EVER KNOWN TO SAVE A PLANET AND A PEOPLE HE HAS BARELY MET.

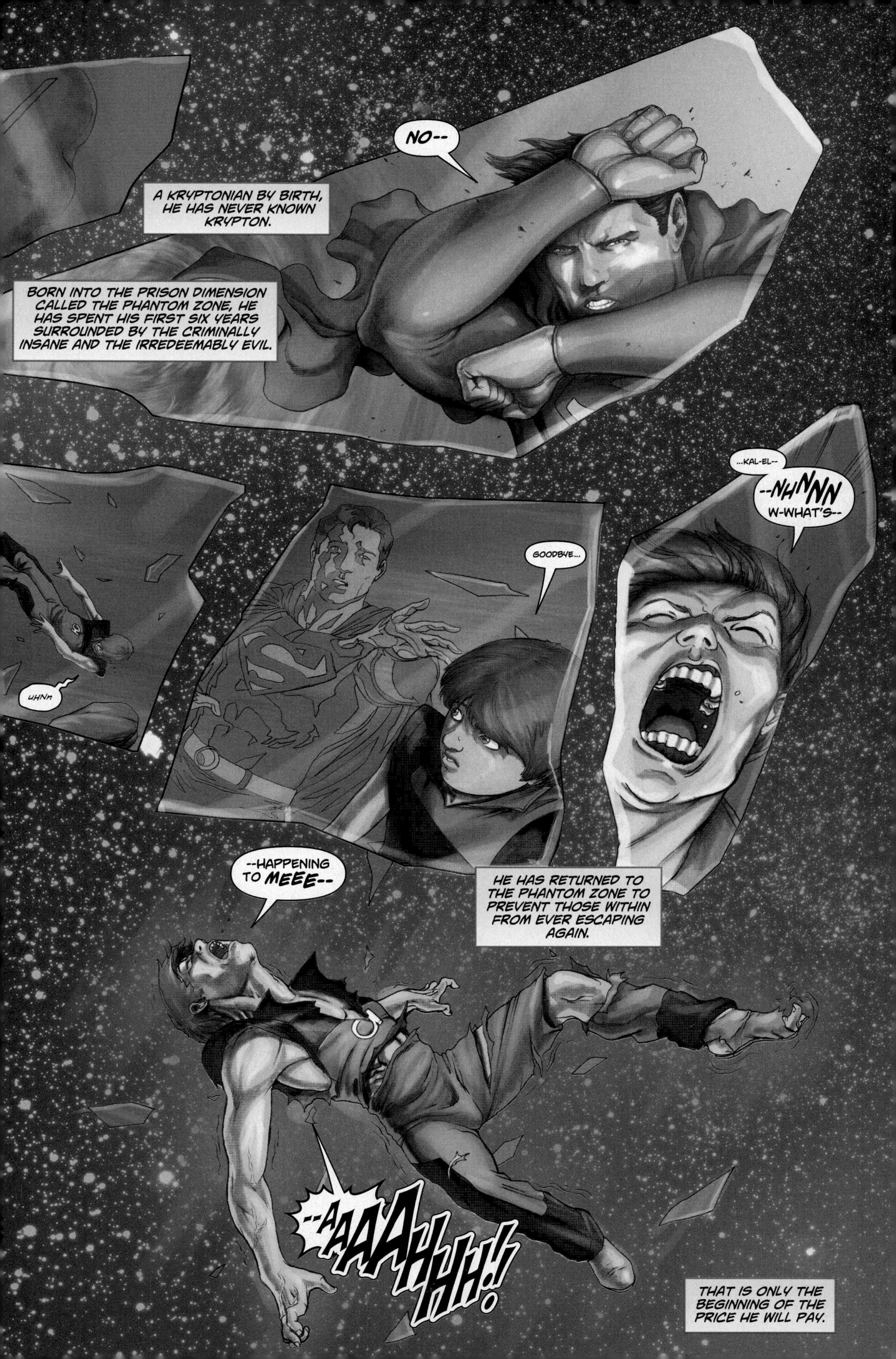
NO--
A KRYPTONIAN BY BIRTH, HE HAS NEVER KNOWN KRYPTON.
BORN INTO THE PRISON DIMENSION CALLED THE PHANTOM ZONE, HE HAS SPENT HIS FIRST SIX YEARS SURROUNDED BY THE CRIMINALLY INSANE AND THE IRREDEEMABLY EVIL.
UHNn
GOODBYE...
...KAL-EL--
--NHNNN
W-WHAT'S--
--HAPPENING TO MEEE--
HE HAS RETURNED TO THE PHANTOM ZONE TO PREVENT THOSE WITHIN FROM EVER ESCAPING AGAIN.
--AAAAHHHH!!
THAT IS ONLY THE BEGINNING OF THE PRICE HE WILL PAY.

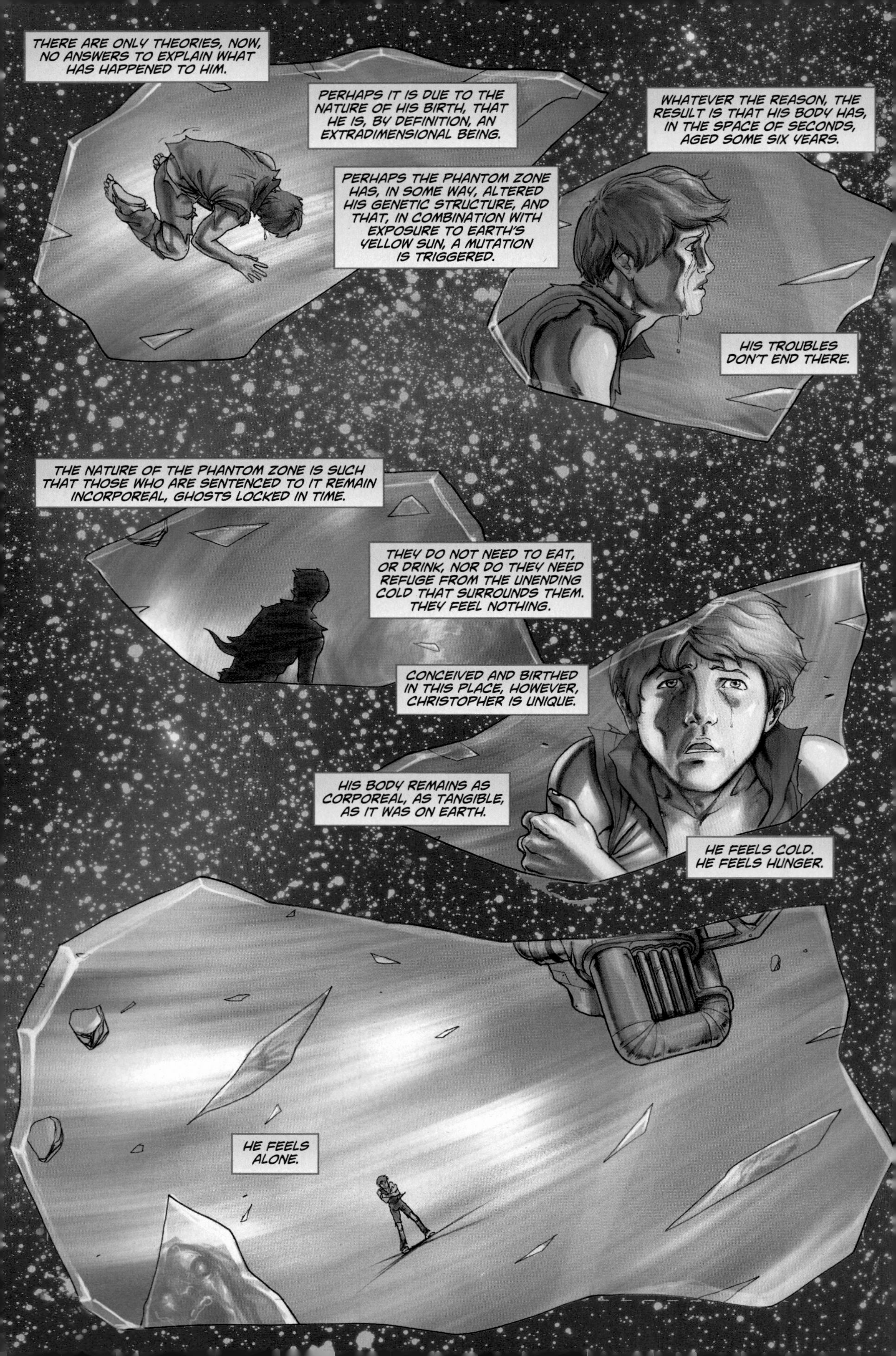
THERE ARE ONLY THEORIES, NOW, NO ANSWERS TO EXPLAIN WHAT HAS HAPPENED TO HIM.
PERHAPS IT IS DUE TO THE NATURE OF HIS BIRTH, THAT HE IS, BY DEFINITION, AN EXTRADIMENSIONAL BEING.
PERHAPS THE PHANTOM ZONE HAS, IN SOME WAY, ALTERED HIS GENETIC STRUCTURE, AND THAT, IN COMBINATION WITH EXPOSURE TO EARTH'S YELLOW SUN, A MUTATION IS TRIGGERED.
WHATEVER THE REASON, THE RESULT IS THAT HIS BODY HAS, IN THE SPACE OF SECONDS, AGED SOME SIX YEARS.
HIS TROUBLES DON'T END THERE.
THE NATURE OF THE PHANTOM ZONE IS SUCH THAT THOSE WHO ARE SENTENCED TO IT REMAIN INCORPOREAL, GHOSTS LOCKED IN TIME.
THEY DO NOT NEED TO EAT, OR DRINK, NOR DO THEY NEED REFUGE FROM THE UNENDING COLD THAT SURROUNDS THEM. THEY FEEL NOTHING.
CONCEIVED AND BIRTHED IN THIS PLACE, HOWEVER, CHRISTOPHER IS UNIQUE.
HIS BODY REMAINS AS CORPOREAL, AS TANGIBLE, AS IT WAS ON EARTH.
HE FEELS COLD. HE FEELS HUNGER.
HE FEELS ALONE.

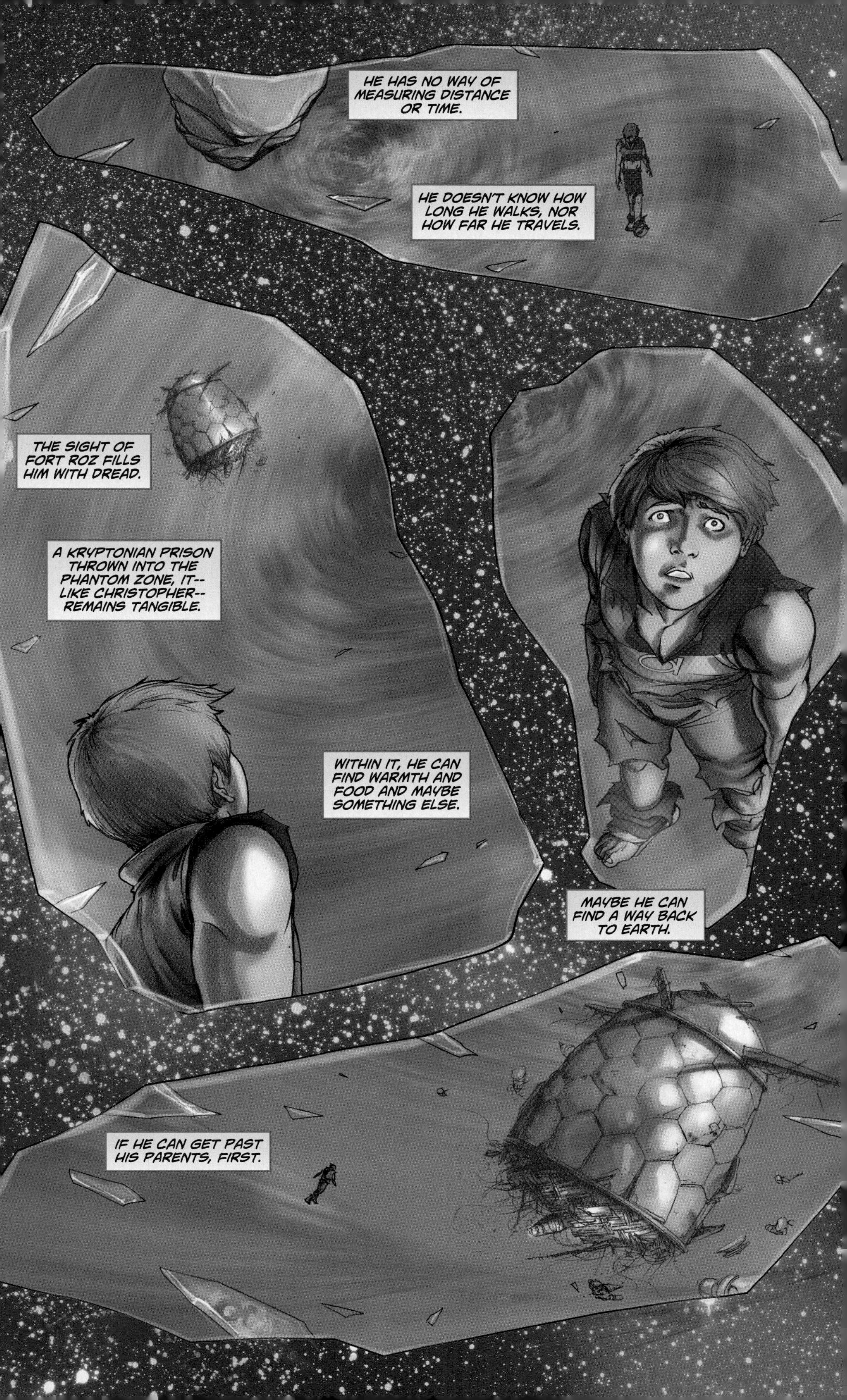
HE HAS NO WAY OF MEASURING DISTANCE OR TIME.
HE DOESN'T KNOW HOW LONG HE WALKS, NOR HOW FAR HE TRAVELS.
THE SIGHT OF FORT ROZ FILLS HIM WITH DREAD.
A KRYPTONIAN PRISON THROWN INTO THE PHANTOM ZONE, IT-- LIKE CHRISTOPHER-- REMAINS TANGIBLE.
WITHIN IT, HE CAN FIND WARMTH AND FOOD AND MAYBE SOMETHING ELSE.
MAYBE HE CAN FIND A WAY BACK TO EARTH.
IF HE CAN GET PAST HIS PARENTS, FIRST.

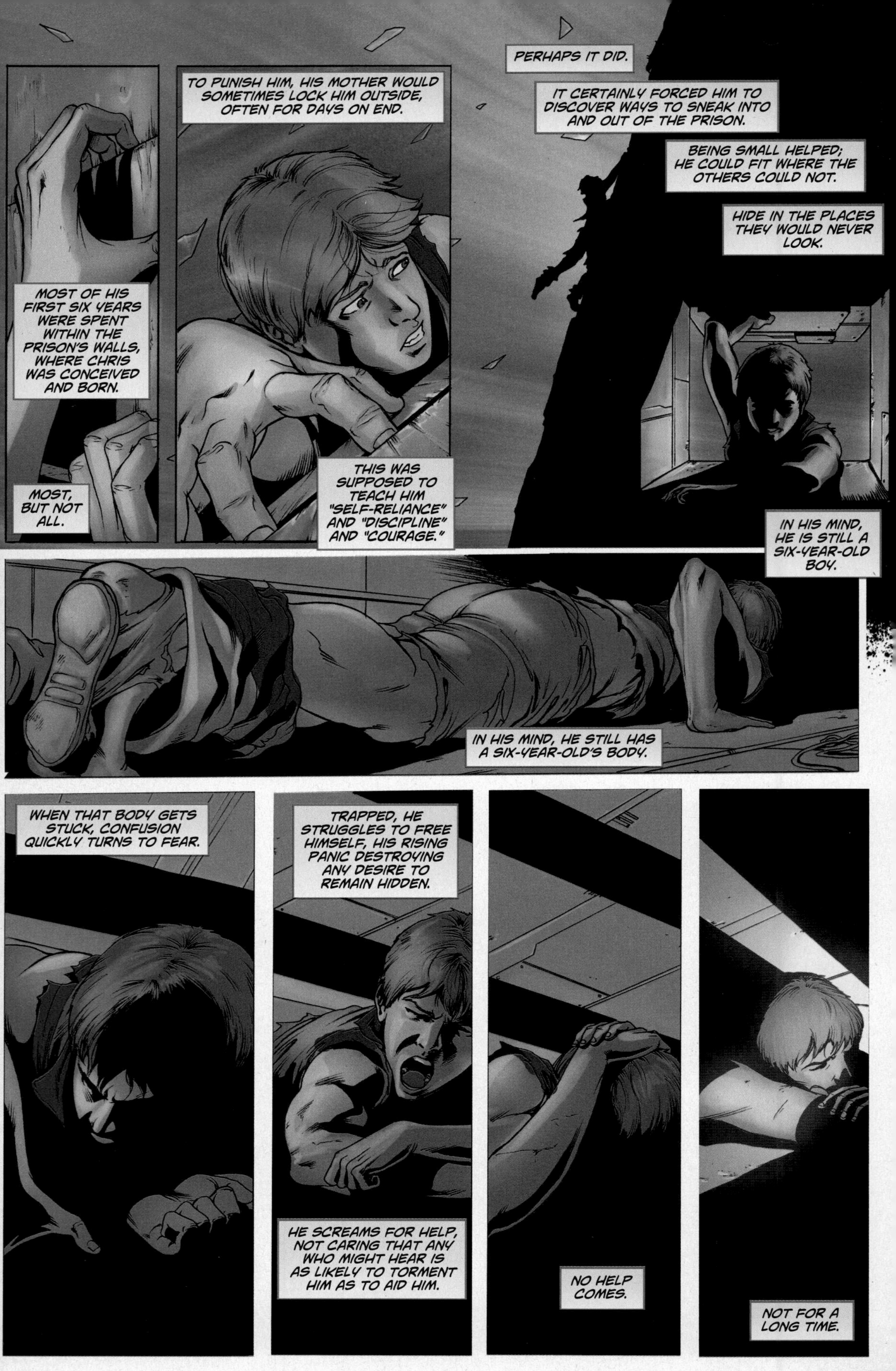
MOST OF HIS FIRST SIX YEARS WERE SPENT WITHIN THE PRISON'S WALLS, WHERE CHRIS WAS CONCEIVED AND BORN.
MOST, BUT NOT ALL.
TO PUNISH HIM, HIS MOTHER WOULD SOMETIMES LOCK HIM OUTSIDE, OFTEN FOR DAYS ON END.
THIS WAS SUPPOSED TO TEACH HIM "SELF-RELIANCE" AND "DISCIPLINE" AND "COURAGE."
PERHAPS IT DID.
IT CERTAINLY FORCED HIM TO DISCOVER WAYS TO SNEAK INTO AND OUT OF THE PRISON.
BEING SMALL HELPED; HE COULD FIT WHERE THE OTHERS COULD NOT.
HIDE IN THE PLACES THEY WOULD NEVER LOOK.
IN HIS MIND, HE IS STILL A SIX-YEAR-OLD BOY.
IN HIS MIND, HE STILL HAS A SIX-YEAR-OLD'S BODY.
WHEN THAT BODY GETS STUCK, CONFUSION QUICKLY TURNS TO FEAR.
TRAPPED, HE STRUGGLES TO FREE HIMSELF, HIS RISING PANIC DESTROYING ANY DESIRE TO REMAIN HIDDEN.
HE SCREAMS FOR HELP, NOT CARING THAT ANY WHO MIGHT HEAR IS AS LIKELY TO TORMENT HIM AS TO AID HIM.
NO HELP COMES.
NOT FOR A LONG TIME.

GENERAL ZOD LED TWENTY-NINE OF FORT ROZ'S PRISONERS IN HIS CONQUEST OF EARTH.

SEVEN DIED IN THE BATTLE TO DRIVE THEM BACK INTO THE PHANTOM ZONE.

OF THE TWENTY-TWO WHO REMAINED, ONLY ONE OF THEM EVER SHOWED CHRISTOPHER ANYTHING APPROACHING KINDNESS.

NON HAS BEEN CALLED MANY THINGS: SIMPLE; A BRUTE; AN ANIMAL; A SAVAGE.

HE WASN'T ALWAYS THAT WAY.

ONCE, HIS MIND WAS AS BRILLIANT AS ANY KRYPTON HAD EVER KNOWN.

ONCE, THAT BRILLIANCE WAS ONLY MATCHED BY HIS COMPASSION.

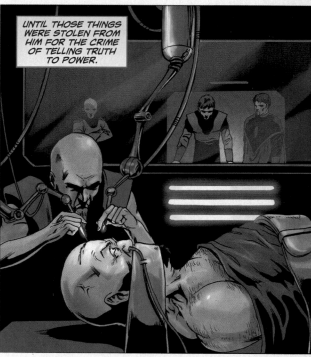

UNTIL THOSE THINGS WERE STOLEN FROM HIM FOR THE CRIME OF TELLING TRUTH TO POWER.

NON HAS THE DISTINCTION OF BEING THE ONLY PERSON IN FORT ROZ TO TREAT CHRISTOPHER WITH CONSISTENT KINDNESS.

AND IF THEY WERE KINDRED SPIRITS BEFORE, THE CHILD AND THE CHILDLIKE MAN...

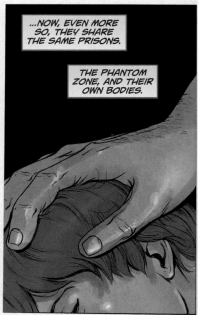

...NOW, EVEN MORE SO, THEY SHARE THE SAME PRISONS.

THE PHANTOM ZONE, AND THEIR OWN BODIES.

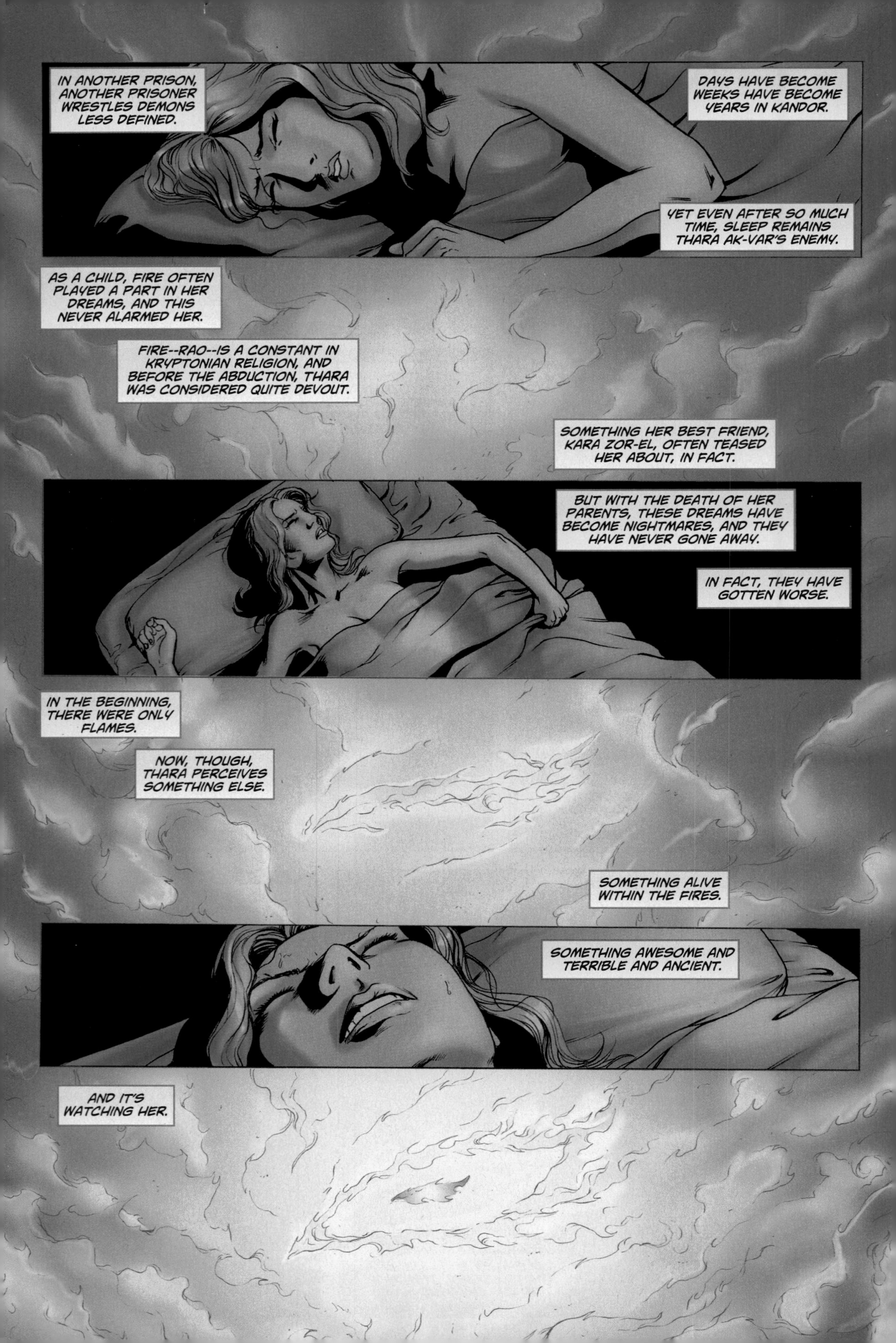
IN ANOTHER PRISON, ANOTHER PRISONER WRESTLES DEMONS LESS DEFINED.
DAYS HAVE BECOME WEEKS HAVE BECOME YEARS IN KANDOR.
YET EVEN AFTER SO MUCH TIME, SLEEP REMAINS THARA AK-VAR'S ENEMY.
AS A CHILD, FIRE OFTEN PLAYED A PART IN HER DREAMS, AND THIS NEVER ALARMED HER.
FIRE--RAO--IS A CONSTANT IN KRYPTONIAN RELIGION, AND BEFORE THE ABDUCTION, THARA WAS CONSIDERED QUITE DEVOUT.
SOMETHING HER BEST FRIEND, KARA ZOR-EL, OFTEN TEASED HER ABOUT, IN FACT.
BUT WITH THE DEATH OF HER PARENTS, THESE DREAMS HAVE BECOME NIGHTMARES, AND THEY HAVE NEVER GONE AWAY.
IN FACT, THEY HAVE GOTTEN WORSE.
IN THE BEGINNING, THERE WERE ONLY FLAMES.
NOW, THOUGH, THARA PERCEIVES SOMETHING ELSE.
SOMETHING ALIVE WITHIN THE FIRES.
SOMETHING AWESOME AND TERRIBLE AND ANCIENT.
AND IT'S WATCHING HER.

WHEN ZOR-EL, ELECTED WITH ALURA TO HEAD KANDOR'S GOVERNMENT, ASKED THARA TO BECOME HIS HEAD OF SECURITY, MANY WERE SURPRISED.

CERTAINLY, THERE WERE OTHERS IN THE MILITARY GUILD MORE QUALIFIED.

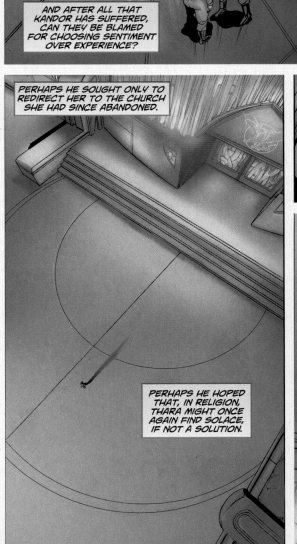

BUT IN THARA, BOTH ZOR-EL AND ALURA SEE THE MEMORY OF THEIR LOST DAUGHTER.

AND AFTER ALL THAT KANDOR HAS SUFFERED, CAN THEY BE BLAMED FOR CHOOSING SENTIMENT OVER EXPERIENCE?

WHETHER ZOR-EL SAW RELIGIOUS SIGNIFICANCE IN WHAT THARA TOLD HIM WILL NEVER BE KNOWN.

PERHAPS, UNABLE TO OFFER AN ANSWER TO HIS SURROGATE DAUGHTER THROUGH SCIENCE, HE OFFERED PHILOSOPHY.

PERHAPS HE SOUGHT ONLY TO REDIRECT HER TO THE CHURCH SHE HAD SINCE ABANDONED.

PERHAPS HE HOPED THAT, IN RELIGION, THARA MIGHT ONCE AGAIN FIND SOLACE, IF NOT A SOLUTION.

WHAT SHE FOUND WAS SOMETHING ELSE ENTIRELY.

WHAT SHE FOUND WAS A LEGACY.

KRYPTONIAN RELIGIOUS BELIEF HAS BEEN CHARACTERIZED AS POLYTHEISTIC, AKIN TO HINDUISM ON EARTH. THIS IS INACCURATE.

A BETTER ANALOGUE MIGHT BE CATHOLICISM, WITH RAO, THE SUN GOD, AS A MONOTHEISTIC DEITY, SURROUNDED BY NAMED "ANGELS," CYTHONNA, YUDA, AND THE LIKE.

OTHER ASPECTS OF THE RELIGION MIGHT BEST BE LIKENED TO TERRAN CABALS, OR EVEN CULTS, WITH LAYERS OF SECRETS CONCEALING FURTHER MYSTERIES.

THIS MAY EXPLAIN WHY THE RELIGIOUS GUILD IS SO SMALL IN COMPARISON TO THE OTHER GUILDS, AND WHY SO LITTLE IS KNOWN ABOUT THEM.

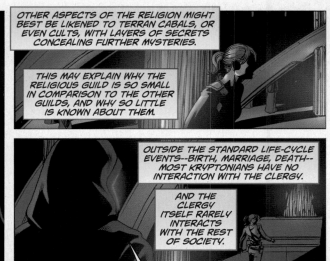

OUTSIDE THE STANDARD LIFE-CYCLE EVENTS--BIRTH, MARRIAGE, DEATH-- MOST KRYPTONIANS HAVE NO INTERACTION WITH THE CLERGY.

AND THE CLERGY ITSELF RARELY INTERACTS WITH THE REST OF SOCIETY.

AK-VAR.

IT SHOULD BE NOTED, HERE, THAT KRYPTONIAN NAMING CONVENTION USES A PERSONAL--"AK"-- TO PRECEDE A FAMILIAL--"VAR."

AK-VAR.

AK-VAR.

FOR MALES, THIS SUFFICES. THUS THE HOUSE OF VAR WOULD HAVE SONS NAMED "KEM-VAR" OR "BYN-VAR."

FEMALE NAMES, HOWEVER, TAKE A PERSONAL--"TES" OR "THARA"--TO PRECEDE A HUSBAND OR FATHER--"AK-VAR."

AK-VAR.

AK-VAR.

AK-VAR.

THIS VARIATION MAKES THE GENERATIONAL REPEAT OF A SPECIFIC NAME, IN THIS CASE "AK-VAR," INCREDIBLY RARE.

YES.

TO HEAR THARA AK-VAR TELL IT, THEY KNEW SHE WAS COMING.

TO HEAR THARA AK-VAR TELL IT, THEY HAD BEEN WAITING FOR HER.

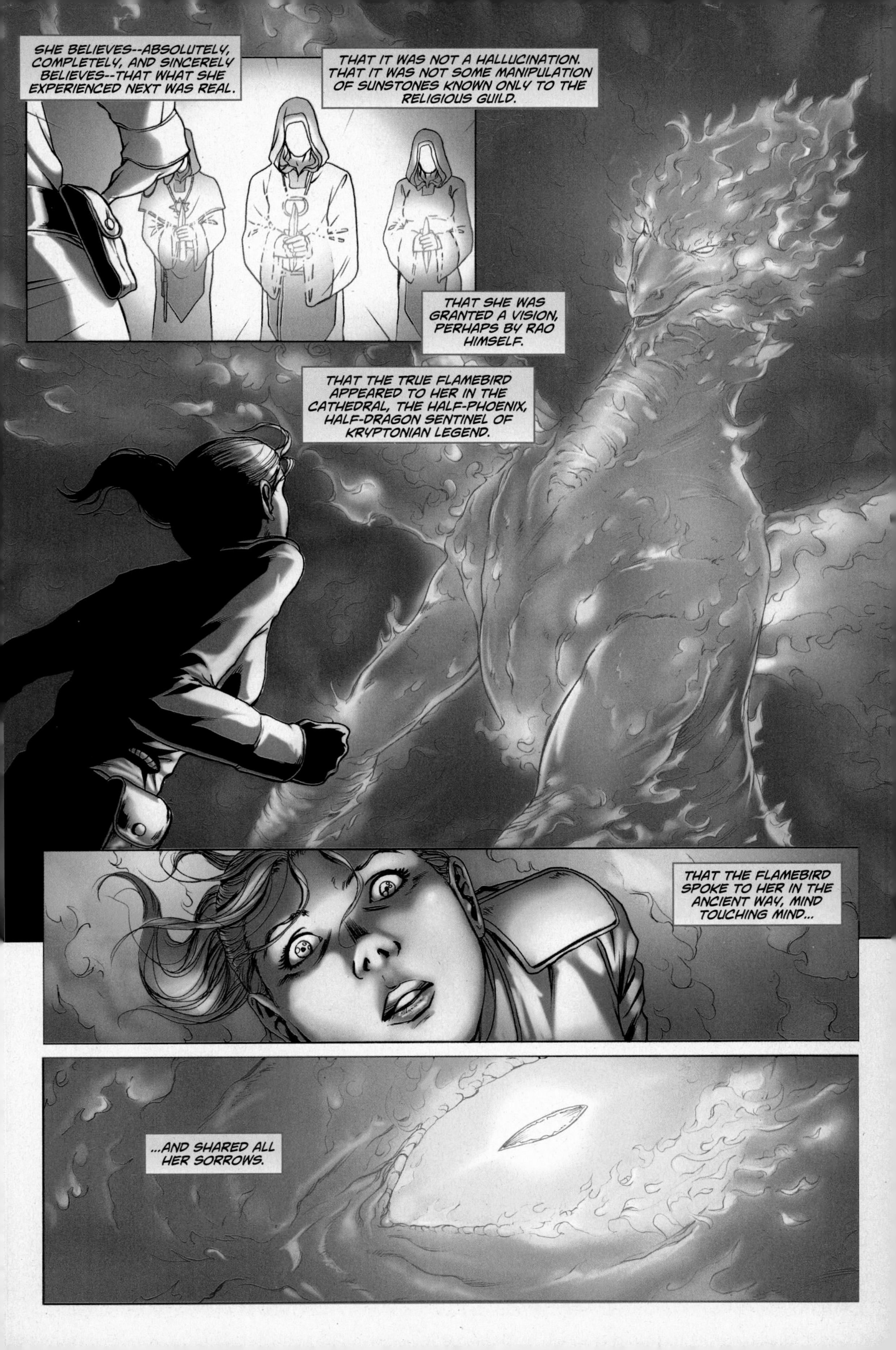
SHE BELIEVES--ABSOLUTELY, COMPLETELY, AND SINCERELY BELIEVES--THAT WHAT SHE EXPERIENCED NEXT WAS REAL.
THAT IT WAS NOT A HALLUCINATION. THAT IT WAS NOT SOME MANIPULATION OF SUNSTONES KNOWN ONLY TO THE RELIGIOUS GUILD.
THAT SHE WAS GRANTED A VISION, PERHAPS BY RAO HIMSELF.
THAT THE TRUE FLAMEBIRD APPEARED TO HER IN THE CATHEDRAL, THE HALF-PHOENIX, HALF-DRAGON SENTINEL OF KRYPTONIAN LEGEND.
THAT THE FLAMEBIRD SPOKE TO HER IN THE ANCIENT WAY, MIND TOUCHING MIND...
...AND SHARED ALL HER SORROWS.

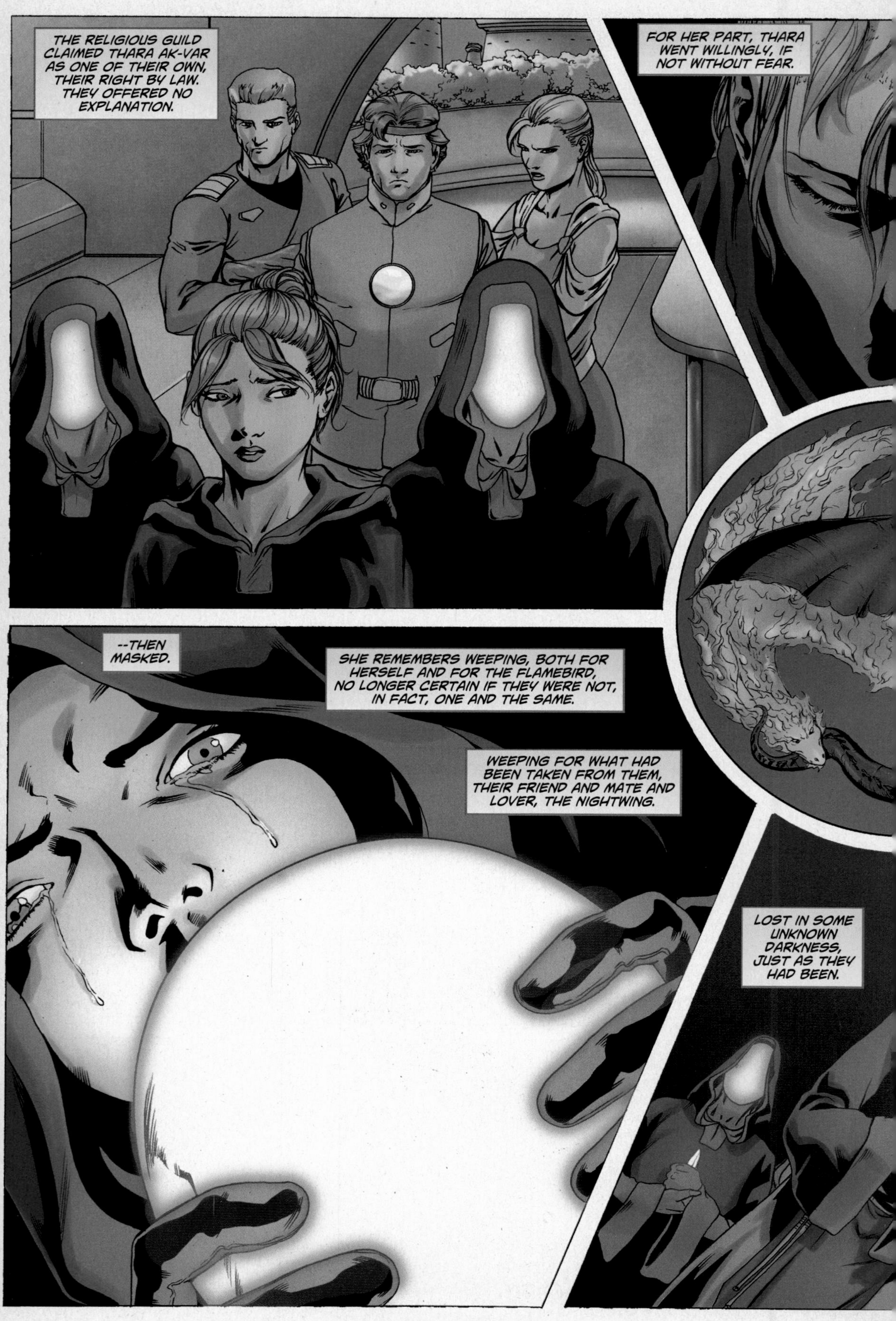
THE RELIGIOUS GUILD CLAIMED THARA AK-VAR AS ONE OF THEIR OWN, THEIR RIGHT BY LAW. THEY OFFERED NO EXPLANATION.
FOR HER PART, THARA WENT WILLINGLY, IF NOT WITHOUT FEAR.
--THEN MASKED.
SHE REMEMBERS WEEPING, BOTH FOR HERSELF AND FOR THE FLAMEBIRD, NO LONGER CERTAIN IF THEY WERE NOT, IN FACT, ONE AND THE SAME.
WEEPING FOR WHAT HAD BEEN TAKEN FROM THEM, THEIR FRIEND AND MATE AND LOVER, THE NIGHTWING.
LOST IN SOME UNKNOWN DARKNESS, JUST AS THEY HAD BEEN.

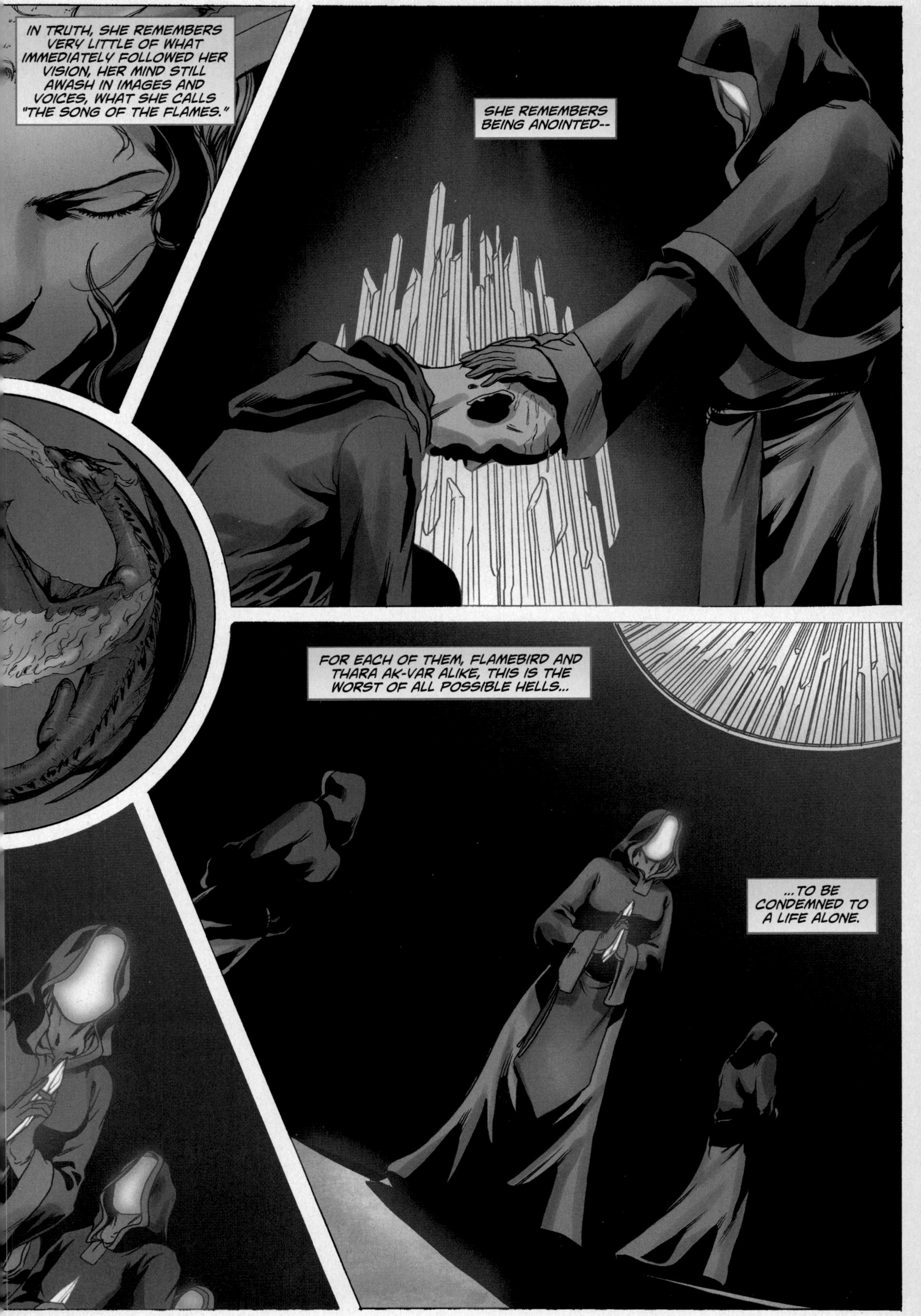
IN TRUTH, SHE REMEMBERS VERY LITTLE OF WHAT IMMEDIATELY FOLLOWED HER VISION, HER MIND STILL AWASH IN IMAGES AND VOICES, WHAT SHE CALLS "THE SONG OF THE FLAMES."
SHE REMEMBERS BEING ANOINTED--
FOR EACH OF THEM, FLAMEBIRD AND THARA AK-VAR ALIKE, THIS IS THE WORST OF ALL POSSIBLE HELLS...
...TO BE CONDEMNED TO A LIFE ALONE.

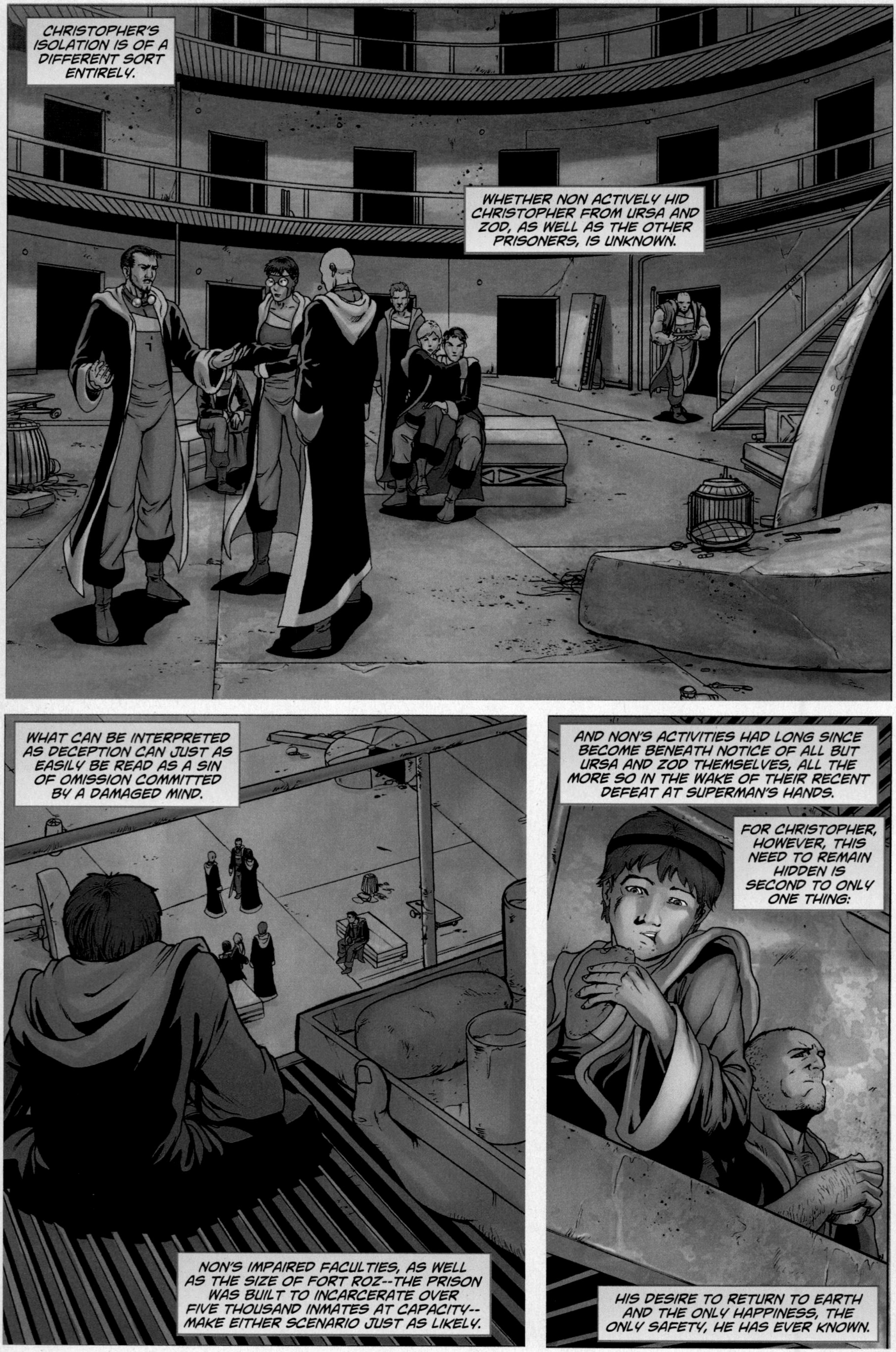
CHRISTOPHER'S ISOLATION IS OF A DIFFERENT SORT ENTIRELY.
WHETHER NON ACTIVELY HID CHRISTOPHER FROM URSA AND ZOD, AS WELL AS THE OTHER PRISONERS, IS UNKNOWN.
WHAT CAN BE INTERPRETED AS DECEPTION CAN JUST AS EASILY BE READ AS A SIN OF OMISSION COMMITTED BY A DAMAGED MIND.
NON'S IMPAIRED FACULTIES, AS WELL AS THE SIZE OF FORT ROZ--THE PRISON WAS BUILT TO INCARCERATE OVER FIVE THOUSAND INMATES AT CAPACITY--MAKE EITHER SCENARIO JUST AS LIKELY.
AND NON'S ACTIVITIES HAD LONG SINCE BECOME BENEATH NOTICE OF ALL BUT URSA AND ZOD THEMSELVES, ALL THE MORE SO IN THE WAKE OF THEIR RECENT DEFEAT AT SUPERMAN'S HANDS.
FOR CHRISTOPHER, HOWEVER, THIS NEED TO REMAIN HIDDEN IS SECOND TO ONLY ONE THING:
HIS DESIRE TO RETURN TO EARTH AND THE ONLY HAPPINESS, THE ONLY SAFETY, HE HAS EVER KNOWN.

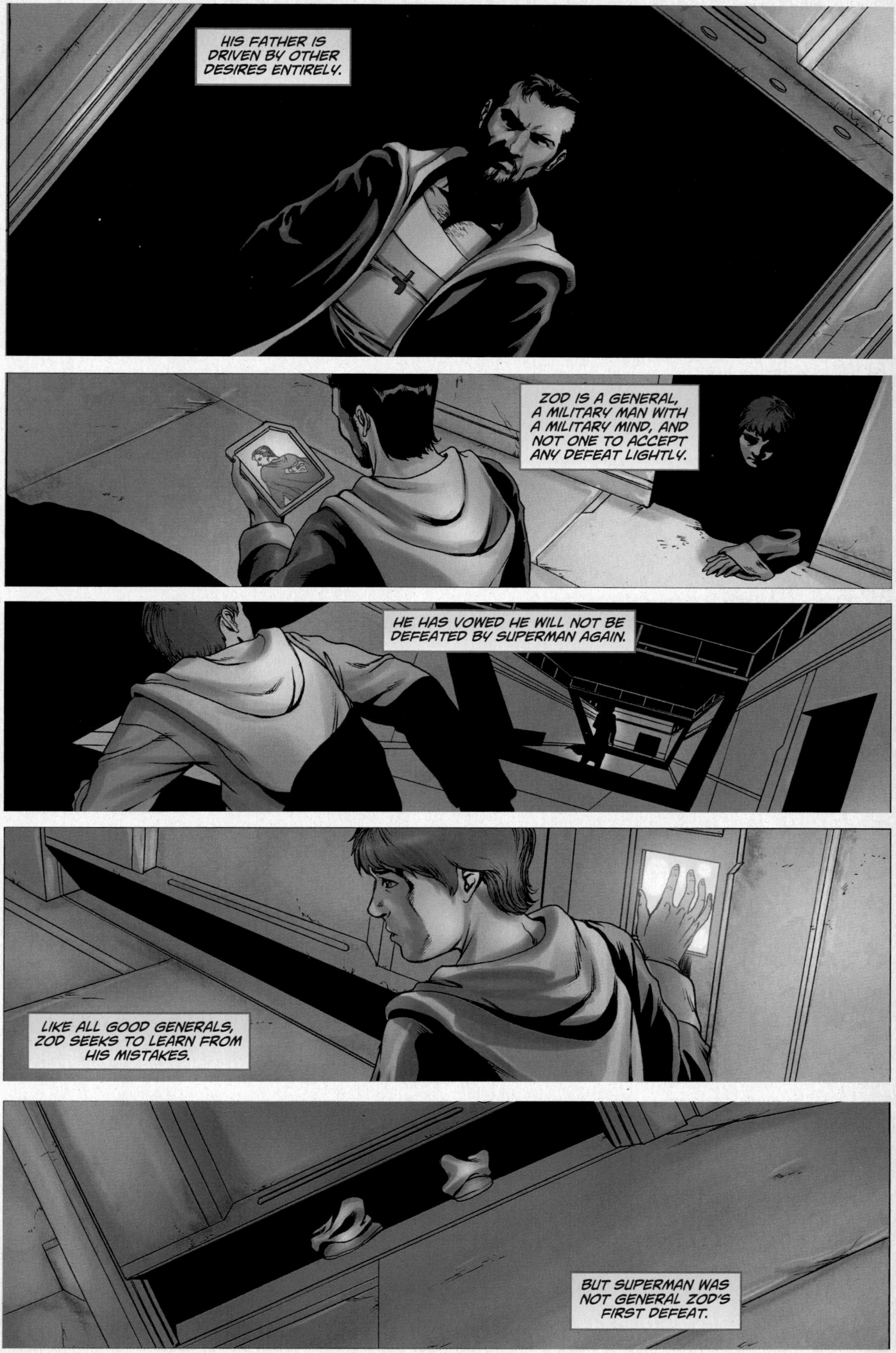
HIS FATHER IS DRIVEN BY OTHER DESIRES ENTIRELY.
ZOD IS A GENERAL, A MILITARY MAN WITH A MILITARY MIND, AND NOT ONE TO ACCEPT ANY DEFEAT LIGHTLY.
HE HAS VOWED HE WILL NOT BE DEFEATED BY SUPERMAN AGAIN.
LIKE ALL GOOD GENERALS, ZOD SEEKS TO LEARN FROM HIS MISTAKES.
BUT SUPERMAN WAS NOT GENERAL ZOD'S FIRST DEFEAT.

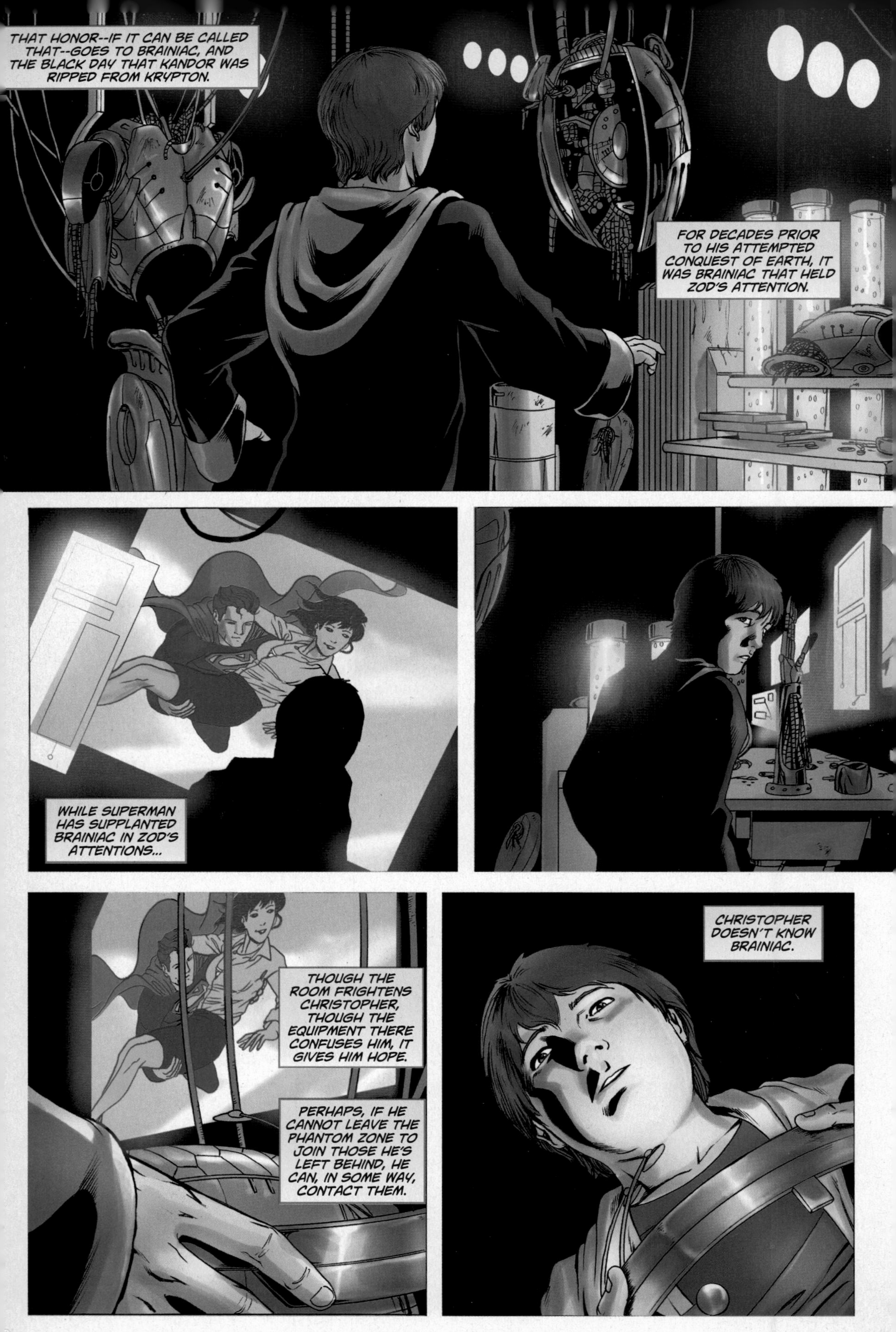
THAT HONOR--IF IT CAN BE CALLED THAT--GOES TO BRAINIAC, AND THE BLACK DAY THAT KANDOR WAS RIPPED FROM KRYPTON.
FOR DECADES PRIOR TO HIS ATTEMPTED CONQUEST OF EARTH, IT WAS BRAINIAC THAT HELD ZOD'S ATTENTION.
WHILE SUPERMAN HAS SUPPLANTED BRAINIAC IN ZOD'S ATTENTIONS...
THOUGH THE ROOM FRIGHTENS CHRISTOPHER, THOUGH THE EQUIPMENT THERE CONFUSES HIM, IT GIVES HIM HOPE.
PERHAPS, IF HE CANNOT LEAVE THE PHANTOM ZONE TO JOIN THOSE HE'S LEFT BEHIND, HE CAN, IN SOME WAY, CONTACT THEM.
CHRISTOPHER DOESN'T KNOW BRAINIAC.

FOR YEARS, HE DEVOTED HIMSELF TO THE STUDY OF HIS ENEMY.

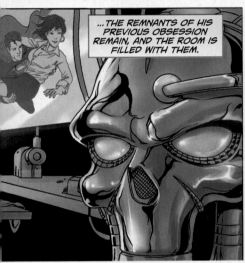

...THE REMNANTS OF HIS PREVIOUS OBSESSION REMAIN, AND THE ROOM IS FILLED WITH THEM.

THOSE BITS AND PIECES OF BRAINIAC TECHNOLOGY THAT HAVE "WASHED UP" WITHIN THE PHANTOM ZONE DURING THE LONG YEARS OF IMPRISONMENT.

EVERYTHING ZOD COULD FIND, ANYTHING THAT MIGHT HELP HIM UNDERSTAND HIS ENEMY, ALL GATHERED HERE.

HE DOESN'T KNOW KANDOR.

BUT WITH ONE DECISION...

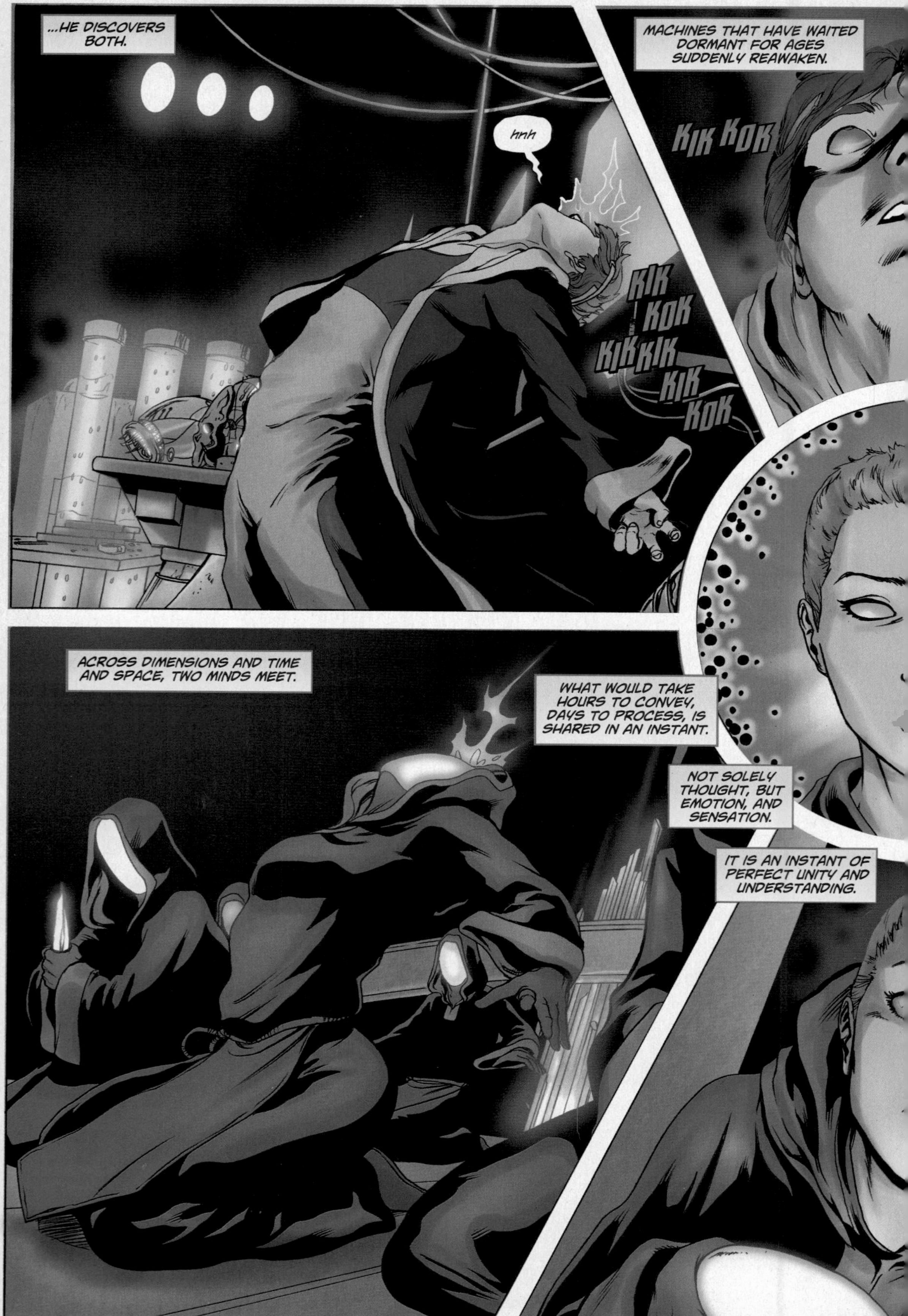
...HE DISCOVERS BOTH.
hnh
MACHINES THAT HAVE WAITED DORMANT FOR AGES SUDDENLY REAWAKEN.
KIK KOK
KIK KOK KIK KIK KIK KOK
ACROSS DIMENSIONS AND TIME AND SPACE, TWO MINDS MEET.
WHAT WOULD TAKE HOURS TO CONVEY, DAYS TO PROCESS, IS SHARED IN AN INSTANT.
NOT SOLELY THOUGHT, BUT EMOTION, AND SENSATION.
IT IS AN INSTANT OF PERFECT UNITY AND UNDERSTANDING.

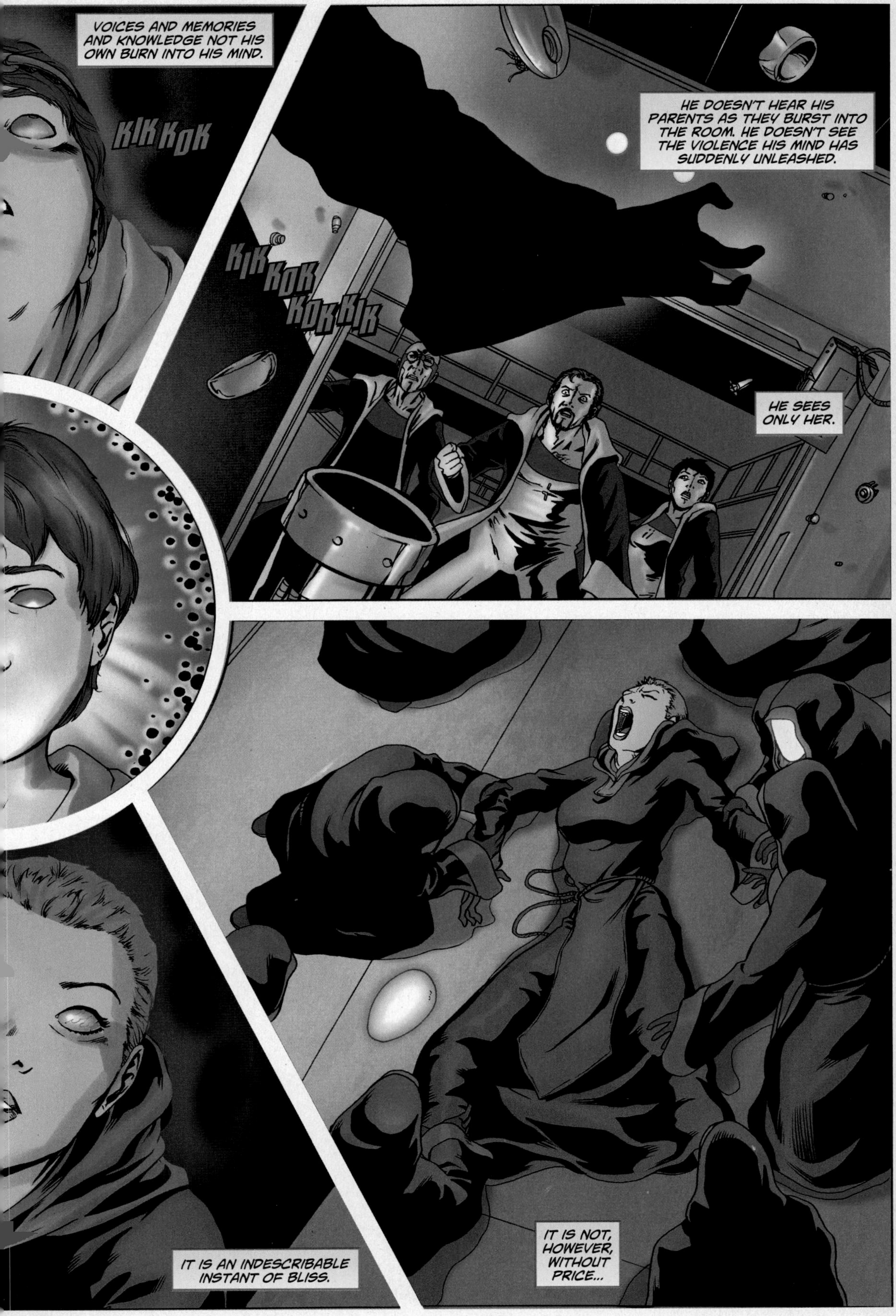
VOICES AND MEMORIES AND KNOWLEDGE NOT HIS OWN BURN INTO HIS MIND.
KIK KOK
KIK KOK KOK KIK
HE DOESN'T HEAR HIS PARENTS AS THEY BURST INTO THE ROOM. HE DOESN'T SEE THE VIOLENCE HIS MIND HAS SUDDENLY UNLEASHED.
HE SEES ONLY HER.
IT IS AN INDESCRIBABLE INSTANT OF BLISS.
IT IS NOT, HOWEVER, WITHOUT PRICE...

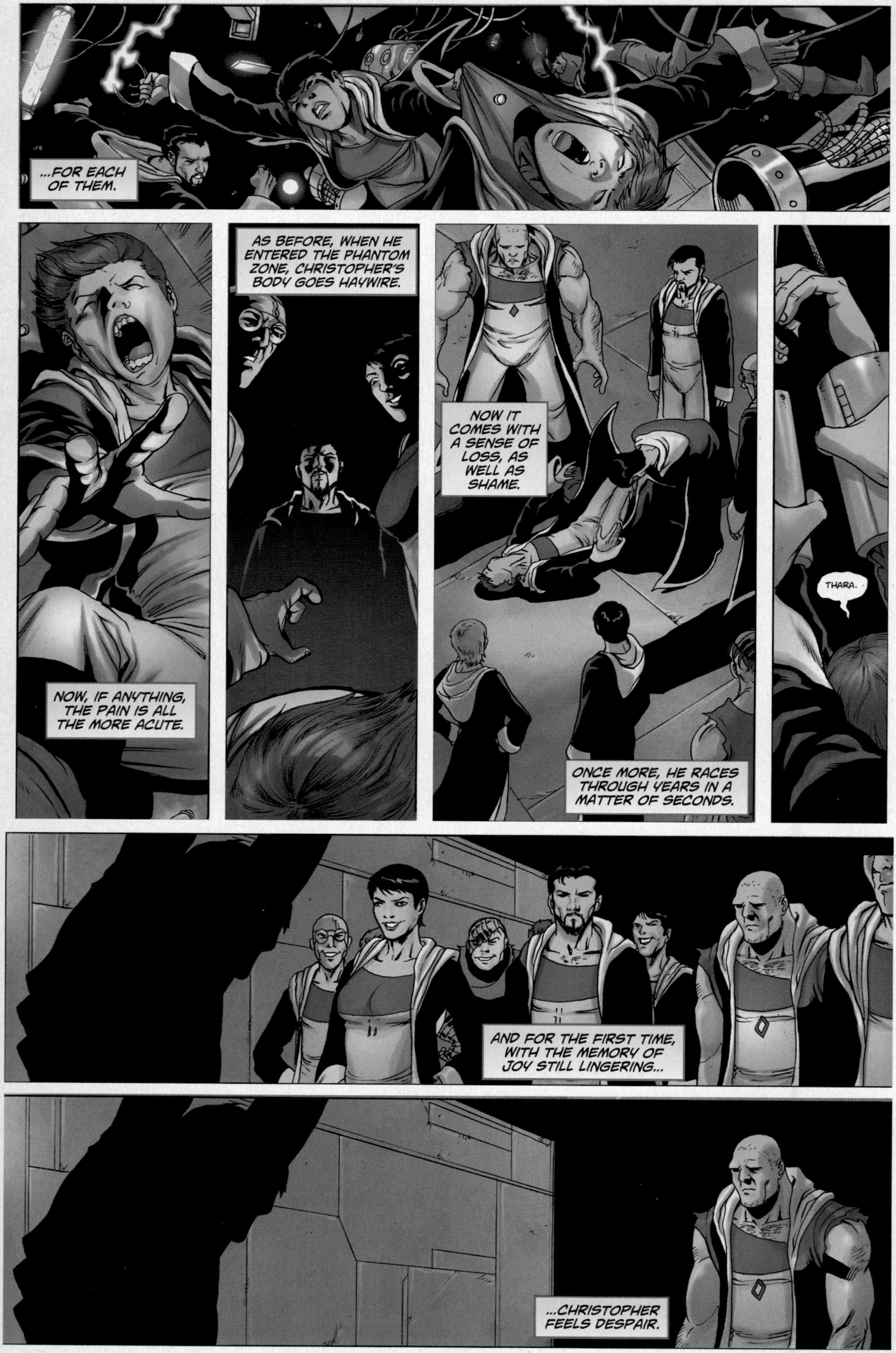
...FOR EACH OF THEM.
NOW, IF ANYTHING, THE PAIN IS ALL THE MORE ACUTE.
AS BEFORE, WHEN HE ENTERED THE PHANTOM ZONE, CHRISTOPHER'S BODY GOES HAYWIRE.
NOW IT COMES WITH A SENSE OF LOSS, AS WELL AS SHAME.
ONCE MORE, HE RACES THROUGH YEARS IN A MATTER OF SECONDS.
THARA.
AND FOR THE FIRST TIME, WITH THE MEMORY OF JOY STILL LINGERING...
...CHRISTOPHER FEELS DESPAIR.

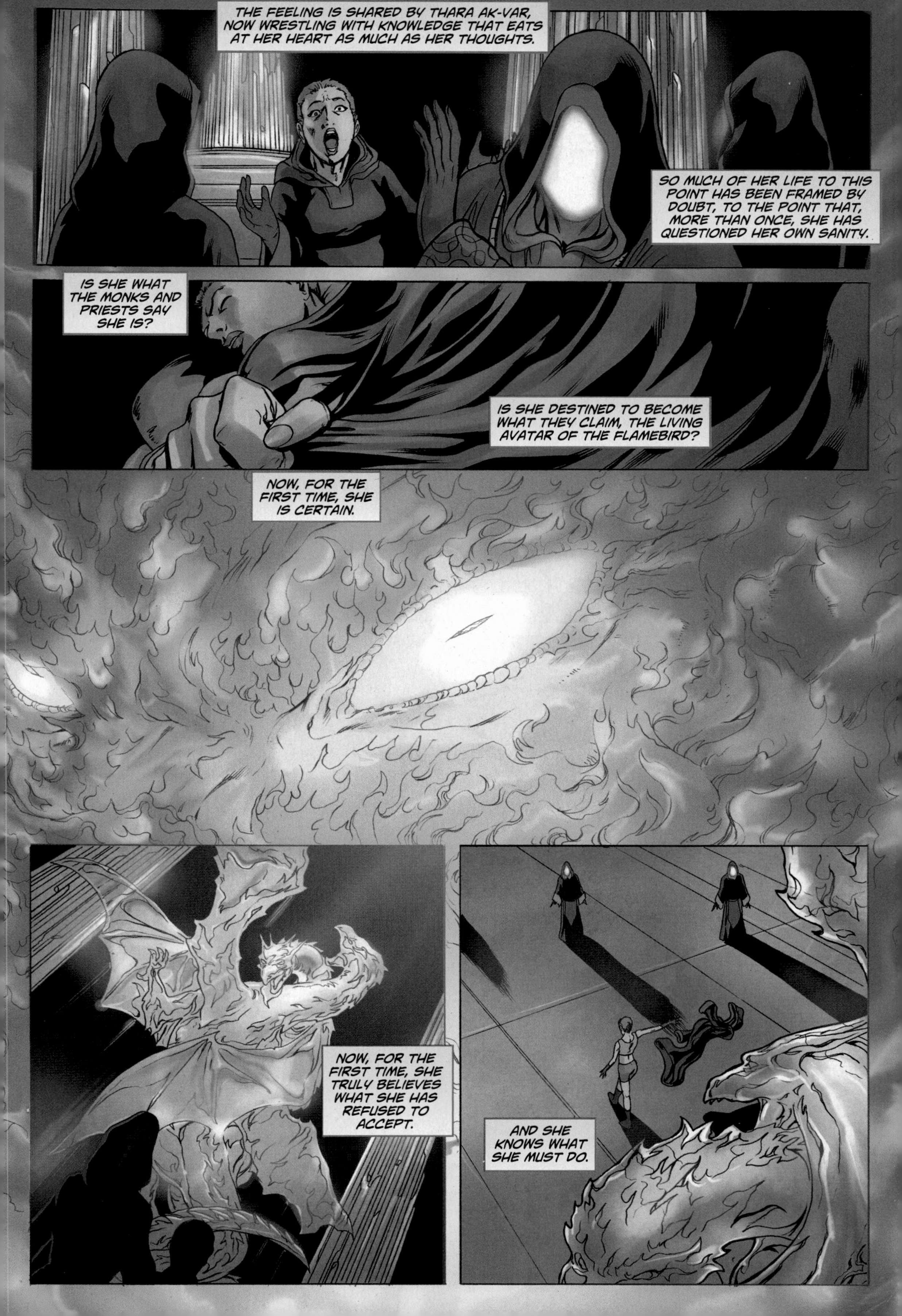
THE FEELING IS SHARED BY THARA AK-VAR, NOW WRESTLING WITH KNOWLEDGE THAT EATS AT HER HEART AS MUCH AS HER THOUGHTS.
SO MUCH OF HER LIFE TO THIS POINT HAS BEEN FRAMED BY DOUBT, TO THE POINT THAT, MORE THAN ONCE, SHE HAS QUESTIONED HER OWN SANITY.
IS SHE WHAT THE MONKS AND PRIESTS SAY SHE IS?
IS SHE DESTINED TO BECOME WHAT THEY CLAIM, THE LIVING AVATAR OF THE FLAMEBIRD?
NOW, FOR THE FIRST TIME, SHE IS CERTAIN.
NOW, FOR THE FIRST TIME, SHE TRULY BELIEVES WHAT SHE HAS REFUSED TO ACCEPT.
AND SHE KNOWS WHAT SHE MUST DO.

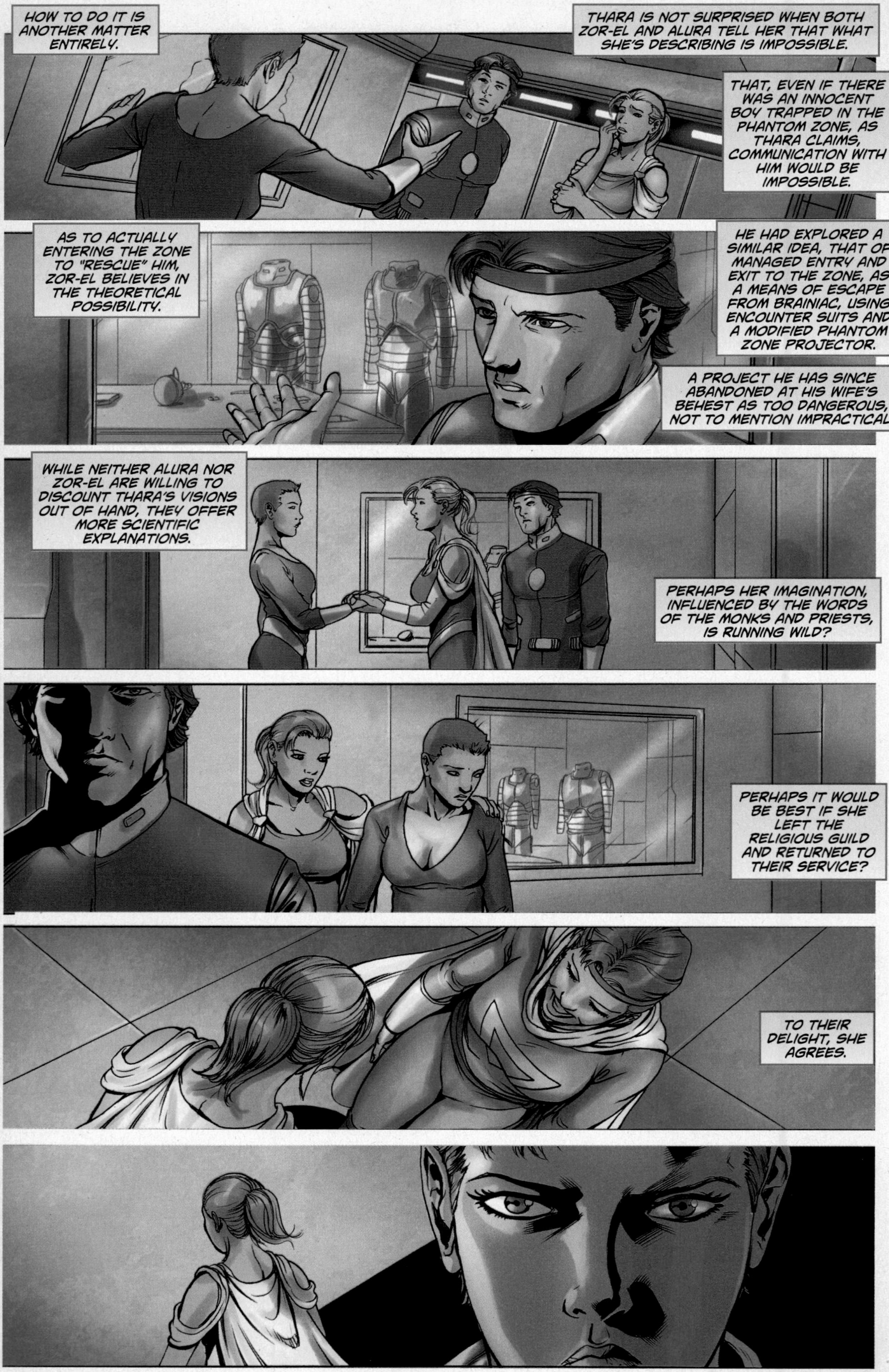
HOW TO DO IT IS ANOTHER MATTER ENTIRELY.
THARA IS NOT SURPRISED WHEN BOTH ZOR-EL AND ALURA TELL HER THAT WHAT SHE'S DESCRIBING IS IMPOSSIBLE.
THAT, EVEN IF THERE WAS AN INNOCENT BOY TRAPPED IN THE PHANTOM ZONE, AS THARA CLAIMS, COMMUNICATION WITH HIM WOULD BE IMPOSSIBLE.
AS TO ACTUALLY ENTERING THE ZONE TO "RESCUE" HIM, ZOR-EL BELIEVES IN THE THEORETICAL POSSIBILITY.
HE HAD EXPLORED A SIMILAR IDEA, THAT OF MANAGED ENTRY AND EXIT TO THE ZONE, AS A MEANS OF ESCAPE FROM BRAINIAC, USING ENCOUNTER SUITS AND A MODIFIED PHANTOM ZONE PROJECTOR.
A PROJECT HE HAS SINCE ABANDONED AT HIS WIFE'S BEHEST AS TOO DANGEROUS, NOT TO MENTION IMPRACTICAL.
WHILE NEITHER ALURA NOR ZOR-EL ARE WILLING TO DISCOUNT THARA'S VISIONS OUT OF HAND, THEY OFFER MORE SCIENTIFIC EXPLANATIONS.
PERHAPS HER IMAGINATION, INFLUENCED BY THE WORDS OF THE MONKS AND PRIESTS, IS RUNNING WILD?
PERHAPS IT WOULD BE BEST IF SHE LEFT THE RELIGIOUS GUILD AND RETURNED TO THEIR SERVICE?
TO THEIR DELIGHT, SHE AGREES.

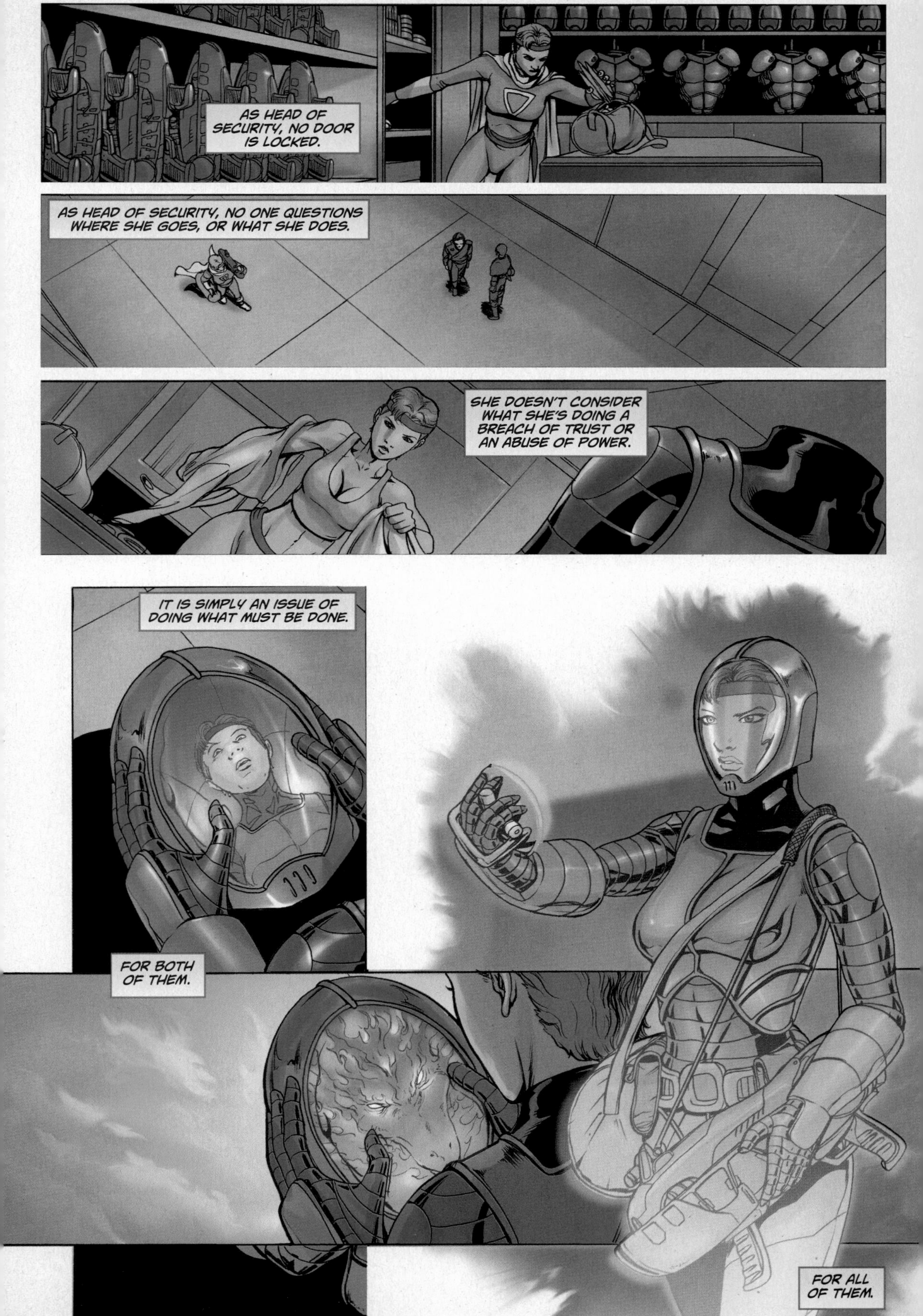
AS HEAD OF SECURITY, NO DOOR IS LOCKED.
AS HEAD OF SECURITY, NO ONE QUESTIONS WHERE SHE GOES, OR WHAT SHE DOES.
SHE DOESN'T CONSIDER WHAT SHE'S DOING A BREACH OF TRUST OR AN ABUSE OF POWER.
IT IS SIMPLY AN ISSUE OF DOING WHAT MUST BE DONE.
FOR BOTH OF THEM.
FOR ALL OF THEM.

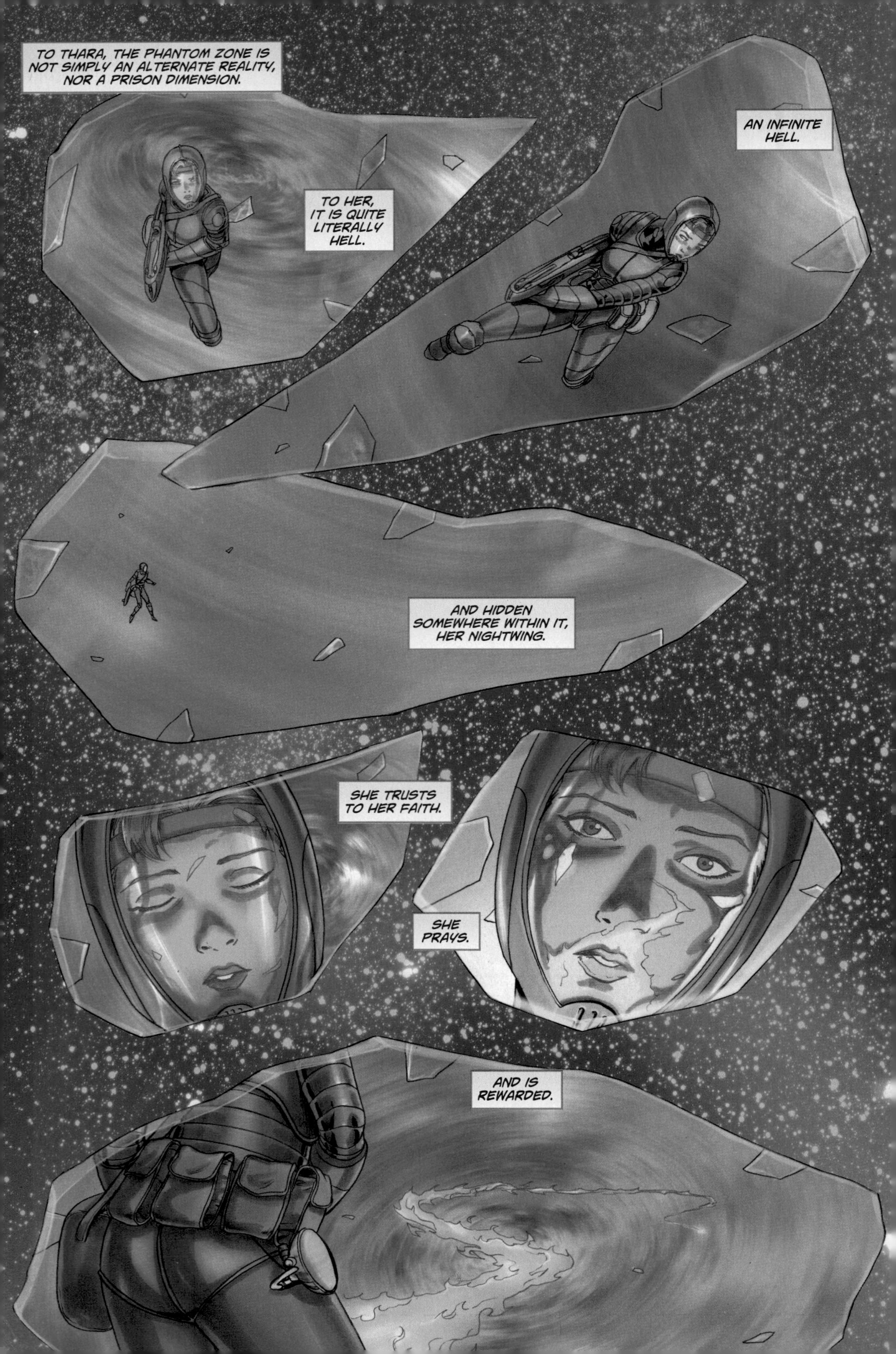
TO THARA, THE PHANTOM ZONE IS NOT SIMPLY AN ALTERNATE REALITY, NOR A PRISON DIMENSION.
TO HER, IT IS QUITE LITERALLY HELL.
AN INFINITE HELL.
AND HIDDEN SOMEWHERE WITHIN IT, HER NIGHTWING.
SHE TRUSTS TO HER FAITH.
SHE PRAYS.
AND IS REWARDED.

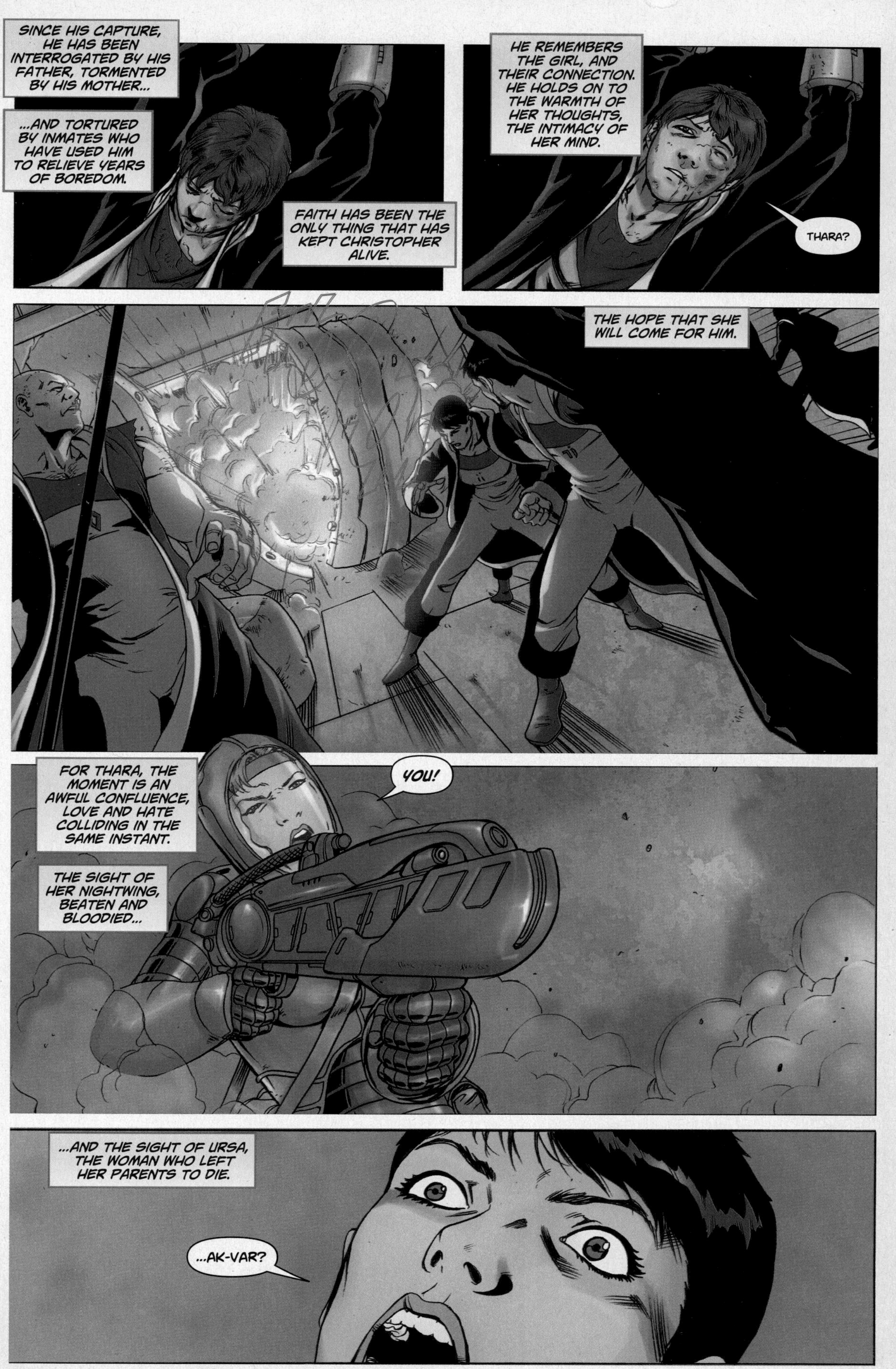
SINCE HIS CAPTURE, HE HAS BEEN INTERROGATED BY HIS FATHER, TORMENTED BY HIS MOTHER...
...AND TORTURED BY INMATES WHO HAVE USED HIM TO RELIEVE YEARS OF BOREDOM.
FAITH HAS BEEN THE ONLY THING THAT HAS KEPT CHRISTOPHER ALIVE.
HE REMEMBERS THE GIRL, AND THEIR CONNECTION. HE HOLDS ON TO THE WARMTH OF HER THOUGHTS, THE INTIMACY OF HER MIND.
THARA?
THE HOPE THAT SHE WILL COME FOR HIM.
FOR THARA, THE MOMENT IS AN AWFUL CONFLUENCE, LOVE AND HATE COLLIDING IN THE SAME INSTANT.
YOU!
THE SIGHT OF HER NIGHTWING, BEATEN AND BLOODIED...
...AND THE SIGHT OF URSA, THE WOMAN WHO LEFT HER PARENTS TO DIE.
...AK-VAR?

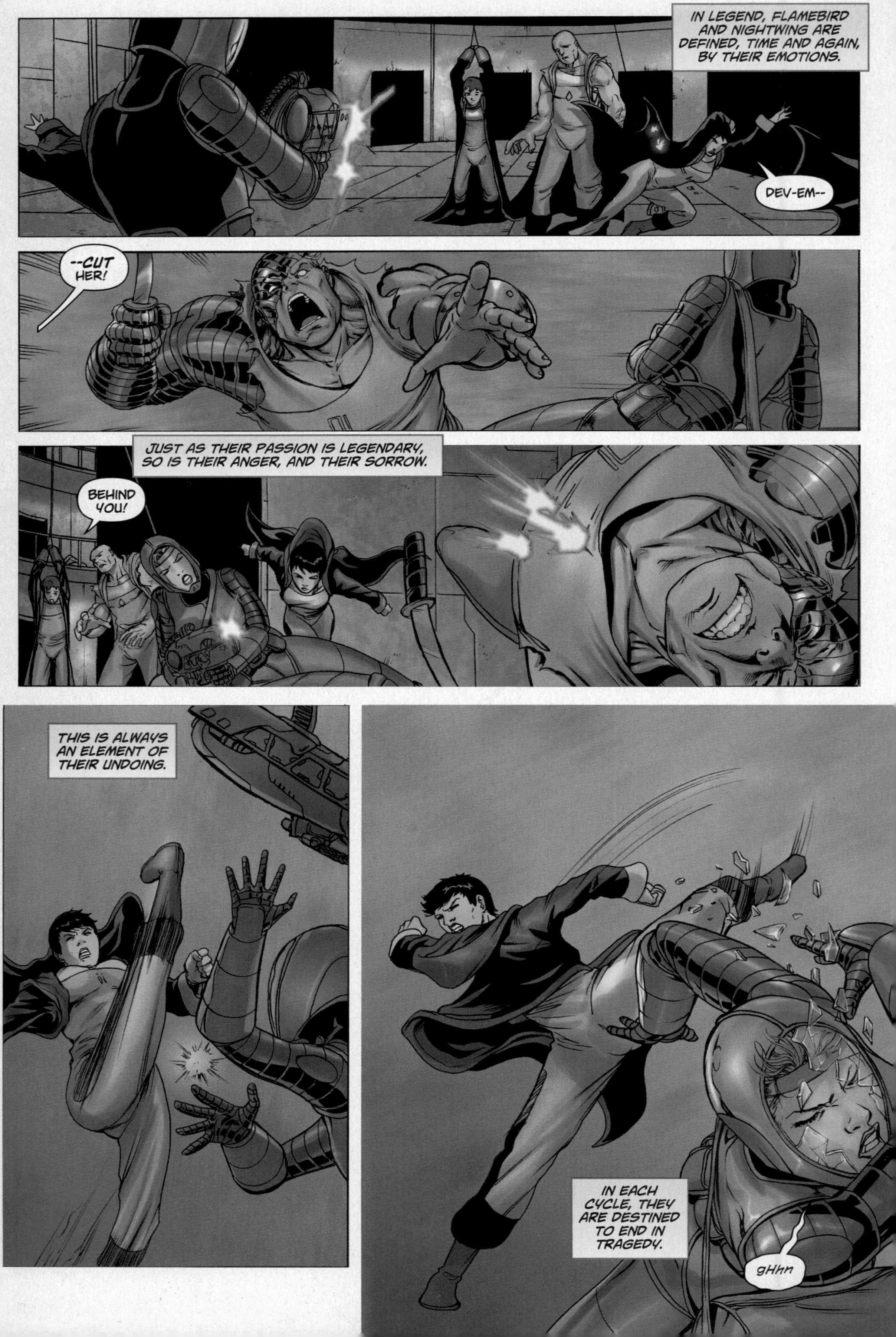
IN LEGEND, FLAMEBIRD AND NIGHTWING ARE DEFINED, TIME AND AGAIN, BY THEIR EMOTIONS.
DEV-EM--
--CUT HER!
JUST AS THEIR PASSION IS LEGENDARY, SO IS THEIR ANGER, AND THEIR SORROW.
BEHIND YOU!
THIS IS ALWAYS AN ELEMENT OF THEIR UNDOING.
IN EACH CYCLE, THEY ARE DESTINED TO END IN TRAGEDY.
gHhn

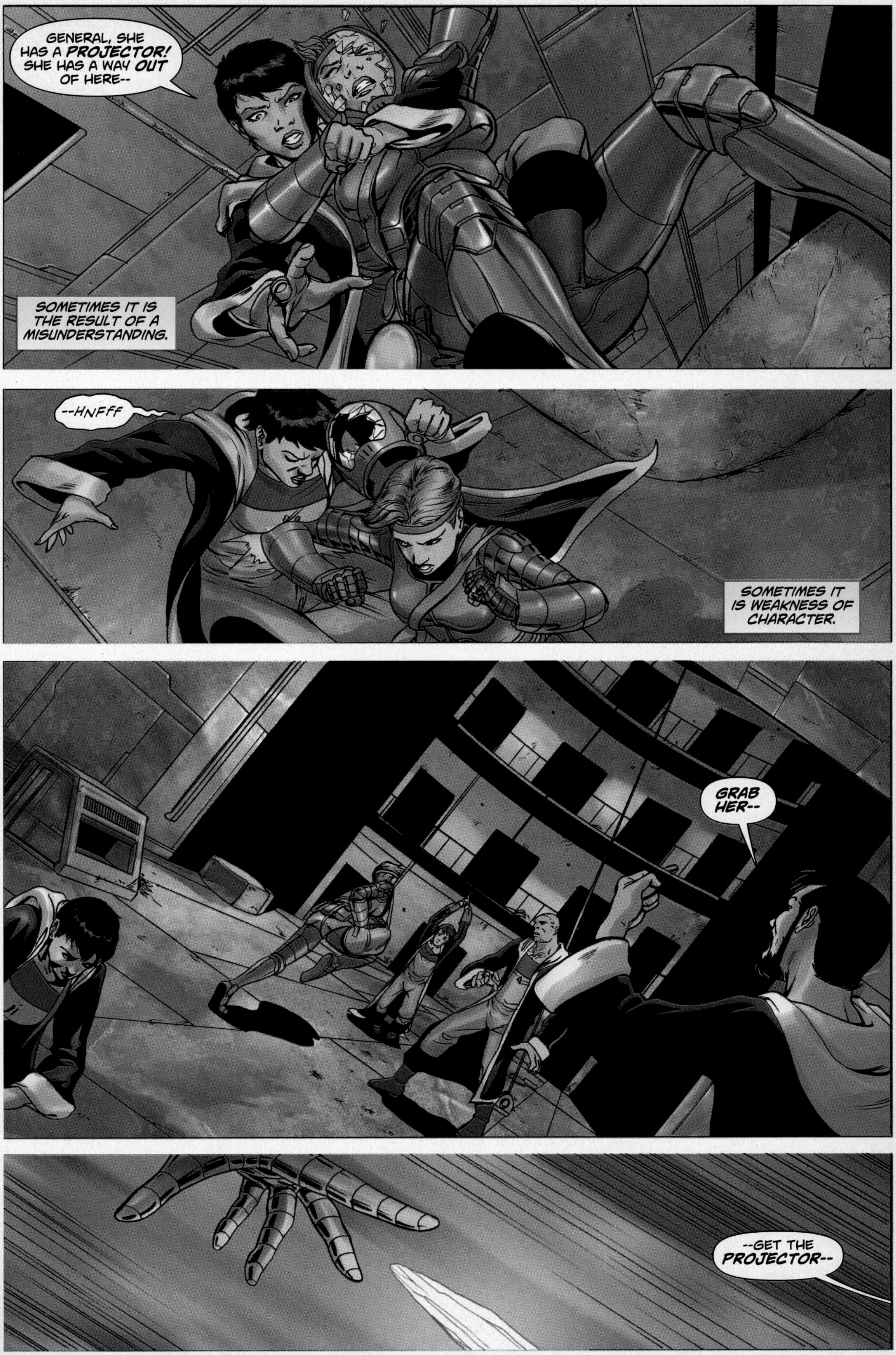
GENERAL, SHE HAS A PROJECTOR! SHE HAS A WAY OUT OF HERE--
SOMETIMES IT IS THE RESULT OF A MISUNDERSTANDING.
--HNFFF
SOMETIMES IT IS WEAKNESS OF CHARACTER.
GRAB HER--
--GET THE PROJECTOR--

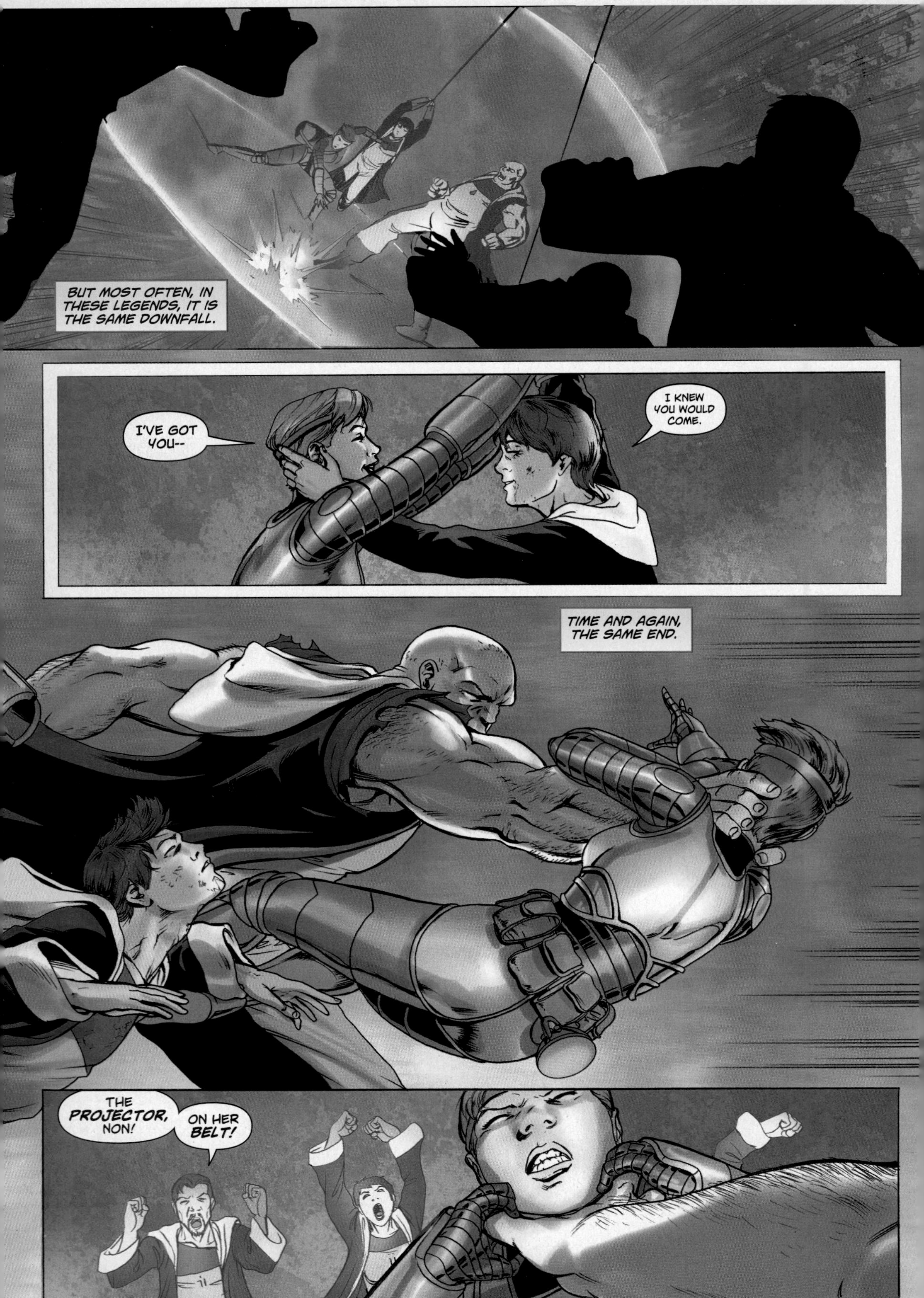
BUT MOST OFTEN, IN THESE LEGENDS, IT IS THE SAME DOWNFALL.
I'VE GOT YOU--
I KNEW YOU WOULD COME.
TIME AND AGAIN, THE SAME END.
THE PROJECTOR, NON!
ON HER BELT!

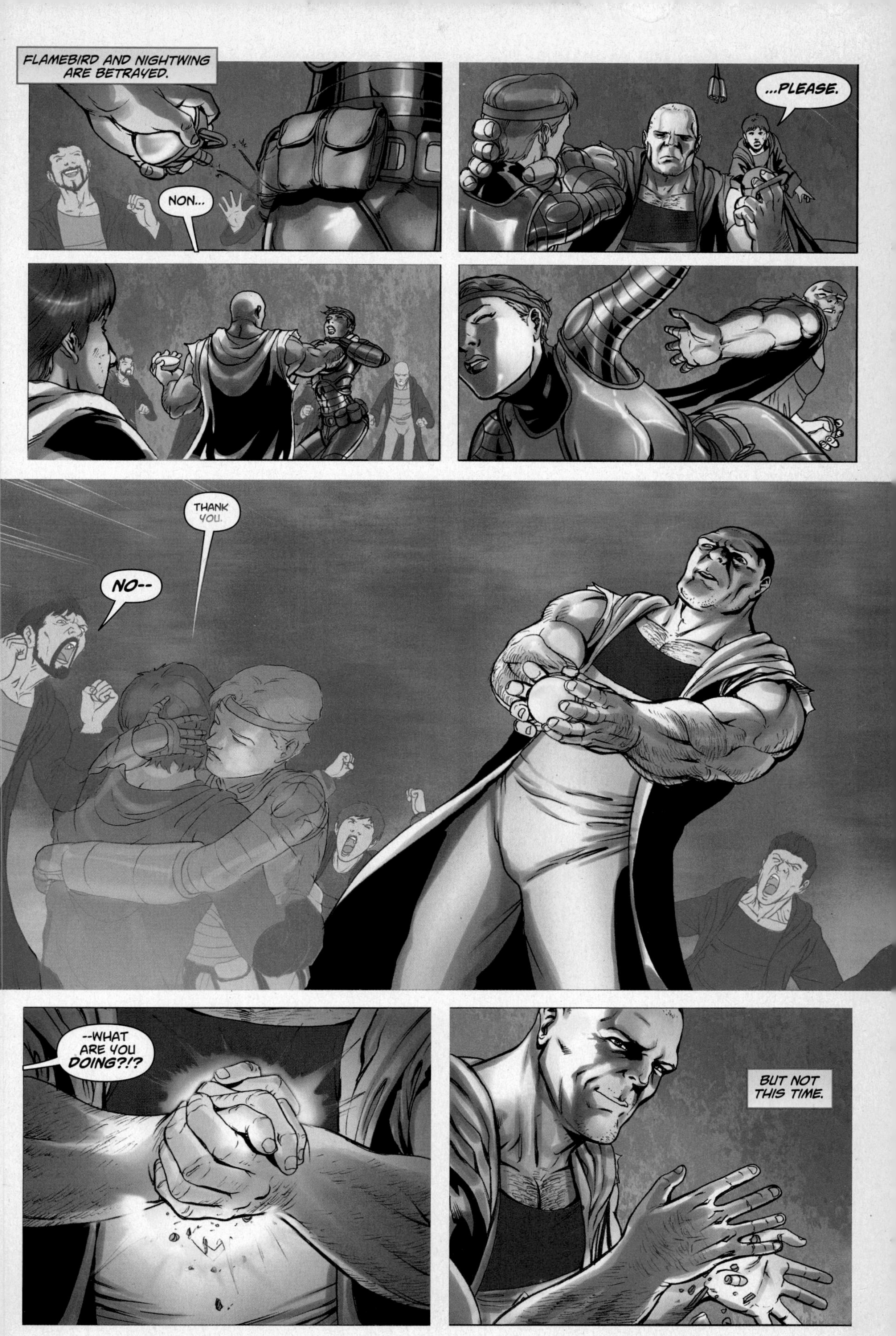
FLAMEBIRD AND NIGHTWING ARE BETRAYED.
NON...
...PLEASE.
THANK YOU.
NO--
--WHAT ARE YOU DOING?!?
BUT NOT THIS TIME.

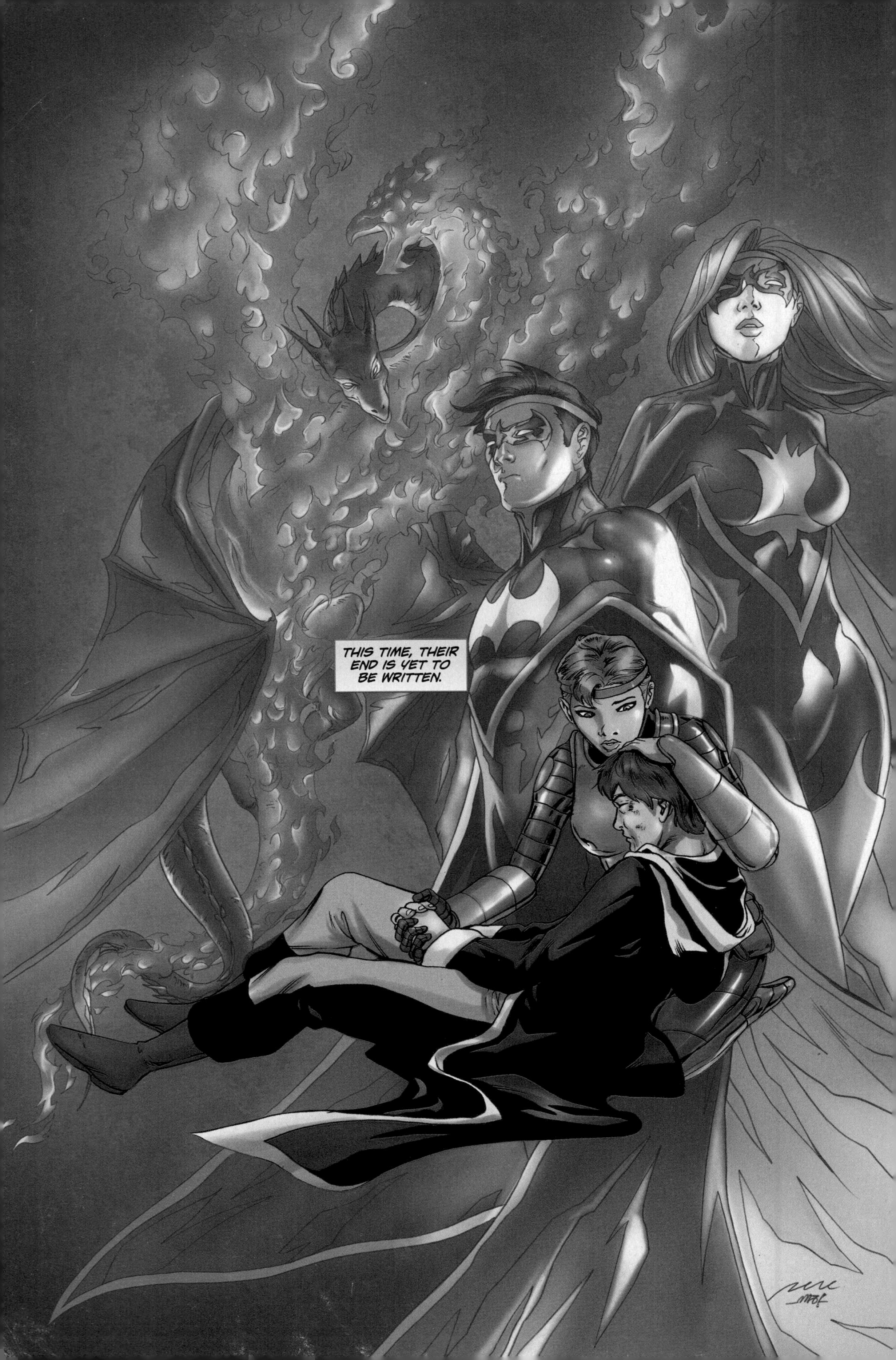
THIS TIME, THEIR END IS YET TO BE WRITTEN.

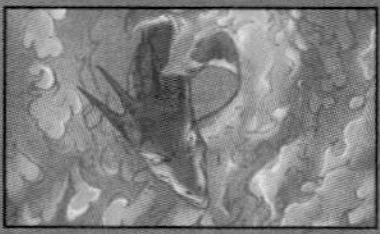

NIGHTWING

ALTER EGOS: Lor-Zod, Christopher Kent

BASE OF OPERATIONS: Mobile; formerly the Phantom Zone

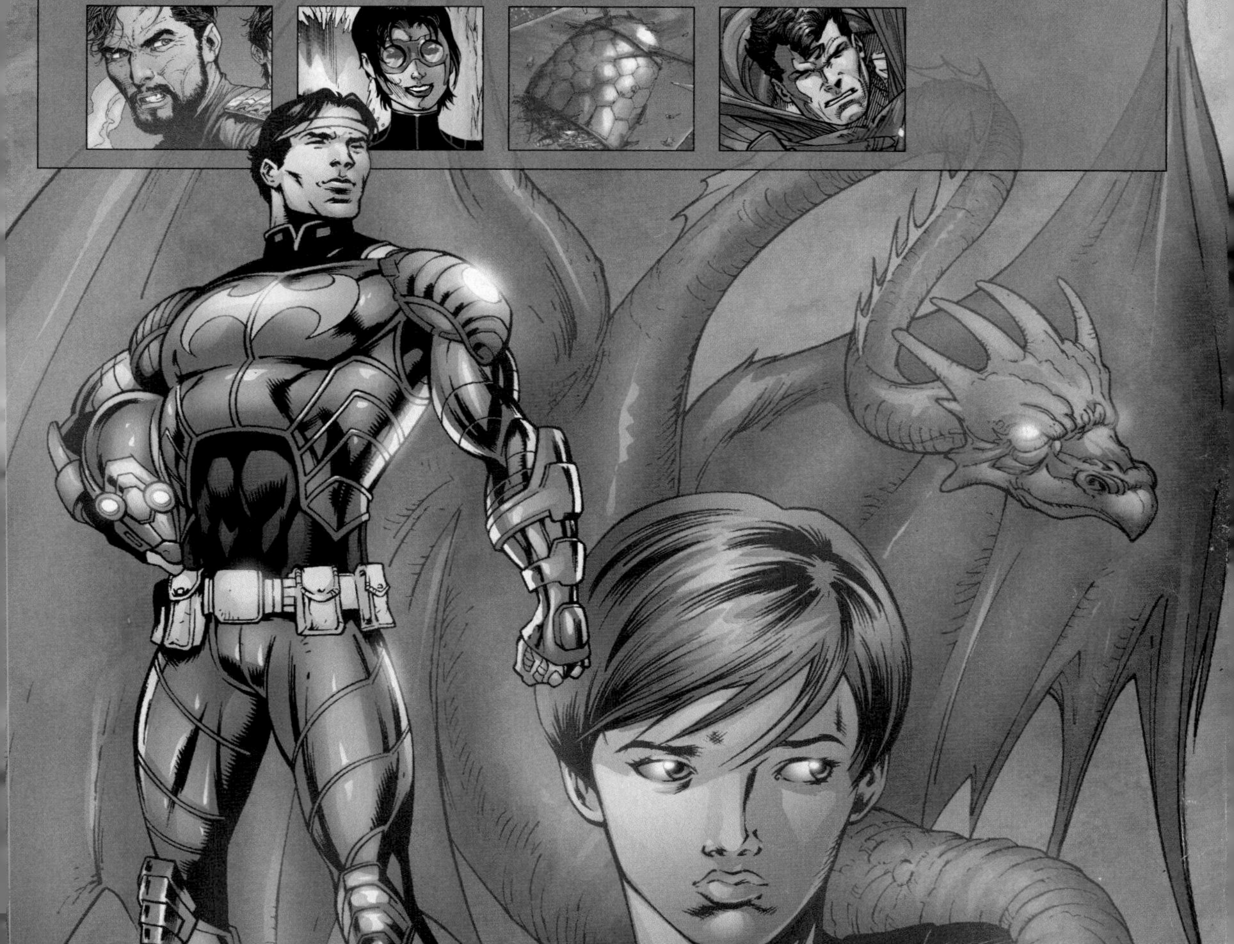

POWERS/ABILITIES: A Kryptonian by birth, Nightwing's genetic structure was mutated as a result of his conception and birth in the Phantom Zone. Possessed of the standard Kryptonian power set, he is marginally, if demonstrably, weaker than the rest of his race when under Earth's yellow sun. Kryptonite, while still lethal to him, takes longer to reach full effect. Nightwing has exhibited tactile telekinesis, though if this power is the result of his Phantom Zone birth or his interaction with Brainiac technology, none can say.

HISTORY: Lor-Zod is the only child of **GENERAL ZOD** and **COMMANDER URSA**, born and raised in **FORT ROZ**, in the Phantom Zone. Surrounded by some of Krypton's worst criminals, he would certainly have become one of the most evil creatures the universe had ever seen, but for the machinations of his father. When General Zod used his young son to spearhead an attempted invasion of Earth, the child was discovered by **SUPERMAN**, who immediately forged a strong bond with the boy.

In the care of Superman and Lois Lane, Lor, renamed "Christopher," began a new life, free from the trauma and hardship he had previously experienced. His education by both, along with time spent among Earth's mightiest heroes, had an immediate and profound effect, and instilled in him the passionate desire to follow in Superman's footsteps.

To repel Zod's invasion, Christopher sacrificed his life on Earth, voluntarily returning to the Phantom Zone. Upon reentry, he suffered the first of three bouts of "burst-aging" he has since undergone, his body growing the equivalent of several years in mere seconds. The source of this disorder is unknown, and Nightwing is quite concerned when the next "episode" will occur.

He is currently working with Flamebird, attempting to stop Kryptonian sleeper agents placed on Earth by his father Zod.

GREG RUCKA, art by FERNANDO DAGNINO & RAUL FERNANDEZ, color by PETE PANTAZIS

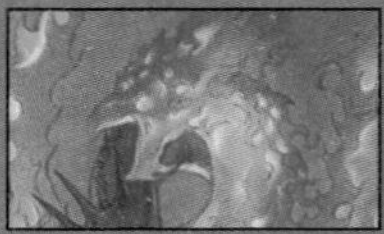

FLAMEBIRD

ALTER EGO: Thara Ak-Var

BASE OF OPERATIONS: Mobile; formerly Kandor

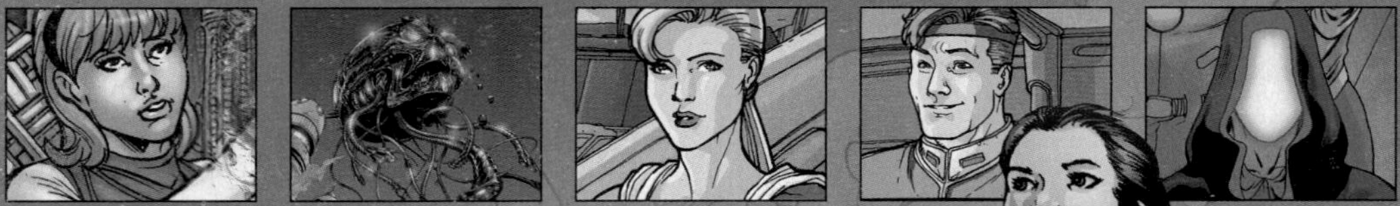

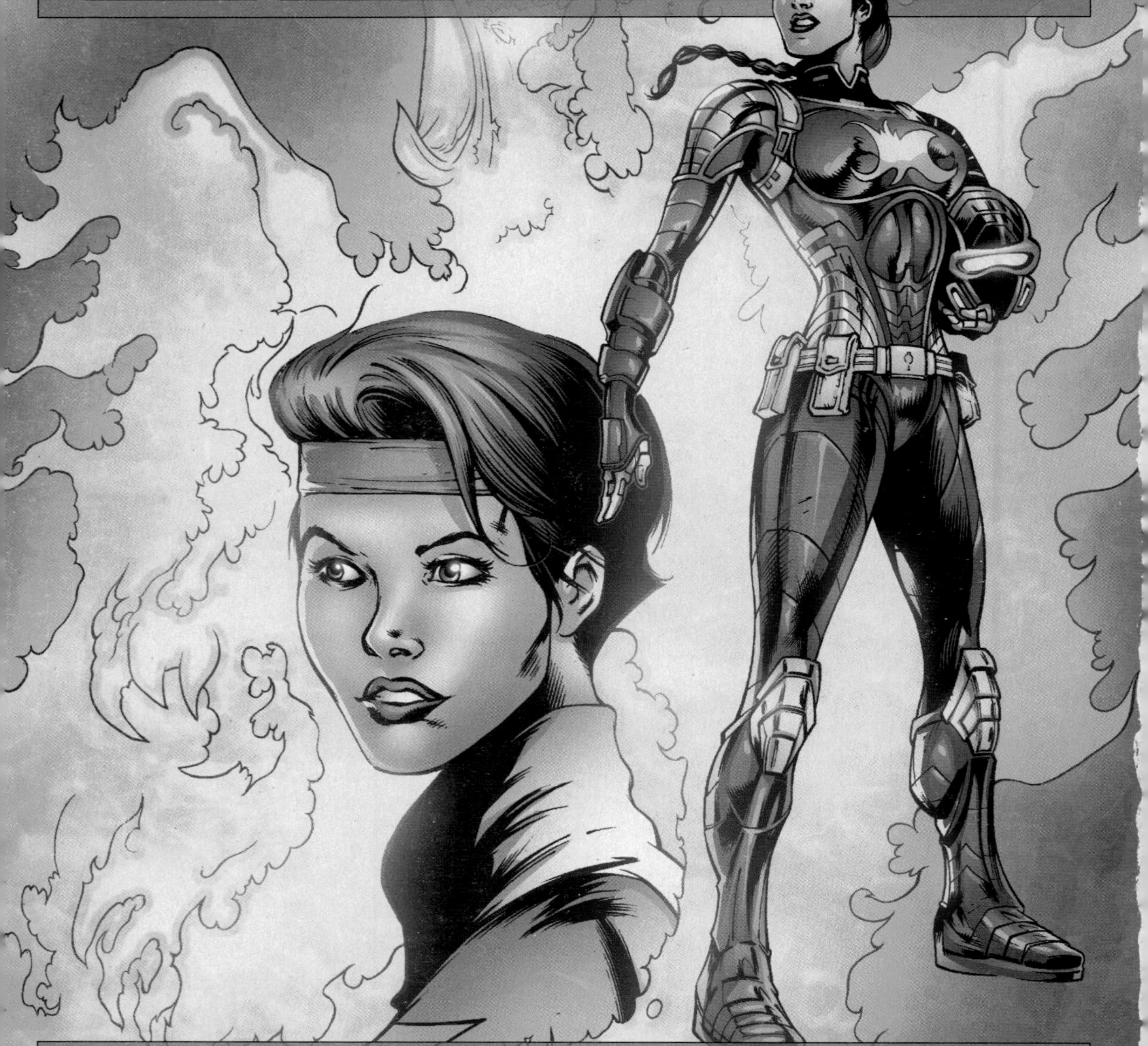

POWERS/ABILITIES: Standard Kryptonian power set and vulnerabilities. Additionally, Thara believes herself to be the avatar of the ancient Kryptonian Flamebird, a quasi-religious/mythical beast from the Kryptonian pantheon, best described as a fusion between a phoenix and a dragon, and the eternal mate of the Nightwing, a similar creature composed of shadow and night.

HISTORY: Thara Ak-Var has dreamt of the flames all her life. Born to members of the Military Guild's elite unit Black Zero, Thara was raised on Krypton, with time divided between Kandor and Argo City, the home of her best friend, **KARA ZOR-EL**. The two made an odd pair, Kara a far more scientifically minded girl than her devoutly religious friend. At fourteen, Thara was abducted along with thousands of other Kryptonians when **BRAINIAC** stole the city of Kandor from planet Krypton. The trauma of that event, as well as witnessing the death of her parents (and their subsequent abandonment by their commanding officer, Ursa) in an attempt to rescue her, affected her deeply.

When Brainiac incorporated the captured populace of Argo City into Kandor, Thara was reunited with Kara's parents, **ALURA** and **ZOR-EL**, and became a surrogate daughter to them. It was Zor-El who directed her back to the **RELIGIOUS GUILD** in an attempt to help her recover her faith. Entering the House of Rao, Thara experienced what she maintains was a vision of the Flamebird. Inducted into the Religious Guild and initiated in its mysteries, she shortly after experienced a seizure, and emerged from it convinced that there was a young man trapped in the Phantom Zone – her Nightwing. She effected his rescue, and the two have been together ever since, though Thara has yet to share with him the depth of her feelings, or her religious convictions, for fear of rejection or – worse – that he might believe her insane.

Text by GREG RUCKA, art by FERNANDO DAGNINO & RAÚL FERNANDEZ, color by PETE PANTAZIS

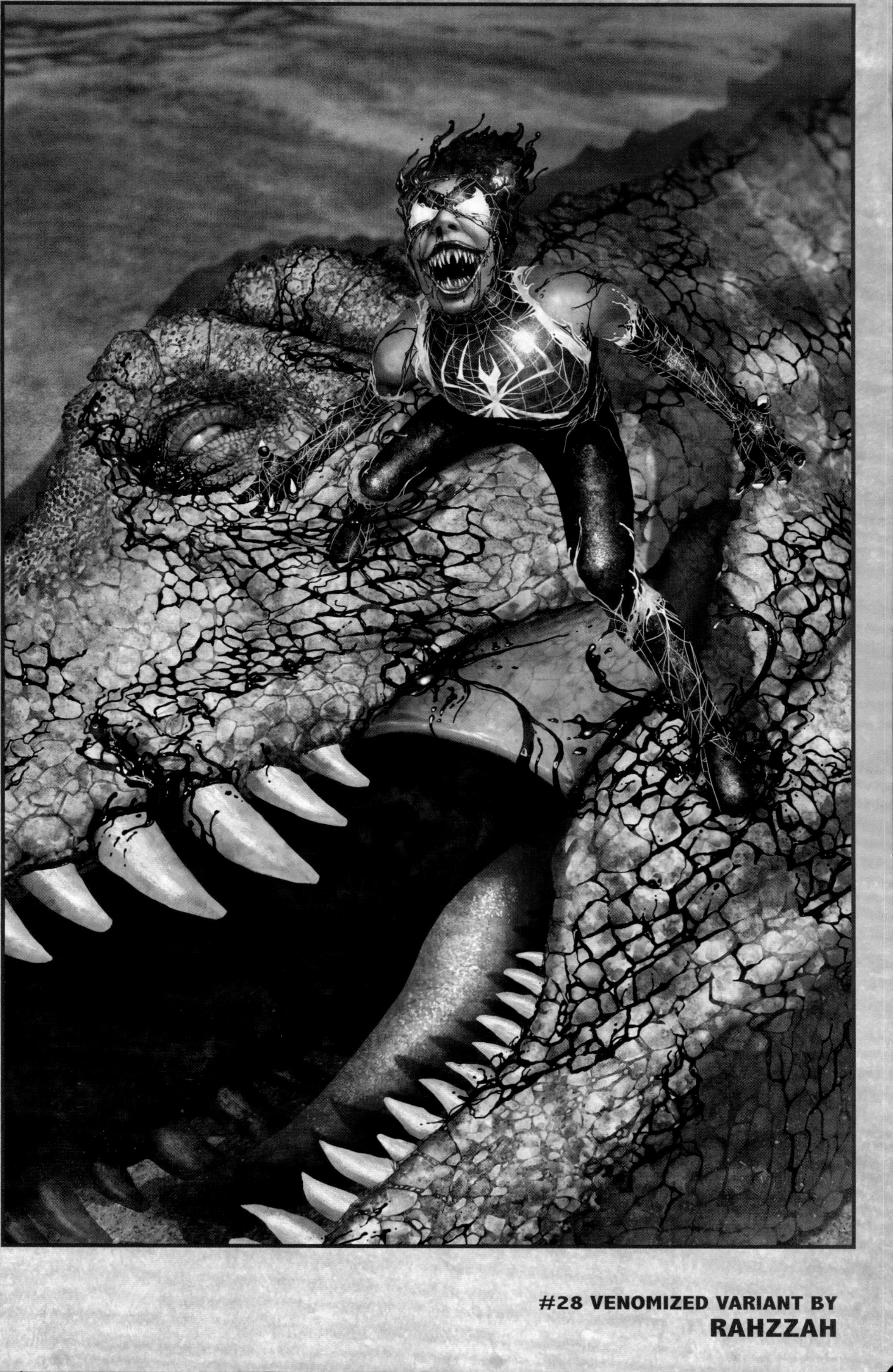

#28 VENOMIZED VARIANT BY
RAHZZAH